W9-ARC-683

Contraception
and Abortion
in Nineteenth-
Century America

DISCARD

Contraception and Abortion in Nineteenth-Century America

JANET FARRELL BRODIE

Cornell University Press

ITHACA AND LONDON

Copyright © 1994 by Cornell University

All rights reserved. Except for brief quotations in a review, this book, or parts thereof, must not be reproduced in any form without permission in writing from the publisher. For information, address Cornell University Press, Sage House, 512 East State Street, Ithaca, New York 14850.

First published 1994 by Cornell University Press.
First printing, Cornell Paperbacks, 1997.

Printed in the United States of America

Library of Congress Cataloging-in-Publication Data

Brodie, Janet Farrell
    Contraception and abortion in nineteenth-century America / Janet Farrell Brodie.
        p. cm.
    Includes bibliographical references and index.
    ISBN 0-8014-2849-1 (cloth: alk. paper)
    ISBN 0-8014-8433-2 (pbk.: alk. paper)
    1. Birth control—United States—History—19th century.
2. Contraception—United States—History—19th century. 3. Sex customs—United States—History—19th century. I. Title.
HQ766.5.U5B76 1994
363.9'6'097309034—dc20   93-30515

⊗ The paper in this book meets the minimum requirements of the American National Standard for Information Sciences—Permanence of Paper for Printed Library Materials, ANSI Z39.48-1984.

Cloth printing   10   9   8   7   6   5   4   3   2   1

Paperback printing   10   9   8   7   6   5   4   3   2   1

To Bruce, Jedediah, and Nathaniel

Contents

Prologue

This book is the first extensive look at the full range of options for contraception and abortion in the decades when the birth rate of white American couples plunged most dramatically, the years between 1830 and the last third of the nineteenth century. Many couples were desperate to learn effective and safe ways to prevent conception and to induce abortion. Yet the subject was clothed in secrecy, for reproductive control was just beginning to emerge into the public domain. As it became more public, Anthony Comstock and other reformers secured, in the 1870s, the passage of the "Comstock laws"—the legislation that prohibited the mailing of birth control information and products. As a consequence of this secrecy, at first cultural and later legalized, considerable silence has surrounded historians' questions about how couples limited their families—for, after all, many did—and what motivated them to do so.

I began my investigation of these questions expecting to find only sparse information, and thinking that I might find useful models in the sociological literature on the communication of taboo knowledge. Yet it quickly became apparent that in the second quarter of the nineteenth century information on American reproductive control was neither all that rare nor all that tabooed. In the decades after 1830 women as well as men, rural folk as well as urban, and the laboring classes as well as the middle classes had access to new information about old and new methods—withdrawal, douching, and the rhythm method, as well as to condoms, spermicides, abortion-inducing drugs, and early varieties of the diaphragm. Beginning in the 1830s reproductive control became a commercial enterprise in the expanding market economy of Jacksonian America. Information about the safety, morality, and effectiveness of various methods became part of the public grid of meanings, or part of, to use Michel Foucault's useful term, public "discourse." The archives contain a wealth of advice published in books and pamphlets, an extraordinary diversity of advertisements for products, drugs, and literature, of business and credit-rating records dealing with reproductive control entrepreneurs, of druggists' records and catalogues. What began in the 1830s as the focus of a small group of social and health reformers—Robert Dole Owen and Charles Knowlton especially—by the 1860s was the province of a diverse assortment of entrepreneurs and business people. The central motivation for the dispersal of reproductive control shifted from morals to money.

The diffusion process I trace differs from the two chief models that earlier histories and demographic studies have used to explain the nineteenth-century fertility decline. Few scholars today accept the model of birth control diffusion proposed in Norman E. Himes's 1936 *Medical History of Contraception*, in which Himes posited a direct relationship between the scientific and technological advances in contraception (invented by medical men) which became "democratizated" and the consequent decline in the birth rate. It is more commonly heard today that birth rates fell because couples began to want fewer children or longer intervals between children—that is, that birth control practices depended on the diffusion of new attitudes and values. In this model, changing values led to behavioral changes, as couples called out of the large repertoire of perennially available folk knowledge simple methods for family limitation—withdrawal of the penis before discharge of sperm, sexual abstinence, and abortion.[1]

This book does not follow either model. First, while withdrawal can be an effective method, the varying knowledge about this technique in the nineteenth century affected both its practicality and its "psychological" availability. Nor do I believe that sexual abstinence was as widely practiced to limit fertility as some historians have argued. It is the historian's job to document the specificities of time and place and to question assumptions about universal behaviors.[2] Not all peoples at all times believed that they could promote or curtail reproduction. Magic, medicine, and superstitious behaviors may suggest the existence of desire for reproductive control but not the existence of beliefs that such control was feasible. Women and men might use magical incantations and herbs and potions or appeal to a god to bring about or to prevent birth, but such actions did not necessarily entail the actual belief in one's personal ability to intervene in natural processes.

Nor can the decline in white marital fertility be directly attributed to the availability of new knowlege or techniques, for the relationship was not that simple. Motivation to control pregnancy and birth and the increasing availability of efficient techniques, devices, and information were mutually reinforcing. In a spiraling process, demand and supply stimulated one another. Himes wrote that contraceptive knowledge in the nineteenth century saw only a "limited percolation downward" to the general public until the publicity from the 1877 trial of freethinking British editors Charles Bradlaugh and Annie Besant for reissuing Charles Knowlton's earlier book, *Fruits of Philosophy*, created "an inundation."[3] This book argues that the inundation began earlier and was more complex and convoluted. Transformations in knowledge were not a gradual percolating downward. The process of diffusion of ideas, information, and products resembled a web more than a percolator, but a web that twisted, knotted, and even folded back upon itself. Some of the new techniques made reproductive intervention safer and more reliable, but unsafe and unreliable methods, some of them also new, coexisted with them for decades. Access to effective information at times expanded and at times contracted. Contraception did become more effective over time, and popular awareness of contraception did grow. But one cannot say with any definitiveness that the knowledge of safe and reliable contraception steadily "advanced" between 1830 and 1880; it evolved, rather, by fits and starts.

The process of unraveling the different meanings that methods held for different people at different times, of grasping the competing and fluctuating significances of safety, reliability, morality, and "psychological availability," and the material accessibility of diverse techniques, proved to be complex. To some extent these are problems many historians deal with, to some extent they are singular to a study like this, of a subject in the process of shifting from the clandestine to the commercial. One problem lay in determining who constituted the various publics for reproductive control: who bought the advice literature, who came to the lectures, who received the unsolicited advertisements. Closely related were the interpretive issues: how can we reconstruct what nineteenth-century audiences understood from literary texts or formal verbal pronouncements in lectures by self-declared experts? What did the advice offered in Owen's *Moral Physiology* or Knowlton's *Fruits of Philosophy* mean to a journeyman printer or a farmer's wife or a newly married city couple, and how can we detect those meanings today? Did what they read or heard change their reproductive behavior?[4]

Much of the language surrounding contraception and abortion today is highly politically charged. Much of it, too, is ahistorical. I have tried, for example, not to rely on the term "birth control" for the techniques, ideas, devices, and behaviors described in this book, although it is a temptingly convenient shorthand. Margaret Sanger coined the phrase early in the twentieth century to refer to her movement, and she and her colleagues explicitly excluded abortion as a form of birth control. Mary Ware Dennett explained in 1924 that contraception and abortion were separated by a "deep abyss."[5] My book, following nineteenth-century thought, includes both practices as reproductive control. I have not distinguished between contraceptive methods that required behavioral changes (withdrawal, the rhythm method) and those requiring the use of appliances or drugs. I consider them all to be contraceptive methods even though, in this case, many nineteenth-century opponents and proponents regarded appliance methods as less "natural." Unlike demographers, I include child spacing and attempts to increase the intervals between pregnancies as family limitation. It seems to me ahistorical to consider family limitation as only involving attempts to stop childbearing when so many couples could succeed only in delaying pregnancies. Nor have I differentiated between "parity dependent" and "parity independent" reproductive control techniques (the former being contraceptive practices that can be employed or altered depending on the number of children already born, and the latter—breastfeeding is defined this way by some demographers—methods that cannot be altered even as family size grows) because, as I argue in Chapter 2, even breastfeeding was susceptible to more deliberate alteration than such a view allows.

Obviously a book on reproductive control will have relevance to the ongoing historians' debates about nineteenth-century marriages, sexuality, and gender relations. For some time, historians have disagreed about whether marriages were becoming more affectionate and companionable and whether nineteenth-century couples were more sexually passionate than stereotypes would have us believe. My work, illustrating the availability of so much contraceptive and abortifacient information in the nineteenth century, challenges conventional explanations that sexual abstinence was one of the chief means by which American couples achieved their low birth rates. But it does not support the view that changes in reproductive control methods fostered closer, more intimate marriages, for although these changes afforded couples the security of sexual expressiveness with less risk of pregnancy, they also highlighted unresolved tensions in gender relations.[6] Contraception and abortion affected many aspects of marriage and sexuality, holding threats as well as promises.

One final explanation: I make no claims to being neutral about issues concerning the self-determination of reproduction. I am intensely aware of the fact that my own ability to plan and time my children and to control my fertility has given me extraordinary freedom and an autonomy and control over my life which is unavailable to many women today and which was uncertain for women in the past. It is good if couples are able to work together to decide about fertility control, but I believe that it remains fundamentally a woman's prerogative to decide if and when she wants to bear children and that such essentially private decisions are fundamental personal rights. I have tried, nevertheless, to be empathetic to those women and men who, in nineteenth-century America, held no such assumptions, just as I continue to try to understand and to be sensitive to the complexity of factors behind the politically, emotionally, and intellectually charged cultural battles over reproductive rights today.

JANET FARRELL BRODIE

Pacific Palisades, California

Acknowledgments and Sources

M y work deals primarily with source materials from the 1830s to 1880s, yet it has been greatly enriched by others' histories of reproductive control. Linda Gordon's 1976 book, *Woman's Body, Woman's Right: A Social History of Birth Control in America*, one of the first to examine the many-layered politics of nineteenth-century contraception and abortion, raised crucial, and still pertinent, issues about the gender politics, class politics, and reform politics of reproductive control. I have also found helpful Gordon's 1982 essay "Why Nineteenth Century Feminists Did Not Support 'Birth Control' and Twentieth Century Feminists Do: Feminism, Reproduction, and the Family." My work has been aided as well by James W. Reed's *From Private Vice to Public Virtue: The Birth Control Movement and American Society since 1830* (1978), Carl Degler's *At Odds: Women and the Family from the Revolution to the Present* (1980), and James Mohr's *Abortion in America: The Origins and Evolution of National Policy* (1978). James Reed generously shared some of his early work on Charles Knowlton with me. The many histories of family limitation among nineteenth-century Europeans and Canadians have also been immensely useful, as have been certain earlier works, such as Norman E. Himes's *Medical History of Contraception* (1936), and Peter Fryer's *The Birth Controllers* (1966).[1] Historians of women's history, family history, and the history of sexuality are now studying the behavior and fertility patterns of particular demographic groups, and many of these studies have been helpful to me: my notes suggest their range and scope.

The single most significant sources I used in writing this book were the advice books and pamphlets on reproductive control in their variant editions scattered in libraries around the country. These included some sixty-two titles, most with at least two or more variant editions. *The National Union Catalog of Pre-1956 Imprints*, although not infallible, was valuable in my search for the most important of these editions and as a source in itself, for it contains useful information for my purposes about publishers, printers, and book sizes of works that are no longer available. The Rare Book Room of the Francis A. Countway Library of Medicine of the Harvard University Medical School has the largest number of nineteenth-century works giving reproductive control advice. There are also important holdings at the American Antiquarian Society, the National Library of Medicine, and the Library of Congress. Librarians at Wayne State University Library, Lane Medical Library at the Stanford University Medical Center, and the University of Southern California kindly mailed me copies of significant documents. I also relied heavily on articles in nineteenth-century medical journals. In both systematic searches and random browsing, I found valuable information in the rich collection of well-known and obscure journals in the Countway stacks. Druggists' catalogues and contemporary medical almanacs yielded details about products, prices, and availability. The research libarary of the Boston Public Library, Harvard's Widener Library, the Library of Congress, the research libraries of the University of Chicago, the University of California at Berkeley and at Los Angeles, the Bio-Med Library at the UCLA Medical School all provided me with a wealth of nineteenth-century sources ranging widely from folklore and folk medicine to popular health reform, women's history, and nineteenth-century business history. It is a joy to work in a library where, when I stumbled across a brief reference to an otherwise completely unknown mid-nineteenth-century physiological lecturer, within fifteen minutes I was reading the equally obscure, privately printed biographical sketch written by his wife.

The Poor Family Papers at the Arthur and Elizabeth Schlesinger Library on the History of Women in America at Radcliffe College were inestimably useful, as were the Lydia E. Pinkham Medicine Company Records. The R. G. Dun and Company Collection in the Historical Collections at the Baker Library of the Harvard Graduate School of Business Administration yielded treasures of information on the entrepreneurs involved with diffusing birth control literature and products. Their scrapbook of "unprintable" advertisements in the E.C. Allen Company Papers was also important. The Norman E. Himes

Archive at Countway, particularly his notes on a projected companion volume to *Medical History of Contraception*, had useful gleanings, and the Horatio Robinson Storer manuscript letters, also at Countway, were crucial for an understanding of his campaign against abortion. The Houghton Library at Harvard University gave me access to the "Notes on the Abner Kneeland Controversy." At the Library of Congress Manuscript Division I used the Joseph M. Toner Collection, the Collection of the New York Society for the Suppression of Vice, the Blackwell Family Papers, and the Elizur Wright Papers. I am grateful to these libraries and to the R. G. Dun Company for permission to quote from their manuscripts, and I am especially indebted to Alfred D. Chandler for his gracious permission to quote from the Poor Family Papers.

The American Antiquarian Society's unsurpassed newspaper collection permitted me the great luxury of reading actual copies of the *Boston Investigator*. In other places I also found important information: in the *Free Enquirer*, the *Cleveland Liberalist, Day's Doings, Sporting Times and Theatrical News*, and the *New York Tribune*. At the Patent and Trademark Office of the U.S. Department of Commerce I found fascinating patent records for vaginal and intrauterine devices, most of which I did not, in the end, include in the book.

✦ The staffs of many libraries have been patient with my requests for esoteric, sometimes long-buried materials. Richard J. Wolfe and the staff in the Rare Book Room at Countway Library gave courteous and prompt attention to my many requests. The staff of the Historical Collections of the Baker Library was exceptionally kind during the weeks I poured over the volumes of the R. G. Dun Collection. Eva Moseley was thoughtful during the months I worked in the collections at the Schlesinger Library. Women and men too numerous to thank individually have aided me at the Library of Congress, the U.S. Patent Office, the Boston Public Library, the Boston Athenaeum, the Massachusetts College of Pharmacy Library, the American Antiquarian Society, the Minnesota Historical Society, the New York Academy of Medicine Library, the University Research libraries at the University of California at Los Angeles and Berkeley, and the Medical Library at UCLA. Among librarians, the late Robert Rosenthal, curator of Rare Books and Archives at the University of Chicago Library, was a friend as well as a wonderful boss.

I count myself extraordinarily fortunate to have had Larry Malley and Peter Agree as editors. This book has been greatly improved by the attentive editing of Jeanette Hopkins and Marilyn Sale.

My most heartfelt pleasure as I finish this book is to acknowledge the help and support I have received from friends, family, and colleagues. Some have read drafts and redrafts of chapters. Others have read the entire manuscript more than once. Their suggestions have enriched and enlivened every part of the book and have saved me from errors of fact and judgment. I am especially grateful to Robert Dawidoff, Ellen DuBois, Betty Farrell, Nancy Hewitt, Wayne Hobson, Harold Meyerson, David Pivar, Jennifer Radden, Helena Wall, and Leila Zenderland for scrupulously thorough readings and detailed comments. Ellen Chesler, Jeffrey Kirk, James Reed, and Sarah Stage gave me helpful advice on early versions of chapters presented at the Berkshire Conference of Women Historians, the Mid-West Conference of Women Historians, and the Western Association of Women Historians. Neil Harris, giving encouragement and guidance oversaw this project from its earliest stages in graduate school. The generous responses of Dana Cuff, Barbara Davis, and Janet Levin reassured me of the interest of professionals in varied disciplines. Edwin Brown gave generously of his time and expertise with computers when I still distrusted anything more modern than a manual typewriter. Edward Sellers nobly tried to speed up my writing with business management techniques.

My sisters Deborah Farrell and Patricia Farrell provided research assistance at crucial stages, and Betty Farrell has read and reread the manuscript, improving it with her sociological perspective and elegance of style. My parents, Mary and Kenneth Farrell, my sister Lisa, and my brother Bob mastered the art of warm interest in the book without pressing questions about when it would be finished.

Without my sons, Jedediah and Nathaniel, and the restoratives of their humor, their worlds of soccer and medieval fantasies, and their posters urging me to "Keep on Working, Mom," it would have been much harder to persist. To Bruce I owe more than I can possibly express here.

J. F. B.

Introduction

If we want to know how nineteenth-century couples limited reproduction, we learn almost nothing by turning to contemporary fiction. Only occasionally was the subject referred to. In *Sunset Song*, Lewis Grassic Gibbon's classic novel about country life in early twentieth-century Scotland, Mistress Mutch warns the heroine Chris Guthrie at her wedding reception about having too many children: "'Don't let Ewan saddle you with a barn full of bairns, Chris, it kills you and eats your heart away . . . you won't steer clear of the first or the second. But you belong to yourself, mind that.' Chris went hot and cold and then wanted to ask something of Mistress Mutch and looked at her and found she couldn't, she'd just have to find the thing out for herself."[1]

Like Chris Guthrie—who wanted to ask how to avoid having a child she did not want but could not bring herself to ask aloud—most nineteenth- and even early twentieth-century novelists could not openly address contraception and abortion. Readers may wonder yet have to remain ignorant about how Dreiser's Sister Carrie avoided pregnancy. Even the boldest French novelists skirted the subject, and readers never learn how Madame Bovary or Zola's courtesan, Nana, controlled their fertility. In a rare exception, the American writer Mary Austin daringly had the turn-of-the-century heroine of her semiautobiographical novel, *A Woman of Genius* (1926), question her mother about "how to interpose between marriage and maternity ever so slight an interval in which to . . . leave off shrinking from the looming terror of childbirth." The simple query, however, struck "the dying nerve of long since encountered dreads and pains," and her mother would not help her.[2] Tolstoy's *Anna Karenina* is one other rare exception, for Anna's fecund sister-in-law Dolly was shocked to learn from Anna that there were ways to keep from having children: "To her it was one of those discoveries which lead to consequences and deductions so enormous that at first it is quite impossible to grasp it all, and one that one has to think about a great deal first."[3] Anna's own technique, either contraceptive or abortion-inducing, depended on her own actions, not her lover's. Tolstoy truncates Anna's explanation to Dolly by using ellipses—a highly symbolic example of the stifled communication process surrounding reproductive control in America as in Russia: the control of reproduction known by some was secret information, spread by whispered intimacies along friendship or acquaintance networks, sometimes directly but often by innuendo—a cautious and reticent dissemination of sought-after but almost illicit knowledge.

Intimate letters and diaries of nineteenth-century American women and men, like the hints in fiction, provide only fragmentary detail on who used what and how and why, and how they learned about it. Married couples sometimes discussed contraception and abortion in letters; women occasionally confided to their diaries; advice passed between women friends in letters, but few such exchanges seem to have been preserved. The evidence is scattered, impressionistic, and hence frustrating to a historian.

Yet in spite of this circumspection about reproductive control, the nineteenth century saw a decline in marital fertility throughout the Western industrializing world. In parts of late-eighteenth-century France, in the United States by the mid-nineteenth century, and in Britain, Germany, Australia, and New South Wales by the final third of the century, both fertility and marital birth rates declined significantly.[4] After France, the earliest decline in marital fertility occurred in the United States, where the birth rate of white native-born married women was reduced almost by half between 1800 and 1900. In 1800 the average number of children born to white women whose marriages lasted through menopause was 7.04. By 1900 the average was 3.56, a 49 percent decline. In the United States, 80 percent of the century's total decline occurred before 1880, with 55 percent in the decades between 1840 and 1880—decades important in this book.[5]

The most dramatic decline in birth rates occurred among native-born white married couples. Demographic data on fertility were compiled in these years only for married couples, not for the unmarried, and they are much more reliable for native-born whites than for other racial and ethnic groups, whose fertility patterns therefore are not easy to document. In England, early birth-control propagandists were motivated by Malthusian fears that the population, unless checked, would outstrip food supplies. They were also more sensitive than Americans, because of Britain's earlier industrialization, to class and labor problems, so their writings focused on the working classes and the unmarried. In the United States, in contrast, public discussions of reproductive control centered on the behavior of the married, the middle class, and often solely on married middle class women.

This book also does not specifically explore the reproductive control practices among immigrant groups. Although I believe that many in the mid century had access to the same information available to the native-born—and certainly German-Americans had access to much in their own language—I have not systematically examined the subject. Demographers point out a typical pattern in that immigrant fertility was often high for the first generation and declined after that, although there were many differences, depending on the group, the era, and the region.[6] But how this decline was accomplished requires another book. By the early twentieth century, east European immigrant women were among those waiting in line outside Margaret Sanger's Brooklyn, New York, birth control clinic.[7]

This book, similarly, does not address the issues of whether, how, and why slaves and free people of color may have practiced reproductive control in the nineteenth century. Although some individual slaves obviously knew techniques for fertility intervention, for some practiced infanticide and abortion, and although the subject of reproductive control among nineteenth-century African Americans needs investigation, I decided early on that it was beyond the scope of this book.[8]

The decline in fertility among white couples occurred over a wide geographic area, first in areas of urban and commercial growth, particularly in New England, but soon thereafter in rural and frontier areas in the rest of the Northeast, the West, and even the South. On farms and in frontier areas family size was bigger and had farther to fall over the course of the century, but declined steadily.[9] Historians disagree about the degree to which antebellum white married southerners limited fertility. Catherine Clinton and Anne Scott believe that members of the planter class did not practice family limitation, but historians Jan Lewis and Kenneth A. Lockridge disagree, arguing that southern planter-class women born from 1800 to 1839 reduced their childbearing by persuading their husbands to practice withdrawal and sexual

abstinence even at the price of lessening physical intimacy and of presenting an image of women as frail and weak from the sufferings of
pregnancy.[10]

Scholars disagree about the significance of deliberate family limitation in contributing to the nineteenth-century decline in the birth
rate. Other factors may account for changes in census data (the declining ratio of children under age ten to women in the population):
changes in the numbers of people marrying, changes in women's age
at marriage, changes in the overall age structure of the population,
and fluctuating rates of involuntary sterility may all have played a role.[11]
Yet few historians and demographers discount the role of deliberate
contraception and abortion. Historian F. M. L. Thompson, for example, attributes 50 percent of the declining British birth rate to birth
control and the rest to delayed marriage and marital celibacy.[12] It is
not my purpose in this book to argue the relative importance of reproductive control compared to other factors; rather, I explore what was
known about reproductive control techniques and how that changed. I
certainly believe, however, that in the market economy of industrializing America the abundant supply of information, products, and services for contraception and abortion indicates demand.

The potential market for reproductive control in the nineteenth
century was enormous, but knowing how to control fertility did not
necessarily entail being willing to do so. Significant stages in the process included the dawning of notions that reproductive control might
be possible, learning methods that might work safely and consistently,
selectively accepting knowledge, and putting it into practice. Twentieth-century population experts concerned with the effectiveness of
birth control practices in developing countries learned that formidable
barriers prevent people from practicing reproductive control even
when it is available.[13] Yet it is also apparent that even those who in
public express aversion to birth control in private may practice it. The
pioneering contraceptive-advice author Charles Knowlton claimed
that four out of five of the people he met on his travels in the 1830s
approved of his book on contraception, *Fruits of Philosophy*, but he
explained later that they hesitated to express such support in public:
"Indeed in my travels I have introduced the work and the subject it
treats of to strangers promiscuously . . . and most have been very
interested. But people won't speak out for it in public—they are too
afraid."[14] Knowlton was found guilty of selling his "obscene" book, but
immediately after voting for conviction one of the jurors begged him
for a copy of the work. One of Knowlton's harshest critics, the Presby-

terian minister Mason Grosvenor, who tried to have him run out of town for his writings, purchased a copy of *Fruits of Philosophy* after his own marriage.[15]

In the nineteenth century there was no established language for what today we call "birth control." Before Margaret Sanger succeeded in the early twentieth century in introducing that forceful and assertive label, birth control was referred to in more labored language as "the prevention of conception," "the limitation of offspring," "the prevention of pregnancy," "the anti-conception art," "preventives," "regulating reproduction," "limitation of the family," "regulators," "checks," and "the laws regulating and controlling the female system." The water-cure physician Thomas Low Nichols in 1853 called it "the means and processes for the healthy regulation and voluntary control of the maternal function."[16] Elizabeth Cady Stanton, in the early 1870s, called women's rights in the decision to have children "self-sovereignty" and spoke of "the gospel of fewer children and a healthy, happy maternity." In 1886, the reformer and entrepreneur Edward Bond Foote spoke of "methodiz[ing] conjugal relations."[17] Those who opposed such control used such pejorative labels as "evasions of nature's laws," "crimes without names," "conjugal frauds," "marital masturbation," "obstacles to fecundation," and "artificial methods of preventing fecundation."[18]

Every contraceptive method had its own synonyms, many of them an obscure and transitory argot. Some devices had as many as a dozen names. Early versions of the contraceptive diaphragm for example, were known as "womb veils," "female preventatives," "female protectors," "Victoria's protectors," the "French pessary," the "Pessaire Preventif," or simply "F.P." The coded rhetoric of today's "pro-choice" and "pro-life" movements had forerunners in the many-layered meanings associated with abortion in the nineteenth century. Opponents of deliberately procured miscarriage labeled it "feticide," "criminal abortion," "deliberate abortion," "antenatal infanticide," "aborticide," "antenatal murder." The more sympathetic terms were "menstrual regulation," "miscarriage," and "ridding oneself of an obstruction." With abortion we also get a glimpse of the deeply encoded meanings of certain associations. Who today would recognize that casual references to "savin," "rue," "cotton root" compounds or ergot suggested abortion or that words with quite respectable medical connotations for "ladies' relief" or promises to "cure irregularities" carried similarly layered meanings? Advertisements played on the many meanings attached to botanical products, such as that from the Carter Medical Company of

E. Hampton, Connecticut: "Ladies. Carter's Relief for Women is safe and always reliable; better than ergot, oxide, tansy or pennyroyal pills. Insures regularity."[19]

Much of the enormous range and variation in this terminology stemmed from prudery. People relied on euphemisms for subjects of dubious propriety. In the 1870s, when states and the federal government made dispensing information about contraception and abortion illegal, such circumlocution was a way of avoiding legal prosecution. Yet whether legal or not, many Americans found it exceedingly difficult to give direct, clear names to sexual anatomy, to sexual intercourse, and to reproductive control. Early-nineteenth-century writers on contraception found it so difficult to identify female and male sexual anatomy in print that they offered profuse apologies for speaking of "the female parts" at all and justified their attention to such subjects with title-page apologies that "To the pure, all things are pure."

The wild extravagance of the diction of reproductive control stemmed as well from the idiosyncracies that locale, region, class, gender, and time exerted over a covert arena of culture. Before the emergence of a mass market and mass culture, before advertising made standardized labels a national phenomenon, variety spiced the terminologies for many aspects of culture. Just as words for food and drink, medicinal plants, items of clothing, and furnishings varied enormously with gender, occupation, class, and region, little standardized nomenclature existed for sexuality.[20]

◆ Jacksonian America was being transformed by economic and social forces beyond the ken of most contemporaries, who often recognized that change was in the air, who longed to have greater control over its impacts, but who could scarcely comprehend how. The desire for reproductive control was only one expression of a much larger impulse rampant in the culture: to gain some degree of control over something, somewhere, somehow. By mid century, available contraceptive and abortion methods promised women and men a degree of control over their lives and destinies unimaginable to earlier generations. Tolstoy was correct in calling reproductive control a discovery of such import "that at first it is quite impossible to grasp it all." Yet a sense of personal control did not come automatically or easily to everyone. It was, to a large extent, still a tenuous notion in a culture in which the majority lived a rural existence, dependent on weather, soil, and centuries-old farming techniques, and in which urban workers faced the daily uncertainties of early capitalism's boom and bust cycles. A deeply ingrained sense of life's precariousness prevailed. Even as farmers increasingly became part of the market economic system, even as they began to "become modern" in some areas of life, a sense of personal efficacy over life and death took root only slowly. Given, too, the primitiveness of medicine, still largely in its bleeding and purging stage, any notions by urban or rural Americans that a woman might be able to control her reproductive functions or that a couple might have a say in shaping family size were so revolutionary that many of even the most ardent social reformers and feminists of the day avoided saying so publicly.

Reproductive control illustrates a second important thread in mid-nineteenth-century American culture: the ongoing cultural attempt to redefine and reshape what was public and what was private. The earlier, eighteenth-century, libertine tradition had accorded—to white men—a limited but nevertheless public discussion of sex.[21] But during the Jacksonian and antebellum decades an ideology of privacy took deep root as the middle class emerged. Bourgeois rituals and sense of identify required withdrawal into a private domestic world—into the parlor, the kitchen, and the bedroom—away from the social whirl of life on the streets and other public arenas.[22] The idea was being established that there existed "separate spheres," with men occupying the public spaces and women, children, and the family inhabiting the private.[23] Reproductive control created confusion for, in the decades covered in this book, moralists and cultural advisers of all persuasions argued that it should be a private matter, yet it was simultaneously increasingly commercial and public. Unlike that of the earlier libertine tradition, this public visibility was aimed at women as well as men and at the respectably genteel more than at the rakish. Thus the whole thrust of middle class culture was challenged, and it is no wonder that contemporaries were bedeviled about how to conduct a discourse on the subject. Should it be reserved only for private moments? Between whom? When and where and under what circumstances could it be public? Given such cultural confusion, Thomas Low Nichols's 1853 warning to readers that his book *Esoteric Anthropology* was "to be private and confidential," not a book for the "centre-table, the library shelf, or the counter of a bookseller," makes sense. But the book was, after all, published and sold. So were other books. There were many public forums on the subject, and devices for reproductive control were advertised and available for sale—until, that is, the Comstock laws of the 1870s and 1880s established the legal right to force Americans to put the question of reproductive control back in private once again.

Certainly reproduction posed grave personal and economic consequences for single women and men, especially for women in the labor force. Domestic servants (most of whom were not married), factory operatives, and women hucksters and peddlers would have benefited greatly from reliable reproductive control advice and apparatus. Such women were especially vulnerable to seduction and to rape, but histories of domestic servants and of other working women in America have not discussed their practices, if any, with regard to reproductive control.[24] Although prostitutes have often been assumed by their contemporaries and by scholars to have held special knowledge of contraception and abortion, again, there is almost no historiographic documentation of what prostitutes knew and did to control pregnancy.[25]

"Reproductive control," in this book, refers almost wholly to attempts to curtail fertility, not with efforts to cope with impotence, sterility, or inability to carry a healthy fetus to term. The misery caused by undesired sterility is not hard to document for the nineteenth century, but it is dwarfed by the anguish of those who bore more children than they wanted, or who lived in constant fear that they would. In the United States the nineteenth-century debate about fertility intervention focused overwhelmingly on how to limit reproduction, and this book follows suit.

1

A Story of Love
and Family Limitation:
"×" for Sexual Intercourse

Mary Pierce Poor and Henry Varnum Poor were educated, upper middle class Americans of the mid-nineteenth century, but though at times they were exceedingly well off, at other times money was tight. They had seven children, a large family for their generation. Mary felt the typical ambivalence of married women of her day: a love of children coupled with a dread of pregnancies and the pain and danger of childbirth. Her husband, a pioneer financial analyst, empathized with her fears but did not always succeed in consoling her. Her diaries and letters provide an intimate view of one couple's sexual life and possible attempts to limit family size.

Efforts to Limit and Space Pregnancies:
Blessings and Surprises

After a three-year engagement, Mary Pierce had married Henry Varnum Poor in 1841, when she was twenty-one and he twenty-nine. She left her family and their prominent social position in Brookline, Massachusetts, for the newer, essentially frontier, community of Bangor, Maine, where they spent the first eight years of married life. In 1849 they moved to New York City, living until 1855 surrounded by "literary ladies and authoresses" on a street Mary identified only as "Cottage Place" and for the next nine years at St. Marks Place in a three-story house with a study, a nursery, and hot and cold running water. In 1864, Mary and the children moved back to Brookline while

Henry remained in New York to recoup financial losses in the railroad houses. He commuted regularly by train to Brookline on weekends to stay with his family. In retirement in 1873, he was able to rejoin his family, and the Poors spent the last twenty-five years together in a house on a tree-lined street surrounded by Mary's extended family. Henry died in 1905 at the age of ninety-three, and Mary in 1912 at ninety-two.

In her small, pocket-sized diaries, now in the Schlesinger Library at Radcliffe, for sixty-five years Mary Poor kept lists of her social calls, of mending completed and books read, of her family's health, and banal notes about the weather. She did not use her diary to ruminate or philosophize, and she very rarely allowed public events to intrude onto its pages. Beginning in 1845, four years after her marriage, she penciled small pluses in the margins of her memoranda. The pluses appear with regularity nearly every twenty-eight days, ceasing for nine months before every childbirth and reappearing three to eight months postpartum, becoming irregular after 1864 and ceasing altogether in 1868 when she was forty-eight.[1] Clearly these plus marks are a code for her menstruation. She kept her private record dilatorily right after the wedding, but recorded it with diligence after the birth of her second child until menopause relieved any anxieties about more pregnancies.[2]

Early in 1849, shortly after the birth of their third child, Mary Poor began to keep another coded record in her diary. Throughout the next twenty-eight volumes of her diary she marked small penciled ×'s by certain dates. The ×'s never appear when Henry was away, although they recur with notable frequency just before he departed for a business trip and as soon as he returned. When Mary and the children went on summer vacations the ×'s appear only on days when Henry joined them. In 1858, when Henry was in Europe from 19 May to 15 October, the only ×'s, for example, appear on 18 May and 15 October. When Mary and the children spent the summer in rural Maine, the ×'s occur only on those days when Henry commuted by train from New York to join them, usually on the day Mary noted in her diary that "Henry arrived" and "Henry left." They cease completely for one month after every childbirth and they rarely appear during the first five days of Mary's menstruation. This is clearly a record of the dates on which she and her husband had sexual intercourse, although, as with the menstrual pluses, the ×'s are nowhere explained. Few ×'s appear during times when Mary or Henry or any of their children were sick. During Mary Poor's severe illness as she recovered from a miscarriage in the summer of 1851 no ×'s occur from August until 17

September, when Mary must have been recuperating, because three days later the nurse left. In 1863, Henry himself was sick with an unidentified ailment through much of September and there are no ×'s until 4 October, when Mary noted that Henry was "decidedly better."

Frequency of intercourse was consistent over the years, with no weekly or seasonal patterns. In 1849, when the Poors had been married eight years and had three children, they had sexual intercourse an average of once every five days. By 1868, when they had been married for twenty-seven years and had six children, the ×'s appear once every 7.2 days. In the twenty-two years between 1849 and 1871, after which the record becomes increasingly sporadic, the Poors had sexual intercourse, on average, 58 times a year, or 4.8 times a month. This average is remarkably similar to the frequencies of intercourse among white, middle class couples reported in 1970s family planning studies.[3]

The many crises in the Poors' lives do not appear to have affected the regularity of intercourse. There are no more and no fewer incidents of intercourse after the deaths of their children or after the death of Mary's father in 1849, one of the most painful events in her life.

The sexual markings are not easy to read. Many of the ×'s recorded after 1852 are erased—likely when Mary Poor gathered the family papers together—but in most cases they are decipherable because the original pencil mark was too firm to be completely obliterated.[4] Although the fact that she erased them suggests that this was a very private record, perhaps of some embarrassment to her, she overlooked many. Because of these erasures, however, the timing and frequency of sexual intercourse cannot always be ascertained; I have based my interpretation of the Poors' sexual behavior on two countings of the ×'s, one that counts only the indisputable marks that were never erased or are still clearly visible, and a second that also includes the less-decipherable ×'s.[5]

Why Mary Poor kept these records is open to conjecture. Like many of her contemporaries she probably relied on menstruation as a sign that she was not pregnant, and when she missed a month she began to be alert to other symptoms of pregnancy; at such times she made special note in her diary and sometimes in letters to her sisters of feeling faint or nauseated. She may also have kept the record to remind her to take special precautions in her diet, her exercise, and her clothing when menstruation was due. Physicians urged women to take menstruation very seriously, believing that serious illness, even death, could result from a delay in menstruation caused by factors other than pregnancy (amenorrhea), excessive menstrual flow (dysmenorrhea), or menstrual cramps (menorrhagia).

The record of sexual intercourse may have been an attempt to make dating a conception easier. Although the careful record keeping came later, during her first pregnancy Mary Poor looked back over her diary and tried to calculate when she had conceived, basing her estimate both on menstruation and on her memory of when she had had sexual intercourse. She decided that she had conceived 9 February 1842 and wrote in the margin, "Begin from here." One week later she began numbering the weeks until one day after week thirty-nine, when Agnes was born. She followed a similar procedure with her second and third pregnancies, but must have found it unsatisfactory to rely solely on a memory of dates of intercourse so she began to keep a record of these dates as well. Mary Poor stopped marking the "×'s" after 1877 when she was fifty-seven and Henry was sixty-five. If the markings were begun to date conceptions or perhaps as part of a "rhythm" method of reproductive control, they continued a long time past when there was any procreative or contraceptive reason to keep track. This practice suggests that sexual intimacy with her husband played an important role in Mary Poor's life and that she wanted a record of it in a way that particularly suited her needs for modesty and privacy.[6]

Whatever the reasons, Mary Poor's diaries offer the historian a rare glimpse into the sexual and procreative lives of a Victorian couple. Scholars trying to reconstruct individual fertility histories in earlier centuries usually must rely on birth intervals and not on far more useful conception intervals. Nor is it common to find information about miscarriages, postpartum amenorrhea (the length of time following childbirth before menstruation resumes), and breastfeeding behavior. Mary Poor's records, to the contrary, permit us to relate at least one woman's menstruation, pregnancies, and childbirth. They allow us to weigh the impact of advice literature—the Poors, for example, seem to have ignored contemporaries' warnings against sexual intercourse during pregnancy but they did wait one month after childbirth. And the records offer suggestions about the motivations, ambivalences, and frustrations of a Victorian couple attempting to control their reproductive destinies. The value of these records for scholars far outweighs any scruple about violation of Mary Poor's privacy.

Henry Varnum Poor was born in Andover, Maine, in 1812 into one of the state's most prominent families. He was graduated in 1835 from Bowdoin College and moved to Bangor, where he speculated in lum-

Table 1. Conception and birth intervals of the children of Mary and Henry Poor

Child	Birth date	Birth interval* (in months)	Conception interval† (in months)
Agnes	10 Nov. 1842	14 (from marriage)	5 (from marriage)
Henry William ("Willie")	16 June 1844	19	10
Robert (d. 1849)	21 Oct. 1848	52	43
Miscarriage 1 **			
Mary Evangeline ("Eva") (d. 1871)	28 Aug. 1853	58	45
Lucy Tappan	17 Dec. 1855	28	19
Mary Merrill ("Quita")	9 Feb. 1860	50	41
Charles Lowell ("Charlie") (d. 1869)	11 Nov. 1861	21	12/13
Miscarriage 2††			

*Number of months between previous child's birth and birth of subsequent child.
†Number of months between previous child's birth and subsequent child's conception.
**Miscarriage 1: 1851 (May-June). There were 31 months from Robert's birth to the miscarriage and 14 months from the miscarriage to Eva's conception.
††Miscarriage 2: 1863 (May-June). There were 18 months from Charlie's birth to the miscarriage.

ber, promoted the building of railroads, and intermittently practiced law. Just after the Poors bought a house in Bangor, a financial depression forced them to move to New York, where, in 1849, Henry took over editorship of the *American Railroad Journal* from his brother, a job he held until 1861. He helped found the American Geographical and Statistical Society, dabbled in the stock market, and after sharp stock losses in 1864 joined a railroad brokerage firm. He spent much of his time after that lobbying for railroads before Congress until his firm went bankrupt in 1867, when Henry and his oldest son, Henry William, a recent graduate from Harvard, formed a railroad commission house to provide railroad insurance and financial data. Their firm, H. V. and H. W. Poor, was a resounding success, and their annual organ, *Manual of the Railroads of the United States*, was the forerunner of the compilations of business statistics and advice later published by Standard and Poor's.

Mary Wild Pierce was born in 1820, youngest daughter of Rev. John Pierce, who for fifty years was the minister of the Unitarian First Parish of Brookline. As minister and also as secretary of the Harvard Board of Overseers for thirty-three years, secretary of the Massachusetts Convention of Congregational Ministers, and member of the Massachusetts Historical Society and the Massachusetts Statistical Society, he held a commanding presence in the community. Her mother, Lucy Tappan Pierce, was the sister of Benjamin Tappan, a senator from Ohio, and of Arthur and Lewis Tappan, New York businessmen whose abolitionist zeal and mercantile fortunes were important to the New York Antislavery Society. Through her parents and her older married sisters, Mary Pierce grew up surrounded by Boston's intellectual, reform, and religious elite. Ralph Waldo Emerson, George Ripley, Margaret Fuller, Elizabeth Peabody, and other Transcendentalists were old family friends. Even in her teens she joined their discussion groups and read their works;[7] all the rest of her life she prided herself on a continuing self-education, keeping note in her diaries of lectures she attended (anatomical lectures, lectures on maternity and the care of infants, lyceum lectures), sporadic language lessons in French, German, Latin, and elocution, and lists of the popular novels and essays she read.

The Poors were Unitarians. In Bangor they attended the church of Mary's brother-in-law and Henry's dearest friend, Frederic Henry Hedge, one of the foremost Unitarian ministers in America, a scholar of German literature, and a Transcendentalist. In New York City they joined the congregation of Thomas Lake Harris, where they met newspaperman and reformer Horace Greeley, writer Catharine Sedgwick, and Elizabeth Blackwell, the first formally licensed woman doctor in the nineteenth-century United States.

The Poors were caught up in the fervor of the reforms of antebellum America. They opposed slavery and attended lectures of the New York Antislavery Society. For a while in New York Mary Poor helped edit a women's temperance paper and, in 1853, joined the Prison Reform Society, later devoting time and money to a "home" founded by the Ladies' Society to rehabilitate female ex-convicts. She helped raise money at charity fairs for the Blackwell sisters' New York Infirmary for Women and Children and in 1856 attended sessions of Elizabeth Blackwell's Sewing Society, a group she referred to in her 1856 diary as the "energetic and strong-minded females of New York." She loved New York, writing to her sister Lucy Hedge, "I feel much happier than I have in a long time because there is work I can do and I can do it with all my energies."[8] Drawn to women of "liberal sentiments," as she wrote to a sister, she was nonetheless not deeply engaged by women's rights, noting of Emily Blackwell: "it strikes me she is not exactly a woman. I would rather my daughters would love and marry after the 'law of their kind' than to turn out quite so strong-minded."[9] Both Poors were interested in communitarian settlements, and, as a guest at Horace Greeley's North American Phalanx in Red Bank, New

Jersey, in 1851, Mary renewed an acquaintance with old family friends, Sarah Grimke and Angelina Grimke Weld. The next summer Henry joined her at the Phalanx and also at abolitionist Theodore Weld's Fourierist community near Eagleswood, New York.

The Poors dabbled in phrenology, and Mary wrote to her sister that she had just had her head examined by a phrenologist who reported, much to her amused acknowledgment, "This person is not practical."[10] She enthusiastically converted to the water cure when she was trying to regain the weight and strength she lost grieving over the deaths of her father and her infant son, Robert, who died of "cholera infantum" in 1851. Perhaps also as an aid to getting pregnant, she followed the hydropathic regimen then at the height of its mid-century popularity, took salt water baths and sitz baths, wrapped herself in "rubbing sheets," took douches, and consulted several of New York's leading water-cure practitioners, among them Mary Gove Nichols and Joel Shew, the publisher of the *Water-Cure Journal*, who had married one of Mary's childhood friends. In the summer of 1853, Mary stayed at the Highland Water Cure Resort and in 1854 at the "immense establishment" of her water-cure physician, a Dr. Wellington, in Orange Mountain, New Jersey. For a while the Poors even followed the vegetarian and dietary instructions of Sylvester Graham, whose theories about the preservation of health through careful management of diet, sexuality, and other "appetites" had aroused particular interest among New England reformers since the late 1830s.[11] Together they attended séances and spiritual rappings; at one, Mary believed that she conversed with her dead father. The appeal of spiritualism to many well-educated and religious Americans in mid century, in the Poors' case, was short-lived. Henry began to scoff at its premises and Mary concluded, with regret, that it was "not a dignified way to converse."

Of Mary Pierce and Henry Varnum Poor's seven children, three died before becoming adults: Robert at nine months of "cholera infantum," Charlie at seven years after a fall, and Eva at nineteen from heart disease. Mary Poor had two miscarriages in twenty-one years and bore her last child when she was forty-one. The Poors were doting and affectionate parents who took seriously their responsiblities for their children's physical, moral, and mental development. Mary, especially, took her maternal duties to heart, writing to her parents when she had two children: "It requires great wisdom and tact to direct aright these different dispositions and I often fear I shall commit some error that shall affect them for life and forever."[12] Although they loved each child, the Poors did not welcome each pregnancy with equal pleasure and delight; at times for reasons of Mary's health or family finances, or for concerns less easily articulated, they wanted to prevent conception.

The Poors' attempts to limit and to space Mary's pregnancies had mixed results. Three of the intervals between a birth and the next pregnancy were long and deliberately contraceptive, as we know from piecing together evidence from her menstrual and sexual records and her writings. Other intervals early in their marriage and, surprisingly, near the end of her childbearing years, were clearly contraceptive failures, judging by their shortness and from the internal evidence in letters and diaries.[13] (See Table 1.)

If the Poors did try to space or delay the conception of their first two children, they were not efficient: their first child, Agnes, was conceived only some five months after their marriage. The short interval between their marriage and this first conception, substantially shorter than any subsequent conception intervals, suggests that the Poors, like so many couples at the time, took no precautions to prevent a first child.[14] The pregnancy and birth were difficult and Mary was sick most of June, reporting from her parents' home in mid-July that she was better. Not until twenty-four days after delivery did Mary take a walk. The nurse stayed five weeks. Although she had "a girl" to help with housework, Mary found breastfeeding and infant care unexpectedly exhausting. It is unlikely that her second pregnancy was planned, following as it did only ten months after Agnes's birth. Just before Mary was certain she was pregnant again, Henry wrote to her in Maine, where she had gone to regain "flesh and strength": "I have tried in vain to find those things which you seem to think so very monstrous in your first letter. Always write dearest just as you think and feel. You always tell me your own heart and you always must. Of course no one sees your letters but myself. I am very glad that you have got a girl to hold the baby etc. etc." Mary's letter of complaints has been lost, but it seems likely that it concerned the interrelated trials of a baby, breastfeeding, and continued postpartum ill health, and possibly news of a suspected new pregnancy that may have been the source of her breastfeeding difficulties.[15]

Although Mary Poor wrote to her parents twenty-one days after Willie's birth that she had "never felt so well"—she had already walked out three times and ridden out twice—she had a difficult winter and spring in 1845.[16] She was lonely because Henry was away much of the time, working on the railroad coming from Montreal, but she was also increasingly preoccupied with her own health. Willie was eight months old in February when her menstruation resumed. She cannot have forgotten that she had conceived him when Agnes was only ten months old. On her doctor's orders she began to wean Willie in April, and this action may well have intensified her anxieties about her fertility. By May she was writing to her parents, "I have been a complainer myself this spring—All the time H. was away I was quite unwell and laid [sic] on the sofa, but the doctor didn't consider me sick enough to take the trouble to cure me."[17] Not until late June, returning from an extended visit to Brookline, was she able to write, "My own health has very much improved by my journey, indeed I feel quite well and strong though easily fatigued."[18]

The sense that Mary Poor was anxious about her health and fearful of a new pregnancy is underscored by several references in her diaries. In a letter to her parents written when Willie was five months old, she wrote that Agnes and Willie were close in age but "it will probably be better for them to be so near of an age than if a longer space intervened between their ages." Apologizing for writing so short a letter, she added, "It is meritorious for a mother of two babies to write at all."[19] The notion of families with three and more children was not far from her mind. She wrote to her parents when Willie was eight months old that she had taken care of a friend's child and found it "very difficult to have three."[20] After she resumed menstruation, she began to keep a meticulous menstrual record, recording her menstruation every month. Her sense of restored health during her visit with her parents in June may, indeed, have been abetted by the arrival of her menstruation 25 June.

The Poors successfully prevented a third pregnancy for forty-three months, a long interval significant because for thirty-three months Mary did not have even the minimal natural protection breastfeeding provides. On 9 January 1848, Mary menstruated for the last time that year. On 16 February when her period was one week late and Henry was away on a short business trip, she overturned the sleigh while driving alone, and was sick for a week. She recorded frequent rides and walks in her diary through the rest of February and March, often when Henry was away, but her diary makes no direct references to her pregnancy or to her health except for unexplained problems in September when a doctor was called in several times. Robert was born on 21 October 1848. Apparently the childbirth weakened her; she did not sit up in bed for eight days or venture downstairs for twenty. During this convalescence Henry and a nursemaid took the infant to Boston for two operations to correct a harelip. With his father's attentive care and the medical expertise available in Boston, he survived the journey and the medical treatments. Because Mary did not accompany the infant to Boston she could not breastfeed him and began to menstruate within three months of his birth. She resumed her diary's menstrual record and also began keeping track of sexual intercourse, an indication of the intensity of her desire to understand and to control her fertility.

With three children under the age of six, Mary did not want another soon. Henry left no evidence about his feelings, but Mary wrote to her parents six weeks after Robert's birth about a friend of hers with four children, all too young to talk: "It would be a great trial to some to have so many, but she does not seem to mind it."[21] There are other reasons why the Poors would have wanted to delay the birth of a fourth child, if, indeed, they wanted any further children at all. In 1849 and 1850 they had suffered considerable financial and emotional distress, crises that left them ill prepared for added familial burdens. An economic depression hit Bangor in 1849, and they were forced to put their house on the market, although it did not sell quickly. It was at that time that Henry moved to New York, hoping to establish himself in a new career and leaving his family in Maine. Mary coped alone with the harsh weather and with their three young children; Robert was still exceptionally delicate. In the spring the family joined Henry, living at first with Mary's brother and his family in Williamsburg and then renting a parlor, bedroom, and adjoining water closet in a New York City boardinghouse. Under financial constraints, and cramped in the small rooms, Mary was restless and unhappy. There was more sorrow to come; that autumn her father died, a loss from which she never fully recovered. Then, a mere three days later, Robert, only eleven months, died from dysentery and "cholera infantum" after hovering between life and death for most of the summer. Mary sought solace at séances, where, for a while, she believed that she was communicating with her father and her son. Mary wrote later to a sister that she had not thought she was "capable of bearing all that I have lived through"; she had "passed through the depths of mental anguish for a year."[22] Her letters do not mention Henry's feelings, but he appears to have tried to bury his own grief in work.

In the summer of 1851 Mary was pregnant again, a pregnancy that miscarried. Although she told her mother and her diary that she had "brain fever," the evidence of miscarriage, though indirect, seems to me conclusive. On 17 May 1851, Mary had menstruated, the twenty-ninth month of regular menstruation following Robert's birth. One month later, on 15 June, she noted in her diary that she was "sick" and, always alert to the possibility of pregnancy, noted on 17 June that it had been "one month" since she last menstruated and on 17 July "two months." On 25 July she became gravely ill, writing two days later that somehow she had "got through." She remained seriously ill from 27 July until 5 August and made no further diary entries. On 21 August a Miss Price arrived to care for her, a trained nurse who stayed for one month and who later attended Mary in every one of her subsequent pregnancies, arriving each time to help with the delivery and staying for exactly one month. The presence of Miss Price with her midwifery skills further suggests Mary's illness was a result of a miscarriage and not simply a severe summer fever.

Mary was in delicate health for several months before regular menstruation resumed. After fourteen months of regular menstrual cycles, she became pregnant again, and in August 1853 Eva, their fourth child, was born.

Interpreting the Poors' intentions about reproductive control in the forty-five-month interval between the birth of Robert and the conception of Eva is difficult because the evidence is ambiguous. It is unlikely, considering their financial and boarding arrangements and also the nursing care that Robert required, that either Henry or Mary wanted a fourth child between 1848 and early 1851. Yet after Robert's death in September 1851, they may have decided to have another child as a hedge against the possible loss of other children and as a replacement for Robert. In any case, Mary became increasingly anxious about losing their other children, writing in her diary—although Agnes had no recorded health problems whatsoever—that it was "almost a certainty" that Agnes "will not live to grow up."[23]

Mary may well have miscarried a pregnancy she wanted in the summer of 1851, although her incoherent diary entries during the illness suggest that she and Henry may have disagreed about its desirability, for she had scribbled "never no more money," and "no more just now comman[d]." The last entry is particularly interesting. Did Mary think it was Henry's wish ("command") that they have "no more children just now"?[24] Her attendance at a lecture by the water-cure physician, Mary Gove Nichols, 8 February 1851 called "Maternity and the Care of Infants" suggests that she had not ruled out future pregnancies. Her active involvement in the water cure that year—her reliance on hydropathists Joel Shew and "Dr. Wellington" for minor family and personal illnesses, her use of water-cure therapies such as douches and wrapping herself in wet sheets, and even her advocacy of the Sylvester Graham diet of wholewheat "graham" crackers and vegetables may have come from a concern over health which had at its root her failure to become pregnant. Water-cure practitioners were known to give contraceptive and abortive advice, but in dealing with women's gynecological and obstetrical concerns they were more generally associated with alleviating the pains of menstruation and the dangers of childbirth. Water-cure remedies such as douches, sitz baths, and wet sheets were recommended for any of a dozen different complaints.[25] Although Mary Poor reported to her mother that she was cured of "inflammation of the lungs" by wearing rubbing sheets three times a day and although elsewhere she recommended that a niece "brace and excite [her] whole system" by using the water cure, she did not leave evidence about what she believed was wrong with her when she "fainted away taking injection" on 26 March, or when she "called at Lesdernier & Shew"—a water-cure establishment—on 17 June. On the other hand, she weighed only ninety-nine pounds in July 1851— her more normal weight, recorded five years later, was 136 pounds— and her concerns may have been entirely related to her general lack of strength and vigor.

Mary's next pregnancy, with Eva (Mary Evangeline), was unusually easy, although when she was about sixteen weeks pregnant she slipped on the stairs in the rain and was "sick" the next day. She wrote in a letter in May, when she was about five months pregnant, that she was "never better in my life." During her ninth month she added, "It has been very unhealthy here, but I have borne the heat etc. better than usual, and am as well and better, I think than ever before in the same situation. My preparations are all completed and Miss Price is staying a few steps from here, ready to come at a moment's notice. For medical attendant I expect to have Miss Blackwell & repose the greatest confidence in her experience and skill."[26] Her letters nevertheless express fears about the future; she wrote in June, "If our lives and health are spared, we shall enjoy [the grapes] very much. I try to have no anxious thoughts for the future, but to remember that we are in the hands of One who doeth all things well."[27] And to a sister, "If we could take no thought for the morrow and cast all our care upon Him who cares for us, we should be happier than we are" and "[I] try to have faith that whatever comes, all will be for the best."[28] Eva was born 28 August; one day later Mary, the infant, and Miss Price, the nursemaid, went to the Highland Water Cure establishment for nearly one month. Even in early November she was writing, "I have not recovered my strength so fast as I have done after previous confinements, which is owing in part I suppose to my living in this crowded city and in part to my being older than I used to be," adding that the baby was thriving and "I wonder how we have got along without one."[29]

Although Mary doted on Eva, "my darling little baby blessing," she did not welcome a new pregnancy nineteen months later. She continued to be anxious about Eva: "she is a precious treasure to us . . . we hope and pray she will be spared."[30] Perhaps it was her despair over the new pregnancy that caused her to destroy the diary for 1855 or to fail to keep one. In sixty-five years of married life Mary Poor failed to keep, or destroyed, her diary only three times: during her 1855 pregnancy with Lucy and in 1905 and 1906, after her husband died.[31] Also, in 1855, she wrote few letters. The day before Lucy's birth she did write to her mother, "I have everything to cheer me and try not to dread the future. Pain is the lot of man & we ought not to shrink from our individual share of it. I do not think any character can be disciplined without it. 'Perfect through suffering' is a significant text."[32]

The Poors successfully prevented another pregnancy for forty-one months after the birth of Lucy, their fifth child, in December 1855, when Mary was thirty-five. We know this was an interval of successful reproductive control—the second longest for the Poors—because they had regular sexual relations randomly during Mary's menstrual cycles. Nearly one-third of all the incidents of their sexual intercourse occurred in mid menstrual cycle when the probability of conception was greatest, and yet Mary did not become pregnant. The Poors could have afforded another child from 1855 to 1860 when they were financially secure; they were living in a large house staffed by three full-time servants and a nursemaid. Mary Poor led an active social life in those years, attending charity fairs and sewing circles, paying and receiving calls from friends, and there were many reasons why she would not have wanted another child. In any case, the Poors succeeded in preventing pregnancy.

In the spring of 1859, after forty-one months without even a pregnancy scare, Mary Poor became pregnant with their sixth child, Mary Merrill ("Quita"). She was thirty-nine, and it is entirely possible that she or both she and Henry did want one additional child before Mary approached menopause, perhaps a second son. Still, whether the pregnancy was desired or whether it was the result of complacency after years of careful contraception, it is impossible to tell because almost no manuscripts about this pregnancy have survived.

After Quita's birth in February 1860, Mary's letters and diary leave no doubt. She wanted no more children and became obsessively alert to the slightest possibility of pregnancy; she was worried about any bout of nausea and alert to any menstrual delay whatsoever. For most of July, even though it was only five months after the last birth, she feared she was pregnant. Interpreting one "bilious attack" as a possible symptom of a new pregnancy, she was filled with despair. That she even suspected a pregnancy so soon after childbirth when she had not yet resumed menstruating and when she was actively breastfeeding an infant suggests that the Poors had had sexual intercourse without what Mary considered to be sufficient contraceptive protection. Still weakened from Quita's birth and convinced she might not survive another pregnancy, she wrote to Henry from Andover, Maine: "If things be as I imagine I will be resigned—the pure air of Andover will perhaps give me strength to live through it. At any rate I will not worry about the future."[33] Six days earlier she and the children were almost killed when their horse bolted on a bridge and their cart overturned. Despite the accident and despite—or because of?—the suspected pregnancy, she walked or rode every day and took one particularly arduous hike with friends to a nearby waterfall, where they were caught in a rainstorm. She wrote to Henry the next day:

> I went to Dunn's Notch yesterday with the Barlows and found it a MUCH MORE fatiguing jaunt than it was when I had you to take care of me. I do not know whether I ought to have gone or not. I had felt SO VERY WELL for a few days that I concluded I had been MISTAKEN and had only suffered from a bilious attack. I HOPE IT WAS SO. . . . Perhaps I did wrong to go, but do you think I ought to stay home all summer on a mere possibility? I do not feel sure that that was the case with me. . . . If I did wrong and ill consequences ensue, forgive me. . . . I feel rather like writing today. . . . I hope yet to have opportunities to show you how much I love you.[34]

Ill consequences did ensue. She was sufficiently ill that Henry had to be telegraphed to come. By 31 July, however, she was convinced that she was not pregnant and wrote Henry, "No SHADOW OF DOUBT now disturbs me and my rosebud Mary grows and thrives." Those two statements suggest why, despite the fact that her menses did not appear for another week, Mary was reassured that she was not pregnant. The Poors used the word "thrives" in conjunction with breastfeeding and the fact that Mary's milk was sufficient to feed her infant convinced her that she could not be pregnant.

Two years later she endured another pregnancy alarm during the summer, and she signaled her relief to Henry on the day she menstruated in a postscript to her letter: "P.S., Events have *proved* my fears to be groundless."[35] She had four pregnancy alarms, including this one, between Quita's birth in February 1860 and menopause in 1868 at age forty-eight. Twice (in 1860 and 1862) her fears were groundless for she was not pregnant, but twice she was: only eighteen or nineteen months after Quita's birth she was pregnant with Charlie; and eighteen months after his birth she was pregnant again, but miscarried in the summer of 1863.

Charlie was conceived sometime after Mary's menstruation of 4 March 1861. In a 15 April letter to a sister, Mary mentioned that she had fainted several times lately, though she said nothing more directly about pregnancy. Only after Charlie's birth did she write explaining:

> Was I not cunning about my expectations? I was *obliged* to tell Elisabeth [another sister] because she wrote and told me she expected to visit me in November and I knew I could not enjoy her society at that time. Sister Sarah and my little Agnes proved as true as steel . . . so I was able to surprise you for once in my life.[36]

In the same letter she noted, revealingly, "altogether I felt very happy and I trust not ungrateful to the Giver of all good who has thus blessed me."

Perhaps it was to effect a "cunning" surprise that she did not reveal the pregnancy. It may not have been welcome and Mary Poor may have hoped it would end prematurely (as the subsequent pregnancy did) or that it would prove to be a false alarm (as had happened the preceding summer). Her words, "I trust not ungrateful" suggest some guilt over her attitude. In April, when her period was eleven days late, she had written to another sister, "We don't know after all what to be anxious about. . . . We go on blindly. If it would only teach us to walk humbly and meekly with our God it would be well with us. I often think of the Bible saying that the 'trials of faith work patience,' but they don't seem to with me. Little troubles wear on me and make me moppish [sic] instead of patient."[37]

The anguished letters before she miscarried in 1863 attest to her intense desire to bear no more children. By then she was forty-four, her seventh child was eighteen months old and had been weaned for two months. Then, after twelve months of regular menstrual cycles she suddenly skipped June, July, and August, only to resume menstruating September 11, after weeks of nausea and despair. Mary and the children were at the Andover, Maine, farm of Henry's oldest brother, and Henry was at work in New York City. Their frequent letters reveal their confusion: Henry did not believe that she was pregnant, his sister Martha believed that she was, and Mary sometimes believed Martha, sometimes Henry, and occasionally suspected that her symptoms marked the onset of menopause. She did not describe her symptoms in her letters; we know only the major one—lack of menstruation—from her diary. That this three-month lapse was a miscarriage seems likely because menopausal irregularities did not set in until two years later, and because this was the opinion of Dr. Elizabeth Blackwell, Mary Poor's main obstetrical and gynecological adviser after 1853.

After menstruating in May 1863, Mary vacationed in Brookline. Henry came on weekend visits and, 26–28 June, to help his family journey to Andover. It is likely that Mary told him then that she was two days late with her period. It was the only time she was with him and she did not write until 30 June, with the postscript, "Prospects do not brighten with me but I do not complain."[38] On July 1 she wrote again, adding below her signature with a penciled hand pointing to it, "(no change)." "*I sympathize most deeply with you*," Henry wrote the next day. "I know that you will not repine. . . . I will do all I can to console you." She was not consoled, and wrote, "I think I am resigned to my lot," and "I feel pretty well, considering." On 14 July she wrote, despondent that there was no mail. The rain was "falling, falling": "Occasionally we are cheered by Charlie pulling Mary's hair or Mary scratching Lucy's face. Life is a warfare. He comes out best who has the toughest skin and the dullest nerves. . . . Mrs. Dr. Ingalls fainted away in church yesterday. So you see my lot is common."

For the next month she took long hikes, horseback and carriage rides, and occasionally noted in her diary, "I felt ill" and "slight illness." Her 16 August letter told Henry, "I am *not yet well* and begin to think that your sister Martha may be right and you wrong. I will try to feel resigned to the fate that Providence assigns to me. It may all blow over after all." Two days later she asked him to send her Elizabeth Blackwell's address in New York so she could write for her opinion. She added, "I do not dare to walk or ride." The next day, however, she wrote in her diary, "I rode out and did not feel so well after it." She wrote to Elizabeth Blackwell and then to Henry that his sister Martha's theory was probably right, but "when it is all over we may be very thankful and years hence may rejoice over this issue of this little trial."[39]

Though he was worried about his wife's health and state of mind, Henry did not share her despair. He felt, for one thing, that she was wrong in her suspicion about a new pregnancy. He wrote, "If you are right, I shall not regret it; on the contrary I think I shall be not a little pleased. We are well off and can take things very comfortably. . . . How happy you will be in clasping the offspring of such love a thousand times to your bosom . . . [with] your growing promise of a new life I shall clasp you with tenfold warmth and affection to my bosom."[40]

Elizabeth Blackwell's answer to Mary has not survived, nor has Mary's letter telling Henry of the physician's opinion. But one of his own letters provides ample clues that Dr. Blackwell believed Mary had miscarried a pregnancy. Henry wrote:

> I am relieved to learn Dr. Blackwell's conclusions, but somewhat surprised; but I do not know why I should be, you have always been so regular in your habits that I ought to have drawn the natural inference from any interruption of them. It is fortunate that you have got along as well as you have. I see now that you ought not to have taken those long rides with me. . . . Shall we never learn wisdom? I should have been pleased than otherwise to have had it gone on. Another baby would not have been one too many, I think. But we must take things as they are."[41]

On 11 September Mary's menstruation resumed, and her diary entries become more cheerful: "Perfect day," "lovely day." She wrote to Henry, "I have had a pretty hard summer but the clouds have all lifted now and everything is bright."[42]

Although the Poors left no direct evidence about how they managed their long intervals between pregnancies and why they had occasional failures, their records do offer us glimpses into this question of *how*, the most elusive of all the issues connected to Victorian reproductive control.

Sexual Abstinence and Unwelcome Advice

Although historians have long argued that nineteenth-century couples controlled fertility by sexual abstinence, the Poors at no time in their marriage were sexually abstinent. Over the course of their married life they had sexual intercourse with great regularity even when Mary was most fearful of another pregnancy. They may have tried at times to restrict the frequency of intercourse both for reasons of health (part of the Graham dietary regimen was to teach people to curb their passions) and for reasons of reproductive control. They may even have resorted to deliberate physical separation as a means of preventing conception during one summer, when Mary, staying in Andover with Henry's family, wrote to her husband: "I do not like to be long separated from you. We are happiest together, do not let us try absence again. I want to be with you, wherever you are, the rest of the summer and the rest of my life."[43] It is even possible that sexual inter-

Table 2. Frequency of coitus before and after resumption of menstruation, Mary Poor, 1854–62

Date menses resumed	Coital frequency (4 months prior)	Coital frequency (4 months after)
4 May 1854	18	21
20 May 1856	31	20
7 Aug. 1860	31*	17*
11 June 1862	25*	15*

*Questionable data because the actual numbers in the diary were especially well erased for these months.

course once or twice a week was an attempt at moderation, although the consistency of their frequencies suggests otherwise. Still, in 1860 and 1862 the Poors may have tried to prevent pregnancy by deliberately reducing the number of times they had sexual intercourse in the months after Mary resumed menstruating after childbirth. (See Table 2.)

Sleeping together was important to both of the Poors. Henry once complained to the vacationing Mary that it "is hard to sleep alone," and even in 1868, after twenty-seven years of marriage, Mary annotated the first page of her diary with the lament, "Of 365 nights Henry spent at home 123." She was not counting the days absent, but the nights.[44] Mary's attitudes toward intercourse may well have undergone more dramatic shifts than Henry's did over the years, given her fears of pregnancy, but even so it appears that sexual intercourse was simultaneously an occasion for an intimate bond and a time of dread and anxiety. The very fact that she kept the careful sexual record suggests that sex held diverse and possibly conflicted meanings for her (she wanted a record but she wanted to erase it), meanings that Henry may or may not have shared or, given the weighted reticences of this couple, not even been aware of. The ×'s may have started out as a way of determining the exact conception date of a pregnancy, but the persistence with which she maintained the notations, even after menopause when she was no longer fearful about pregnancy, suggests that this had become a record with many layers of connotations, some of which she may have been unable even to articulate.

In the first half of the nineteenth century, advisers commonly urged couples not to have intercourse during pregnancy lest it cause abortion or somehow mark the fetus. In 1853, Thomas Low Nichols, husband of Mary Gove Nichols, warned against any sexual activity during pregnancy in his popular book *Esoteric Anthropology: A Comprehensive and Confidential Treatise on the Structure, Functions, Passional Attractions and Perversions, True and False Physical and Social Con-*

Table 3. Frequency of intercourse during pregnancies, Mary and Henry Poor, 1852–1860

Pregnancy	Frequencies during pregnancy*	Frequencies 8 months prior[†]
Pregnancy 4 (Eva) 1852–53	49	42
Pregnancy 6 (Quita) 1859–60	49	40
Pregnancy 7 (Charlie) 1861	35	33

*For the first eight months only, excluding the month before delivery.
[†]The sexual records did not exist for pregnancies 1, 2, 3 and are not extant for 5.

ditions, and the Most Intimate Relations of Men and Women.[45] But the Poors did not significantly vary their sexual frequencies when Mary was pregnant, apparently not curbing their sexual appetites even in the ninth month. (See Table 3.) The only times the Poors appear to have deliberately restricted sexual activity was immediately after childbirth, when they were abstinent for exactly one month after delivery (which was usually the day the nurse attending Mary left), during illnesses (but not always), and, as noted earlier, in the first three days of Mary's menstruation.

Many historians maintain that coitus interruptus or "withdrawal" was one of the best-known and most effective of all methods of birth control in the nineteenth century. Later chapters in this book take issue with such assumptions, but though the Poors may well have relied on withdrawal at times, there is no evidence in their papers to suggest that they did or whether they found it effective. When other contraceptive options were available, couples seem to have preferred them to withdrawal.

Henry Poor himself ought to have had considerable access to condoms—the newly invented rubber varieties or the traditional "skin" condoms known for centuries in Europe—but again there is no evidence that he did in the Poors' letters or in Mary's diaries. His college training in classical economics and political and economic theory had exposed him to Malthusian doctrines about the dangers of overpopulation, and he may possibly have read the European theorists, such as Francis Place, Jeremy Bentham, and Richard Carlile, who rebutted Malthus's emphasis on delayed marriage, urging contraception as a way to stem the dangers of excessive population and a dwindling food supply. More directly however, Poor's Nassau Street office as editor of the *American Railroad Journal* placed him daily in the heart of a neighborhood that openly offered for sale sexual and reproductive control publications, erotica, contraceptives, and abortion services. Several times a week he walked by a dozen such establishments, among them probably T. W. Strong's bookstore at 98 Nassau Street, from which Strong sold condoms and tracts on reproductive control and sexual advice.

The Rhythm Method

Mary Poor's menstrual and sexual records provide no clear-cut evidence about whether the couple relied on any of the variants of the nineteenth-century rhythm method. As Chapter 3 develops in greater detail, many Victorians believed that women had an infertile period sometime between each menstrual flow. Physicians did not agree exactly when it occurred, and their advice differed about how women could recognize this "agenetic" period each month, but, in general, women who wanted to avoid pregnancy were advised to avoid sexual intercourse just before, during, and especially just after menstruation while the ovum was in the uterus ready to pass from the body. The safe period was believed to be anywhere from eight to sixteen days after cessation of the menstrual flow. A mid-century woman who wanted to avoid pregnancy would have tried to concentrate sexual intercourse in mid cycle with low frequencies before and after menstruation.

Mary Poor left no direct evidence to indicate her beliefs about rhythm-method theories. She certainly had access to such ideas, living as she did in New York City at the height of the popularity of Frederick Hollick, one of the chief lecturers and writers about the monthly infertile period. She attended lectures on anatomy, maternity and the care of children, which probably included hints about the infertile period. She was a close personal friend of the family of physician Augustus K. Gardner, and she read at least one of his books, *Old Wine in New Bottles*, an account of his year in Paris. She may have had a special familiarity with his rhythm-method recommendations. Gardner had published his views in 1858, arguing that "conception cannot take place except during the ten days subsequent to the appearance of menstruation."[46] According to his theory, then, Mary Poor would have believed herself safe from pregnancy from around Day 10 until her next menses neared. One month in 1845 Mary made a special note in her diary the day she believed she ovulated, writing in the margin the word "egg" next to 16 March. Unfortunately, her menstrual mark is unclear for that month (she marked three dates with a " + "), so we cannot know clearly which day in her cycle she believed she ovulated, but it was either Day 3, Day 8, or one day before menstruation.

A graph plotted according to what day in Mary's menstrual cycle the Poors had sexual intercourse suggests that they did try to concentrate their sexual activity in what they believed was the safe period: from Day 9 through 15.[47] They had sexual intercourse relatively infrequently during menstruation (although they were not totally abstinent, especially on Day 1) and frequency levels did drop off sharply just before menstruation every month. (See Figure 1 on the sexual frequencies in the menstrual cycle for the years 1849–1864 when Mary was not pregnant.[48]

A review of her individual conception intervals illustrates the same

*The day MPP marked a " + " in her Diary is Day 1.

Figure 1. Frequency of coitus by day in menstrual cycle for the years with no pregnancies, Mary Poor, 1849–64

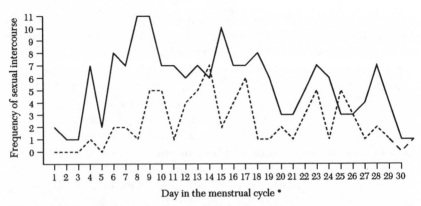

*The day MPP marked a "+" in her diary is Day 1.

The solid line represents the interval from January 1849 to May 1851; the dotted line represents the interval from 20 September 1851 to November 1852.

Figure 2. Frequency of coitus by day in the menstrual cycle for two intervals, Mary Poor, 1849–52

general pattern. Figure 2 shows the timing of sexual intercourse according to Mary's menstrual cycles for two intervals: from January 1849 (when Mary resumed menstruating after the birth of their third child, Robert, and when she began to keep her sexual record), until her miscarriage in May 1851; and second, from September 1851, when she resumed menstruating after the miscarriage, until her November 1852 conception of their fourth child, Eva. Both were exceptionally long contraceptive intervals.

The graphs underscore one important point clearly: the Poors must have been practicing some type of contraception in addition to the rhythm method because they had sexual intercourse roughly one-third of the time in mid menstrual cycle when, by today's calculations, Mary was most likely to have been ovulating and was, therefore, most fertile. The risk of conception from a single coitus increases from almost zero early in the menstrual cycle until its highest peak three days before ovulation. After ovulation the risk again falls near zero.[49] The Poors' peak sexual frequencies, in Figure 1, are Days 9 and 15. With Mary's average menstrual cycle 28.7 days long during those years, ovulation would probably have been around Day 14. Because the five days preceding Day 14 and the one following were the most fertile, she stood her greatest chance of conceiving on the days they most frequently, in fact, had sexual intercourse.[50] Although the Poors appear to have tried at times to limit their sexuality to what they thought were her infertile days, they did not follow such prescriptions conscientiously, perhaps from carelessness, but more likely because they were using other preventive methods, with the rhythm method as a means of additional protection.

Douching: Vaginal "Injections"

Mary Poor's water cure was a major source—although indirectly—of contraceptive information. She learned how to give herself vaginal douches and occasionally noted them in her diary.[51] She did not record how often she douched, but water-cure advisers did specify frequent and thorough vaginal douching. She may have heeded the advice of Mary Gove Nichols, whose lectures she attended, to douche as often as four times a day for a variety of menstrual and general medical complaints.[52] It required little experimentation or even imagination to move from douching for medicinal and hygienic purposes to douching for contraception. She did not record the solutions she used or the type of douching apparatus. She may have used spermicides, such as weak carbolic acid, vinegar, baking soda, and vegetable astringents, all recommended for gynecological problems, and many of them recommended also for gynecological infections and menstrual irregularities. Possibly frequent douching, even if not with deliberate contraceptive intent, reduced her chances of conceiving and delayed pregnancy, especially if she and Henry were simultaneously practicing other forms of reproductive control.

Breastfeeding as a Means of Delaying Pregnancy

So pervasive was the belief in mid-nineteenth-century American culture that breastfeeding provided contraceptive protection that some could even joke about it. A young married woman, Priscilla Cooper Tyler, wrote laconically to her sister in 1840, "I suppose you have heard that Victoria [the Queen of England] is expecting again. Poor thing! So much for not nursing!"[53] Medical advisers differed substantially over the efficacy of maternal breastfeeding as a means of family limitation. Some, including those who opposed other methods of reproductive control, promoted it as a natural way to prevent conception, while others urged women not to rely on lactation. Physician and women's medical adviser George Napheys, who supported the limitation of offspring and the practice of child spacing, urged women in the

1870s not to prolong nursing over twelve months. That his advice was largely ignored is clear from the abundance of complaints in medical literature against women who "sometimes nurse their children for eighteen months or more, even when they know they are pregnant in the hope of aborting" or women who "for various reasons wish to nurse as long as they can to the point of exaggerating their good health."[54]

Breastfeeding can lower the probability of conception—by lengthening the period before menstruation resumes after childbirth and possibly by increasing the number of anovulatory menstrual cycles. The contraceptive effect, however, diminishes over time; it is further reduced when menstruation returns and when supplemental foods are substituted for full nursing.[55] To Mary Poor's misfortune, she relied too often throughout her fertile life on the faulty contraceptive protection of breastfeeding.

When, after the birth of her later children, Mary Poor relied on breastfeeding as a means of reproductive control she had many pregnancy scares and unwanted pregnancies. (See Table 4.) She breastfed all her children, and for most she kept notes about when she began and completed weaning. Eva was the first who did not have to be weaned early. Mary breastfed her for thirteen and a half months and delayed weaning even though her own health was not robust. She breastfed Lucy for nearly sixteen months, longer than she had nursed any previous child. In addition, after the disastrously short birth interval between Eva and Lucy, she doubled the length of time of breastfeeding once she began to have regular menstruation. She breastfed Eva, for example, for five months after menstruation resumed, but Lucy for ten.

Although medical advisers differed in their advice about weaning, sixteen months was in the upper range of their recommendation, and almost every one of them urged mothers to stop nursing with the renewal of menstruation. Russell Thacher Trall, one of New York's

Table 4. Weaning practices: Mary Pierce Poor, 1842–63

Child	Duration of breastfeeding	Duration after menses resumed
Agnes	10 months	5 months
Willie	9 months 2 weeks	6 weeks, 2 days
Robert	ca. 3 weeks	not applicable
Eva	13 months 2 weeks	5 months 10 days
Lucy	15 months 3 weeks	10 months 18 days
"Quita"	13 months 1 week	7 months 9 days
Charles	16 months 2 weeks	9 months 14 days

leading water-cure physicians in the 1860s and a good friend of Mary's hydropathists, was even more emphatic, writing that, for the sake of her own health and that of her child, no woman should nurse beyond nine or ten months.[56]

The increasing length of time Mary Poor breastfed her children suggests a decision, corroborated by other evidence about her despair over later pregnancies, to try to prolong lactation as a contraceptive aid. Not only did she nurse her children longer than many medical advisers recommended, but she felt obliged to justify her actions to her mother and sisters. She delayed weaning Eva beyond the time her mother thought advisable and postponed weaning Lucy well beyond even that.[57] In December 1856, Mary continued to breastfeed the twelve-month-old Lucy three times a day even though the nursemaid, a *Mrs.* Anne Seymore, may well have been capable of wet-nursing. In November, Mary felt that she had to explain to her mother why Lucy was not yet weaned: "It is always sad to me to wean my babies and Lucy is doing so very well now I cannot bear to make any change and have concluded to continue to nurse her for the present." She did follow a sister's advice to wean Lucy at nights.[58] Later, in spite of the unanimous medical opinion that women should cease nursing immediately after recognizing the onset of a pregnancy, she continued to nurse Quita between June and August 1860 even though she suspected (wrongly, as it turned out) that she might be pregnant.

Abortions or Accidental Miscarriages?

For many mid-nineteenth-century women, abortion was an ever-present alternative to an undesired pregnancy. Indeed, the abortion rate, particularly among the middle class, was sharply on the increase. American women had considerable access to diverse sources of information about abortion and abortion drugs and instruments, and to different sorts of persons offering abortion services. Although Mary Poor left no evidence of any kind that she ever sought out a "professional" abortionist or bought and used any of the widely marketed drugs to induce abortion, Victorian women did have many ways to procure miscarriage relatively easily and safely. There was little outcry about abortion's being immoral or unethical until the American Medical Association began a campaign to curb it in mid century. Nor were abortions illegal so long as quickening (fetal movement) had not yet occurred, generally in the second trimester. Neither of the Poors ever broached the subject of deliberate abortion in letters nor did Mary in her diary, and Mary's chief medical advisers disagreed vehemently about the subject. Blackwell disparaged the very idea of deliberately induced miscarriage; she detested the long association of "female physicians" with abortionists. Mary Gove Nichols, on the other hand, probably shared her husband's opinion that a woman had the right to her own ova and the right to abortion if she did not want to bear a child.[59] Yet Mary Poor's actions in 1860 and in 1863 are highly suggestive and she may well have induced more than one abortion. Despite fears that she was pregnant, despite bouts with nausea and "sickness," despite inclement weather, she persisted in taking vigorous exercise—walks, climbs, cart rides. Henry warned her, "Be careful not to overdo, whatever may be your SITUATION."[60] Later, when it was clear she had miscarried, he wrote, "I see now that you ought not to have taken those long rides with me. . . . Shall we never learn wisdom?"[61] Yet Mary does not seem to have hesitated in taking the arduous exercise, even though she noted in her diary several times that she did not feel well after a walk or ride. More significantly, she wrote to Henry once that her symptoms of pregnancy made it so "I do not dare to walk or ride," yet her diary for the very next day shows that she took a ride "and did not feel so well after it."

Women's Options

This story of the Poors' marital sexual experience illustrates important issues about reproductive control in Victorian America. Mary Poor's discontent with her reproductive life took place in a marriage that in all other ways appears to have been loving and intimate. Yet love and affection in a relationship did not preclude disagreements, even conflict, over sexual issues and reproduction. Even happy marriages could involve differences of opinion about the number and timing of pregnancies, family size, and sexuality. Historians Jan Lewis and Kenneth A. Lockridge have similarly noted in connection with attitudes about family limitation and practices among Virginia gentry women that as much as husbands and wives loved each other, men could not share and often did not empathize deeply with a wife's articulated fears and deep despair about pregnancies and childbirth.[62] Men's and women's interests in such matters were distinct and often antagonistic in an era when reproductive control was far from being absolutely reliable and when every sexual encounter could lead to pregnancy. How did the Poors decide when and whether to practice contraception, and if so what methods did they adopt? Who would be responsible for preventing pregnancy? What happened when pregnancy resulted anyway? Who determined when and how often to have sexual intercourse? Raising such issues, much less resolving them, created the potential for deep anger, as well as the possibility of joy and harmonious agreement. Communication difficulties contributed to the problem, for no such issues were easy to discuss even between the closest of couples.

Reproductive control affected women and men as individuals, as heterosexual couples, as families, and as members of other social groups. Although there was no publicly articulated politics of "birth control" at the time, and no organized social movement for or against it, any issue that involved such expressions of power, however subtle or quiet, that required such negotiation, compromise, victories, and losses between husband and wife—however unarticulated or unconscious—obviously had a private politics. Although much of this book focuses on the relations between reproductive control and public activities—the marketplace, for example—we should not lose sight of the underlying fact that contraception and abortion involved a personal, a gender, a marital, and a sexual politics of enormous significance.

Mary Poor is a good illustration of some of the dilemmas motherhood posed for Victorian women. She did not challenge or question the importance of maternity, although at times she chafed at the demands of the role and feared the consequences of bearing and raising children. It is also clear that she was convinced that even with three young children she could find other roles for herself, for she took up reform activities and pursued her own further education. Conventional in most respects, devoted to her children and husband, she did not find the domestic sphere enough, but made forays into the wider public world. She based her attempts to space and restrict her pregnancies in part on her sense of maternal duties, her concern that more children would interfere with her ability to nurture those already born, and her deep fear that she would die in childbirth and leave her family motherless. Motherhood took on ambiguous meanings for her quite quickly in her married life: both a job and a pleasure, a burden, a means of self-definition, a legitimate social role and a limitation and threat to health and life itself. Her life, then, illustrates some of the ways that marriage circumscribed a woman's life more than a man's and the ways that maternity, even to a woman who loved her children and found joy in the maternal role, became a burden, an ever-looming threat, and even a curse.[63]

In a number of ways the Poors do not fit the historical demographers' profile of a couple practicing family limitation at mid nineteenth century. They had seven children. Mary did not stop childbearing before menopause. The Poors used child spacing as a form of family limitation, though some demographers give short shrift to spacing as family limitation.[64]

The Poors also illustrate that motivation is never easy to assess. Historians who boldly attribute one or the other cause to family-limitation practices in the nineteenth century are in danger of oversimplifying. For all their records—and the Poors left far more direct evidence about their reproductive behaviors and attitudes than did most nineteenth-century couples—their motivations remain elusive. The Poors do not appear to have had any desired number of children in mind when they began married life. Rather, their attempts to control fertility resulted from many factors: Mary's health, fluctuations in their economic position, and the number and health of the children already born. What is abundantly clear is that they changed over time and occasionally differed as a couple in their perceptions and goals. Early in their marriage, buoyed by youthful optimism, both Henry and Mary had convictions about their abilities to shape events and to live the kind of life they wanted. Their openness to the yeasty mixture of social and cultural reforms of the 1850s and Mary's zest and assertiveness in health regimens illustrate their shared belief in the power of individuals to perfect and control. Both showed confidence that life's exigencies could be regulated and made more predictable. Whether it was Henry's gathering of business statistics about lumber and railroads, or Mary's attempts to gain control over disease by the water-cure regimen, by a vegetarian diet, or by tracing her menstrual and sexual patterns, the Poors believed that one could gather data, analyze them to find the underlying patterns or laws, follow their lessons, and thereby gain power and control.

Henry's beliefs in this respect increased as the marriage progressed; Mary's followed a different trajectory. The vicissitudes of Henry's career did not alter his youthful assumption that men could chart their lives by rationality, by work, and by decisive action. Time only reinforced such confidence and he remained a committed economic reformer—writing treatises on the need for free trade, silver coinage, an interstate commerce commission. Mary, however, experienced no such reaffirmation of youthful beliefs in power and control. Her liberal reform activities, like those of many other Americans, declined after the Civil War. In spite of her menstrual and sexual records, in spite of her fears of pain and death from excessive pregnancies, in spite of experiences proving that sometimes she and Henry could control reproduction, her fertility wore her down. Her growing passivity is nowhere more evident than in the language she began to use to refer to her suspicions of pregnancy. She referred to "trials of faith," "my lot to be borne," to "the fate Providence assigns to me." Mary lost confidence in her ability to effect change. Fate took over. Her sense of control and individual power was fragile and dissolved slowly but inexorably in the face of contraceptive failure, age, and personal setbacks. Given the unreliability of nineteenth-century reproductive control, her fatalism no doubt increased her failure rate and led to more pregnancies. Menopause may have aided her descent into even deeper passivity. So, too, the tragedies of seven-year-old Charlie's death from a fall downstairs in 1869 and of nineteen-year-old Eva's from heart disease, when all Mary could do was helplessly record in her diary the dying girl's pulse rate may have furthered her sense of a lack of control. The diaries of the last third of Mary Poor's long and fruitful life show little more than endless, mindless games of whist and social exchanges with other leisured ladies of Brookline.[65]

In the Poors' failures to attain the measure of fertility control they so clearly wanted lie the outlines of deeper issues in nineteenth-century reproductive control. Beyond intense desire for fewer pregnancies and successful or unsuccessful practice of family limitation lay a host of other factors—financial, psychological, moral, medical—pertaining to specific contraceptive and abortive methods and to reproductive control in general. These made choices more difficult.

2

Strategies in
Colonial America

The reproductive control options of the Poors, like those of other nineteenth-century Americans, built on earlier traditions. Some colonists in the seventeenth and eighteenth centuries knew about and practiced contraception and abortion, although the cases that made it into the historical record generally involved men and women in illicit sexual activities rather than married couples. Cases of fornication (sexual activity between unmarried people), adultery, or seduction occasionally elicited attempts at contraception, abortion, and infanticide. Plymouth Governor William Bradford recorded in his journal, kept between 1630 and 1650, the case of a local minister, a Mr. Lyford, who seduced a young woman ostensibly while determining her fitness to marry one of his parishioners.

> [Lyford] promised faithfully to inform [the parishioner], but would first take other knowledge of her and have private conference with her and so [did at?] sundry times and in conclusion commended her highly to the young man as a very fit wife for him, so they were maried together. But some time after mariage, the woman was much troubled in mind and afflicted in [countenance?], and did nothing but weptd and mournd and long it was before her husband could get of her what was the cause, but at length she . . . prayed him to forgive her, for Lyford had overcome her, and defiled her body before mariage affor he had comended him onto her for a husband, and she refused to have him when he came to her in that private way.[1]

The young woman did not want to tell her husband the full circumstances "for they would offend chast ears to hear them related, for though he satisfied his lust on her, yet he endeavored to hinder conception." In the village of Pomfret, Connecticut, in 1742, young Amasa Sessions convinced his pregnant lover, nineteen-year-old Sarah Grosvenor, to "take the trade"—take an abortive drug—and then hired a local "practitioner of physick" to perform an abortion. When she died, Sessions and Hallowell, the physician, were charged with "highhanded misdemeanor," but only Hallowell eventually stood trial. Found guilty, he fled the colony before being punished.[2] It seems quite clear that the young people involved in this case—Sarah Grosvenor, her sister and sister-in-law, her lover and his confidantes— were familiar with the idea of abortion and even with its slang, although Sarah herself apparently did not want the abortion and only reluctantly consented because her lover "So very earnestly perswaided her," for he would "take no denyal."[3] Colonial records also illustrate that some women, generally marginal and desperate women, were executed for committing infanticide, and other women secretly and by their own devising aborted unwanted pregnancies.[4] Many women who found themselves unmarried and pregnant simply got married because colonial authorities did not punish fornication as severely if the couple married. Premarital pregnancy rates in the American colonies varied considerably in the seventeenth and eighteenth centuries, but at times one-third of all brides in a given area were pregnant at marriage.[5]

So rare and so hushed was any public discussion of reproductive control that no laws or statutes proscribed contraceptive practices. Abortion, on the other hand, was a serious offense, in the eyes of both the law and the church. Puritans, in particular, condemned it as a sin—a man or woman trying to induce miscarriage was usurping the prerogatives of God by daring to intervene in life and death—and abortion was not uncommonly linked with witchcraft accusations against women.[6] Convictions for abortion, however, were rare. Middlesex County in Massachusetts had only four convictions for attempted abortion between 1633 and 1699.[7]

The question of whether reproductive control entered into marital relations—that is, whether married couples in colonial America used methods to space or limit the size of their families—continues to challenge historians, many of whom believe that such deliberate family limitation was rare. New England fertility rates were relatively high by European standards, and the spacing of children and the length of most women's childbearing span are not suggestive of successful attempts at family limitation. Many colonists, Puritans especially, even if they knew of the use of contraceptives among the aristocats in England, may well have believed the godly route was to follow the biblical injunction to multiply and replenish the earth.[8] It is, however, by far more accurate to state that the historical record is silent about what married couples tried than to argue that they attempted no reproductive control at all. The existence of large families and the absence of evidence about fertility intervention do not prove that couples did not *attempt* some form of child-spacing or family limitation, although with great secrecy and little success, especially in their later years. Nor do they prove anything about couples' motives. Few wives or husbands would have had reason to publicize practices that they believed their neighbors and the authorities associated with lewdness and immorality. If they talked with each other about wanting fewer children or longer intervals between children, or if one sought to persuade the other, or if they tried contraception or abortion, married women and men did so very quietly. We do not have neighbors' gossip or servants' reports in court records attesting to such practices. That married couples' interest in reproductive control did not make it into court records is hardly conclusive proof that it did not exist. Still, because there was little privacy in any of the seventeenth-century colonies,[9] married women must have been very careful if they took actions or used any of the botanical products with reputations as abortives, products that in parts of America by the nineteenth century were called "character spi'lin'" because any woman seen taking them was suspected of trying to prevent conception or induce miscarriage.[10]

The claim by historians John D'Emilio and Estelle Freedman that in colonial America "married couples had little motive to prevent or terminate pregnancy" is too sweeping. Fears about land scarcity and declining properties to leave to children affected many New Englanders as early as the second half of the seventeenth century, and women may have had their own motives for wanting greater intervals between children.[11] The economic situations in England and New England differed, but an English example is suggestive here. Historian Alan Macfarlane writes of a mid-seventeenth-century English clergyman, Ralph Josselin, and his wife, Jane Constable Josselin: "Children were greatly desired, and welcomed, until they became an economic burden to their parents; then there are indications that a brake was put on the enlarging family, though not a very effective one." The gaps between the Josselins' last children were greater than between their first, but more significantly, Jane Josselin appears to have recognized her pregnancies within two months of conception, and the three miscarriages she had after the birth of nine children "coincided almost exactly with the earliest point at which [she] could have known she was pregnant and have used some form of abortion."[12]

By the late eighteenth century, married women and even their husbands openly expressed displeasure over unchecked pregnancies. In the village of Hallowell, Maine, midwife Martha Ballard wrote in her diary about a forty-five-year-old neighbor who, in historian Laurel Thatcher Ulrich's words, "was overwhelmed by her last pregnancy, an unexpected and probably unwelcome event."[13] Abigail Adams "openly lamented her daughter Nabby's repeated pregnancies, declared that her sister Elizabeth was 'foolish' to start 'a second crop' of children at the age of forty, and in 1800 welcomed the news of a young relative's miscarriage because 'it is sad slavery to have children as fast as she has'."[14] As much as women's and even some men's letters and diaries reflect distress and concern about "excessive" childbearing, they reflect, at the same time, a sense of its inevitability.[15] Whatever may have been the desire for greater control, and whatever their individual attempts, the prevailing view among colonial Americans was that they had little real ability to intervene in such issues.

What Colonial Americans Used

When and if they did intervene, the three reproductive control methods with which colonial Americans were the most familiar were coitus interruptus, abortion, and breastfeeding. Coitus interruptus, or withdrawal, was clearly known and practiced by some colonists. In 1710, in an exceptionally unusual case, a married woman in Massachusetts, Abigail Emery, accused her husband of Onan's "abominable sin," which she claimed he practiced because "he feared the charge of children."[16] In this case, the practice of withdrawal was clearly contraceptive, and it is noteworthy that the husband used it over his wife's protests. In another case, a colonial Massachusetts man, charged in court with fathering an illegitimate child, protested his innocence by telling the court that the child could not be his for he had always "minded my pullbacks."[17] He was apparently correct in expecting this veiled reference to be readily understood.

Women in widely different cultures have often had means available to end unwanted pregnancies by the deliberate induction of miscarriage. The methods—violent exercise, cervical or uterine insertions, drugs—were often so dangerous that they threatened the woman's life, and a large percentage were ineffective. Other methods worked and even those that appear horrifyingly dangerous today may not have appeared so in past eras when compared to the evidence of women's deaths in childbirth or from pregnancy-related problems. Modern medical opinion holds that it is difficult to self-induce an abortion, but folklore annals are filled with the contrary view. John Gerard, whose book *The Herball or Generall Historie of Plantes* was one of the most influential medical authorities in seventeenth-century New England, believed some plants to be so powerful that he put sticks around them in his garden "lest any woman so much as step over [them]."[18] Many plant products were believed to bring on a miscarriage, prevent conception, ease menstrual cramps and the pains of childbirth, speed labor, and cure a multitude of "female complaints." Even in the seventeenth century, when books were not readily available, many families owned the popular herbals of Gerard, John Parkinson, and Nicholas Culpeper. Culpeper's *The English Physician* and *Complete Herbal* recommended more than a dozen preparations of botanicals common to English and New England gardens, any of which would "bring on a woman's courses." He cited pennyroyal, sage, common groundpine, bistort or snakeweed, gladwin, brake fern, calamint, and honeysuckle and listed six to twelve he believed would cause abortion.[19]

Women from the colonial era through the nineteenth century who wanted to abort took a variety of steps. A woman who did not want to be pregnant might first drink an herbal tea or soak her feet in hot water mixed with special herbs, breathe hot herbal vapors, or apply herbal mixtures or mustard plasters to her breasts. If taking mild herbal solutions and slightly strenuous exercise did not bring on menstruation quickly at its due time, women would increase both the intensity of their exercise and the drug dosage, perhaps for two or three months, until menstruation resumed or pregnancy was confirmed by other signs.[20]

Husbands and lovers were sometimes known to be involved both in the decision to seek miscarriage and in the procurement of drugs. In one seventeenth-century abortion case, community suspicions were first aroused when a young man was observed reading in an herbal about the aborting properties of juniper berries.[21] Alan Macfarlane concluded after studying seventeenth-century English women and fertility that "the date of conception appears to have been accurately and quickly discovered in mid-seventeenth century."[22] Once a pregnancy "quickened" and movement could be felt, some women abandoned miscarriage attempts, but others used increasingly desperate means, including, by the seventeenth century, use of instruments inserted into the cervix. By the nineteenth century, slippery elm bark had become associated with abortions.

Colonial Americans knew of an especially diverse botanical materia medica reputed to affect fertility. Among the herbs the earliest Dutch and English settlers saw growing luxuriantly in the American woods were several with already well-established European reputations as contraceptives and abortives: pennyroyal, tansy, savin, and rue, among them.[23] In four cases of alleged abortion in late-seventeenth-century Middlesex, Massachusetts, the drug of choice was savin boiled in beer. The remedy did not work as an abortive in three of the four cases. In 1666 a twenty-four-year-old Mary Davis accused a John Phillips, thirty-three, of attempted rape. Phillips told her "he could have his desier and not get her with child and could give them steele powder." The "steele powder" was presumably a contraceptive.[24] Tansy, especially, had an ancient association with fertility intervention. The writings of the well-known seventeenth-century herbalist Culpeper reported that tansy seeds would destroy stomach worms, stop fluxes, stop miscarriages when applied externally to a woman's navel, yet when served in wine, tansy would "procure women's courses." Culpeper considered it an herb to aid conception: "Let those women that desire children love this herb, it is their best companion.[25] This is probably the reason for the Cape Cod saying that "every woman should curtsy on passing tansy, it has done so much for the female sex."[26] It is neither uncommon nor illogical in folk medicine that the same plant would be believed capable of preventing and also of inducing miscarriage. Because a menstruating woman was presumably a fertile woman, promoting menstruation was a means of ensuring that a woman was ready to conceive. On the other hand, inducing menstruation might abort a newly conceived pregnancy. Thus, remedies to induce menstruation had dual uses.[27] Later, entrepreneurs advertised their commercial preparations by playing deliberately on this well-known association.

Mint species had a reputation dating to the Greek medical writers as being capable of inducing menstruation, hindering conception, producing abortion, and expelling a dead fetus. Galen wrote of marjoram, which he called "Organy," that a decoction "provoketh urine and bringeth down the monthly courses," and Culpeper wrote that "there is scarcely a better remedy growing for such as are troubled with a sour humour in their stomach." In Europe and America more than a dozen species of the Labiate (mint) family—including pennyroyal, summer and winter savory, peppermint and spearmint, rosemary, marjoram, European lavender, American horsemint, catnip, balm, horehound, and hyssop—retained this reputation as emmenagogues (remedies capable of stimulating a menstruation delayed for reasons other than pregnancy) and abortives. Minty herbs were believed capable of killing and expelling stomach worms (remedies known as "anthelmintics"), and the logic linking such properties with the ability to induce abortion is primitive but obvious.[28] In American folk medicine, pennyroyal, of all the mints, has had one of the longest associations with abortion. John Gerard's *Herball* recommended pennyroyal to destroy stomach worms, provoke urine and menstruation, expel a dead fetus, and hinder conception.[29] Interestingly, Native American tribes also considered pennyroyal to be an abortive and remedy for general gynecological problems, as its colloquial name "squaw mint" suggests. Charles Millspaugh, a late-nineteenth-century authority on American medicinal plants, wrote that pennyroyal "will often bring on the menses nicely; and, if combined with a gill of brewer's yeast, it frequently acts well as an abortivant, should the intender be not too late with her prescription."[30]

Some remedies used were out-and-out poisons; women presumably took them hoping desperately to kill an unwanted fetus without killing themselves. Taking poisons to kill the invading ill humour causing an illness was an established part of medical theory in the eighteenth and nineteenth centuries, so it should not be surprising that women tried such dangerous poisons as aloes, oil of savin, oil of tansy, oil of cedar, oil of pennyroyal, cottonroot compound, or teas made of rue, tansy, and nightshade to abort an unwanted pregnancy. Fourteen of the most important toxic plants in the United States were linked to abortions in folk medicine, among them, foxglove (*Digitalis purpurea* of the Figwort family), white hellebore (*Veratrum viride* or American hellebore or veratrum of the Lily family), mayapple (*Podophyllum peltatum*), boneset herb (*Eupatorium rugosum* of the Composite family), *Aconitum* (a species of the Crowfoot family), mistletoe (*Phadendron villosum* and *P. flavescens* of the Mistletoe family), Bloodroot (*Sanguinaria canadensis* of the Poppy family) and castor bean (*Ricinus communis* of the Spurge family).[31]

The single largest category of plants in colonial and nineteenth-century medicine, cathartics, inevitably figured prominently as abortives in folklore through the primitive but obvious logic that abortion could be induced by reflex action of severe intestinal contractions. The single most common cathartic used as an abortive, aloe, could induce severe intestinal cramps. Ely Van de Warker, a well-known New York gynecologist, explained in an 1871 article why and how aloes worked as an abortive. He believed that aloes worked only because women overdosed, taking aloetic pills two and three times a day for up to two weeks, severely harming their health in consequence.[32]

Breastfeeding versus Marital Duty

Colonial women who breastfed their children probably managed to increase the spacing between their pregnancies, thereby reducing the total number of children they bore. The precise physiological mechanisms by which lactation makes a woman less fertile are not clearly understood even in contemporary medicine, but breastfeeding does reduce the probabilities of conception for a while after childbirth, possibly by as much as 25 percent. It may work by delaying ovulation, and it is known to increase the duration of postpartum amenorrhea (the suppression of menstruation).[33] It may be that the stable population growth associated with early hunter-gatherer societies was caused by physiological mechanisms, including a long lactational amenorrhea. When agriculture enhanced nutritional levels, these mechanisms no longer functioned as well to restrict population growth, so that additional social and cultural controls over sexual activity and reproduction were necessary.[34]

Elizabeth Drinker, a Philadelphia Quaker, lamented in 1790 in her diary that her daughter had given birth to a stillborn child. It was a twofold tragedy, she wrote, for her daughter, "who lost what may be called the reward of her labor, and promising [sic] a good breast of milk, may pass a year sooner for the loss."[35] In her own mothering, Drinker had made decisions about how often to nurse and how long, when to supplement breast milk with infant food, and when to wean her children. She weaned them at different ages, some quite late by the standards of her peers, for she weighed in her decision such factors as the infant's health, her own health, the season, and the weather. She had been forced to wean nine-month-old Nancy early when she became pregnant. Sometimes illness compelled her decisions: she grieved at falling ill and thus having to send an infant son to a wet-nurse. Yet she does not appear to have derived a sense of control over fertility from such changes in breastfeeding practices, though she clearly believed lactation would help prevent another too-quick pregnancy. Breastfeeding was part of the natural order of a married woman's life, and her comments suggest that she viewed nursing's temporary protection from a new pregnancy as serendipity rather than empowerment.

Twenty years earlier, in Virginia, Landon Carter complained that his ailing daughter-in-law (he did not give her name or her illness) was risking her infant's health by continuing to breastfeed, all because she feared a new pregnancy if she stopped nursing. Carter wanted her to arrange for a wet-nurse and he wrote, "The poor little baby Fanny is every time to share her Mamma's disorder by sucking her, and this because she should not breed too fast. Poor children! Are you to be sacrificed for a parent's pleasure? I have been a parent and I thought it murder and therefore hired nurses or put them out."[36] Writing from New York to his wife, Pamela, in 1786, Theodore Sedgwick worried that she was ruining her health by continuing to nurse their son, adding tellingly that "a certain reason why he was not earlier weaned ceased when I came from home."[37]

Female neighbors, mothers, aunts, all proffered advice, and in the eighteenth century much published advice began to appear. Even the most submissive woman had to make some of her own choices, however. Women left few records detailing the minutiae of their breast-feeding practices, but historical studies of weaning suggest great diversity. The age at which infants were weaned varied from one to two years, slightly longer than such influential medical writers as William Cadogan advised; he told women to feed children regularly four times a day and to wean them slowly at twelve months, advice repeated in William Buchan's widely circulated *Advice to Mothers*.[38] Some women weaned some of their children earlier than they weaned others. We do not have sufficient evidence to weigh whether such practices were meant to limit family size or not, but certainly there is diary evidence that the later children were breastfed for the longest period, although a mother's experience may have played a part in that, with women finding it easier to nurse longer once they had had practice and, too, because women approaching menopause may have felt especially tender toward what they assumed would be their last or penultimate infant.[39]

The increasing availability of wet-nursing may have altered women's attitudes toward breastfeeding. In the colonies, most women breastfed their own infants unless they were ill, and then a relative or friend "suckled" the infant. Because the colonists came from countries where wet-nursing was a form of employment for poor women who, with infants of their own, could gain financially from a full breast of milk, they were familiar with the practice. By the eighteenth century, wet-nurses were more readily available for hire in towns in the New England and middle colonies; the spread of chattel slavery in the southern colonies, too, gave some white mothers similar options. In 1754, however, in New York City, wet-nurses cost three to six shillings a week—no small sum. There were other disadvantages. In 1771 a Philadelphia Quaker woman who had to wean her four-month-old son and hire a wet-nurse grieved because he was sent to live with the nurse—not an uncommon practice—and was away from her until he was a year old. Nurslings apparently often did live with their wet-nurses. In 1851 a "clean, tidy woman, own baby recently weaned," advertised in the *New York Daily Tribune* that she would prefer taking an infant into her own house but would "come to parents if required."[40]

By the mid nineteenth century in France even the lower middle class provincials of small towns hired wet-nurses for their infants and "farmed" children out to commercial wet-nurse establishments. But the business of wet-nursing developed unsavory undertones of "baby farming" in Britain and France, never assumed in the American colonies. The extraordinarily high mortality rate of infants sent to some of those establishments in Europe led contemporary critics to charge that parents were using them to rid themselves of unwanted children.[41] Indeed, in Britain, physicians in the mid nineteenth century mounted a campaign against what they believed to be a rising tide of infanticide; their campaign appears remarkably similar in imagery, symbolism, and motivations to a concurrent American Medical Association crusade against abortion—and similarly raised a hue and cry against the wet-nursing "business."[42] No such charges were made against wet-nurses in America although later in the nineteenth century some concern was expressed about depriving the wet-nurse's own infants. Emily Blackwell wrote in 1876 about the death of a wet-nurse's child: "Wet nursing is a cruel sort of thing, for it almost always means saving the nursling and the death of the abandoned child. But Mrs. Clarke is a rather unfeeling woman and was I think glad to be rid of the trouble and expense of the child."[43]

By the nineteenth century some American women had an option of feeding their infants without suckling, with rubber nursing nipples and baby bottles commercially available from druggists and apothecaries, peddlers, and even by mail order. One New York druggist in 1871 offered forty varieties of nursing bottles.[44] These, along with cow's milk and arrowroot, made it possible to bring up an infant "by hand." In 1849, Mary Poor wrote to her mother from Bangor, Maine, that she was buying cow's milk for her three-month-old infant, whom she had been unable to breastfeed, adding, "It is much more common here to bring up babies by hand than in any place I was ever in before and they seem to do as well as those who nurse."[45] The growing number of options for replacing or supplementing breastfeeding at the same time that many couples were managing to reduce the size of their families is corroborative evidence that they had forms of family limitation other than breastfeeding to rely on.

Demographers sometimes omit breastfeeding from a list of birth control practices because it affects women in different ways and be-

cause its effectiveness varies depending on how long a woman breast-
feeds, on when her menstruation resumes after childbirth, and on how
long and how often the infant suckles.[46]

Nevertheless, sufficient numbers of mothers in a given population
breastfeeding their young will have an impact on population growth.[47]
The historical demographic literature that analyzes birth spacing as it
relates to maternal breastfeeding does not discuss other possible explanations for the decline in average birth intervals after infants died,
although it is possible, of course, that behaviors other than maternal
lactation accounted for faster pregnancy. Perhaps couples had intercourse more often to replace a dead child; perhaps they practiced coitus interruptus less carefully or not at all. In addition, demographers
fail to consider breastfeeding to be a family limitation method because
it is not "parity-dependent," that is, because demographers do not
believe that women were able to change their breastfeeding behavior
once the desired number of children was attained. According to this
argument, although breastfeeding functioned as an involuntary type of
population control because it enabled a woman to space pregnancies
and ultimately to reduce family size, it does not qualify as a deliberate
family limitation technique because most women had no alternative to
nursing their children and could not alter that behavior even if they
did not want more children.[48]

These demographic arguments overlook the number of choices
women actually had with respect to breastfeeding and they mistake
the significance of breastfeeding as a woman's contraceptive. Breastfeeding was neither an unconscious mechanism nor an effective birth
control method such as coitus interruptus or abortion. It was a behavior most women had to adopt for reasons that had nothing to do with
fertility control; it was a behavior applauded by society as promoting
familial and civic good, as being "natural" and, to the religious, ordained by God; yet it was also a behavior that enabled a woman to
make some choices and decisions. And, after all was said and done, it
provided some control over pregnancy. Women could prolong breastfeeding their children, hoping to delay another pregnancy. They could
nurse more often or longer than cultural sanctions suggested, or resist
supplemental foods that might lessen milk supply. What if a woman
decided to delay weaning several months for her contraceptive protection? Was it a sin against nature? What if she did not wean an infant
just because her menstruation returned, or because she fell ill? The
most effective contraceptive protection from lactation was at the time
when an infant was not receiving any other foods; so what if a woman
decided to delay those foods? At what point did making decisions

about breastfeeding become interference with what moralists called "the laws of God"? At what point did they seem to women to be deliberate intervention in reproduction?[49] Decisions such as these may have been the first stages in a long and complex process by which individual women took the first tentative steps to intervene in and to control their fertility.

A French historian, Jean-Louis Flandrin, has postulated a somewhat different trajectory in which in eighteenth-century France issues surrounding breastfeeding also contributed to the emergence of a changed consciousness about family limitation. Flandrin argues that as maternity and child nurture began to be accorded importance in eighteenth-century France, women were caught in a dilemma about breastfeeding. If a woman became pregnant while breastfeeding she was supposed to wean the nursling so as not to harm the child in the womb, but early weaning, especially before the age of one, increased the chances that the nursing child would die. Moralists increasingly held mothers responsible for their infants' welfare and blamed mothers for not breastfeeding. Mothers—and possibly fathers—began to feel greater personal responsibility—and guilt—about infant mortality. As maternal responsibilites for infant welfare became a larger part of the culture, the teachings of the Catholic church that a wife owed her first allegiance to her husband and his desire for sexual intercourse did not change. The church urged a woman torn between the maternal duty of breastfeeding and sexual duty to a husband to send the infant to a wet-nurse. This dilemma led, in Flandrin's view, to a changed consciousness and next to the practice of contraception in marriage. Women began to have—and to exert—some power over sexual relations, and their husbands acquiesced by practicing coitus interruptus, which "might have been a means of alleviating the conflicts, a means more convenient for everybody than maternal nursing plus sexual abstinence."[50]

How Reproductive Control Became Known

The processes by which ideas, information, and attitudes about reproductive control spread into more widespread acceptance, by which individuals or couples became motivated to take action to intervene in reproduction, remain exceptionally difficult to trace. We can see the results: in eighteenth-century America, as in pre-Revolutionary France, the first changes in behavior appeared abruptly among a few couples. Then slowly over the ensuing decades additional couples, motivated either by new ideas or by new practices, or by a combination of both, began to practice fertility control.[51] In farming and fishing villages in Massachusetts and in the Connecticut Valley some couples marrying after the 1740s began to have longer birth intervals, younger ages at last birth, and fewer children per marriage—all indexes of deliberately restricted fertility.[52] Historian Edward Byers argues that a discernible change occurred in marital fertility on Nantucket Island in 1740 and that a second major downturn is evident between 1780 and 1800. Forty percent of the fertility decline over the 160 years on Nantucket occurred because women, on average, began to marry slightly later, but the remainder of the decline was probably caused by deliberate family limitation.

Other historians dispute this finding, arguing that what appears to be deliberate family limitation was actually the result of increasingly long spousal separations caused by the growing importance of whaling in the island's economy.[53] Among the Pennsylvania Quakers, women born before 1730 were one of the first groups whose fertility patterns demonstrate statistical evidence of family limitation. The fertility patterns of women of the next generation also suggest that couples were deliberately intervening in reproduction.[54]

What changed the motivation and attitudes of such couples or individuals remains mysterious and complex, perhaps more in the realm of the poet or novelist than the historian, but some of the ways by which specific information was diffused can be suggested.

How Colonial Americans Learned Lore about Reproductive Control

The earliest European settlers in North America brought with them from their native countries a store of remedies and actions they believed would affect fertility. Some involved magical actions, charms, and incantations, while others were based on plant lore or manipulations of the body. Some of the remedies promoted fertility for those suffering from sterility or impotence, but others were intended as contraceptives and abortives.[55] The lore the Europeans packed to the Americas was quickly enriched, deepened, and even challenged by their intercultural contacts, chiefly with Native American tribes and with African-Caribbean slaves, for both had their own traditions and information about reproductive control.

The Native American tribes with whom colonial and nineteenth-century white settlers came into contact had cultural practices and specific knowledge that enabled them to maintain small families. The fact that something was in use among Indian tribes could have been deduced from the consistent reports of outsiders about the small size of Indian families (never more than four to six among the Delaware Iroquois in the eighteenth century, four on average among the Kickapoo in the Sugar Creek, Illinois, area in the early nineteenth century, at a time when white settlers averaged eight.)[56] Unfortunately, it is exceedingly difficult to reconstruct what the Indian tribes knew and did. White observers then and now longed to know what Native Americans used, but the historical record provides little specific or detailed information. Some practices contributed to long intervals between births. In many tribes women breastfed their children for over two years, and some forbade sexual intercourse with a nursing woman.[57] The practice in the Micmac tribe, as well as in other northeastern tribes, that a woman induced abortion if she became pregnant before weaning a nursing child suggests, however, that proscriptions on sexual intercourse were far from universally followed. Infanticide and voluntary abortion were common, although not universal, in the Native American cultures of North America.[58]

Because the tribes did not keep written records and only a few white travelers and priests recorded any detailed information about any tribal medicines (and then they used colloquial names for plants), it is difficult to trace Indians' beliefs about plant contraceptives, abortifacients, and parturients (remedies to ease and speed childbirth). Some, however, did at least try. In 1769 a Connecticut physician, Benjamin Gale, wrote to a Protestant missionary among the Oneida tribe asking him to "make Enquiry, what Medicines the Indian Parturient Women take antecedent to Delivery which occasions so easy a Travail—they have given some of our [English] Captives Medicines which have had very Extraordinary Effects to Ease their Travail Pains."[59] Whatever answers Gale learned he did not leave for posterity.

By the nineteenth century Native American fertility-inhibiting herbal lore had penetrated deeply into American folk medicine. Native American plant lore included effective obstetrical botanicals, especially plants known in European medicine as oxytocics—products believed capable of directly stimulating contractions in the smooth muscle of the uterus and thereby speeding childbirth. *Cimefuga racemosa* of the Crowfoot family of plants, known colloquially as "black cohosh," "black snakeroot" and "squaw root" was used by eastern tribes throughout North America to stimulate menstruation, cause abortion, or stimulate labor by causing "rapid expansion of the [uterine] parts." It came to be widely regarded in American sectarian and official medicine for similar purposes.[60] In some tribes, Indian women drank a tea made from blue cohosh (*Caulophyllum thalictroides* of the Barberry family) for up to two weeks before childbirth to lessen the duration of labor. Blue cohosh was one of the Indians' principle medical remedies and their best parturient. Millspaugh noted that the dried powdered root of blue cohosh was extremely irritating to the female generative organs, causing intermittent contractions rather than the longer ones associated with ergot.[61] Senecio (of the Composite family, known colloquially as "ragwort," "liferoot," and "female regulator") was also known as an oxytocic.

Slaves from Africa and the Caribbean brought involuntarily to North America an abundance of medical lore which included plant contraceptives and information about substances to abort a fetus. Slave expertise permitted white colonists to cultivate indigo, rice, and cotton, and there is no reason to doubt that slaves just as readily transferred to their New World surroundings their knowledge of fertility-inhibiting plants. Such information may have been passed down from generation to generation, particularly among those women renowned for their healing and midwifery. By the eighteenth century, slave botanical lore from Africa was intermixed with what slaves had learned from Native Americans and from whites. The entire history of this aspect of slave culture needs much further investigation. White colonists feared slaves' botanical knowledge—their familiarity with vegetable poisons, for example[62]—and believed that slaves had secret knowledge allowing them great power over reproduction. A West Indian planter noted in 1815 what he considered to be a typical occurrence with his slaves:

> This morning (without either fault or accident) a young, strong, healthy woman miscarried of an eight months [old] child; and this is the third time she has met with a similar misfortune. No other symptom of childbearing has been given in the course of this year, nor are there above eight women upon the breeding list out of more than 150 females. Yet they are all well clothed and well fed, overworked at no time, and when upon the breeding list are exempted from labor of every kind. In spite of all this, and their being treated with all possible care and indulgence, rewarded for bringing children, and therefore anxious themselves to have them; how they manage it so ill I know not, but somehow or other certainly the children do not come.[63]

A Georgia physician, E. M. Pendleton, reported in 1849 that slave women had far more abortions and miscarriages than did his white patients, either because of the excessive work slaves were compelled to perform or, "as the planters believe," because slaves were "possessed of a secret by which they destroy the fetus at an early stage of gestation."[64] In May 1860 physicians of the Rutherford, Tennessee, County Medical Society listened to a paper about the means slave women used to prevent conception and procure abortion. In the discussion after the paper, one physician described a plantation on which abortion was rampant: "Every conception was aborted by the fourth month." After persistent questioning, the master finally learned that his slave women took "medicine," and they showed him "the weed which was their favorite remedy."[65]

Slaves imported into North America had a high rate of natural increase from the eighteenth century throughout the antebellum period, so any reproductive interventions that slaves practiced remained individual, possibly discernible at the plantation level but rarely widespread enough to have affected overall demographic patterns. At some places and times—in the upper South in the early nineteenth century, for example—fertility levels among female slaves neared human capacity, yet at other times and places fertility fell. Historian Jacqueline Jones notes, "At the regional level, a decline in slave fertility and increases in miscarriage rates during the cotton boom years of 1830 to 1860 reveals the heightened demands made upon women."[66]

Children were valued and loved in the slave community, but slave women's attitudes toward children and motherhood were complex and were not necessarily the same as those of white women or those of free women of color. Fecundity assured slave women that they were valuable to the master and offered some hope against being sold. Yet preventing the birth of new slaves for the master could be a form of resistance to slavery.[67] Some mothers smothered infants rather than see them grow up in slavery or be separated by sale. Others aborted their pregnancies. Decisions about abortion no doubt depended on who the father was, and pregnancies resulting from rape by a master or his kin may have been aborted more commonly than those by slave husbands.

Whatever the degree of herbal and botanical knowledge among some slaves at some times and on some plantations, we cannot assume that there was constancy or universality in slaves' practices and knowledge of reproductive control. In her autobiographical narrative, *Incidents in the Life of a Slave Girl*, the young antebellum slave woman who called herself Linda Brent did not know reproductive control techniques although her master, a white physician who wanted to make her his mistress, clearly did. To escape her master's increasingly insistent sexual attentions, Brent took another white man as her lover and became pregnant by him. When her master learned of the pregnancy, his angry response suggests that he would have taught her preventive methods, although what they were—whether contraceptive or abortive—is unknown:

> He talked of the disgrace I had brought on myself. . . . He intimated that if I had accepted his proposals, he, as a physician, could have saved me from exposure. . . . He then went on to say that he had neglected his duty; that as a physician there were certain things that he ought to have explained to me. Then followed talk such as would have made the most shameless blush.[68]

It is beyond the scope or purpose of this book to explore the ways in which contraceptive and abortive knowledge and ideas were exchanged between Native Americans, African Americans, and European settlers in the two centuries of colonial interactions, although such a study would be a valuable contribution to a growing body of literature on just such cultural and intellectual interactions.[69] From the indigenous knowledge and practices of each group and from the interactions among them, an American folk medicine was created.

The chief mode of communication about reproductive control in colonial America was snatched whispers or terse exchanges in quiet corners. The chief diction was probably homely metaphors conveyed with ribaldry, laughter, and knowing winks. People appealed to same-sex friends and relatives for guidance, but seeking or giving information on such embarrassing subjects had to be done warily. Unmarried and married couples alike had to be careful if they sought contraceptives or abortives. Unlike some Native American and European cultures, however, American colonial society did not have taboos about who could dispense reproductive control information. The Cherokee tribe in the Carolinas, for example, allowed only non-kin to tell each other about a particular herb capable of preventing pregnancy. Mothers and mothers-in-law were expressly forbidden to tell their daughters about it.

There were other possible ways for some to learn methods of curtailing fertility, both oral and written. Midwives, a logical but also problematic source, might be sympathetic to whispered pleas for contraceptive or abortifacient advice, but just as likely not. Much depended on the circumstances, and on who did the asking. The extraordinary power some midwives attained as guardians of community norms may have made approaching them hard. Even in the twentieth century, the degree of their help was far from assured. A twentieth-century midwife advised a Georgia woman who was seeking an abortive to drink copious quantities of a strong tea made from blackhaw roots she had dug in the woods. The midwife admitted lying to her patient: "I tell her it will help her and it do but not the way she thinks it will. Though I don't tell her then, it will make her baby hold on tighter and wait till the right time to get born."[70]

Sometimes informal oral communications were so valuable that they were recorded in treasured family bibles or cookbooks.

Pennsylvania Germans in the eighteenth and nineteenth centuries copied household and farm recipes from oral tradition and other printed sources, secreting them in commonplace books, family account books, school and copy books, in collections of family letters, and in the cubbyholes of furniture. Much of this information came from conversations about fertility and women's medical concerns, including "secret and mysterious remedies" for menstruation, pregnancy, and childbirth.[71]

Herbals and medical almanacs occasionally contained gleanings of information about pregnancy, childbirth, and fertility. Almanacs, too, particularly those specializing in medical information, provided advice on fertility restriction and fertility promotion. At least fifteen hundred medical almanacs, in French, German, Dutch, and English, circulated in the colonies before the American Revolution.[72]

The most famous printed sources of advice on sexual and reproductive matters in the eighteenth century were four anonymous titles attributed to Aristotle, often published in a single volume as *The Works of Aristotle, the Great Philosopher*. The most widely read of the four, *Aristotle's Master Piece*, with at least twenty-seven American editions between 1766 and 1831, was a compendium of magic, superstition, and herbal lore already centuries old by the eighteenth century.[73] Some of its advice, especially some of the botanical suggestions for inducing miscarriage, worked on occasion, apparently, but any effective advice was interspersed with the ludicrously ineffective.

Even in the mid seventeenth century the audience for printed lore and for folk medicine included women as well as men, young as well as old. One nineteen-year-old girl, Elizabeth Holmes of Cambridge, reproved by the courts in 1661 for "some imodest speeches about the nature of womene," asked where she had learned such things, replied that "some girles in the towne had bookes that learned them prity things."[74] By the eighteenth century, almanacs and home medical guides were so readily available that all but the poorest colonists in New England and the Middle Atlantic areas had access to advice literature.[75] A few gave advice on reproductive control.

♦ John Adams called the period from the 1760s to 1775 the "first" revolution "in the hearts and minds" of colonists, a reference to political sentiments, to ideas of liberty and independent institutions, to the growing sense of an American identity separate from Britain, to the beginning of a revolution against authority. But those decades were even more revolutionary than Adams believed; economic, political, and ideological culture brought changes in the most intimate matters of married life and sexual behavior. A few men and some women did begin to value rational planning and calculation in economic life, moving away from the fatalism historians have so long associated with colonial life. Historians of colonial American women have long noted their acquiescence toward the natural rhythms of the reproductive cycle,[76] but that acceptance began to change in the decades after 1790.

If the late eighteenth century saw the first stage in the spread of reproductive control among a few families in a few communities, the early Victorian period saw the beginning of a rapid dispersion of information among many families in many communities.

3

The "New" Reproductive
Control

From 1892 to 1912, Clelia Duel Mosher, a physician and re-
searcher at Stanford University, conducted a small but extraordinary
survey of her women patients' reproductive control and sexual practices. Forty-seven married women, 57 percent born in the 1850s or
1860s, responded to her detailed questionnaire. The candor and intimacy of their responses is remarkable, and historians have found this
evidence invaluable,[1] for it gives us a retrospective view of three contraception practices that had become widely used by the last half of
the nineteenth century. Specific devices—especially sponges, condoms, and pessaries—began to be advertised widely by mid century,
as I show in later chapters, but here I focus on more conservative
measures.

The women in Mosher's study were especially open about their experiences with birth control. Among these women, douching was the
most common contraceptive method (cited by 42.2 percent), followed
by the rhythm method (24.4 percent) and coitus interruptus, also
called "withdrawal" (20 percent). Most couples relied on a combination of methods to prevent conception—particularly those couples
born the latest—though others relied principally on a single method.

Among the forty-five usable Mosher questionnaires, four wives married between 1854 and 1882 reported that their sole birth control
method had been their husbands' withdrawal. Five more, born and
married later in the century, relied on withdrawal plus other methods.
The oldest woman in the study (born in 1832), reported that her husband used withdrawal but was "worn out the next day." After the birth

of the second of their three children, she and her husband slept apart (Case 9). Another woman (born in 1844 and married in 1869) said that six of twelve pregnancies in her twenty-nine years of marriage had ended in miscarriage. Her husband practiced withdrawal "sometimes" (Case 35). Another woman (born in 1859) opted for "incomplete intercourse," but complained that its effect on her health was "not good"; a woman (born in 1862) had avoided withdrawal in thirty years of marriage because "I know it is better to use something than to have the husband withdraw. That is dangerous to his health" (Case 41). Instead, they found the "French method of prevention perfectly successful"— probably meaning condoms—after failing with the rhythm method and douching: "Practiced the rule of no intercourse ten days after menstruation and three days before, which served my mother, with douche immediately after. Did not answer in my case."

For more couples the wife's douching to prevent conception was the strategy of choice. They used a variety of douching solutions. One woman (born in 1868) found a sulphate of zinc douche "not infallible"; she had had two accidental pregnancies in thirty months of marriage. Another, born in 1846 and raised in the "country," had had two accidental pregnancies in her twenty-seven years of marriage as a result of sexual intercourse "near the menstrual period"; she used a douche of water and "sometimes a solution of alum" or "a little alcohol [and] a teaspoon of powdered alum in a pint of water" (Case 19). A third, whose father was a farmer and her mother a "nervous invalid for twenty-two years," had been married for fourteen years with no children. She said that she had used no birth control at all, but then added an afterthought: "I have always used as a measure of cleanliness an injection of warm water and borax or soap suds" (Case 18). A fourth respondent (born in 1874) had been married twenty-four years and had had three conceptions. She used a "pure water douche practically always" with no ill effects on her health (Case 30).

Of those who used the rhythm method, most who answered the Mosher study said that they thought they did have an infertile period, but they differed about its timing. Few were precise about it. One woman (born in 1849) told Mosher that her birth control method consisted of "confining intercourse to the latter part of my month" (Case 14). Another (born in 1850) and married for eight years with one accidental pregnancy, denied using any preventive means except "selection of the time for intercourse" (Case 12). One born in 1862 reported that her second child died of a "cerebral derangement" because she, the mother, had persisted in nursing her first child even when she was six weeks pregnant. She had kept close track of her menstrual cycles, calculating that her first child was conceived immediately before menstruation and her second "after the eighteenth day from the first appearance of the menses" (Case 24).

The strategies of coitus interruptus, douching, and the rhythm method developed somewhat differently in the nineteenth century, and had different supporters and opponents, as well as varying efficacies.

Coitus Interruptus, Coitus Reservatus

The ancient contraceptive practice of coitus interruptus took on new meaning in nineteenth-century America. It became increasingly well known and openly discussed, and it appears to have been widely practiced well into the twentieth century. Its growing public visibility can be seen in the number of synonyms it garnered, from the derogatory "conjugal onanism," "marital masturbation," and "coitus imperfecti," to the more benign "withdrawal," "the pullback," "the drawback," "the method of retraction," "incomplete coition," or simply "the way." Lecturing and writing on health, marriage, and sex in antebellum America, William Andrus Alcott expected audiences to understand his references to a reproductive control method that was "a species of self-denial on the part of the husband, which though it should be in its essential form like that of Onan, would be without his particular form of guilt."[2] This was "withdrawal." In 1831, Robert Dale Owen, son of the founder of New Harmony in Indiana and a pioneer in publicizing reproductive control, described a Quaker couple who had been married for twenty years. They had six children and claimed that they would have had twelve if they had not practiced withdrawal.[3]

Couples in these case studies who discussed the need for spacing or preventing any further pregnancies whatsoever cited motivations that were primarily health concerns—a wife's or couple's fears about a wife's health, fears about a husband's overwork—and, secondarily, financial concerns. The late-eighteenth-century Quaker couple was greatly pleased to have only six children, but couples in the 1860s and 1870s found two children in four years or two children in seven years too many.

Coitus interruptus, for all its seeming simplicity, was not a uniform contraceptive technique. Historians have paid too little attention to the variations. Historians also disagree about whether withdrawal is one of those simple folk contraceptives that individuals can invent easily on their own or whether it needs special circumstances to be learned.[4] In Victorian America some said they had "invented" withdrawal, much like the young man who, after his marriage in the 1820s, wrote to Robert Dale Owen explaining that he had used withdrawal successfully for seven years to improve his economic circumstances and his health before having a family. He had learned about it, he claimed, when "withdrawal presented itself to my mind."[5] In the 1930s a white tenant farm woman in Appalachia told a WPA interviewer that withdrawal was easy to understand: "If you don't want butter, pull the dasher out in time."[6]

Others needed instruction. Owen described the visit to his New York newspaper office in the early 1830s of a man who lived "west of the mountains." He had used withdrawal successfully for nearly eight years after the birth of three children. Owen asked if his neighbors also found it effective, but his visitor had not thought it prudent "to speak with any but his own relations on the subject, one or two of whom, he knew had profited by his advice and afterwards expressed to him their gratitude for the important information."[7] Such reticence apparently did not bother an Upstate New York farm woman, Calista Hall, who wrote to her husband, Pliny, in 1849 to reassure him she was not pregnant, to commend him for using withdrawal so effectively, and to suggest that he instruct a friend or relative in its advantages: "The old maid came at the appointed time. . . . I do think you are a very *careful* man. You must take Mr. Stewart out one side and learn him."[8]

The publication in 1831 of Owen's pamphlet *Moral Physiology* made it easier to learn about withdrawal. It was concise and plainly written, without the many euphemisms and metaphors that cloaked so many discussions. A letter Owen said he had received from a young mechanic after the initial appearance of *Moral Physiology* reported that the young man heard Owen speak about reproductive control but he was unable to understand Owen's advice because "like the Nazarene Reformer, you spoke in parables." He concluded despairingly, in consequence, that he could do nothing to limit his rapidly growing family: "I had apparently nothing left but to let matters take their own course when your *Moral Physiology* made its appearance. I read it; and a new scene of existence seemed to open before me. I found myself, in this all important matter, a free agent, and in a degree, the arbiter of my own destiny."[9]

In its many editions and through its many imitators and competitors, Owen's tract put coitus interruptus in the culture. Almost all contraceptive advice literature from the 1830s through the 1880s gave explicit or tacit recognition to coitus interruptus. Much of it disparaged withdrawal because it competed with other methods such as douching, condoms, rhythm, or abortion, which they themselves were touting, but few ignored it.

Twentieth-century studies of the effectiveness of various contraceptive methods show that, under optimal conditions, coitus interruptus can be quite reliable but also that there is great variation in success rates.[10] It ranks in some studies as more effective than douching and nearly equal to spermicidal suppositories, contraceptive jelly, and condoms.[11] Its reliability depends on the care with which withdrawal is practiced— no sperm at all may be left in or near the vagina, even on the external labia, because sperm move quickly and can fertilize an ovum within minutes. Knowledge of sperm mobility grew only slowly in the last century.

Partial withdrawal, that is, ejaculation as far as possible from the cervix but possibly still in the vagina, appears to have been as widely known as complete withdrawal both in Europe and in America. Because it required less concentration from men, it may have been more widely practiced. Richard Carlile advocated partial withdrawal as an effective pregnancy preventative in his *Every Woman's Book*, first published in England in 1826, and Robert Dale Owen believed the method well enough known in 1830 to justify his warning that it was "by no means an infallible preventive of conception."[12] It is especially ironic that the 1858 edition of *Moral Physiology* updated by his colleague and friend, Gilbert Vale, promoted the partial withdrawal method Owen himself had warned against. Vale's publisher's notes in 1858 stated that it was safe to deposit semen within the vagina as long as it was not near the womb and as long as a syringe [a douche] was used immediately afterwards.[13]

When people believed, as many did in earlier centuries, that conception occurred only if a woman experienced orgasm or if the sperm were thrown forcefully against the cervix, partial withdrawal appeared a logical method. But by the mid nineteenth century, new theories about how sperm reached the ovum (by their own motility, by absorbent vessels in the vaginal lining) convinced some that partial withdrawal could not work.[14] Yet well-established ideas and practices change slowly, and, apparently—or why were there so many continuing warnings against it?—at least some Americans continued to rely on partial withdrawal. Frederick Hollick, a social reformer and Owenite, listed partial withdrawal in his 1850 book, *The Marriage Guide*, as one of the era's least desirable preventive methods, but even he believed that it sometimes worked.[15]

Withdrawal of any degree fell into increasing disfavor as time went on, and medical professionals, promoters of reproductive control, and the middle class public began to raise doubts about it, or worse. Medical opponents claimed that withdrawal caused in men "general debility of brain and brawn," "tubercula foci" in the prostate and seminal vesicles, and symptoms like gonorrhea; and, in women, hysteria, degeneration of the womb, neuralgias, and a host of "local and constitutional disorders."[16]

Physicians frequently commented negatively on coitus interruptus. In 1876, Nicholas Francis Cooke, a physician and birth control critic, wrote *Satan in Society: A Plea for Social Purity. A Discussion of the True Rights of Woman, Marital and Social* chiefly "to stigmatize . . . conjugal onanism," which he deplored as a "deeply rooted vice . . . a national curse, a reason for the widespread moral degradation and a powerful reason for the decline of the native population."[17] Some doctors included case histories of patients who practiced withdrawal. William Goodell, professor of clinical gynecology at the University of Pennsylvania Medical School and an active opponent of family limitation, described an 1872 case of "conjugal onanism." His patient had two children in the first four years after her marriage. She and her husband wanted no more children but neither did they want to abstain from sex, so for six years they relied on withdrawal three to five times a week. They succeeded in preventing pregnancy, but the woman came to Goodell complaining of dizziness, loss of appetite, heart palpitations, and jealousy. He attributed her ailments to withdrawal and advised her to stop. She begged Goodell to recommend another method, saying she would leave her husband rather than have more children. Goodell told his medical colleagues that he had refused to help her, for she was nearly insane, her health was shattered, and her morals were perverted from the couple's contraceptive practices.[18] In an 1882 discussion among physicians, a Doctor Coles reported that a patient who did not want more than two children took "a napkin to bed and practiced withdrawal." Neither the husband nor his wife reported satisfaction with the method, but they had no further children until Dr. Coles persuaded them to stop.[19] L. Bolton Bangs said that a male patient who came to him in 1893 with unspecified complaints had used withdrawal at least three times a week for the previous sixteen years because his wife wanted only the two children of their first seven years of marriage. Like Goodell, Bangs told the patient that his health problems stemmed from withdrawal.[20]

Some physicians late in the century reported that withdrawal caused psychological disorders. A Philadelphia doctor who had advised a delicate female patient who was about to be married not to have children immediately and her husband-to-be to practice withdrawal, reported that the couple had no children for three years and the wife had become healthy and robust, but the husband "nervously affected" and "rendered delicate." Although Sigmund Freud later changed his mind, in the early stages of his developing theory of anxiety neuroses in the 1890s, he believed that coitus interruptus precipitated neurasthenia, hysteria, and other anxiety neuroses because it created sexual dissatisfaction. In 1895 he wrote, "I do not think I am exaggerating when I assert that the great majority of severe neuroses in women have their origin in the marriage bed."[21]

Yet the public may well have paid scant attention to the negative onslaught. The remark of a farmer in pre–World War I Germany (where withdrawal and postcoital douching were the most common forms of contraception among the working class) may be equally applicable to nineteenth-century Americans. Asked if he believed medical reports that withdrawal is harmful, the farmer replied no, "otherwise everybody would be sick."[22] Annie Besant wrote in her pamphlet *The Law of Population* in 1878 that although doctors said that withdrawal might be injurious to women, its universal practice by the French attested to its safety.[23]

Dislike of withdrawal became more openly expressed over the course of the century as other contraceptive and abortive options emerged in the commercialization of reproductive control. Men, in particular, began to express complaints about it more openly, centering on how difficult coitus interruptus was to practice and how much it lessened their sexual pleasure. Owen had been sufficiently troubled by such questions to address them in the first edition of *Moral Physiology*, trying to reassure his readers that all but a very few men could master withdrawal quickly even though "the slight deprivation" in sexual enjoyment might make it difficult at first: "I can readily imagine that there are men who have little control over their passions and who might find it difficult if not impossible to practice it. Yet I do believe the number of these to be very small; not a tenth part of those who at first may IMAGINE such to be their case."[24] He considered the issue of reduced sexual pleasure a mere "trifling restraint." By the 1850s, however, Owen altered his text, writing testily: "I can readily imagine that there are men who in part from temperament, but much more from the continued habit of unrestrained indulgence, may have so little command over their passions as to find difficulty in practicing [withdrawal] and some it may be who will declare it impossible (which I very much doubt). I am at least convinced that the number is exceedingly small; not a fiftieth part of those who may first *imagine* such to be their case."[25]

When Gilbert Vale, Owen's fellow freethinker, published an edition of *Moral Physiology* in 1858, adding his own publisher's notes at the end, he said that withdrawal was difficult for any but mature men in "the decline of life." Younger men could not be expected to have sufficient control to practice withdrawal and so should use condoms or rely on partial withdrawal, followed by the wife's douching. The pirated edition of *Moral Physiology* put out in 1846 by the unknown "physician" Ralph Glover, too, played on the discontent, commenting, "How frequently do we hear the mothers say, I have all the family I want and am determined to have not more children if I can prevent it; but alas: she has not the power when the partner of her bosom loses the self-control of his passions."[26] A. M. Mauriceau, a pseudonym for Joseph Trow—brother of Ann Trow Lohman, also known as, "Madame Restell," a New York abortionist—in 1847, wrote *The Married Woman's Private Medical Companion Embracing the Treatment of Menstruation or Monthly Turns during Their Stoppage, Irregularity or Entire Suppression, PREGNANCY and How IT MAY BE DETERMINED: With the Treatment of Its Various Diseases, Discovery to PREVENT PREGNANCY: Its Great and Important Necessity Where Malformation on Inability Exists to Give Birth. To Prevent Miscarriage or Abortion When Proper and Necessary. To EFFECT MISCARRIAGE When Attended with Entire Safety, CAUSES AND MODE OF CURE OF BARRENNESS OR STERILITY.* In this book he claimed that withdrawal posed insurmountable difficulties. Men's anxieties about losing control made coition unsatisfying, because even the most careful might lose control occasionally with some semen escaping inadvertently. "Mauriceau" warned, therefore, that the problem of diminished pleasure was compounded by ineffectiveness.[27] An 1854 Boston book, *The Young Married Lady's Private Medical Guide*, noted: "All that practice [withdrawal]—and a very great many do, for want of knowing how to obtain something better—feel its uncertainty."[28]

Women had their own reasons for disliking withdrawal. A woman had to have great confidence in her sexual partner's reliability, self-control, good will, and judgment. This dependence was not satisfactory for many women. A man's reliance on coitus interruptus might actually have increased a woman's level of anxiety because a man who became more confident about his ability to "pull back" effectively may have become less willing to be abstinent or to be overruled in the timing and frequency of sexual intercourse. Still, family-limitation

critic Nicholas Francis Cooke was lamenting in 1876 that a husband
who practices coitus interruptus is "eulogized by his wife and applauded by her friends."[29] Ten years earlier in his advice booklet *The
Book of Nature, containing information for young people who think of
getting married, on the philosophy of procreation and sexual intercourse; showing how to prevent conception and to avoid child-bearing. Also, rules for management during labor and child-birth,* James
Ashton, who referred to himself as a "lecturer on sexual physiology,"
praised withdrawal as "indeed a refinement of social intercourse."
Women, he said, liked withdrawal for its "cleanliness." He listed it
first among the ways "to avoid child-bearing," yet ended his paean
with the warning that a wife "would need other plans to give her confidence."[30]

Unlike men, women did not leave a record of complaints about
withdrawal's interference with their sexual pleasure, but it can hardly,
one assumes, have had any other effect. And fears that the pullback
would not be in time can only have increased their anxiety. Nevertheless, husbands and doctors occasionally blamed wives for making their
husbands practice withdrawal. L. Bolton Bangs, a physician opposed
to contraception, wrote in 1893 that his male patients felt anger and
disgust toward their wives at the moment of withdrawal. Other historians have seen the practice of withdrawal as an example of the increasing power of women within marriage. Daniel Scott Smith's well-
known article "Family Limitation, Sexual Control, and Domestic
Feminism in Victorian America" argues that women in mid-nineteenth-century America gained considerable power within marriage to
control the timing and frequency of sexual intercourse and thereby
to control reproduction.[31] The young Philadelphia physician George
Napheys, whose very popular medical-advice books generally expressed some sympathy toward reproductive control, warned wives in
The Physical Life of Woman (1872 and later) that withdrawal was so
dangerous to a man's health that "no wife who loves her husband will
ask or permit him to run this danger."[32] Wives who employed more
subtle stratagems to persuade husbands to practice withdrawal ran
even more insidious risks than being considered heartless harridans.
The historians Jan Lewis and Kenneth Lockridge have pointed out
that the gentry women who succeeded in restricting their fertility in
the early-nineteenth-century South did so by playing on prevailing
cultural images of women as frail, weak, and greatly endangered by
pregnancies and thus that husbands, in sympathy for their plight,
agreed to practice abstinence or to use coitus interruptus.

In what may be viewed as another variant of withdrawal in that it,

too, involved a man's control of ejaculation during the sexual act, coitus reservatus was known and practiced by some in nineteenth-century America. Coitus reservatus (prolonged coition with no emission of
semen and with gradual loss of the erection while the penis is still in
the vagina) is an ancient sexual practice, but Americans believed that
it was invented in the 1840s by John Humphrey Noyes, the leader of a
New York communitarian group, the Oneida Perfectionists.[33] Noyes,
who called the practice "male continence," explained that he invented
it after his wife, Harriet, suffered six pregnancies but only one live
birth in the eight years after they were married in 1838. He promised
Harriet she would never again have to suffer the pain and anguish of
childbirth even if they had to sleep apart. Worried by such a prospect,
he "studied the subject of sexual intercourse in connection with my
matrimonial experience and discovered the principle of male continence."[34] This then became the way conception was prevented at the
Oneida Community, which from 1848 until the mid 1870s proved to
be the longest-lasting, most publicized, and most financially successful
of all the nineteenth-century American experiments in communal living. It apparently worked remarkably well, for there were only thirty-
one accidental pregnancies from 1848 to 1869, although the community grew from some eighty-seven to 219 by 1874. To Noyes, for
whom the method was as much a spiritual as a contraceptive practice,
its advantages were manifold: it preserved men's health by preventing
the loss of semen; it freed women from "the curses of involuntary and
undesirable procreation," a freedom that, he believed, would promote
happier relations between the sexes and happier maternity for
women, who now regarded childbearing as a burden and a curse.
Above all, it enabled both men and women to enjoy sexual intercourse.[35]

Male continence was probably never widely practiced in the United
States except at Oneida, but it received considerable publicity and
was far from unknown. Noyes first described it in a chapter of his book
The Bible Argument in 1848.[36] In 1866 the Perfectionists decided that
American society would benefit from a wider knowledge of male continence, so Noyes published as a four-page leaflet a letter he has written
to a young medical student who requested detailed information on
how the community controlled reproduction. They mailed the leaflet,
*Male Continence; or, Self-Control in Sexual Intercourse. A Letter of
Inquiry Answered by John Humphrey Noyes*, only in response to specific requests for information, but even so it went through four editions. In 1872 rather than issue a fifth edition, Noyes revised and enlarged the leaflet, adding twenty pages on the history of his discovery

of male continence. This he published in 1877, and it was sold by general booksellers and agents. Ezra Heywood, who stood trial and served a jail term for breaking the laws against dispersing birth control information by selling his own book, *Cupid's Yokes*—an antimarriage tract—and Russell Thacher Trall's *Sexual Physiology*, sold *Male Continence* without any trouble.[37]

In some years over two hundred visitors a month passed through the Oneida Community, and all had access to freely given information about its beliefs and practices. The community's newspaper, the *Oneida Circular*, with a weekly circulation of two thousand in the 1860s, discussed male continence in its columns. Later birth control publicists included discussions of it in their books,[38] and critics of fertility intervention disparaged it. John Harvey Kellogg's *Plain Facts for Old and Young*, in 1880, labeled male continence "double masturbation" and warned readers that it was as destructive to health as withdrawal.[39] Members of the Boston Gynaecological Society in 1871 discussed "the pathological results of conjugal fraud as practiced in so disgusting a manner at the so-called Oneida Community."[40] In his advice tract *American Womanhood*, in 1870, physician James Caleb Jackson wrote that men must learn to live "continently" if abortion rates were to decline. Couples did not have to forego all "conjugal enjoyment," Jackson added, for continence did not involve great self-denial.[41] Jackson's use of the word "continent" is ambiguous, for it could have referred to moderate sexual intercourse, to male continence, or to a nineteenth-century variety of the rhythm method.

Douching: "Prevention Powders," and "Female Remedies"

From the 1840s until the last third of the century, commentators described the growing popularity of douching as a method of reproductive control. William Goodell, one of the era's most prominent gynecologists, wrote in 1872 that it was preceded in popularity only by withdrawal. A physician from the small town of Warsaw, New York, said in 1888 that the most common family limitation method was the use of the vaginal syringe with a strong astringent.[42] A gynecologist writing in the 1880 *Michigan Medical News* advised his colleagues to poll their patients about contraceptive practices, suggesting that they begin by bluntly asking the husband whether he used withdrawal, then turn and ask the wife whether she was "accustomed to spring from her couch and douse the engorged uterus and vagina with cold water? . . . Has she dosed with remedies calculated to do violence to the uterine tissues?"[43] In 1884 the editor of the *Kansas City Medical Record* commented on the widespread knowledge of douching:

> So common has the art become that we are safe in saying a respectable minority of the society ladies, while providing for their wedding also provide themselves with a perfectly adjusted syringe, which is at once given a place in their toilet and kept within reach for the purpose of washing the spermatozoids from the vagina as soon as possible after copulation. They seem to have the information that in this way fecundation may generally be prevented. How this knowledge has become so widespread we are unable to say.[44]

By the late nineteenth century, middle and upper class women reported vaginal douching as their most common birth control method. Of the nineteen women in Mosher's study who listed the douche as one of the methods the couple had used to prevent conception, eleven relied solely on the douche.[45] The other eight used a combination of methods. One douched with water unless she had intercourse near menstruation, which she believed was her fertile period, in which case she added alum to the water. Another woman used hot water except in the fertile period, which she did not define, when her husband used withdrawal. Although two reported that they did not use preventive methods, elsewhere in their questionnaires they mentioned douching, one with tepid water and another with water plus borax or soap suds.

In nineteenth-century America, douching was considered to be both several contraceptive techniques and also an abortive technique. The advice literature on reproductive control frequently advised douching with water on the theory that sperm would be washed away before fertilization could occur. A second technique was closely related in theory to the use of occlusive devices such as the sponge or diaphragm: it recommended douching with astringent solutions to close the cervix to sperm penetration, a plan that had considerable logic in the 1830s and 1840s when a theory of William Potts DeWees held sway. DeWees believed that a special set of absorbent vessels in the vaginal lining carried sperm to the ovary or uterus to fertilize the egg. Because astringents were thought to constrict the vaginal lining as well as the cervix, few or no sperm would then be able to reach either the vessels or the uterus itself.

A third douching method, and the most effective, was use of spermicides. The idea was to inject into the vagina substances that would kill or immobilize sperm rather than just wash them out or prevent their access to the ovum. Physician Charles Knowlton, author of one of the most important contraceptive advice tracts in the nineteenth century, claimed to have invented the idea in 1831. J. Soule, author of *Science of Reproduction and Reproductive Control: The Necessity of Some Abstaining from Having Children, the Duty of All to Limit Their Families . . . , in* 1856 listed douching as fourth in a list of ways to prevent conception, but Soule clearly envisaged three types of douching: the use of the vaginal syringe and an astringent before intercourse to close the mouth of the uterus (he believed that even five to six hours before coitus was safe); the use of water to expel semen (cold water up to four or five hours after intercourse); and the addition of tannin, powdered opium, prussic acid, iodine, or strichnine dissolved in water to destroy the "animalcules."[46]

Other writers linked douching with abortion. Eugene Becklard's *Physiological Mysteries and Revelations in Love, Courtship, and Marriage* (1844 and 1845) said, for example, that a woman could produce abortion in the first two months of a pregnancy if she douched with a "female syringe" filled with warm water and white vitriol. Cold-water douches, too, he said, would induce abortion, but later in his book he said cold water douches would *prevent* abortion. His book was a jumbled mixture of superstition, ancient folklore, and plagiarized ideas. In an 1875 case in California a husband who was suing his wife for divorce cited the fact, if it was, that she had aborted herself four times using "injections of pure water." The wife's defense was that none of the pregnancies had quickened.[47] The hydropathist Russell Thacher Trall, who generally disapproved of reproductive control by any method other than abstinence, said in the 1860s that a cold-water douche would cause immediate contractions of the uterus—an oblique recommendation for one as a contraceptive. Some readers doubtless believed that uterine contractions would induce miscarriage at any stage of pregnancy.[48] Indeed, medical journals sometimes carried terse reports of attempts, such as that of the twenty-three-year-old widow who, in 1885, died after trying to abort a five-month pregnancy with a Davidson syringe and cold water.[49] The association between douching and abortion was furthered by the use of douching in official medicine and by the general availability of intrauterine syringes that could be used to cause miscarriage. A Rockland, Massachusetts, physician noted in 1879 that "in justifiable abortion the method of inducing uterine contractions by the use of the intrauterine douche, known as Cohen's Method, was advocated and practiced to some extent thirty years ago but today is almost universally condemned on account of its danger." It could be fatal to inject any substance—air, gas, or any liquid—into a pregnant uterus, he said, talking of the recent death of a black cook, seven months pregnant, caused by an abortion induced by a "common rubber syringe" filled with a mixture of tincture of aloes and myrrh and a fluid extract of cotton root.[50]

There was a proliferation of brands, sizes, and styles of vaginal douches. In the 1820s, when the first medical reference appeared in *Index Medicus*, "female syringes" was the description. By the 1840s they were known by other names such as "irrigators," "injections" (also the term for the douching solutions), "syringes," "vaginal syringes," "intra-uterine syringes." In 1871, W. H. Schieffelin & Co. in New York advertised 201 different styles of douching syringes—some for irrigating ears, eyes, noses, throats, but fifty-three specifically for vaginal or uterine douching. George C. Goodwin in Boston offered forty-seven douching syringes in 1874, twenty-eight designed exclusively for female use. In 1876 he offered 11l styles, in 1885, 145. Pharmacists from St. Louis to Cleveland to Chicago to Portland, Maine, offered similar quantities and choices.[51] Some manufacturers sold "combination syringes" with adjustable nozzles and pipes to be used for a variety of purposes. Albert H. Essex, the manufacturer of National Syringes, said that his 1885 model, with a change of nozzles, could be used for vaginal douching or for watering house plants.[52] Douching syringes were also available from physicians, itinerant peddlers and by mid century, through the mail from diverse retail establishments. As availability increased in the market, prices fell.

More than two dozen drug and vegetable products were believed to work as spermicides or as astringents, among them such common household products as vinegar, bicarbonate of soda ("saleratus"), and salts. Even the women traversing the Overland Trail in the middle decades of the nineteenth century had access to spermicides if they had wanted them. An average family of four took about eight pounds of baking soda on the trail.[53] Some women manufactured douching solutions at home from common roadside or garden botanicals, from preparations of dried roots, leaves, and flowers. One 1844 home recipe guide included a recipe for "Hannay's Preventive Lotion": "Take Pearlash, one pt.; water, six pts. Mix and filter. Keep it in close bottles and use it without soap immediately after connexion."[54]

By mid century, drug companies and entrepreneurs were selling commercial douching preparations. Some were generically labeled as "injections" (ambiguously either douching solutions or cures for venereal disease); others were more explicitly "vaginal douches" or carried names connoting their uses as contraceptive "checks" for douching or for moistening contraceptive vaginal sponges: "carbolic purifying powders," "soda powders," "Matico injections," "sanative washes," generic "antiseptic douching liquids," and the ubiquitous "female remedies." Chicago's Fuller & Fuller Drug Company offered, in 1885, "Ade's White Clover Injection," "Bradfield's Female Regulator," "Bradfield's Mother's Friend," "Burrough's Antiseptic Liquid," "Cadet's Injection," 'Dr. Caton's Tansy Regulator," "Cre-Ozone disinfectant fluid," and fifteen brand-name "injection" solutions at from six dollars to nine dollars for a dozen bottles. The Boston druggists Rust Brothers and Bird in 1880 sold seven kinds of "injection" solutions as well as American, English, and French brands of "female pills," and "periodical drops" costing from one dollar to $1.50 a bottle. In New York, McKesson & Robbins in 1879 sold "Foster's complete vaginal douche" for four dollars each, Scott's vaginal douche" for three dollars, and "S & D's" vaginal douche" for two dollars.[55]

Expensive bottles of "toilet vinegars" and brands with suggestive names such as "Rimmel's Medicated Vinegar" and the French "Société hygiénique vinegar" were available at drugstores. From New Orleans to Vicksburg the Genuine Medicine Warehouse sold "soda powders," "rose injections," "Cullen's Female Specific," "Billings Astringent," and "Lamotte's French Remedy."[56] Before the 1873 Comstock Law, which outlawed contraceptive advertising, some of these commercial douching solutions were marketed openly for reproductive control, labeled "prevention powders," "defertilizing solutions," "infecundating powders," and "anti-conception compounds." The 1854 Boston booklet *The Young Married Lady's Private Medical Guide* advertised an "Anti-conception compound" for ten dollars.[57] The nineteenth century often failed to draw a fine line between contraception and abortion, and there was some ambiguity over whether "prevention powders" were to prevent pregnancy or birth. Frederick Hollick's *The Marriage Guide, or Natural History of Generation: A Private Instructor for Married Persons and Those about to Marry Both Male and Female; in Every Thing Concerning the Physiology and Relations of the Sexual System, and the Production or Prevention of offspring, including All New Discoveries Never before Given in the English Language,* warned readers not to buy an extensively advertised "prevention powder" because it was exorbitantly priced and consisted merely of inexpensive powdered alum or sulphate of zinc. The vendor called himself a "French professor," but Hollick said that he was actually associated with a notorious New York abortionist.[58] Hollick was almost certainly referring to Joseph Trow ("A. M. Mauriceau"), whose *The Married Woman's Private Medical Companion*, carried advertisements for a drug to induce abortion, also astringent douches to cure prolapsus of the uterus, condoms, and a powder to prevent conception, "Desomeaux's method for neutralizing the fecundating power of semen."[59] The "prevention powders" his sister Madame Restell advertised so widely from the 1840s through 1860s for one dollar to five dollars a box may well not have been for abortions at all.

Spermicides and contraceptive astringents were sold in various forms: as vaginal suppositories (known as "soluble pessaries," "medicated pessaries," "gels," and "solubles"); as ointments (also called pastes, salves, and cerates); and as tablets (also known as "troches"). Suppositories were used as contraceptives in ancient Egyptian, Greek, and Roman medicine, but were not widely recommended in nineteenth-century advice literature except in Thomas Hersey's *The Midwife's Practical Directory; or, Woman's Confidential Friend*. Hersey, an early follower and publisher of the medical theories of Samuel Thomson, the founder of the Thomsonian medical sect, had read Charles Knowlton's douching advice and instructed his women readers to insert a small piece of alum in the vagina before coitus to prevent conception.[60] By the end of the century, commercial contraceptive suppositories were being sold quietly by some druggists and by mail-order entrepreneurs. The publisher of an 1889 New York edition of Annie Besant's *The Law of Population* placed advertisements for contraceptives inside the text. Henry Sumner advertised quinine suppositories, antiseptic sponges, condoms, and "check pessaries." He explained how to use a quinine pessary (a dollar for a box of twelve):

> A most ingenious contrivance, one which can be used by the wife without the knowledge of the husband (and this is often desirable) is the Quinine Pessary. This article is very portable and is invariably efficacious when properly applied. The modus operandi is to introduce the Pessary into the vagina as far as possible, some ten or fifteen minutes before connection takes place. During that interval the Pessary melts and permeates or coats the whole of the interior of the vagina so that the semen on its entrance is enveloped, so to say, with an antifertilizing material, which destroyes its fecundity and precludes the possiblity of conception. The vehicle employed is merely cocoa-butter, a demulcent in itself so that no irritation is set up in either the male or female organs.[61]

One Boston drug company in 1880 sold twenty-five kinds of troches, made of carbolic acid, tannin, salicylic acid, and other compounds, and eleven kinds of "tablets," made, for example, of carbolic acid, bicarbonate of potash, and borax. The Fuller & Fuller Company in Chicago in 1872 sold seven kinds of troches, including "Edey's carbolic," for $1.85 a dozen, and in 1885 sold three sizes of "Anderson's Vaginal Capsules," "Bouchard's French capsules," and "Le Roy's Female Capsules," and capsules of oil of pennyroyal and oil of turpentine. George C. Goodwin & Co. in 1880 Boston advertised an oil of turpentine and matico injection, eleven kinds of injection solutions, four kinds of suppositories, eleven kinds of tablets, all for prices ranging from twenty-five cents to one dollar a box, troches of carbolic acid, buchu, tannin, or salicylic acid.[62]

Reputable birth control advisers today state firmly that contraceptive douching is both dangerous and ineffective. Many safer and more reliable methods are available. Douching is discouraged for birth control because sperm can swim fast and may reach the egg before a woman can douche. Too much pressure from the douching syringe can actually push sperm into the cervical opening, while an insufficient pressure may leave sperm untouched in the folds of the vaginal walls, potential fertilizing agents for their remaining lifespan. Too much pressure from the douching syringe can be dangerous by forcing air or fluid into the uterus or abdominal cavity.[63] Douching is generally said to range in failure rate from a low estimate of 21 pregnancies per 100 woman-years to a high of 41 pregnancies.[64] But douching was not necessarily ineffective by the standards of an earlier era. Early-twentieth-century studies suggest that even those women who said they douched "for cleanliness only" shortly after intercourse and who used no other contraception bore children at intervals two times longer than did women who did not douche at all.[65] A birth control method that reduces pregnancies by 50 fifty percent, while far from adequate given today's options, is still extremely significant.

The choice of douching syringe was important. Douching apparatus came in three basic models: the "elastic bulb" (sometimes called the "syphon syringe"); the "fountain" or water-bag syringe; and the simplest model, a tube of metal, glass, or rubber with a bulb at one end. The hand-squeezed bulb model appears to have been particularly popular by mid century, although early-twentieth-century birth control clinics advised using it or the fountain model. Some syringes may have been too small to assure an adequate supply of the spermicide unless the woman douched repeatedly; some rubber bulbs may have had too little force to reach sperm lodged in vaginal folds.[66] In the 1830s, Charles Knowlton recommended a "female syringe" like that women bought to cure "sinking of the womb," and in 1856 birth control adviser Asa Soule mentioned only a "vaginal syringe." This was vague advice. H. D. Grindle was more precise; he advised his patients in the

1860s not to use glass syringes but to buy a five- or six-ounce vulcanized gutta percha syringe with vaginal pipes at a right angle to the
rest of the syringe so the vagina could be thoroughly washed.[67] Physician Orris E. Herrick in Grand Rapids, Michigan, in 1882 told other
doctors that women should always use the vaginal syringe with a large
glass speculum pipe and elastic bulb at one end. All a woman needed
to do, he wrote, was to squeeze the contents of a previously filled
douche into the vagina, then gradually let the syringe bulb expand in
her hand so that the entire contents would be redrawn into the syringe. In this way a woman could remain in bed and use the douche
without fuss or mess.[68]

The choice of spermicide was also crucial. Not all substances worked
as the publicity said they did; indeed, some women who douched only
with plain water may actually have increased the chances of conception by helping sperm reach the cervix faster. Still, data from twentieth-century studies suggest that water douches can have a contraceptive effect, possibly by lowering the number of sperm available for
fertilization after a single act of intercourse. Because nineteenth-century women were counseled to douche frequently—some of the water-cure literature advised four times a day and so did some physicians—many may have altered their normal vaginal pH sufficiently to
prevent conception even if the contraceptive douching practices themselves were flawed.

Simple water douches were certainly less effective than spermicides
or astringents added to the douching water, for example, "vitriol
drops," alum (known as sulphate of potassium and used medically as
an astringent), sulphate or chloride of zinc, copper water, tannins,
baking soda, vinegar, metallic salts, borax, bichloride of mercury, and
"vegetable astringents" such as nutgalls and white oak bark.[69] But some
of the acidic solutions, which worked by increasing the acidic environment of the vagina, may well have been painful or even dangerous
when used frequently. Women used acidic solutions as spermicides,
especially carbolic acid, household vinegar, white vitriol (sulphate of
zinc), boric acid, and bichloride of mercury (which Knowlton and
others called "corrosive sublimate"). Several of these solutions would
have worked well: common household vinegar, even in weak solution,
is a good spermicide,[70] and lactic acid, boric acid, and tartaric acid are
sufficiently spermicidal to have been common ingredients in commercial contraceptive jellies in the 1930s.[71] With even the normal acidic
properties of the vagina inhospitable to sperm, anything that increased
those properties facilitated contraception. Normal vaginal fluids have a
pH of 4 to 4.7, and sperm are killed if acidity increases, particularly if
the pH gets to be lower than 3.5.[72]

Strongly alkaline substances can also be spermicidal not only because they create a vaginal environment hostile to sperm, but because their viscousity and adhesion help spread them quickly through the vagina and over the cervix, thus blocking sperm motility. The soaps and plants with soaplike properties—some six hundred plant species in North America—often used in folk medicine and as nineteenth-century spermicides may have worked as contraceptives. Even a small amount of soap—one-quarter- to one-half-inch cube dissolved in one quart of water—would do.[73] Saponin compounds in soaplike plants produced foaming suds, found by at least one later study (1938) to be spermicidal.[74] Among the plants with saponin was the widely used trillium (also known as birthroot, wakerobin, and squaw root) of the Lily family, used by Indian tribes as a remedy to ease childbirth and to staunch hemorrhage. One of the principal ingredients in Lydia E. Pinkham's "Vegetable Compound and Uterine Tonic" was helonias, high in saponin, also of the Lily family.

The salts women used in douching, although sometimes causing vaginal irritation and pain, altered the alkalinity of the vagina.[75] Knowlton advised women to douche with a weak solution of corrosive sublimate (he specified five to six grains in a pint of water), an inorganic salt (mercuric chloride) that a later study (1935) did find to be an effective spermicide.[76] In a later edition he also suggested that women make use of common household ingredients, such as "liquid chloride soda" and "old-fashioned pearlash and sal soda used in washing clothes," and warned that "whereas for an hour or so after zinc or alum have been used, there is a roughness about the parts which would not be agreeable to the male on a second copulation."[77] The astringents women used for contraception may also have worked, especially alum, so, too, tannin-containing substances such as nutgalls, pearlash (a white solid made from crude potash), and the white oak bark Knowlton recommended. Plant astringents may actually have constricted the cervical opening, so that it was more difficult for sperm to pass into the uterus; these may not really have served as spermicides. It does seem that vegetable astringents made pregnancy less likely.

The directions in advice literature varied so greatly about when and how to douche that it is impossible to arrive at any agreement about its impact. The best contraceptive advice (although certainly not the most healthful in other respects) urged women to use as strong a spermicide as they could stand in a douche and to douche before and after intercourse. The precoital douche may well have altered the vaginal pH sufficiently to be spermicidal, while the postcoital douche further reduced the concentration of viable sperm.[78] Thus Thomas Hersey's mid-1830s advice to douche with water or with alum and sulphate of zinc and water immediately before and after intercourse was relatively good.[79] So was the advice in the anonymous pamphlet *Reproductive Control* published in 1855, unusually explicit. The author (self-identified as a man) advised that a woman's first step was to "provide yourself with a Female Syringe, which can be had of the Agent selling the work." Women should buy the largest and longest syringe available. Then:

> Provide your bed-chamber, at all times, with a basin of pure, cold water. Immediately after sexual intercourse, let the female arise, fill the syringe with cold water and, placing herself over the basin, introduce the syringe the whole length, and inject the cold water, with moderate force, into the vagina or birth place. Repeat the operation several times in quick succession until a slight chill, or sensation of cold is experienced. Then but not till then, wash the external parts and wipe dry with a towel."[80]

In 1874 a New Orleans physician told his medical colleagues that if it was necessary to give contraceptive advice he would "order the female to thoroughly wash her vagina out with cold water and would further order an acid wash to be used immediately after, with a view to the destruction of the vitality of any remaining semen." But, he added, a more reliable method would be to "[prevent] the semen coming into contact with the mouth of the uterus. . . by forming a barrier. . . ."[81] Orris E. Herrick, a physician in Grand Rapids, Michigan, thought douching the only sure way to prevent conception, and advised his patients that water was sometimes effective but that the best results came from adding carbolic acid.[82] Webb J. Kelley, a physician in Indianapolis, Indiana, reported in 1883 three case histories of women who douched with carbolic acid and water. One was a thirty-nine-year-old woman, already the mother of five, who feared that she would die from another pregnancy. She had successfully douched with carbolized water for four years. In a second case a twenty-year-old woman, married for one year, successfully prevented conception by douching with carbolic acid, using up to four ounces a week, a technique she had learned from her mother. A third woman, a young prostitute, like the other women in her brothel, used vaginal injections of carbolized water to prevent conception and to protect her from venereal disease. When the frequent douching caused vaginal irritations and "nervous symptoms," they abandoned the carbolic acid for a while and douched with plain water instead.[83] A Taunton, Massachusetts, physician reported in 1890 that women used injections of bicarbonate of soda, borax, alum, and potassic bitartrate.[84] A Maryland physician in 1895 described a patient who prevented conception to avoid having a fourth child by using suppositories made of cocoa butter and 10 percent boracic acid. He taught another patient, with her husband present, how to slip a "borated cotton pledget" the size of an English walnut attached to a short string into her vagina. Although the effectiveness seems dubious because the cotton was not to be used until *after* coitus, the doctor was reporting that it had already worked for the couple for three years. His main advice, however, was to use a vaginal suppository before sexual relations and a vaginal douche afterwards.[85]

Lack of privacy, lack of indoor bathrooms, lack of heat in a bedroom, must have discouraged many women from douching on cold winter nights or from douching with frozen solutions. Knowlton heard complaints along these lines, for in the 1833 second edition of *Fruits of Philosophy* he tried to smooth over the difficulties: "I do know that those married females who have much desire to escape [pregnancy] will not stand for the little trouble of using this check, especially when they consider that on the score of cleanliness and health alone, it is worth all this trouble."[86] In the shared intimate spaces of colonial houses where servants, children, and even adult strangers slept in the same room, withdrawal would have been easier. But between the 1840s and 1880s, housing styles and ideals changed for "middling" groups of Americans, giving a new emphasis on privacy in middle class familial and marital life, with separate parental bedrooms in the larger houses, bedroom doors with locks, private "water closets"—all made douching more possible.[87] One 1894 medical discussion of "prevention" noted that most women douched with plain water while standing over a commode, thought to be ineffective. The author, a physician, recommended "one to two triturates of bichloride of mercury" and use of a bedpan so that a woman would not have to leave the bed. Douching took time and was troublesome, "but considering the fact that nearly every woman has the intelligence and means at her disposal for completely washing out the vagina after conjugal relations it is her own fault if she sees fit to disregard measures intended for her own protection."[88] Some doctors argued that it was dangerous to a woman's health if she left a warm bed to douche for contraception.[89]

Doctors recommended douching as a cure for a broad array of vaginal and uterine problems and taught their patients how to douche. By the 1870s and 1880s William Goodell, had personally taught thousands of women at the University of Pennsylvania Medical School, to take daily vaginal douches of solutions of tannin, lead, zinc, slippery elm bark, potassic chlorate, or salt. Although he was opposed to family limitation, ironically he recommended douching solutions similar to the spermicides birth control advisers themselves had popularized. He even recommended the type of Davidson or fountain models widely used in contraceptive douching, and, for "chronic metritis [inflammation of the uterus] and endometritis" he advised that women use vaginal suppositories, particularly those of tannic acid, before going to bed at night. Goodell estimated in 1879 that at least two thousand women annually had been receiving "uterine applications" for years either at the University of Pennsylvania Hospital or in his own private practice. Uterine applications called for a particularly hazardous procedure, involving uterine probes and the swabbing of the uterus with acidic solutions. All these patients were taught afterward to give themselves douches and to use suppositories.[90]

Not only such well-known gynecological pioneers as Goodell taught generations of women how to use vaginal douches and suppositories. An obscure Newton, Massachusetts, physician in 1872 said that he had been freely prescribing suppositories to women for diverse medical complaints. He even recommended suppositories to women *before* they developed signs of vaginal problems so that they would not put off treatment when problems developed because they dreaded calling in a physician. Some doctors, he wrote, "think we should not teach women to introduce things into their vaginas." He considered it "whimsical . . . to fear [that we] shall tell her something which she ought not to know."[91] An article in the 1882 *Columbus Medical Journal* reported that any woman could give herself cheap and easy vaginal douches in only one minute, and told how.[92]

Douching for general health was a token of faith for many physicians from the 1830s through the 1860s. Medical self-help manuals, advertisements, and physicians in their daily practice and written correspondence with patients advised the practice. Lydia E. Pinkham, who did not intend to give contraceptive advice, nonetheless often suggested that women douche and use medicated suppositories every night. When women wrote to her privately, Pinkham advised regular use of suppositories made of carbolic acid or boric acid, or small vaginal sponges dampened with carbolic acid. We know this because Pinkham kept manuscript notes of her responses to women who wrote for medical advice. An 1895 pamphlet published by the Pinkham Company advised women to take a vaginal douche with the company's "Sanative Wash" nightly before bed. It also recommended using a fountain syringe.[93]

Indeed, many who opposed reproductive control and who regarded contraceptive douching as dangerous inconsistently advocated therapeutic douching. It is difficult to gauge how effective such critics were in convincing women that *contraceptive* douching was dangerous when respected medical advisers were advocating *noncontraceptive* douching as a cure for ailments.

Douching offered a man the chance to relinquish primary responsibility for prevention of a pregnancy to his wife and the chance to abandon coitus interruptus or sexual abstinence. It also promised men greater sexual pleasure. They therefore had good reasons to be early advocates of the method. Women may have had reservations, yet many, eager to reduce the number of pregnancies, found douching more certain than breastfeeding, and less dangerous. It gave a woman action to take *before* turning to efforts to induce abortion.

In America, the roles of middle class women were changing, and when ideologies about motherhood, marriage, and the family were subtly shifting, middle class women, who had never been wholly relegated to the "domestic sphere," now expected to become efficient household managers and mothers. They began to be deluged with advice on how to be good homemakers, how to cook nutritious meals, how to raise children correctly, and now how to time their pregnancies to protect their own health and the well-being of children already born. Reproductive control became part of a woman's duty to her family. While some male writers, such as Henry Clarke Wright, argued that men bore the responsibility for their wives' pregnancies, feminists opened a campaign of moral and peer pressure to sanction women's control of the timing, and also the frequency, of sexual intercourse. Douching had appeared at a critical time. It gave women a new power over reproduction, but also a new burden. They were expected to learn the intricacies of using a vaginal syringe, the spermicidal properties of substances, and the rudiments of sexual physiology. It brought household technology into the bedroom and made women its primary agents. This reproductive control method simultaneously permitted women new biological (and perhaps marital) independence and increased the burden of failure. To plan and execute the method improperly could result in an unwanted pregnancy, a failure that left women blaming themselves.

The New Rhythm Methods: A "Safe" Period, but When Is It?

A new contraceptive technique introduced in the 1840s and 1850s was the rhythm method. Not the same method practiced in the twentieth century, it was known by euphemisms—"the agenetic period," "periodical continence," "the physiological rule of abstinence," "certain intervals," "the laws which regulate the female system," and the "sterile period." It revolved around the concept that at certain times in every woman's menstrual cycle conception is impossible. Since antiquity, medical advisers had wrongly believed, for example, that women were particularly likely to conceive immediately after menstruation. Much of the new information on timing was simply wrong. Many women were told that they were safest from conception in mid cycle—that is actually the time when women are most likely to conceive.

Several scientific discoveries in the 1840s had led to this new rhythm method of contraception. Although the existence of eggs in mammals had been known since 1827, the process by which human ova matured and were discharged from the ovary was imperfectly known until the 1840s, when several European scientists published the results of their investigations into "spontaneous ovulation" and the relationship between ovulation and menstruation. A French physician and professor of zoology, Felix Archimede Pouchet, claimed to have discovered that human ova matured and were discharged periodically rather than in response to coitus, sexual excitement, or contact with sperm. In 1842 he published his *Théorie positive de la fécondation des mammifères*, and in 1847, the *Théorie positive de l'ovulation spontanée . . .*, the latter arguing that the discharge of a mature ovum occurred in relation to menstruation every month.[94] Therefore, he said, it is easy to state exactly every month when conception is possible and when it is not. He said that women can *always* conceive on the eighth or tenth day after menstruation, and more rarely on the tenth to twelfth day, and after that they are absolutely safe from pregnancy until the next menstrual period.[95] By 1847, Pouchet was advising readers that conception could never take place "except from the first to 12th day which follows the menses." For any who did not want to count, he suggested that it was sometimes possible to identify the *moments* after which conception became physiologically impossible. He did not specify what they were, writing only that "there are signs which announce the fall of the egg and other signs which attest that the uterus is no longer able to retain the product of the ovary and that it has passed away without being fertilized."[96]

It fell to another doctor in France to forge a more explicit link between this new "ovular theory of menstruation" and birth control. In 1844, Adam Raciborski, at one time chief of the clinic of the Faculté de Medecine in Paris, noted that the delayed marriage recommended by Malthusians as a means of controlling population was not a feasible method in France. Couples burdened by a too-rapid increase in their families would also not find much satisfaction with the recommendation that women prolong lactation for three years; this, he argued, is rarely effective and dangerous to a woman's health. He also rejected "the abortion of beings ready to live."[97] His solution was to put "a certain order into sexual relations": couples should abstain from sexual intercourse for two to three days before menstruation and for the eighteen days following the end of the menstrual flow.[98] This schedule was more effective than that in Pouchet's advice because it increased the length of time of sexual abstinence and enhanced the probability that sexual intercourse would be resuming in the postovular phase of a woman's cycle. The writings of Pouchet and Raciborski, and to a lesser degree the analogous theories of the German T. G. G. Bischoff, influenced American birth control writers and lecturers, who further popularized the ideas for widespread audiences.[99]

In the United States, beginning in the late 1840s, numerous books and lectures publicized the notion that sometime in their menstrual cycle women have infertile days. By mid century, the rhythm method appeared to be nearly universally approved as a birth control technique. It required no devices or drugs, with their attendant dangers and expenses, and like breastfeeding it appeared to be a natural way— some said Nature's own way—to curb fertility. The medical establishment, even those who disliked all other forms of fertility restriction, embraced the notion of a "safe period." The New York gynecologist Augustus K. Gardner, who disparaged contraception and abortion, in 1856 noted that "the human female is capable of being impregnated only for a few days every few weeks, subsequent to her usual menstrual period."[100] Even Horatio Storer, the man most identified with the mounting medical opposition to abortion, and unsympathetic to contraception, wrote in 1867 that any portion of the intermenstrual period is safe from conception, although for a "central ten days or fortnight . . . the risk is slight." Concerned about illicit intercourse, as he continually was, he added, "So far as the public morals are concerned it is well that it is so."[101]

Even the Roman Catholic church gave tacit approval to the rhythm technique, foreshadowing its later support for the twentieth-century model of the rhythm method. In 1853 the French bishop of Amiens asked the Penitentiary, the office of the Holy See that dealt with cases of conscience, if couples should be rebuked by the church for abstaining from sexual intercourse on the days which, in the opinion of skilled doctors, conception was likely. Ignoring or forgetting the teachings of Saint Augustine that reliance on a sterile period was a contraceptive method (and therefore a sin), the Penitentiary replied that "those about whom you ask are not to be disturbed provided they do nothing by which conception is prevented."[102] When, in 1867, Dr. Avrard, a French physician who was disseminating information about the sterile period, asked a preeminent Catholic moral theologian to reconfirm the morality of the rhythm method, the theologian replied that he could not condone the practice but that the confessors should not disquiet those of their flock who were practicing it.[103]

Medical physicians, phrenologists, Perfectionist reformers, and feminists who argued for women's absolute control over the timing and frequency of intercourse—all found the concept of the sterile period reassuring. John H. Kellogg's *Plain Facts for Old and Young* in 1880 claimed that the only truly tolerable method for family limitation was absolute sexual celibacy, but that sexual intercourse during the infertile period was acceptable. Nicholas Francis Cooke's *Satan in Society* (editions from the 1870s through 1890s) agreed that the only legitimate method of family limitation other than total abstinence was restriction of intercourse to the infertile period.[104] Eliza Bisbee Duffey's 1873 *What Women Should Know* castigated abortion, coitus interruptus, and contraceptive douching, yet noted that if there were any safer or better methods than total abstinence or use of the sterile period she did not know of them. Even Elizabeth Blackwell, who detested abortion and disliked most contraception, advised in 1884 that if the sterile period was not always reliable it was, at least, one way of helping to reduce the probability of conception.[105]

In one 1849 study a British physician and professor of medicine, Henry Oldham, analyzed the dates when the wives of sailors conceived, concluding that "the human female is susceptible of impregnation at any time between her monthly periods." He disputed the widespread theory that conception could occur only one or two days before and about ten days after menstruation: "The truth is that this theory has been prematurely shaped into a law."[106] The pseudonymous authors "Dunne and Derbois," who were touting their own abortion-inducing medicine and their abortion services in 1854, wrote:

> There is an erroneous impression among a certain class of persons . . .
> that impregnation or conception will not take place at other times
> than 2 to 3 days before, or about six days after her month turn or
> courses. . . . This is not true and very many ladies have proved, in
> their own persons the false-hood of this statement. . . . It has been
> the fruitful source of much mischief and unhappiness. . . . There are
> no facts *which prove or even render it probable* that the human

female is not susceptible to impregnation AT ANY TIME BETWEEN her monthly turns if sexual intercourse takes place.[107]

As the decades passed, the medical community began to express more doubts about whether menstruation actually marked ovulation. In the second edition of his *Clinical Lectures on Diseases Peculiar to Women* (1873) Loombe Atthill wrote of menstruation that it "marks the period of ovulation." But in his fifth edition five years later he omitted these words.[108]

Almost no one repudiated the idea that women had an infertile period *sometime* in their menstrual cycle; they simply began to doubt that the time of greatest fecundity was around menstruation. An Illinois specialist in women's diseases, A. Reeves Jackson, put the issue succinctly in 1876:

> If the ovular theory were true conception could take place only at or near a menstrual period; but there is abundant evidence to show that it may and does occur at times quite remote from it. My own experience has furnished me with a number of instances where married women, anxious to prevent an increase of family, have observed the "physiological rule" of abstinence for a fortnight after a period and who have found to their chagrin after a time that their precaution had been unsuccessful.[109]

The key words here are "after a time." When the Philadelphia gynecologist Goodell, in 1872, criticized the "widespread delusion" that women were infertile beginning the tenth day after menstruation, he did not dispute that there was an infertile period, but simply questioned its absolute reliability: "Ovulation is not necessarily menstruation, and he who constructs domestic time-tables or trusts to his almanac will find that accidents may happen in the best-regulated family."[110]

It became harder and harder to believe that for all women the same number of days each month were absolutely safe from the possibility of pregnancy or that every individual's safe period could be calculated according to instructions in an advice manual. But very few people argued that the rhythm method *never* worked. Even the most severe critics believed that women had days when the probability of conception was slight. Each was expected to experiment with the timing of those days until she found one that worked for her or shift to another method. At the very least the conflicting advice spurred women to interest themselves in their fertility cycles, which may, in turn, have led to greater self-confidence and knowledge.

Certainly a number of women in mid century appear to have been satisfied with one or another of the rhythm strategies. Russell Thacher Trall, with a thriving practice and a large correspondence, wrote in 1867 that for fifteen years "thousands" of married people had relied on the advice he gave in *The Hydropathic Encyclopedia* (1852). He advised that the fertile period "as a general rule" occurred from the "commencement of menstruation through twelve days" after. By 1867, however, he added the warning that the mid-menstrual period, though generally safe, was not infallibly infertile. He therefore advised waiting ten to twelve days after menstruation.[111] In 1867 he cited statistics collected from "several hundred" patients to prove that for none of the women had an ovum passed into the uterus before the third day after menstruation or after the fourteenth.[112] The satisfaction Trall's patients appear to have found with the sterile period probably did not come from his timetables as much as from his careful instructions to women about how to discern their own ovulation. He recommended: "By noticing the time for two or three successive periods at which the egg or clot passes off she will ascertain her menstrual habit."[113]

Eleven of the forty-five women who responded to the Mosher questionnaire reported that they relied on some version of the rhythm method. Still others believed that there was an infertile period although they did not state specifically that they used it for family limitation. Four of the eleven had relied on fairly accurate versions, four on poor versions, and three did not mention what they understood the infertile period was.[114] Yet the women who had relied on unreliable versions do not appear to have been less satisfied with the results than those with a more accurate understanding. One woman with an essentially correct understanding relied on it successfully for two and a half years; after her pregnancy, her husband had begun to use condoms. Another woman with an accurate understanding noted that she had three children in ten years, a "mixture of choice and accident."

The modern rhythm method advises couples to avoid sexual intercourse in the days just before ovulation and during the twelve to twenty-four hours the ovum is capable of being fertilized after being released from the ovary. Once an unfertilized ovum has passed into the uterus, the possibility of pregnancy has passed until near the time of the next ovulation. The "safe period" is, therefore, after ovulation, through menstruation, and for a few days following menstruation. Women with an "average" menstrual cycle of 28 to 32 days, are told that their fertile days are Day 10–18 (for a 28-day cycle) or Day 15 through 22 (32 day cycle). Ill health or psychological factors can affect ovulation, so that every woman is at times at risk to erratic menstrual cycles. Women whose cycles deviate from the standard of 28–32 days are also at greater risk of accidental pregnancies with the rhythm method. In spite of these problems, studies report a wide range in effectiveness, from zero pregnancies per 100 woman years to 38.5–the highest recorded for the modern calendar rhythm method.[115]

The nineteenth-century women with the greatest probability of success in controlling pregnancy no matter what version of the rhythm method they followed were those who had regular cycles, shorter cycles, and a long rather than a short menstrual flow.[116] The most significant factor in success, however, was the advice a woman followed to determine her safe period. The best advice urged waiting the longest time from the end of menstruation, because doing so increased the length of time in which a couple refrained from sexual intercourse and increased the probability that sexual activity would resume postovulation. Almost all advisers told women to begin counting from the "cessation" of menstruation, a much better recommendation than of those few—A. K. Gardner and Russell Thacher Trall were the best known—who recommended counting from the first day. Seth Pancoast, in *The Ladies' Medical Guide and Marriage Friend* (1859), told women to count five days from the start of the menstrual flow, then to wait twelve to fourteen days for the ovum to pass from the body. Women may have had difficulty judging when menstruation had actually stopped each month and when to begin counting, yet even this uncertainty may have functioned more to their contraceptive advantage, because women who wanted to prevent conception might have been inclined to wait longer. The very confusion in the advice literature may have bred caution.

The era's worst advice told women to wait the shortest time, usually only one to eight days after menstruation. A few women with very short menstrual cycles might have found this advice helpful if they waited a full eight days after menstruation ended and had already ovulated; following any advice to wait longer than eight days began to enhance the probability for birth control. Most women, however, would have felt secure resuming sexual intercourse just when they were most fertile.[117] The most common advice in the 1850s through 1870s was to wait eight, ten, or twelve days after menstruation ended.[118] For many women this advice would have been disastrous, bringing on unwanted pregnancies.

The very abundance of conflicting advice about exact timing, mixed with the pervasive belief in a determinable safe period, encouraged experimentation to find the correct timing. Failure brought pregnancy and the complicated weighing of abortion versus having another child.

Some couples may have learned from failures to rely on combinations of contraceptive methods: using a rhythm method but also using condoms, douching, or withdrawal. One essential result of the literature was to encourage couples to seek out and study advice, to modify their behavior at least to some extent.

At least as important as technological improvements in the effectiveness of reproductive control was a growing awareness in the public mind of the possibilities for greater self-determination in reproduction. Awareness of new methods stimulated hopes of control; desire for fertility control reinforced the demand for better methods.

4

The Private Debate
Goes Public

In 1866, William Andrus Alcott, a New England physician and critic of reproductive control whose books and lectures on sexuality, marriage, and physiology were popular for decades after the 1830s, worried that "tens of thousands" of pregnancies were "destroyed yearly" by "means of a certain book clandestinely circulated."[1] He blamed Charles Knowlton's *Fruits of Philosophy* for teaching women how to douche to control their fertility. Horatio Robinson Storer, a physician in Boston who led the antiabortion campaign in the 1860s, charged that "popular authors and lecturers" were spreading "erroneous doctrines" that were encouraging abortions.[2] Even after the passage of the Comstock laws, another Boston physician, Hugh S. Pomeroy, complained that ideas about contraception and abortion—which he called "the perversion of marriage," "the crime against parenthood," and "the American sin"—were disseminated by books, by newspaper advertisements "which a respectable woman would prefer not to be seen reading," and by "lectures to ladies only," all of which constituted "a school of instruction in the art of avoiding parenthood."[3]

How Americans learned about ways to control or prevent pregnancy was radically transformed in the decades after the 1830s by public lectures and new genres of literature giving contraceptive advice. Discussions that had been mostly private now became more public, more structured, and more accessible. More authoritative publications replaced or supplemented the private, informal face-to-face gossip and dubiously reliable pamphlets and lore of the recent past. The topic was legitimized, in effect, by the proliferation of public communication, and information about reproductive control itself became less taboo.

A recurrent theme in the 1830s and 1840s was the need to control sexuality. Fears of unleashed sexuality permeate much nineteenth-century literature, much abolitionist polemical literature, as well as advice publications on marriage and family, dress, health, hygiene, and diet.[4] Whether or not they were inhibited or uninhibited in private sexual behavior, many Americans found sexuality profoundly disturbing, and in seeking its control, they sought symbolically, too, larger powers to harness social change in a time of vast social and economic transformation.

Much of the deep ambivalence about sexuality which found expression in the early nineteenth century lay, of course, in the relationship of sexuality to reproduction—finding ways to achieve a modicum of reproductive control, and determining who was to exert control over sexuality and reproduction. As contraceptive and abortive options became available and more reliable, Americans had to cope with the implications of a separation between sexuality and reproduction. The promise was liberating yet disquieting. To some it was a religious issue. Did not God condemn such a separation? Was not sex for the purposes of procreation alone? Was not coitus without the possibility of pregnancy "unnatural," sinful just as masturbation was? If women and men need no longer fear pregnancy as an outcome of sexual intercourse, what would keep wives faithful and daughters chaste? Some feared that readily available reproductive control would make women easier prey to male seducers. And if men were not blocked by fear of fathering a child, or by concerns about the effect of pregnancy on their female sexual partner, what restraint would there be, if any, over their sexuality?

The 1830s, then, was one of those decades that occasionally occur in the history of the United States when social forces seem to come together with a rush, when the pace of change, often slow and accretive, becomes dizzyingly overt, when social movements are born. The 1830s saw the birth of William Lloyd Garrison's newspaper the *Liberator*, whose motto "I will be heard" symbolized a panoply of social and cultural voices. The decade experienced shifts to immediatism in abolitionism, to a far more radical phase in the temperance movement, to mob violence, to new cruelties imposed on Native Americans, to a widening of the gap between rich and poor in urban areas, to expansion of religious revivalism: it was a period of economic adventurism and severe financial panic, of ominous political foreshadowings in the Nullification crisis—and of increasing public debate over women's and men's control of reproduction.

The Debate in Print and in Court:
Moral Physiology and Fruits of Philosophy

The decade brought literature of all types—pamphlets and tracts, novels, sensationalist penny newspapers—to ever larger publics, as technological improvements in printing made inexpensive, paper-bound literature available on a scale not possible earlier. Advice literature of every type flourished: there was a vast outpouring of temperance literature, a flood of health reform literature aimed at popular audiences, and new genres—notably advice to mothers about child rearing, maternal duties, and housekeeping. The first full-fledged discussion of women's rights by an American woman appeared in 1837: Sarah Grimke's *Letters on the Equality of the Sexes*. Especially noteworthy in this outpouring was the genre of advice on sex, sexual physiology, and reproductive control. Sexual-advice pamphlets changed significantly in tone as the ribaldry of the eighteenth century gave way to anxieties about controlling sexual excesses and masturbation.[5] To later eyes the pioneering contraceptive tracts of the period appear as logical pieces of the larger cultural preoccupation with sexual control. But to contemporaries the subject was novel and shocking even though the tracts did not celebrate reproductive control as sexual liberation, but promoted it in sober hopefulness of redressing some of the sense of powerlessness.

The works of two men were especially important in making reproductive control a more public matter. Robert Dale Owen's *Moral Physiology*, published late in 1830 or early 1831, was a concise, careful, logical argument about the need for fertility control, advocating the old method of coitus interruptus. In January 1832 appeared Charles Knowlton's *The Fruits of Philosophy*, full of concrete advice, especially on douching with spermicides. The two methods they emphasized—Owen's requiring primary cooperation from the male, Knowlton's from the woman, became significant methods of fertility restriction throughout the rest of the century.

Owen and Knowlton were motivated to write their tracts by a combination of reform sentiments and personal concerns. Each considered himself a freethinker, a member of an iconoclastic group (discussed more fully in Chapter 5) critical of established authority, especially Christianity. Robert Dale Owen, son of the famed English social reformer Robert Owen, was already well known in the United States as a young and idealistic reformer, a utopian socialist (he oversaw his father's communitarian settlement at New Harmony, Indiana, in its early days, from 1826 to 1829), and a labor activist. He became embroiled in the issue of reproductive control, inadvertently and temporarily, but its notoriety dogged his career for many years thereafter. Charles Knowlton, an obscure young physician in rural Massachusetts, like Owen a fervent freethinker, made a more deliberate bid for fortune and renown by publicizing contraceptive advice. He justified his advocacy of reproductive intervention as a defense of the right to free inquiry.[6] Both men personally experienced the wrenching results of inadequate birth control. By 1830 Knowlton and his wife, Tabitha, had four children after only eight years of marriage; Owen's close friend and colleague in free enquiry, Frances Wright, was forced into exile by an unwanted pregnancy and an undesired marriage. He must have known of her situation; at any rate he wrote his book on reproductive control shortly thereafter. Just as Knowlton's growing family began to be a burden, the young, indebted physician read Owen's *Moral Physiology*, recognized a public demand and need for such works, and decided to write his own book on the subject.[7]

Owen's *Moral Physiology* first appeared in New York City sometime between November 1830 and January 1831, as a standard-sized booklet of sixty-nine pages selling for thirty-seven cents.[8] Owen boldly listed his name as author—not always a common practice when books dealt with controversial topics—and the publishers as "Wright & Owen." It therefore came from the press he and Frances Wright operated at their freethought Hall of Science. In the next five months he issued four further editions from the *Free Enquirer* press in New York City, all with the imprint "Wright & Owen." In the United States at least eight, and perhaps ten, editions of *Moral Physiology* circulated in the 1830s, not all authorized by Owen.[9] There is some confusion over how many editions were issued in the 1840s, but there were at least two pirated editions.[10] One edition was put out in the 1850s, none in the 1860s.[11] Only a few cheap editions were published in the United States in the last third of the century: two editions in the 1870s, put out in Boston by Josiah P. Mendum, freethought editor of the *Boston Investigator*, and one mail-order subscription edition in 1881 from the People's Popular Liberal Library in Chicago.[12]

Owen had become interested in Malthusianism and "the population problem" in the late 1820s and had written two articles for the *Free Enquirer* outlining Malthusian theory on the exponential increase of population in relation to food supply and criticizing Malthus's suggested solution of delayed marriage and sexual restraint. In the second of the essays, "The Population Question," he argued that although overpopulation did not appear to be an immediate problem for the nations of the world, the too-rapid increase in family size was of immediate personal concern to many couples. Owen was convinced that delayed marriage simply encouraged prostitution and argued that knowledge of "checks" to prevent pregnancy at will was essential.[13]

In *Moral Physiology*, Owen concentrated on an extended rationale for reproductive intervention, elaborating broad theoretical and social reform arguments. Like the British Neo-Malthusians Francis Place, Jeremy Bentham, and John Stuart Mill, he worried about the inability of humans to control reproduction, and like them he believed contraceptive methods would provide a solution to Malthus's dire predictions that population would overtake food supply. Like them he had worked for broad political and economic reforms for workers, for trade unionism, and for workers' education, and now he was advocating sexual self-help measures to help them control family size. Unlike those theorists, however, Owen gave less attention to the desperately poor and much more to the upwardly mobile but precariously situated workingmen and their families. He equated the ability of young American couples to prevent a too-rapid increase of family with both their individual well-being and with the well-being of the nation as a whole.

Owen addressed only briefly the issue of reproductive control as essential for women's health; rather, he concentrated on its benefits to society as a whole, not to women specifically. Although he said that women with hereditary diseases and women who could not give birth to living or healthy children should not have to forego marriage entirely, he was more concerned with the impact of such diseases on society than on individuals. Later writers would prefer to focus on the merits of contraception for individual women and men, but Owen promoted contraception primarily as a way to improve American society.

Almost alone among nineteenth-century American advisers, Owen argued the importance of reproductive control for single women, noting that men who seduced women went unpunished by society, while women and their illegitimate offspring had to endure scorn and abuse. Unmarried women needed knowlege of "checks" as a defense against the "social brutality of illegitimate pregnancy." All sons, said Owen, "are not chaste and temperate," nor were all daughters "passionless and pure." A knowledge of preventives would save many from ruin and despair. Owen criticized the argument of some opponents of contraceptive knowledge who suggested that wives and daughters were virtuous only because they were ignorant of ways to prevent pregnancy. Such beliefs, Owen charged, slandered women and libeled the whole sex.[14]

Almost none of the later advice literature repeated Owen's daring advocacy of contraceptives for the young and unmarried. Owen's broader view reflected the influence of his English Neo-Malthusian colleagues and his general social radicalism in 1830, and probably also his distress over the accidental pregnancy of his beloved friend and colleague Frances Wright (whose story is told later in this chapter).

Owen devoted little of *Moral Physiology* to practical contraceptive advice—only twelve of the sixty-nine pages of the first edition. There he discussed three methods of reproductive control: his preference, coitus interruptus, was, he maintained, "in all cases effectual" and only a "trifling restraint" to sexual pleasure. But he appended a warning against the popular variant of withdrawal: "I may add that PARTIAL withdrawal, though recommended in a letter published in Carlile's Republican is by no means an infallible preventive of conception."[15]

He also recommended use of a vaginal sponge, moistened with water, to be introduced before intercourse and withdrawn immediately afterward by means of a small attached ribbon: "the power would thus be placed, where it ought to be, in the hands of the woman. . . . She who is the sufferer, would be secured against the inexperience, the culpable carelessness, or perhaps the deliberate selfishness of him who goes free and almost unblamed, whatever may happen."[16] (Here, as elsewhere in the work, Owen's words can be read in relation to Frances Wright's predicament as well as for their more general meaning.)[17] Owen feared that the sponge method was unreliable, however, having heard from three married men who reported failures with it. He asked to hear further about it: "I could very much desire, for women's sake, to find [it] proved effectual by experience."[18] Readers needed more facts, Owen noted, before they could trust "implicitly" in this method.

His third recommendation was the condom, which he referred to as the "baudruche," "a covering made of very fine, smooth, delicately prepared skin." Better known in Europe as a preventative of syphilis than of pregnancy, he said, the condom "has this advantage, that all persons, whatever their temperament, may find in it an infallible preventative [of conception]." Its greatest disadvantages "according to the testimony of those who have employed it" were its expense, "being fit for use once only and costing about a dollar," and the fact that it was "disagreeable on the score of cleanliness."[19]

Over the next thirty years as at least thirteen editions of *Moral Physiology* circulated in the United States, the only significant textual changes made by Owen or anyone else were the recomendations on contraception. Owen changed his mind, for example, about the reliability and propriety of the sponge and the condom, and in the fourth edition he relegated all mention of both to a short footnote, placing his entire reliance now on coitus interruptus. The only explanation he gave, in a postscript to the preface he added to the fourth edition, was that "communications from intelligent individuals on whose physiological knowledge I place reliance have enabled and induced me to somewhat modify the text and alter the arrangement of the sixth chapter."[20] Throughout the early 1830s he worried about improving his recommendations, fretting about the possible harmfulness of withdrawal and the ineffectiveness of the sponge.[21] Yet he never discussed spermicidal douching, even though he must have been aware of the recommendations on douching by his fellow freethinker Charles Knowlton.[22] Owen's single-minded focus on coitus interruptus and his ultimate refusal further to consider women's need for their own contraceptive method was a great weakness of his advice tract.

In the 1840s Owen lost interest in the subject of reproductive control, as, becoming more immersed in mainstream politics, he tried to rid himself of impedimenta from his past which might stand in the way of political success. He minimized his past connection with *Moral Physiology*, although he could never ignore it completely because political rivals often reprinted damaging passages to use against him in campaign broadsides. Owen did have, in addition, a certain squeamishness about sexuality and may have preferred not to become more deeply embroiled in a search for methods which would require detailed exploration of sexual relations. He thought that Richard Carlile's *Every Woman's Book* contained much "which was repulsive (I will not say revolting, to my feelings on the first perusal)."[23] Owen may have been as much disturbed by Carlile's frankness as by any specific contraceptive recommendations, for Carlile was self-educated and his tone "coarse" rather than genteel.[24] He described "genuine love," for example, as "nothing but the passion to secrete semen."[25] Owen took pains to explain his own abstemious habits in food, drink, and sexuality. Withdrawal, he genuinely believed, would promote moderation in sexual activity. (While writing the book, Owen was practicing Sylvester Graham's dietary system as a means of gaining greater self-mastery of all his appetites.)

Ironically, it was unauthorized—pirated—editions of *Moral Physiology* which gave readers a real variety of advice. Readers learned from these editions about condoms, about douching with spermicides, and about the availability of other literature (notably that by Frederick Hollick and Thomas Low Nichols). Openly plagiarized editions of *Moral Physiology*, published in 1846 and 1847 by a "Dr. Ralph Glover," added fifteen pages promoting an "electromagnetic preventive machine" for women. Glover did not explain how his machine worked, noting only that "like many other mysteries" it was "difficult to explain," but that galvanism "is known to impart a slight momentary impetus to the [woman's] parts, so that the vivifying influence of the semen is destroyed or expelled." Women appear to have mistaken Glover's machine as abortion-inducing, for he protested their "misapprehension of my notice."[26] His advertisements, however, as well as the ambiguity about what the term "preventive" meant contributed to the confusion: "Married ladies will find much to interest them by pursuing *Moral Physiology* written by the Hon. R. D. Owen, with additions by R. Glover, M.D., 20 cents."[27] In 1858, Gilbert Vale, a freethought colleague, published in New York what he called a tenth edition of *Moral Physiology*, probably without Owen's authorization. It may have been a reprint of an edition published in 1833 or 1834 in New York from the office of the *Beacon* (which Vale was then editing)—an edition no longer available, but which in 1936 historian Norman E. Himes saw "in private hands."[28] At some point, either in 1833 or 1858, Vale added text, engravings, and publisher's notes that included new recommendations about reproductive control. It was this 1858 Vale edition that was later republished verbatim (as the tenth edition and with Vale's publisher's notes) in 1873 and 1875 by Josiah P. Mendum, editor of the freethought journal the *Boston Investigator*.

In 1858, Vale's publisher's notes explained the theories of Frederick Hollick about the times of the month when women could assume they were infertile; it advocated partial withdrawal, followed by douching; it warned that though douching with cold water was effective it could lead to rheumatism; it recommended douching with water plus a small amount of alcohol, with "the use of a sponge before, or of a female syringe afterwards, or both, [to] give [women] complete control." Available for sale at his office, he said, were three titles by Frederick Hollick—*The Marriage Guide, Male Organs* (actually titled *The Male Generative Organs in Health and Disease*), *The Matron's Manual*, and two by Thomas Low Nichols—*Esoteric Anthropology* and *Marriage*. He recommended also a new kind of condom made of India rubber and gutta percha.[29]

◆ From the Berkshire hills farming village of Ashfield, Massachusetts, a young physician named Charles Knowlton, who had just hung out his shingle there, authorized the publication of his own contraceptive advice tract between 1832 and 1839. Knowlton, an ardent freethinker whose privately printed first book, *Elements of Modern Materialism,* had already brought him debt and notoriety, was probably inspired by Owen's *Moral Physiology* (a copy of which remained part of his library to be listed by title in his estate inventory when he died in 1850). He knew Owen, for he had lectured on physiology at the Hall of Science in 1829, and the community of active freethinkers from New York to Boston was closely intertwined. (Knowlton admired father or son sufficiently to name his second son Stephen Owen Knowlton.)

Knowlton authorized four editions of his *Fruits of Philosophy* between the first edition in 1832 and his death in 1850. The first edition was published anonymously "by a physician" with no publisher listed, a sixty-four-page tract, copyrighted in Rhode Island late in 1831 and issued in January 1832. The second, "by Charles Knowlton, M.D.," was issued in Boston (probably from Abner Kneeland's press at the *Boston Investigator*) in 1833; the third edition issued in Boston (again probably put out by Kneeland) in 1834; the fourth in Philadelphia by an obscure printer in 1839. Knowlton explained the five-year gap between the third and fourth editions as his deliberate restriction of circulation until he could verify the effectiveness of douching. He may, indeed, have conducted a personal experiment with spermicidal douching, because his wife, Tabitha, did not become pregnant from November 1831 (following the birth of their fourth child) until August 1836 (the conception of their fifth)—a "contraceptive interval," as demographic calculations would put it. (There is no evidence about whether or not Tabitha suffered any miscarriages in the interval.) The gap in editions was also probably caused by Knowlton's continuing legal problems with the book.

Soon after the first edition appeared, Knowlton was indicted for publishing an "obscene" work. At the trial, in Taunton, Massachusetts, early in 1832, he was found guilty and fined fifty dollars. He was not forced to pay the customary court costs, however, because, Knowlton said, the prosecutor was ashamed after the trial and felt "so disagreeably about it that he did not sleep the night before." As noted earlier, one of the jurors, "about forty years of age," told him, "Well, we brought you in guilty—we did not see how we could well get rid of it, still I like your book and you must let me have one of them."[30]

Even before the first trial was over, a new indictment was handed down against Knowlton, based on a complaint filed by a Lowell physician who had seen only a prospectus for the second edition of *Fruits*. Knowlton wanted to plead that it was a "good book and he had the right to publish it," but his lawyer, whom Knowlton later charged was incompetent, said such issues could be settled later and persuaded him to plead guilty of *selling* the book.[31] He was found guilty and sentenced to three months at hard labor in the East Cambridge jail. He served the full sentence in the harsh winter months from January to March 1833. Knowlton took pleasure in hearing that his jailor had changed his mind about *Fruits*. The *Boston Investigator* published articles in his defense, and while he was in jail two Philadelphia free-thinkers organized rallies in their city to raise money for Knowlton and, along with fourteen others, sent him $10.50. A month after he was released the second edition came out containing an appendix Knowlton had written in his cell.

Sometime in 1834 the third edition of *Fruits* was published in Boston, and, in August, Knowlton and his medical partner, Roswell Shepard, were indicted a third time for selling an obscene work. The November trial in the county seat of Greenfield attracted large crowds. Knowlton, pleased with his attorney and with the impartiality of the judge, admitted publishing and selling the work but denied that his motive was to make money, that he had ever sold it to the young (he had never sold it to "anyone but a *man*), and, above all, that it was obscene. After seventeen hours of deliberation the jury came back unable to reach unanimity. Ten jurors voted for his acquittal. His partner, Shepard, also on trial, was also freed by a hung jury. In March 1835 both Knowlton and Shepard were retried (in separate trials) and again the juries failed to reach agreement, although only one vote kept Shepard from a guilty verdict. When the district attorney sought new indictments in August of that year, both cases were thrown out of court by the judge.[32] By the end of the year Knowlton felt reasonably secure against further prosecution, yet he still waited four years to publish the fourth edition, perhaps having had trouble finding a publisher willing to risk taking it on. Abner Kneeland was undergoing his own legal battles in the 1830s, indicted for blasphemy (and indirectly for his association with Knowlton's book and reproductive control), and ultimately he spent three months in jail in the summer of 1838. Kneeland moved to Iowa the next year. Neither Knowlton nor anyone else put out further editions of *Fruits of Philosophy* in the 1840s, 1850s, or 1860s although copies continued to be advertised for sale in freethought newspapers.

Knowlton's pioneering tract continued to be available in the second half of the nineteenth century. In 1877, Annie Besant and Charles Bradlaugh, wanting a test case to challenge the new English obscenity law, published a new edition of *Fruits*. They used an English edition—James Watson's from the 1830s—with medical notes and footnotes appended by the neo-Malthusian physician George Drysdale. The publicity stemming from their controversial court battle spurred sales of the work in England and America. In 1877 a group of physicians from the Harvard Medical School published a subscription edition, their interest piqued by the Bradlaugh-Besant trial.[33] In addition, in the next two decades at least a dozen editions or reissues, most of them based on the Bradlaugh-Besant edition, appeared in the United States: four in the 1870s in Boston, Chicago, and Kentucky; two in the 1880s in Chicago and New York, three in the 1890s in Chicago and San Francisco, and three undated issues from Chicago and New York. Two and maybe more editions of *Fruits* were issued between 1888 and 1891 by a G. E. Wilson, who remains obscure.[34] Two of these were issued as part of a mail-order subscription library—"The Reader's Library"—of paperbound works that Wilson made available for three dollars a year. In 1891 one of the monthly tracts was Knowlton's *Fruits of Philosophy*, and in 1893 the library offered Besant's *The Law of Population*. These were mailed from San Francisco and Chicago as pocket-sized, paperbound volumes. Wilson also used the title "The Wilson Publishing Co." In the 1880s he published a Library of Fiction, of which the third issue of volume four was an eighty-seven-page edition of *Fruits*.[35]

Knowlton's first edition had included a publisher's preface telling readers that the work explained "the idea . . . of destroying the fecundating property of the sperm by *chemical* agents" and that it was "written in a plain, yet chaste style," a "philosophical proem" [sic] summarizing Knowlton's beliefs about materialism and freethought, and four chapters. The first chapter, taken freely and without acknowledgment from Owen's *Moral Physiology*, presented Owen's general Malthusian and sociological reasons for reproductive control. By the fourth edition Knowlton had stopped using Owen's arguments and instead was addressing the criticisms of his own work. Knowledge of how to curb reproduction, argued Knowlton, was no more "against nature," as some had charged, than was cutting one's hair or beard. Nor would it lead to illegal intercourse, as critics claimed, because couples who had "become so familiar" as to use his method would practice withdrawal anyway, even "if no such book as this had ever been written."[36] Knowlton also addressed the criticisms that, apparently, women had made about reproductive control. Women should not "condemn checks but approve of them and when they become common or *fashionable*, the practice of them will not be thought indelicate anymore than it now is to marry or to have a male accoucheur."[37] Women who devoted time and money to creating asylums for prostitutes were ignoring, he said, more important underlying problems. A knowledge of "checks" would allow couples to marry young without fear of excessively large families and would reduce men's use of prostitutes. Knowlton advised women to manage their household affairs in a thrifty, prudent, and rational manner, to avoid parties, servants, and fashion, and to assume the fundamental responsibility of keeping the family size small. If a young wife were prudent and prevented a too-large family, her husband could then accumulate money and their marriage would succeed. Thus as early as 1839 an argument was made that was to become crucial in subsequent decades: reproductive control was a woman's responsibility foremost, prescribed as part of her duty as an efficient and well-organized wife and mother. Even a young bride should think rationally and calculatingly about the future and take precautions to prevent pregnancies as her special responsibility for the family economy.

Knowlton presented the first detailed, explicit, and graphic account to be published in the United States on the "physiology of the female genital system." His purpose, he said, was to "enable the reader to see how the checks effect their intended object." He wanted readers to be able to use contraceptive techniques "more confidently and effectively."[38] He presented, therefore, a brief explanation of the "labia externa," the "external organs of generation," the "internal organs of generation," menstruation (though it has only "slight practical connexion with the main object of this work"), and conception. He did not mention sperm or the male sexual organs until the book's second edition, when he explained, succinctly: "As the seminal animalcules are essential to impregnation all we have to do is change the condition of, or (if you will) to kill them."[39] Because animalcules were small and delicate, Knowlton wrote, it would be easy to do so. By the fourth edition, Knowlton, no longer so reticent about describing the male sexual organs, started the chapter on generation with a remarkably detailed discussion of testicles, the prostate gland, the penis, semen, and the role of "seminal animalcules" in conception.[40] It remained one of the longest and least euphemistic discussions of male sexual anatomy in all the nineteenth-century popular literature offering sexual advice.

Knowlton's understanding of the process of conception was largely inaccurate by today's knowledge, but even so, readers could have practiced more effective contraception for having read his book. He believed that the "animalcules" in the male's semen somehow reached the ovary. Although he did not know how they did so, he liked a theory advanced by a University of Pennsylvania professor of midwifery, William Potts DeWees, that the vaginal lining contained a special set of absorbent vessels that carried sperm to the ovary.[41] Knowlton rejected the common ideas that the semen was thrown into the uterus by the force of ejaculation, that semen was absorbed into the blood, and also that women needed to experience "passion" for conception to occur. When a seminal animalcule "penetrated" a "vesicle" in the ovary, he explained, a "fruitful connexion" occurred and the vesicle "burst from the ovary," traveled down one of the fallopian tubes to the uterus, where it attached to the lining and the fetus developed. Knowlton's explanation may have made contraceptive douching more effective by encouraging prompt use of spermicides or, less usefully, astringents. It may also have made the practice of withdrawal more effective, if only by discouraging the apparently still common practice of partial withdrawal.

His 1839 edition had an entirely new chapter on pregnancy and fetal development, including four pages on the rights of women to have abortions, a subject earlier editions had not broached and one few other writers in the century faced as directly. In a section called "Of the Nature or Life of the Foetus: Has It Any Rights?" Knowlton argued that a fetus, because it was attached to a woman's body, had no more rights than any other extremity. "The laws in this country against abortion were never made by physiologists, and I should hardly think by men of humane feelings."[42]

All editions of Knowlton's book discussed sexuality at considerable length. Chapter 3, first titled "Some Other Things That Ought to Be Known" and later the bolder "Remarks on the Reproductive Instinct," warned young women not to "gratify the sexual instinct" until age seventeen (interestingly, the age of Knowlton's wife, Tabitha, at the time of their marriage.) It counseled sexual moderation for both sexes. Unlike many nineteenth-century sexual advisers, however, Knowlton took a relativist position, acknowledging that individuals differed in how much sexual activity was healthful or harmful.

Just as Owen had done, Knowlton altered the chapter of contraceptive advice the most substantively of all over the years. He tinkered with it, worried about it, queried friends and acquaintances (and even strangers) about its contents. As in other editing changes he became bolder about some things, changing the title from the first edition's simple "Of the Checks," to no title at all in the second edition (when he was under a second indictment for publishing an obscene book), to the bold title of the 1839 edition, "Of Preventing Conception without Sacrifice of Enjoyment." He extended the chapter from six pages to twelve. He changed the emphases and explicit directions of his contraceptive advice. In the first edition he had recommended four "checks": withdrawal, the vaginal sponge, the condom, and his own method—spermicidal douching. (His discussion of the vaginal sponge was far more thorough than Owen's and probably more effective, for he recommended moistening the sponge with chloride of soda rather than with plain water.[43]) The second edition also discussed withdrawal, the vaginal sponge, and condoms but in less detail and more disparagingly. Condoms were now objectionable "on account of cleanliness and expense," and were "by no means calculated to come into general use" because they were associated principally with protection from "syphilitic affections" [sic]. He omitted most of his earlier details about how to use the vaginal sponge, its size, and which spermicides to use for moistening, warning readers that "this check has not proved a sure preventive" because it would not dislodge the semen in the folds of the vagina—an accurate objection. Even if moistened with a liquid that would "act chemically upon the semen" and if the method were "ever so sure," he believed it would fall short of douching in several respects. The fourth edition discussed no methods at all other than douching.

Knowlton acknowledged in later editions that his focus on douching was a consequence of conversations with a friend whose wife had successfully controlled reproduction for an entire decade solely by douching. He claimed, however, that he had personally invented douching with spermicides. This was not actually a first—the idea had been known and used by various peoples since the Greeks—but Knowlton's *Fruits of Philosophy* did diffuse the idea widely throughout the United States of preventing conception by chemically destroying the sperm. He pointed out its advantages: "[It] costs nothing; it is sure; it requires no sacrifice of pleasure; it is used after, instead of before connexion, a weighty consideration, it is conducive to cleanliness."[44] The culminating advantage was that "it is in the hands of the woman." Its only disadvantage: "I know the use of this check requires the woman to leave her bed for a few moments, but this is its only objection, and it would be unreasonable to suppose that any check can ever be devised entirely free of objections."[45]

Knowlton's douching advice was clear, explicit, and useful. It helped women maximize the contraceptive effectiveness of douching (which, as noted earlier, can vary greatly). It took care to list substances believed (with some justification) to be spermicidal: sulphate of zinc, alum, pearlash, salts, solutions of vegetable astringents such as white-oak bark, red rose leaves, nutgalls, vinegar. Knowlton advised syringing the vagina with one of these substances rather than with plain water so as to destroy and not simply dislodge the sperm. In the second edition of *Fruits* he added the advice that women should "syringe carefully two times without delay" or at most within five to ten minutes."[46] He discussed briefly the use of plain water but, though it would probably work, he said, it had been known to fail. It is clear that Knowlton had heard complaints about douching, for at the end of the book he added a paragraph rebutting problems he had grown tired of hearing about: "I do not know that those married females who much desire to escape [childbearing] will not stand for the little trouble of using this check, especially when they consider that on the score of cleanliness and health alone it is worth all this trouble."[47]

In the final edition, Knowlton urged women to use the recommended spermicides in as strong a solution as they could stand without discomfort. He provided specific recommendations about strengths and dosages and added to the list of spermicides a few common household substances including saleratus (baking soda). Baking soda would have been effective. He was much more explicit about how to use the douching syringe and emphatic that it should be used immediately after "connexion," but urged women to douche even if there was a delay because no one understood how long the absorbent vessels took "to take up the semen." Women ought never to omit douching even if they were about to menstruate or even if they had not experienced sexual pleasure. He also explained that using a light was not necessary if women could keep the solutions near the bed, that spirits could be added to the spermicides in winter to keep them from freezing, and that women should view any discomforts of leaving a warm bed as "trifling compared with the pleasure it enables us to enjoy, or with the anxieties and other troubles that must or may arise from not using it."[48] It would "require no great ingenuity so to construct and arrange things that one's sleeping room need not be cold in the evening certainly, if not in the morning."[49]

One additional change Knowlton made in *Fruits* requires comment here. The first edition ignored the problem of infertility, but in the second edition Knowlton began his chapter on "checks" with fourteen pages of advice on how to overcome sterility and impotence. This addition marked an important recognition that for all the couples desperate to curtail the growing size of their families, others were equally desperate to conceive. His advice on this subject was a mixture of traditional folk remedies for bringing on the menses or for creating sympathetic actions between bodily parts and the generative organs— taking cold baths, tonics, or cayenne pepper—and ideas growing in popularity among 1830s reformers—on moderation in food, drink, tobacco use, and in sexual activity itself. By 1839, interestingly, he omitted the discussion of impotence and had moved the discussion of sterility to a later chapter on fetal development. Knowlton's receptivity to changes probably reflected the concerns of his public and the growing assertiveness of the women in his public (probably his patients' as well as female readers') in asking questions. The changes were, in general, concerned more with restricting fecundity than with promoting it.

By 1839, after the court trials, Knowlton's confidence that he would not again be prosecuted freed him to write more explicitly and in more detail. Some of the textual changes stemmed directly from his personal needs; he added several paragraphs to the copyright notice of the 1839 fourth edition complaining bitterly against men he claimed were violating his copyright on spermicidal douching. (He may have gotten the idea that he could copyright his spermicidal douching advice from the precedent set when Samuel Thomson in the early 1830s claimed to have a patent on his medical system and charged a fee to learn "Thomsonianism.") The change in the fourth edition's subtitle from "Private Companion of Young Married People" to "Adult People" probably reflected Knowlton's legal problems and a response to the charge, made several times at his trials, that he made his pamphlet too easily available to the young (however, he also showed audacity in leaving out the word "married").

The textual changes referring to women are particularly noteworthy. Knowlton's earliest editions read as though he hoped that women would be part of his audience, but as though he was not quite certain that they would be. We can assume from his inclusion of a chapter on pregnancy in the later editions, his expressed sympathy for abortion, and his addressing of women's particular complaints about douching that by 1839 he had now more confidence that women were indeed reading his book. He was more knowledgeable about what women wanted. In his medical practice he by now had become a specialist in women's diseases, and over the course of the decade he could scarcely help gaining increased understanding of women's desires and the acceptable language for communicating with women on such subjects.[50] Perhaps he believed that he had exaggerated the prudery of earlier women readers, or that the times were different. At the beginning of the decade neither Owen nor Knowlton appeared confident about either the parameters or the diction for written discourse on reproduction; by the end of the 1830s women were unequivocally assumed to be part of the audience for what Knowlton termed "the anti-conception art."

The shifts in Knowlton's text over the course of a decade showed a growing disparagement of withdrawal. In the first edition he said, "This Check, it is true, requires a slight mental effort and a partial sacrifice of enjoyment."[51] By the second edition he had added further derogatory remarks: "Still I leave it for every one to decide for himself whether this check be so far satisfactory as not to render some other very desirable."[52] By the fourth edition, he did not bother to discuss withdrawal as a reproductive control method at all, although he assumed that it was very well known, noting that any couple wanting reproductive control would already know about it, but douching, he said, was preferable because it enabled "the parties to enjoy a more complete, agreeable, but not a more hurtful intercourse . . . without any risk of conception, whereas the draw-back, as usually practiced is not (probably) quite sure."[53]

Knowlton referred frankly to sexual pleasure in the text of all editions of *Fruits*, although in more detail by the last. In the first page of his first edition he wrote that for years there had been attempts to disseminate "a knowledge of means whereby men and women may refrain at will from becoming parents, without even a partial sacrifice of the pleasure which attends the gratification of the reproductive instinct."[54] In discussing how he came to write the book, he explained that he had wanted to discover a sure, cheap, convenient, and harmless method "which should not in any way interfere with enjoyment."[55] And, under a heading "Of Preventing Conception without Sacrifice of Enjoyment," he referred twice to a man's sexual pleasure: a solution of salteratus was the best and most convenient spermicide, leaving "the parts smooth and agreeable . . . whereas for an hour or so after zinc or alum have been used there is a roughness about the parts which would not be agreeable to the male on a second copulation." His text reflected two attitudes toward sexuality, on one hand expecting his audience, women as well as men—but primarily men—to value sexual pleasure; on the other hand, warning against excessive sexual intercourse, especially during menstruation, after childbirth or miscarriage, or during the early stages of pregnancy.

The messages about sexuality in *Fruits of Philosophy* and *Moral Physiology* took quite different forms. Owen argued that men needed to practice greater sexual self-control and restraint; Knowlton promised "checks without sacrifice of enjoyment," although his concern was primarily with men's sexual pleasure. Sexual intercourse and sexual pleasure, he said, need not be eliminated if women exercised precoital planning.

Owen's tract had argued the importance of a contraceptive method for women. Knowlton's provided it. Owen's gave men a method, but in both his own textual changes and in those of Knowlton, too, we glimpse the unpopularity and perceived difficulties of withdrawal. In their lists of methods and advice and their later retractions and amendments, both Owen and Knowlton encouraged readers to think in terms of reliability and safety. Many Americans were already competent in practicing certain types of fertility control behaviors—white marital birth rates had, after all, declined in the 1820s, well before reliable advice literature came on the scene. Owen's *Moral Physiology* and Knowlton's *Fruits of Philosophy* established far greater public awareness that fertility could be successfully controlled. Thus the meanings of a book, in Lucian Febvre's words, are many. A book "furnishes arguments to those who are already converts, lets them develop and refine their faith, offers them points which will help them to triumph in debate, and encourages the hesitant."[56]

Both *Moral Physiology* and *Fruits of Philosophy* sold well, but not dramatically in the decades after publication; neither would have qualified as a "bestseller."[57] In his autobiographical recollections in 1874, Owen wrote that *Moral Physiology* had a circulation in the United States and England of fifty to sixty thousand copies.[58] Knowlton wrote in 1839 that he had deliberately restricted the circulation of *Fruits* to seven thousand copies; if each of the first three editions was the same size, about 2,500 copies, then demand appears to have been fairly brisk in the 1830s. With fifteen months elapsing between the first and second editions, circulation would have approached 166 copies a month—given the informal ways Knowlton marketed the work, probably a reasonable figure. This is considerably less than the circulation of Owen's pamphlet, which in the early 1830s was selling between three hundred and six hundred copies a month; however, Owen had more advertising sources, more access to established booksellers and dispersal networks, and he faced no court trials. Knowlton's sales do not seem insignificant in comparison. Circulation fell from 1834 to 1839 when Knowlton issued no new editions, although the publicity surrounding his several trials and his "obscene" work may have stimulated demand. When he put out the fourth edition in 1839, possibly larger than 2,500 copies, at least 9,500 copies of *Fruits* would have been in print in the United States. With no further authorized or even pirated editions of the pamphlet until 1877, the work became rarer by mid century, but did not go out of print entirely. The editors of the *Boston Investigator* seem to have continued to have access to it, probably by retaining the plates or the unsold copies themselves. In any case, throughout the 1850s and early 1860s the newspaper carried advertisements for it.

The impact of these two tracts can only be guessed at. Certainly they were bought and passed around, and read, sometimes furtively, sometimes openly. Their advice was weighed and considered; some tried it and succeeded; some tried it and found it wanting; some rejected the contents out of hand. Meanings were obviously filtered according to the age, gender, and marital status of the reader, and to the reader's general attitudes toward the rights of humans to interfere with "nature" or toward sexuality, reproduction, children, and fertility. The two texts were aimed at popular rather than learned audiences, but it was not a literature that polarized prospective audiences by class or gender. It was accessible to elites and nonelites alike, women and men alike.

The size and paperbound format of these pioneering advice tracts was significant in that regard. While Owen's was a common pamphlet size, the first three editions of *Fruits of Philosophy* were almost miniature books, only about three inches by two and a half inches in size. It was designed for private perusal and passing on to friends, not for public display. The fourth edition, still small enough to be easily concealed, was about the size of a three-by-five-inch index card.[59] A product bound in paper may have seemed cheap and shoddy to some—for paperbound literature was usually sensational trash bought for a pittance in disreputable urban areas, filled with news of crime, violence, and sex, but the paper format may also have made the product seem easier to buy and read, less solemn and more accessible. That format may have encouraged workers or the less educated and less literate—men and women more accustomed to buying newspapers than books—to buy them and read them.

The most important contribution made by Owen's and Knowlton's tracts, more important even than the advice they contained, was their very existence in printed form as serious, plainly written, informative, carefully argued treatises. Both tracts proved that advice on reproductive control could be communicated in a new way: not merely in potentially embarrassing verbal face-to-face encounters between friends or acquaintances, but anonymously, through contact with print. Reproductive intervention could be learned soberly and rationally from booklets embodying what seemed to be the most modern and scientific understandings of sexuality and physiology. Above all, such advice could effectively counter the disorderly earlier compilations of centuries of superstition. Unlike their precursors, Owen and Knowlton, concerned with accuracy and reliability, tried to verify the accuracy of their contraceptive advice by speaking with users about their first-hand experiences.

Following Owen and Knowlton, through the 1870s, written advice on reproductive control came in even more structured form, with tables of contents and with indexes. Readers could look up "prevention of conception" or "procuring miscarriage" and turn to the appropriate pages without having to read an entire book. In style and layout, in the sense of the order and rationality of the presentation, the literature seemed reassuringly to have come from experts, from sensible and educated professionals. Not all subsequent works, of course, were models of organization and clarity. Readers still had to decode labels and euphemisms if they did not want to miss information. Mauriceau's *The Married Woman's Private Medical Companion*, in the 1840s, for instance, though it did not have a table of contents, did have an index in which an alert reader might have found hints about reproductive control in five different places under the entries "Conception, prevention of," "French secret," "Portuguese Female Pills," "Pregnancy, prevention of," and "When necessary to effect abortion."[60] Works in the ribald-sensationalist mode continued to be popular, too, as the circulation of the books by "Aristotle," as Eugene Becklard's *Physiological Mysteries and Revelations in Love, Courtship, and Marriage* and Jean Dubois's *Marriage Physiologically Discussed* illustrate.[61]

Few readers of the 1830s would have known from the title alone what the *Fruits of Philosophy* was about. After Owen's *Moral Physiology*, however, references to "physiology" began to carry added layers of meaning so that even the relatively staid publishers Fowlers and Wells carried an advertisement in the back of their 1844 bestseller, *Love and Parentage*, announcing that a list of "special books on physiology" was available privately through the mail. By the second half of the nineteenth century it became more common for titles straightforwardly to reflect contents, as, for example, the anonymous 1855 work simply called *Reproductive Control*.

On the Public Stage: The Itinerant Lecture
Circuit

The lyceum and itinerant lecture circuits were a highly important form of entertainment and education in early nineteenth-century America. Reformers lectured both in the organized lecture series known as the "lyceum" and on the circuit as a way to persuade Americans to take various social actions: to avoid alcohol, to abolish slavery, to fight for women's rights, to follow new health regimens. Lyceum speakers on subjects ranging from Shakespeare to beekeeping helped the public while away long winter months. Lectures became a crucial type of public ritual and a source of self-help and education for Americans still distrustful of the legitimate theater yet longing for amusement and self-improvement.[62]

Itinerant lecturers, who, because they managed their own affairs, rented halls, and paid for and circulated their own advertisements and circulars, were free to address subjects too controversial for the staider lycea—subjects such as marriage and divorce, gynecology and obstetrics, sexuality and even reproductive control.[63] By the time they made reproductive control a subject for the public stage, lecturing was already a well-established practice in many states. In the decades from 1830 to 1860, scores, perhaps even hundreds of itinerant lecturers, crisscrossed the rural and urban Northeast and the West speaking both to formal and informal gatherings, and to large mixed audiences and to small intimate ones, about sexual, physiological and anatomical, marital and maternal matters. Although some dealt with the issue of fertility control obliquely, others discussed it directly, giving advice about specific methods, arguing for the importance of spacing pregnancies. They legitimized ideas about fertility regulation and spread physiological and anatomical information that would facilitate contraceptive practices.

The difficulty for a historian trying to recapture what lecturers said on such covert topics to audiences in antebellum America is great. Lecturers rarely kept notes of their talks, and only a few published their lectures. Even the rare published works must be used with care because we cannot assume that the written words mirror the spoken ones. Newspapers rarely reported what lecturers said, especially if the topics were even remotely scandalous or sensational. Only the most basic information—the name of the lecturer (possibly pseudonymous anyway), the title of the lecture, place and time—can be teased from occasional newspaper reports and advertisements. And no doubt much of the most practical advice at the reproductive control lectures was communicated after the main talk in question-and-answer sessions or in private consultations, or was relayed in careful verbal circumlocutions in the talk itself or in written material handed out at the door. The editors of the *Boston Medical and Surgical Journal* in 1864, for example, derided the popularity of (unnamed) itinerant lecturers on anatomy and physiology in the city: "But let one of these vagrants claim the popular ear and at once crowds flock to hear him, eager to drink in the mysteries which his pretentious exhibition of papier mâché caricatures of the human organism, and his unblushing promises to remove the veil which preserves the decencies of society, lead them to expect the revelation of." They particularly disliked the enticements to private consultations in the lecturer's rooms after the talk.[64] Thus although antebellum Americans began to hear contraceptive advice and rationales for reproductive control in formal public lectures at least as early as the late 1830s, and although this practice continued until the outbreak of war in 1861, we know very little about what audiences actually learned from this new and important mode of communication.

What, for example, did the otherwise obscure lecturer Sarah Coates say about physiology before the audiences of women she spoke to in Ohio from 1849 to 1851? Coates, a young Quaker from West Chester, Pennsylvania, felt she "had a *call*" to study anatomy and physiology with a physician in Stark County, Ohio, and then "to teach women— wives, mothers, daughters & sisters, the laws of health & some of the means of preserving it to themselves & their families."[65] She described in letters to a friend the manikins she used, the advertisements she posted, and the trouble she had composing a lecture on "the peculiar constitution of women and associated topics," by far "that most difficult one to treat aright." She did not explain what the "associated topics" were. They may have been as innocent as the physiological evils of wearing a corset; or they may have dealt with conception, pregnancy, and related subjects that led some listeners to quiet questions after the lecture. Coates herself did not remain a physiological lecturer long; she moved to frontier Minnesota in July 1851, where she conducted a small class, then she married and bore three children over the next eight years.

Or, what did "Dr. Morrill" say when he spoke in New York City in 1851? His newspaper advertisement promised information on "the physiological relations of marriage to the health of the individual and the welfare of the community, involving an exposition of the nature, use and abuses of the sexual instinct, its connection with our social affections, solitary and social licentiousness, hints upon marriage." For the anounced separate lectures for women he promised to present information about "the vital organs, the lungs, tight lacing . . . the premature development of the passions of children, their restraint, etc. comprising a variety of topics which cannot be discussed before a promiscuous audience."[66] Morrill could easily have been addressing reproductive control, and could have given advice about specific methods, but we cannot know.

Lecturers on phrenology often gave advice about marital and parenting decisions, indirectly reinforcing ideas that it was important to plan when, where, and under what circumstances to conceive. Lydia Folger Fowler, the second women to receive an official medical degree in the United States, was married to Lorenzo Fowler, one of the best-known phrenologists in mid century and part of the family comprising the highly successful publishers Fowlers and Wells. Lydia Fowler spoke primarily to audiences of women, but from their marriage in 1845 until they moved to London in the early 1860s, the two lectured together and separately, he primarily on phrenology, she on anatomy, physiology, and hygiene, including "the laws of life and health, physical culture, moral duty and obligation." Husband and wife both may have disapproved of contraception and abortion—we do not know—but like other lecturers they could not always limit the ideas their lectures helped promote. In many cases lecturers were not addressing audiences hostile to reproductive control, and even subjects peripheral to family limitation provided legitimization in the form of rationales and the latest scientific information for what couples were already doing or inclined to do.[67]

It is, however, clear that some lecturers did present reproductive control information, and their styles of presentation and the nature of the contents of their lectures followed some of the same patterns of change as did the reproductive control advice literature. The first lectures veered toward the ribald and sensationalist, and only later did the approach become more serious and staid. Like the authors of contraceptive advice, lecturers varied greatly in the style and respectability of their approach, in their aims and persuasiveness. Some were discreet and dignified, some were not. The lectures of Russel Canfield, for example, appear to have been less than genteel although they were far from unique in their mix of information and innuendo.

Russel Canfield was an irascible free enquirer in Philadelphia, the chief organizer of often rancorous freethought debates in that city and the surrounding countryside from 1835 to 1839, publisher of cheap editions of "liberal" books, and from 1835 to 1837 editor of *The Temple of Reason, Devoted to Free Inquiry, Moral Science, Universal Education, and Human Happiness*. His weekly had a circulation of one thousand copies at its height. Canfield lectured on "sexual physiology," principally in the Philadelphia area in the 1830s, discussing, among other things, contraceptive douching, much to the fury of Charles Knowlton, who considered it a violation of his "copyright" on the method.[68] Canfield appears to have published his lectures on sexual physiology in 1832, according to his later report, although no copy of the book is known to exist. In 1849 he copyrighted a revised edition of the lectures, *Practical Physiology, Being a Synopsis of Lectures on Sexual Physiology, including Intermarriage, organization, intercourse, and their general and particular phenomena.*[69]

Canfield had a history of religious conversions and passionate enthusiasms and hatreds. From 1801 to 1811, he was a Deist; he later was converted to Universalism. In 1829 he stopped preaching and publishing Universalist doctrines in Hartford, Connecticut, and left for Philadelphia, where he moved even more openly into freethought. In 1839 he converted to more traditional Christianity, for he published *Atheism Abjured and the Libels of Infidels Self-Refuted*. Shortly after 1839 Canfield moved to Rochester, New York, where he dropped from public records.[70]

Canfield's lectures were aimed at audiences of men, although some respectable women either attended them or heard about them from their husbands, for he claimed that "a committee of ladies" urged their publication and he wrote that the subsequent book was for the "esteemed ladies." He touched on serious health, marital, and sexual topics, and furthermore addressed topics unlikely to have been raised earlier to a mixed audience of men and women, or to respectable women at all. He spoke, for example, about women who were "deflowered" while asleep, why virginity was not essential, the dangers of men's having sex with prostitutes, and even (extremely rare in any of the nineteenth-century sexual advice tracts) sodomy—"congress of male with male." He emphasized the importance of sexual pleasure, arguing that one reason that "checks to population" were so necessary was that "the object of marriage is mutual pleasure in the sexual embrace" and that early in marriage "the young want uninterrupted private pleasures" though few were well fitted to agree yet about child rearing.[71]

Canfield imparted decidedly mixed information about reproductive control. The tone and reliability of his advice resembled those of *Aristotle's Masterpiece*: a mixture of antique folklore and useful hints, of serious intent and artful pandering. He scattered the reproductive control advice about in several places throughout the book rather than put it all in one chapter where it would be easier to find. His index purposefully enticed buyers with a promised "secret worth 50,000 copies of this work," which turned out to be that "all the pleasure induced by variety may be enjoyed with one individual." His "male check" was a rehash of an old, painful, dangerous, and ineffective folk remedy: a man should tie a string around his penis above the testicles before erection to prevent ejaculation. One of the two "female checks" he advised was also an ancient and unreliable method: coughing violently within two minutes of intercourse and contracting the abdominal muscles to eject "the discharge." His best advice, taken from Knowlton but without Knowlton's superior directions and better examples of spermicides, was: "If before and after the act, or before it only, an injection of brandy and water, or water only, be thrown briskly into the passage by a female syringe, so much the better."[72]

John Wieting, a highly successful lecturer in the early 1850s who gave advice on the rhythm method, offered lectures that were, in fact, "exhibitions and entertainments." His talks were intended to shock and titillate audiences as well as to impart contraceptive information. Although his wife described his style as "modest and quiet" and added somewhat defensively that "his lectures were confined strictly to physiology and the laws of life and health," his rivals on the lecture circuit were offended by the inaccuracy of his advice on reproductive control.[73] Frederick Hollick, for one, disparaged Wieting as a rival much as Knowlton had Canfield, and complained bitterly that Wieting plagiarized from him. To make matters worse, Hollick said, Wieting garbled the information:

> Besides which they had picked up, from my lectures and books, some faint notions of the *new discoveries* I have referred to and knowing that they would interest their audiences, they made them their chief topics. Not being perfectly acquainted with them, however, their explanations were generally erroneous, and always imperfect, so that people who listened were misled thereby, and often to their great disadvantage. This was especially the case in regard to the *time* and the manner of conception. Not knowing practically the laws which regulate this process and having heard only very partial explanations, they both confused themselves and misinformed their audiences."[74]

Wieting came to itinerant lecturing after earlier careers as a surveyor for the New York and Erie Railroad, as an engineer working on the Syracuse and Utica Railroad, and as a street grader who in his spare time "read medicine" with a Syracuse, New York, physician. In the early 1840s, after attending a lecture on physiology given by an itinerant physician from New York City, a Dr. Austin Flint, Wieting bought Flint's "lecturing apparatus"— mainly manikins—and began traveling to the towns and villages of upstate New York. He was a great success. By 1850 he had acquired six life-sized "French mannikens" that could be disassembled on stage to show more than seventeen hundred parts of the human body, colored models of every organ, and twelve skeletons, some six feet tall.[75] Unlike his rival Hollick, whose lectures were praised because they made "no effort to surprise or startle," Wieting placed his own models with care about the stage and punctuated his lectures with dramatic lighting.[76] He amassed a fortune from lecturing and real estate speculation and retired at forty-five to travel around the world.

"Respectable" Public Lectures Become
Respectable

By the 1840s and 1850s the genre of the popular lecture on sexual and contraceptive advice had become more respectable, the path smoothed by public acceptance and an increasingly acceptable diction—including coded terms—for such public discussions. From 1847 through the 1860s Henry Clarke Wright, a Presbyterian minister turned abolitionist lecturer in the 1830s, and in the 1840s a fervent advocate of the water cure and marital and sexual reforms, spoke to sizable audiences about their duties in "parentage," "the crime of undesigned maternity," and the "unwelcome child." Wright probably provided no direct advice on reproductive control, but his repeated message that couples should plan and regulate reproduction was impassioned. Courting couples, he advised, should discuss such issues well before marriage, and maidens should shun suitors who avoided such conversations. If couples wanted healthy, intelligent children and happy marriages, only "designed maternity" would do: "Wives! be frank and true to your husbands on the subject of maternity and the relation that leads to it. Interchange thoughts and feelings with them, as to what nature allows or demands in regard to these." Wright's biographer, historian Lewis Perry, found little evidence about the contents of Wright's lectures in his diary, but believed that his books were an important clue to the lectures.[77] If Wright did not explicitly speak of contraception to the audiences attending his lectures he may well have done so quietly to smaller more informal groups after the actual lecture. He was especially interested in coitus reservatus, the method associated with John Humphrey Noyes and the Oneida Perfectionists.[78]

Other lecturers told women about sexual anatomy, the stages of pregnancy, and the process of conception. Even if they did not impart direct advice about how to control pregnancy, they encouraged a more positive perspective on fertility intervention. Lecturers who argued that couples could affect their children's looks, intelligence, and character by carefully controlling when they conceived a child helped to further the notion that people not only could but had a duty to alter their practice of sexual intercourse for the well-being of the fetus, the family, and society.

Frederick Hollick, one of the most popular and successful of all the nineteenth-century lecturers on reproductive control, contributed to the evolution of the topic's respectability in formal verbal formats. Hollick proved that public lectures given with properly restrained delivery and style and with carefully chosen language could engage and persuade audiences. He had been born in Birmingham, England, and had become a follower of Robert Owen and a devoted worker in the social reform movement Owen inspired.[79] In 1838 he passed the grueling examinations and became one of the first six "social missionaries" the Owenites hired to do grass-roots organizing from the ranks of their self-educated, working class volunteers. From 1838 to 1842 he organized Owenite groups, debates, and lectures in Glasgow and apparently found time to study medicine, although there is no record of the medical diploma he said he had received from Edinburgh.[80] In 1842 the Owenites could no longer afford to pay their social missionaries, and probably about this time Hollick emigrated. He had published one pamphlet in Liverpool in 1840, *What Is Christianity? And Have the Persons Calling Themselves Christians Any Right to Interfere with the Free Expression of Opinions of Other Parties?* and also in 1840 had copyrighted one book in America, *The Matron's Manual of Midwifery and the Diseases of Women during Pregnancy*, but he did not move to the United States until somewhat later. The first book he published in the United States, a work on "slavery, abolition, amalgamation, and aboriginal rights," came out in 1843 and did not sell well. For the next eight years Hollick made a living as a public lecturer, a writer, and a physician with a practice primarily conducted through the mail. Ten other books of sexual, marital, and general health advice, issued between 1840 and 1852, sold well for decades.[81] Yet his reputation was first made in lecturing.

In the spring of 1844, Hollick lectured to New York City men on sexual physiology and anatomy; within three months he had branched out to include separate lectures to women on female anatomy and women's diseases. These proved so successful that he organized a lecture series in the towns of the eastern seaboard and through the Ohio and Mississippi river valleys. From 1845 to 1850 he lectured twenty-six times in Philadelphia, presented a series of addresses in Baltimore and Washington (the latter attended by former president John Adams and congressional leaders), throughout Massachusetts, and in St. Louis, Cincinnati, Louisville, Pittsburgh, Hartford, and as far south as New Orleans—at the request of the passengers, he even lectured on the steamship that was taking him to New Orleans.[82]

Hollick was brought to trial twice in Philadelphia, in 1845 and 1846, on charges of obscenity for his book *The Origin of Life*, for his lectures, and for displaying a realistic maniken of a naked human body on a public stage. Hollick believed the indictments were sought by jealous medical rivals who had first tried to dissuade him from lecturing because he "injured the profession." Later his rivals harassed him by writing anonymous letters to newspapers and by sending letters and obscene drawings forged with his signature to respectable women who had publicly endorsed Hollick. The first trial ended in a hung jury, and Hollick was set free after posting two thousand dollars' bail. After three ajournments in a ten-month period, which Hollick viewed as a continuation of the policy of harassment, he was acquitted on all counts in the new trial in April 1846. The trials, Hollick acknowledged, brought him free publicity, increased attendance at his lectures, and boosted the sale of his books from the hundreds to the thousands. After the acquittal Hollick began to lecture cautiously about ways to regulate pregnancy.

Hollick's specialties included anatomy, the male and female "sexual systems," theories of conception and impregnation, fetal development and nutrition, "the sexual feeling," and (to especially select audiences) the evils of masturbation. The audience interest at his lectures prompted Hollick to put them into book form. He first published them as *The Origin of Life* in 1845. Because the book was organized just like the lectures, we can deduce some of what audiences learned verbally from him. In 1846 he published *Outlines of Anatomy and Physiology* and in 1847, *The Diseases of Woman*, both giving us further clues about what he told his audiences. Before 1847 he did not discuss contraception directly from the public stage—he had read the European literature linking ovulation with menstruation, but saw no contraceptive implications in it.[83] But, alert to shifts in public opinion and recognizing a growing demand for discussion of contraception, beginning in 1847 and continuing with great success for the next five years, Hollick lectured on the need for family limitation and on the rhythm method, which he claimed to have invented.

Hollick lectured about reproductive control in front of mixed audiences of men and women—many of them married couples. His advertising notice in Boston, 20 March 1849, openly hinted at the family limitation content, for he promised a new lecture series for "married persons [who] will readily understand the nature of the topics to be introduced and will see their importance especially to them. The want of such information, at a timely period, is the cause of incalculable suffering and unhappiness."[84] The advertisements announced that he would provide "new information much desired by married couples."

Whatever else he advised couples to do to regulate fertility, he certainly provided information about his version of the rhythm method. At first Hollick's version was relatively effective, because he recommended waiting at least sixteen days after menstruation before resuming intercourse, which would have carried some women safely past ovulation.[85] In 1860 he gave what was later discovered to be less reliable advice: that most women needed to abstain from intercourse only six or eight days after menstruation (just in mid cycle, when most women were more fertile): "In fact it is hardly ever the case that it can take so long as sixteen days after [the flow ceases] because the egg is seldom more than two days in reaching the Womb and if it remains six, as an extreme limit, *eight days* is probably about the average. If the truth could be ascertained, I have no doubt that nine out of every ten pregnant females have conceived within the first seven days after the flow and that impregnation would not follow connection after the *Tenth* day once out of fifty times, but still it is requisite to state the latest *possible* time and that is *sixteen days*."[86]

Hollick also wrote that any intelligent and observant woman could learn to recognize when her egg left her body—an important piece of advice. The signs he gave were an accurate description of the signs of ovulation: he told women to watch for "bearing down sensations" or contractions, what today is called "mittelschmerz" and is a sign of ovulation. He also said that there would be a clear mucous discharge from the vagina, which is also recognized as a sign of ovulation today. Hollick believed that women could actually spot a "clot" that was the egg and decidua.[87] Many women, he said, "have ascertained this time quite readily after the signs had been explained to them and I believe nearly all would do so with a little trouble." Women were encouraged to try to learn by observation when their own safe and unsafe phases occurred. This was an empowering lesson.

Hollick was an avid entrepreneur of products for fertility control; he hawked them in his books and may have hawked them at his lectures as well. He sold condoms and "inflated pessaries" through the mail to customers who sent in five dollars and a sufficiently convincing reason why they needed them. He explained why people needed to know how to control reproduction and weighed the advantages and disadvantages of various methods. A nine-page section on "the prevention of conception" in *The Marriage Guide* provided rationales for family limitation and discussed (*and disparaged*) coitus interruptus, partial withdrawal, douching with water and spermicides, the vaginal sponge, forcible compression of the scrotum before intercourse, and condoms. Alert readers learned that ergot of rye caused women to miscarry and (incorrectly) that Cantharides ("Spanish flies") rendered married people hopelessly sterile. Into his 1849 *The Matron's Manual of Midwif-*

ery he inserted advertising notices for his personal advice by mail, for a "superior" brand of condoms for nine dollars, and for a preventative of syphilis for ten dollars.[88]

Hollick's lectures successfully negotiated the shoals of presenting risqué information from a public stage without compromising his audience's sense of propriety. He managed to give contraceptive information and to display anatomical models yet to stay respectable. The abolitionist and author Lydia Maria Child commended his lectures in 1844 for their "plain, familiar conversations, uttered and listened to with great modesty of language and propriety of demeanor."[89] The *St. Louis Intelligencer* in 1850 called his style "exceedingly lucid and intelligible. There are no tricks of art or oratory, no effort to surprise or startle. . . . They are listened to in silence and with enchained attention."[90] Even when he lectured to men in a saloon, as he did from time to time, "there is nothing improper or in the remotest degree indelicate in the exhibition of his models or in the manner in which the subject is treated." He never missed an opportunity to emphasize such respectability, advertising widely the gold pen, the writing desk, and the gold medal "ladies of the highest social standing" had given to him in gratitude. In the back of his books he reprinted the advertising notices for his lectures from newspapers and signed testimonial letters from a Susan Wood, Sarah Webb, Elizabeth Bunting, and Mrs. R. P. King—respectable women and officers of the "ladies class" attending his Philadelphia lectures.[91]

Hollick made skillful use of full-sized wax and papier-mâché "anatomical models" of the human body ordered from Paris. He was hardly the first to use such models, but his still caused a sensation when he first displayed them on the public stage: "The conviction that they are natural is, at first so strong, that many have even *fainted away* at a first view, from the impression that they were viewing a real body," he reported in his 1846 edition of *The Origin of Life*.[92] The manikens were technologically intricate with removable parts. Notices described them as "brightly colored" and arranged "to bold effect." Throughout the 1840s and 1850s it became a badge of seriousness for female and male lecturers to boast in advertisements that their lectures would be illustrated with life-sized manikens.

The use of such models may have had a significant impact in overcoming prudery. Once a woman viewed a maniken on a public stage she may have been able to face private instruction (oral or written) about her reproductive organs and functions. That more than a few lecturers reported women fainting when first viewing the manikens on stage requires evaluation. The claim was more than self-congratulatory or self-promotion by the lecturers. It was a way to entice audiences with the promise of respectable titillation; no one needed to fear that the talk would be boring, yet even "ladies" (who might faint) would be in attendance.

With the successful publication of his *The Marriage Guide; or, Natural History of Generation* in 1850, Hollick could stop depending on lecturing for his livelihood. After 1852 he devoted himself to writing popular medical books and to his growing private practice, conducted almost entirely by correspondence. About fifty letters arrived daily at his post office box in Manhattan.[93] Lewis Masquier, inventor of a phonetic system and lecturer on the labor reform theories of George Henry Evans, wrote admiringly in 1877 that Hollick was like himself "an advanced thinker" who had "long since discarded the creeds of Christendom" and who had built an immense business from the sale of his books and his consulting. Credit reporters wrote in 1864 that Hollick "is an author and lecturer, principally upon Staten Island, said to own his own residence and is called a smart man in his line of business; of excellent character, very attentive and careful. His means are by no means considered large but his reputation and standing with the [Medical] Faculty is very good."[94] Hollick eventually retired to his Staten Island estate to enjoy a private fortune multiplied by real estate speculations.

Historians sometimes focus on the spread of essentially correct ideas and ignore the fact that information rarely flows directly. As historian Theodore Zeldin notes, the process is much more convoluted: "Ideas took time to be accepted and absorbed; they were usually incorporated into a different set of ideas with more or less superficial reconciliation. . . . People picked up ideas from many sources, which were themselves far from coherent."[95] In many ways the dispersal of information on reproductive control changed and improved in the second quarter of the nineteenth century. In many ways it remained uneven and disorganized and subject to error and exploitation. The career of Alfred G. Hall is a case in point.

Hall, a self-taught botanical physician who had practiced medicine for some twenty years, traveled about upstate New York in the 1840s peddling his medical advice, his patent medicines ("Dr. Hall's Female Hygean Pills . . . for all problems associated with pregnancy from the first months to the last"), and other botanical preparations. A self-described "new school practitioner," he recommended botanical products instead of the mercury and calomel preparations preferred by the "old school" physicians. He probably sold vaginal douching syringes and solutions, for they figured so prominently in his medical advice.

In the 1850s he traveled through Ohio to Washington, D.C., as a "professor of physiology," lecturing on theories of disease and the "nutritive principle and science of fluid physiology." One convert was the phrenologist Orson S. Fowler, who said Hall's advice helped him gain strength and weight. In the 1860s Hall was in Boston editing *The Hygienic Monitor and the Institutes of Medical Jurisprudence.*[96]

In the years of his itinerant selling he was also reaching a wide readership by a book he wrote and published in 1843, *The Mother's Own Book and Practical Guide to Health; Being a Collection of Necessary and Useful Information. DESIGNED FOR FEMALES ONLY.* It contained 144 pages of advice on menstruation, "conception and gestation," "parturition and abortion," and similar topics. Hall sold about two thousand copies in nine months of peddling and lecturing, or so he said. Two years later he published a revised and expanded second edition under a new, enigmatic title, *Womanhood: Causes of Its Premature Decline.* It included engravings of female sexual and reproductive organs and sixty "vegetable and domestic recipes with directions." Both editions discussed menstruation, conception and pregnancy, childbirth and miscarriage, female (but not male) sexual anatomy, and menopause. There was contraceptive and abortion information, too, although a reader needed to be diligent in searching for it—Hall listed neither in the table of contents or in the index. Clearly Hall believed that his readers wanted information about preventing conception. Boldfaced type in the table of contents enticed readers with the promise of "secret information." Later in the book Hall assured "the amiable class of females" for whom he had written the book that it would be a "SECRET counselor much to be appreciated" and "truly worthy" of their "confidence." The secret information changed between the first and second editions, and Hall did not have much information to give, although he was floundering with the implications of some of the era's latest medical beliefs about reproduction. The first pieces of "secret information" were a recipe for an emmenagogue (a remedy to induce menstruation) and the information that pulverized bloodroot steeped in gin might, so some believed, prevent conception "by relaxing the uterus."[97] Both advice and recipe were missing from the second edition. One bit of secret information in both editions said that, of "the first stage of conception," the absorbing ducts or membranes of the vagina extended to its entrance "and therefore any fluid left on the surface, even at the entrance, would be absorbed and produce conception." His purpose was to explain to readers the occasional failure of withdrawal and the frequent failure of partial withdrawal. His final bits of "secret information" (although they were hardly as secret as he claimed) in the second edition, were that conception requires the "unision of two persons," that "little eggs" formed the basis of every fetus, and that without healthy ovaries a woman could not conceive.[98]

Hall's most significant contraceptive contribution was his instruction on "medicinal douching." He provided recipes for homemade douching solutions, many with vegetable astringents; they may have worked if the solutions were strong enough.[99] He recognized the importance of withdrawal, also, and explained the principles to his audience. He believed that conception could occur only if the timing of sexual intercourse (the "commingling" of the female and male life-giving fluids) was right: with an ovule in the ovary having begun to "pulsate with life and vitality" and with the ovaries in a special condition, which he believed was for most women usually in the first few days after menstruation. (He was, of course, wrong in this according to present knowledge, but right in the contemporary mainstream of belief about the timing of the fertile period.) The other conditions he specified illustrate his understanding of why contraceptive douching worked: the male and female fluids had to be of the same consistency and the same temperature if pregnancy was to ensue. Conception could be prevented by douching, which altered both male and female sexual fluids. Ironically, even though he got the reason wrong, his advice might have helped some women avoid pregnancy.

Hall also provided information on how to induce abortion. Like many gynecological advisers, he explained how to bring on a "suppressed menstruation." While he may not have intended the advice to be abortion-inducing—he gave none of the coy warnings beginning to be common from abortion entrepreneurs that the emmenagogues should not be taken in the early months of pregnancy because "miscarriage is bound to occur"—he did advise women to take instant action if their menses were late by so much as a day. His advice on how to encourage menstruation included hot foot baths, hot bricks wrapped in cloth over the navel to induce perspiration, and drinking teas of tansy, rue, featherfew, motherwort, savin, pennyroyal, or thyme. He provided recipes whose main ingredients were savin, black cohosh, pennyroyal, rue, and tansy—botanicals with a long folk medical connection with abortion.[100]

The Triumph and Tragedy of Frances Wright

Historians have tended to pay more attention to women's public roles in antislavery, temperance, and moral reform than to their lectures on health, sex, anatomy, and fertility control, although actually women were extremely important as such lecturers in the antebellum period.[101] Paradoxically, historians have tended both to ignore their role and, at the same time, without adequate documentation and scrutiny of sources, to assert that women lecturers did give information on reproductive control. The difficulty of determining what any lecturer actually said is greatly compounded in the case of women lecturers, and it becomes formidable when we try to reconstruct what they said about reproductive control. This is especially the case with Frances Wright, the first woman lecturer of any consequence in the United States—she spoke publicly as early as 1828—and one of the most celebrated and vilified women in antebellum America. Her story is complex and worth telling in some detail because it reflects, at the extreme, the dilemmas and constraints other women faced.

Fanny Wright came to the United States in 1818 on a visit, a wealthy, orphaned young Scotswoman with literary ambitions. Americans acclaimed her in 1821 when she published her enthusiastic responses to the new nation, *Views of Society and Manners in America*. When Fanny, then twenty-one, and her younger sister, Camilla, came to America a second time in 1824, they were lionized by prominent politicians, social reformers, and intellectuals. Yet within four years Fanny Wright had alienated large numbers with her radical social views.[102] Repelled by what she had seen of chattel slavery on a trip down the Mississippi and inspired by a visit to the Owenite community at New Harmony, she decided to use her personal fortune to establish an interracial community to demonstrate to Americans her plan to end slavery by "compensated emancipation."[103] In late 1825, near what is now Memphis, Tennessee, she purchased land and established Nashoba, settling there along with a fluctuating number of friends and supporters and the slaves she purchased so that they could earn their freedom.

The experiment—courageous, bold, and even noble in its aims— failed. It lacked careful and experienced management; the climate and swampy situation nearly destroyed Wright's health, forcing her to leave for months of recuperation in Europe; but, above all, the members of the community spoke injudiciously to the press, particularly to abolitionist-newspaperman Benjamin Lundy, about their approval of miscegenation and their disapproval of traditional marriage. Scandalized reactions in the religious, reform, and secular press branded Nashoba "a giant brothel," its participants "free lovers." Wright fueled the flames by publishing her opposition to organized religion and her detestation of the indissoluble bonds of traditional marriage and of racial taboos in sexual relations.[104] From then on she became a symbol: to supporters, a gallant and eloquent spokeswoman for much of what was wrong in America; to detractors, notorious: ridiculed and attacked by clergy and the conservative press as a "female monster [who] blasphemes God and advocates licentiousness," "The High Priestess of Beelzebub" whose ideas "on the subject of morality . . . were in the highest degree vicious and immoral."[105] From the ruins of Nashoba early in 1828, Fanny Wright went to New Harmony, where she coedited the *New Harmony Gazette* with Robert Dale Owen, by that time a good friend, and, in 1829 to New York City where they bought (with Wright's money) an old church on Broome Street and turned it into a "Hall of Science"—the center of freethought activity in the city—and the office of their new newspaper, the *Free Enquirer*.

Beginning in 1828 and continuing in 1829, Frances Wright turned to a new career as a public lecturer, meeting both with wild success and with deepening hostility. From the Mississippi and Ohio river valley towns and cities, through New England and New York, crowds of men and women in the hundreds, sometimes numbering nearly a thousand, flocked to hear her proclaim the necessity of state-funded education for all children, better education for women, and married women's property rights, to declaim the horrors of capital punishment and deride organized religion as an obstacle to mental freedom and the unfettered pursuit of knowledge. In Cincinnati, Louisville, and St. Louis no public building large enough to contain the audience could be found. A New York City supporter wrote early in 1829 that with Wright's lectures "there has not been such excitement in the city since the time of Thomas Jefferson's election." New York's *Evening Post* warned that riots and fire might be the result of this "singular spectacle of a female, publicly and ostentatiously proclaiming doctrines of atheistical fanaticism and even the most abandoned lewdness. . . . We presume no modest woman will be seen there."[106]

Historians have assumed that Wright's lectures must have included discussions of reproductive control, but there is little in the available record to bear this out.[107] She was not unfamiliar with the subject, and there are suggestions that early in 1829 she may have been moving intellectually to a more open justification of reproductive control, although she had said nothing publicly on the subject. In a third lecture in New York City in February 1829, in which she challenged the utility of the priesthood and of all religious instruction, a commentator quoted Wright as exclaiming "before an enraptured audience of thousands": "'Turn your churches into Halls of Science, and devote your leisure day—the first day of the week to the study of the anatomy of

your own bodies, the analysis of your own minds, and the examination
of the fair material world which extends around you.'"[108] There is little
to suggest that she ever spoke up on reproductive control in her lectures more directly than that. Indeed, she explained in March 1829
about a subject of deep interest to her: "The marriage contract is a
subject I have never treated [in public lectures] save once in Cincinnati. . . . The marriage contract indeed . . . presents to my mind no
subject for discussion. It forms only *an item in a system of coercive
laws* [her emphases]."[109] In July 1829, Wright reprinted a letter from a
young woman in Kentucky (probably sent to Robert Dale Owen, because it was addressed "Dear Sir") who complained that after four
years of marriage and the birth of three children, her husband, a mechanic, "gets drunk once every three to four weeks" and when drunk
"makes foolish bargains and therefore has almost rendered his family
penniless." She cited her own good health and the industry and the
labor of her husband: "I feel able to bring up these three little cherubs
in decency were I to have no more; but when I seriously consider my
situation, I can see no other alternative left for me than to tear myself
away from the man." She wanted advice about whether to leave her
husband, and also apparently about how to control the size of her
family if she stayed with him. Wright's response could not have been
particularly helpful. She could not "address the particular case" but
would instead give "a few first principles by which to test all actions
and to steer through all difficulties." The pursuit of happiness is a
right, she assured the writer, and in staying with her husband she
injured herself, her children already born, and added "to the number
of those unfortunates who, under the given circumstances, ought not
to be in existence." "I am far from passing censure," Wright said, criticizing individuals "unexercised in self government and blinded to real
duty by false lessons and erroneous habits [who] allow themselves to
become parents when they cannot fulfil the parental duties." Her only
concrete suggestion was of little immediate value to the troubled
woman—parents ought to "educate children to have self-control."
Women in such circumstances should "consider whether they can consistently with rectitude give birth to children who must inevitably be
doomed to a life of ignorance and consequent vice and misery." Only
at the very end did she move away from abstractions with an oblique
aside that the French, often stigmatized by Americans as immoral,
were nevertheless careful "to limit their progency to the means of
provision" by "calculation" and "forethought."[110]

Wright interrupted her hectic schedule of writing and lecturing
when she decided to travel to Haiti with the remaining slaves from

Nashoba to free them and, as a consequence, experienced personal tragedy and exile. William Phiquepal, a friend from New Harmony and its former schoolmaster, went with her. Sometime before his 17 March 1830 departure from Haiti they became lovers, and on her return voyage home in April she recognized her unusual seasickness as a symptom of pregnancy. No stranger to scandal, she knew that even she could not weather the storm of fury that would surround her and her friends and colleagues if news of an illegimate pregnancy became known. Her career as a public lecturer would be destroyed; she would probably not be able to continue writing for the *Free Enquirer*; the scandal would engulf every cause and everyone she held dear. All the slander from her many enemies about her sexual license and promiscuity would now seem corroborated. Yet for Frances Wright, one of the most outspoken critics in America of traditional marriage, to have married Phiquepal solely because of a pregnancy appears to have been equally untenable. So she took a third course and, accompanied only by her sister Camilla (who left her husband, Richessen Whitby, to be with Frances but who was grieving the death of her infant son), sailed for Europe. She told friends and readers of the *Free Enquirer* that she would be away on business for a few months, but when the ship docked in England the two sisters vanished into self-imposed obscurity and no record of their life for the next few months exists.[111]

Eventually Fanny Wright surfaced, living in a small flat outside Paris. She kept up an intermittent correspondence with friends and sent articles to American freethought newspapers, but no word of her pregnancy leaked out. Whatever her friends suspected or knew, none of Fanny's most vengeful critics ever laced their usual cries about her immorality and licentiousness with references to illegitimacy.

In December 1830 or early January 1831, Fanny Wright gave birth to a daughter, Frances Sylva. In February Camilla, who had never recovered emotionally from the death of her child, died in the flat she shared with Fanny outside Paris. The loss of her sister—her closest companion since childhood—following so immediately the birth of an illegitimate daughter were traumas that sent Fanny into a spiral of depression from which it took years to recover. In July 1831 she married Phiquepal (who had begun to refer to himself as d'Arusmont), and a second daughter was born on 14 April 1832. When the infant died early in the summer, Fanny, still hoping to avoid any possibility of scandal, pretended that its birthdate was that of her elder child. There seems never to have been any scandal about her marriage or her daughter.

Owen had known Fanny Wright since her earliest days in America.

He was one of her closest friends and confidantes, an admired mentor. Together they coedited the *New Harmony Gazette* and its successor in New York, the *Free Enquirer*. Their views coincided on nearly every topic. They influenced each other, although Wright appears at times to have been the decision maker and the dominant voice. It was she, for example, who decided to move home base from New Harmony to New York City early in 1829. It was she who rented the communal mansion five miles north of the city, where a fluctuating group of New Harmony friends—at times Robert Jennings, William Phiquepal, and several of his students—in addition to Owen, Fanny Wright, and her sister Camilla, several chickens and two cows, reestablished a serene rural communal life while commuting into the city.

Although they were intellectually and emotionally close for several years and lived together at Nashoba and New Harmony and in New York, Fanny Wright's relationship with Robert Dale Owen was that of a sister, not a lover. To say that they did not have a sexual relationship, however, is not to underestimate the depths of Owen's emotional attachment to Wright and the devastating loss her exile in Europe meant for him. Owen would have realized acutely what her pregnancy signified for Fanny: a forced marriage with Phiquepal, whom Owen considered her intellectual and social inferior, or a public scandal on a scale that even she could not have imagined. It is in this context, then, that his motivation to write *Moral Physiology* must be seen. In July when she left for Europe, Owen became reinvolved in an old controversy over his purported approbation of Carlile's *Every Woman's Book*. His critics had tried before to bait him into its defense, but in vain.[112] This time he fought back, in the way he was most comfortable: with his pen. He wrote and published *Moral Physiology*.

Friends who visited Fanny Wright in the early 1830s described her as silent and unresponsive, eking out an existence with Phiquepal, his adopted son, and their young daughter in a small and squalid flat. In 1835 she tried to effect a comeback on the lecture circuits in America, but it was a failure. Her presentations had become rambling and vague. The woman who had been one of the most electrifying speakers on any stage in America had become a bore. In addition, she quarreled with old friends, even with Owen, and turned an estrangement from her husband into a permanent separation; her daughter chose to remain with her father.[113] She continued to participate in liberal causes and in politics, writing and speaking, but even Tammany Hall found her an embarrassment and a political liability. She traveled back and forth between Europe and America. She died in Cincinnati on 13 December 1852, forgotten and ignored by a public that had once found her both brilliant and formidable.

Frances Wright dared to challenge two of the most sacred institutions in American culture—marriage and Christianity—and to try to remedy the horror at its core—slavery. Yet even she, courageous and boldly iconoclastic, could not raise the controversial issues surrounding reproductive control in any public way. That she appears to have been unable or unwilling to address them privately was her greatest tragedy. Her silencing profoundly underscores the larger public silencing around the issues of reproductive control and the extreme social constraints facing more ordinary women.

The Right to Decide: Early Spokeswomen

Before the 1860s there is little direct evidence that female lecturers disseminated contraceptive or abortive information. The most important of those who did do so was probably Mary Gove Nichols, whose public and private life, like that of Frances Wright, was full of sexual paradox. Mary Gove was intellectually curious and upwardly mobile, but at a young age married, unhappily, a dour Quaker, Hiram Gove. She secretly read medical textbooks and taught herself the rudiments of medicine and the water cure. Six years of increasing marital misery and five pregnancies later (all but one ending either in miscarriage or stillbirth), Mary and Hiram Gove left their New Hampshire farm and moved, in 1837, to Lynn, Massachusetts, where Mary supported the family by operating a boarding school run on the dietary principles of Sylvester Graham, supplementing this income by lectures on physiology and hygiene.[114] Her lectures, in turn, brought her to the attention of the American Physiological Society (founded in 1837 in Boston by William Andrus Alcott and Sylvester Graham).

Because some women attending the first lectures of the American Physiological Society were embarrassed to be in an audience with men, the society decided to hire separate speakers for men and women and create the Ladies Physiological Society. Mary Gove came to Boston in September 1837 and began to lecture on diet, dress, menstrual difficulties, and the dangers of female masturbation, sometimes to audiences of more than four hundred women.[115] So successful were these lectures that she continued throughout New England and as far south as Philadelphia and New York, speaking on "sanitary education," "the laws of life and health," the evils of wearing corsets, the problems of masturbation in girls' boarding schools, and, most radically of all, on the physical and emotional problems resulting from "indissoluble marriage." Desperately unhappy in her own marriage, she spent as much time away from her husband as possible, but he would not grant her a divorce. In 1842 she left him, but feared that he would never allow her to see their daughter and that he would continue to claim her financial earnings. Even though she was immersed in itinerant lecturing, consulting lawyers about her marital rights, and in poor health, she still found time in 1842 to publish some of her lectures as a book, *Lectures to Women on Anatomy and Physiology.*[116] If the book mirrored her lectures (as the title implies), then she did not speak on reproduction except to lament the prevailing ignorance among women on the subject of their bodies, but the book may have omitted such comments. Some of her lectures were given separately to married and unmarried women.[117] Her lectures scandalized some because of her comments on masturbation (the topic alone was shocking) and her references to her own (clothed) body to demonstrate anatomical points. She consulted a favorite cousin, the writer John Neal, whether he thought it proper to speak before men and women on the evils of "tight lacing," but added, "I think I have a *right* to speak on proper subjects in a proper manner before a mixed audience."[118] New York newspaper editor James Gordon Bennett denounced her, but the *Boston Medical and Surgical Reporter* commended her book and her lectures, noting that "useful knowledge becomes a woman, let it embrace whatever department it may," and adding that there is "nothing objectionable or indelicate for one woman to tell another those important facts . . . in a country where ladies have been too negligent of the laws of health, and sometimes apparently proud of being profoundly ignorant of the mechanism of themselves."[119]

Mary Gove supported herself (and her husband, though separated) as a water-cure physician in a series of hydropathic resorts, in Brattleboro, Vermont, Lebanon Springs, New York, and then at the establishment of Joel Shew in New York City, and finally in 1846 at her own water-cure boardinghouse on Tenth Street in Manhattan. In 1847 she met Thomas Low Nichols, a young itinerant novelist and journalist who had studied medicine at Dartmouth College and was absorbed in the theories of John Humphrey Noyes, Josiah Warren, and Charles Fourier. They married the following year when her husband, also wanting to remarry, finally granted a divorce.[120]

In the 1850s Mary and Thomas Gove Nichols became active New York water-cure practitioners and lecturers and writers on sexuality, marriage, and reproductive control. They operated a Reform Bookstore at 65 Walker Street in Manhattan, from which they sold their literature and advertised their services. Mary Gove Nichols probably influenced her new husband in these directions, for only after their marriage did he show any interest in many of the subjects they subsequently wrote about. Both lectured to large mixed audiences, but she specialized in intimate talks to small groups of women. They wrote and lectured on the benefits of the water cure, especially its aid in ameliorating the dangers and pains of pregnancy and childbirth,[121] and advocated easier divorce, women's property rights, and, above all, women's sexual rights. She had long believed that a woman had the right to determine if and when she would bear children and to choose who would father them. When Mary Gove Nichols and Thomas Low Nichols published such views they were branded "free lovers" by critics, although they emphasized the dangers of excessive sexuality, women's rights to *refuse* sex, and the legalized "prostitution" created by contemporary marriage laws.

The book *Esoteric Anthropology* appeared in 1853. Although Thomas Low Nichols is credited as its sole author, the wording of the text—especially the opinions about contraception and abortion—suggests that Mary Gove Nichols wrote parts.[122] In any case, both probably shared its views and may have expressed them in their lectures and, almost certainly, in their private consultations. *Esoteric Anthropology* boldly argued a position she had long held: "If a woman has any right in this world it is the right to herself; and if there is anything in this world she has a right to decide, it is who shall be the father of her children. She has an equal right to decide whether she will have children and to choose the time for having them."[123] She had written to a colleague in health and marriage reform, Stephen Pearl Andrews, that a woman in "indissoluble marriage to a man she abhors is his victim and their children will have all the same lusts of the father. . . . Hundreds of women in such marriages murder their children rather than bear them."[124]

Esoteric Anthropology suggested how women and men could achieve reproductive control, discussing a variety of methods, among them abstinence (it is "unhealthy and unnatural" but "easily done by most women and by many men"); rhythm ("in ordinary cases . . . conception can only take place when connection is had a day or two before or ten, or for safety's sake, say sixteen days after menstruation); complete withdrawal; use of a soft sponge "to cover the upper vagina over the mouth of the womb"; use of condoms or other "delicate coverings of the whole penis"; and "pressing upon the urethra to prevent emission of the semen," effectual but harmful. Above all, it advised an "immediate, very deep, thorough" douche—an "immediate injection of cold water by the vagina-syringe" to "kill and wash away zoo-sperms." Douching was, after all, an important part of the water cure.

In other sections *Esoteric Anthropology* presented enough information about the movement of sperm to enable effective use of withdrawal, noting that "zoosperms can retain power of motion for hours or
days under favorable circumstances" and that they are active enough
to move rapidly "through the entire vagina, uterus, [and] tubes."[125] It
defended more boldly than any nineteenth-century sexual advisor except
James Ashton the right of women to abort:

> [T]he ovum belongs to the mother—she alone has a right to decide
> whether it shall be impregnated. It is the same after pregnancy. It
> still rests with the mother. . . . It is an unnatural thing for her to
> refuse this sustenance—it may be very wicked. But it is exclusively
> her own affair. The mother, and she alone has the right to decide
> whether she will continue the being of the child she has begun. The
> wishes of the father should weigh with her—all obligations, moral,
> social, religious, should control her; but she alone has the supreme
> right to decide.[126]

Esoteric Anthropology included advice about the simplest and least
dangerous abortion method, and warnings about the most dangerous
techniques. The reformist physician Elizabeth Blackwell in 1853 noted
with asperity in a letter to her sister Emily, who was studying medicine in Edinburgh, that "the Nichols set is spreading their detestable
doctrines of abortion and prostitution under spiritual and scientific
guise—they are placing agents with the advertisements of their books
at the doors of the conventions now being held here, worded in the
most specious and attractive manner." In her published autobiography, Blackwell changed the wording of these remarks slightly and referred not by name to the Nicholses but to "an active set of people,"
whose "detestable doctrines of abortion and prostitution" were now
the "detestable doctrine of 'free love.'"[127]

Another lecturer, Paulina Kellogg Wright Davis, an antislavery and
woman's rights activist in the 1830s, became active in health reform
after her husband's death. From 1845 to 1849 she toured throughout
the East and the Midwest speaking to audiences of women on health
reform, anatomy, and physiology. Following the precedent established by Mary Gove Nichols, she used a manikin to illustrate her
lectures; but unlike Nichols, she did not publish them. Davis may not
have felt the personal anguish of excessive fertility; her concerns, indeed, may have been in the opposite direction, for, married twice,
she had no children by either husband. Still, she sympathized with
women's need for greater bodily autonomy. In *Una*, the journal she

published in the early 1850s, were articles about the evils of unrestrained sensuality in marriage and critiques of husbands' excessive marital rights over their wives.[128]

Harriot K. Hunt, another antebellum lecturer, practiced medicine in Boston for more than forty years, trained by a husband-and-wife team of homeopathic physicians, though she was repeatedly denied entry to the Harvard Medical School. One of the best known and most outspoken of the first generation of women physicians and a fervent participant in the early woman's rights movement, Hunt had contact with an unusually wide range of women, from those in Charlestown, Massachusetts, who joined her "Ladies Physiological Society" in 1843 to those in a working class district in Boston before whom she gave free public lectures in 1849. Her goals in medicine—"to trace diseases to violated laws and the science of prevention. That word—preventive—seemed a great word to me; curative was small beside it"[129]— showed her concern with ideas of preventing problems before they occurred, and this, by implication, would have included reproductive control. She may well have raised the matter of women's right to determine the timing and frequency of intercourse, to argue for rational and calculated pregnancies, and to suggest use of specific contraceptive methods. There is no direct evidence that she did so, but she was probably familiar with Knowlton's work on pregnancy prevention and she bought and proudly wrote her name in an 1853 copy of Nichols's *Esoteric Anthropology*. Earlier, in Lynn, she had boarded at Mary Gove's house "for a day or two every month," finding affinity with the water-cure practitioner: "Her deep interest in anatomy and physiology drew me to her."[130]

Hunt severely criticized doctors for conducting physical examinations of their female patients, calling them "skeptics who lived sensually and "contaminated their patients" with examinations "too often unnecessary."[131] She was obviously thinking about what she called "abuses of the marriage relation" and believed that women needed more control over a husband's sensuality. Investigating this complex issue, she visited a Shaker community in the late 1840s but found Shaker celibacy too extreme a response to the problems of fertility and sexuality.

Other women lecturers who left even less direct evidence about public discussions of reproductive control included Jane Elizabeth Hitchcock Jones. Jones was raised in the "burned-over" district of New York; she joined the outspoken Garrisonian antislavery lecturer Abbey Kelley Foster on a lecture tour in the early 1840s. Jones developed a powerful presence and eloquence before audiences and in the

1850s, after studying anatomy and physiology with an Ohio doctor, forged a new career as a health reform lecturer, using a manikin and engravings to illustrate her talks. She attracted large audiences in Ohio, Michigan, Illinois, and other states, garnering five thousand dollars in three years—a large sum by any standards, but especially for a woman. She may not have addressed the issue of reproductive control at all: there was not even a hint of the issue of sexual self-sovereignty or of the sexual abuses of marriage—all of growing concern to feminists—in the "Address to the Women of Ohio," which she almost certainly authored in 1850. Instead she focused exclusively on the need for reform of property laws for married women and on women's right to equal access to education.[132]

Still, reproductive control may have been very much on her mind. She had married Benjamin Smith Jones, a Quaker and antislavery lecturer, in 1846, at age thirty-three and had borne a daughter in 1848. It was after her child's birth that she began to study medicine, and just about the time she would have weaned her daughter Jones began her first extensive lecture tour. A woman could not easily have undertaken such a tour while breastfeeding, and weaning also marked the end of the minimal contraceptive protection offered by lactation. She and her husband were not entirely happy in their marriage, and Jones's reform activities may have provided a useful way to ensure long periods of separation.[133] There is, therefore, only scanty evidence, but it is suggestive nonetheless, that Jones had an interest in reproductive control and that after she undertook medical study she may have passed on some of what she learned to her subsequent female audiences.

General topics connected to reproductive control, such as the need for wives to have control of marital sexuality or to determine the timing and frequency of sexual intercourse, would, no doubt, have been easier than more explicit ones for women lecturers to raise. The rhythm method might well have been discussed without discomfort because of its seeming "naturalness." Withdrawal, on the other hand, might not have been, though it could have come up in connection with comments on menstruation or with recommendations for sexual abstinence. So, too, women lecturers may have found it relatively comfortable to refer to medicinal and hygienic douching or the use of vaginal suppositories or the vaginal sponge rather than measures men might take to avoid insemination of their wives. The freedom of women to speak publicly on sexual matters was greatly enhanced by the woman's rights movement that itself was stimulated by the wartime struggle for emancipation and racial equality.

The Women's Search for Sexual
Self-Sovereignty after the War

After the Civil War increasing numbers of women lecturers on woman's rights linked feminist concerns to issues of health reform, especially gynecological and obstetrical problems, sexual physiology, reproduction, and maternity. They gave particular attention to women's need for sexual self-sovereignty and often veered easily into discussions of "voluntary motherhood," especially in the late 1860s and 1870s.

Elizabeth Cady Stanton undertook a lecture tour of midwestern towns in 1869: her frequent topic, "Marriage and Maternity." At informal afternoon sessions before smaller groups of women she spoke on "enlightened motherhood" and on the "gospel of fewer children and a healthy, happy maternity."[134] Stanton spoke openly about sexual matters, but according to at least one of her coworkers, Frances Dana Gage, this outspokenness alarmed many of her female listeners. Gage wrote that most women "even in the bedchamber or in the most private conversation start back in alarm that cannot be controlled from the immodesty of the thing."[135] Historian William Leach has argued that, in the 1860s and 1870s, feminist hygienists took to lecture circuits to make the public discussion of sexual knowledge by women more open. "Feminist physiological societies" appeared in Washington, D.C., Brooklyn, Chicago, Philadelphia, and New Haven, as they had in Boston in 1837.[136] Although discussions at these public forums were not automatically on the subject of fertility intervention, many were.

One lecturer before such groups, Sarah Blakeslee Chase, was a homeopathic physician specializing in the diseases of women. Divorced in the early 1870s, with a young daughter to raise, she moved from Ohio to Manhattan. Chase edited, from 1878 to 1881, *the Physiologist and Family Physician* (a newspaper of the New York Physiological Society) and, in 1883, the now obscure *Woman's Friend*. She lectured to women on health and physiology in halls and churches in Manhattan and Brooklyn. Unlike others who left few clues about their concerns with reproductive control, Chase was an open partisan, convinced that reproductive control was essential to women's health and to the nation's well-being. An early eugenicist herself, she presented a paper to New York's Liberal Club in 1875 which maintained that no one with hereditary diseases should have children.[137]

To her women audiences she gave information on douching to control pregnancy, and she reinforced it by selling douching syringes from her office and probably after her lectures too. These activities, as well as her association with New York's freethinking "liberal" community, brought a confrontation with the vice hunter and special postal agent Anthony Comstock, who in the 1870s indefatigably pursued violators of the new federal and state laws against the circulation of birth control information and products. Comstock arrested Chase five times between 1878 and 1900. In May 1878 he wrote to Chase, pretending to be a woman who had attended one of her lectures and received "valuable information from them" and who wanted a douching syringe. He went to her home to obtain the syringe and instructions in its use. As a friend and supporter of Chase's (and sworn enemy of Comstock's), DeRobigne Bennett wrote that year that Chase was "of course, willing to sell these valuable syringes to every married lady who wished them." Comstock charged her with selling syringes to prevent conception and with being an abortionist, but a jury found her not guilty.[138] In July, Comstock arrested her again for selling vaginal syringes, but a district attorney dismissed the case. In 1893, when a female patient died from the medical complications of a pregnancy, she was tried for abortion, found guilty, and served six years in the state penitentiary. Released in 1899, Chase continued to promote family limitation in Elmira, New York. Comstock arrested her one last time in 1900, again for selling a vaginal douching syringe. A grand jury acquitted her.[139] Credit reporters in 1883 wrote that Chase was "not a graduate of any [medical] school, not recognized by [the] medical profession, not in good standing. . . . No doubt makes money but probably nothing could be collected from her if she did not want."[140]

➧ While men, in print and lectures, were promoting, in increasingly public ways, information and ideas about reproductive control women who broke the taboos about open communications on contraception and abortion risked greater censure. Even without the vote and with little direct impact on the passage of laws or the workings of the judicial system, armies of women did battle with alcohol, prostitution, and slavery before the Civil War and waged war for "social purity" in the postwar period. In spite of the prevailing ideology that ordained woman's place as the home, women had a public presence and a forceful public voice supporting and opposing many issues—but not reproductive control. In that matter all but a few chose silence, or were silenced. Yet even those women speakers who probably did venture into advice or discussions of fertility regulation at their lectures, as we have seen, left so little evidence that we can only speculate about what they actually said.

It is particularly fitting, therefore, to end this chapter by taking note of Mary Jane Owen and Tabitha Knowlton, the all-but-forgotten wives of the two men who stimulated the earliest formal public discussion of reproductive control. Mary Jane Robinson, whose father was a New York City workingman, married Owen in April 1832 when she was nineteen and he thirty-one. Tabitha Stuart, the daughter of New England farmers, married Knowlton in 1821 when she was seventeen and he twenty-one. Both couples benefited from their growing knowledge of reproductive control, for at times they successfully delayed or limited pregnancy. The Owens had six children in eighteen years of marriage. The last two birth intervals were almost certainly contraceptive—nearly sixty months and thirty-six months, respectively. Mary Jane Owen bore her last child when she was thirty-seven.[141] The Knowltons had five children in twenty-nine years of marriage, with Tabitha bearing her last when she was thirty-three. After the relatively rapid birth of four children early in their marriage, the Knowltons delayed a fifth pregnancy for fifty-seven months from 1831 to 1837, during the worst years of their legal problems.[142]

Mary Jane Owen and Tabitha Knowlton, whether they liked it or not, were linked to reproductive control in another more public way, by dint of their husbands' associations with it. A husband's character, his social standing, his moral repute became perforce a wife's. They may have resented being somehow "tainted" by their husbands' choice of reform topic, for slander and malicious rumors and scandal could hurt a woman's standing even more quickly than a man's, and guilt by association may not have been viewed within their communities as any less powerful a form of guilt than if they themselves had written the tracts.

On the other hand, both women may have been pleased to be associated with such widely sought-after information. Within the world of women's culture, among their friends and kin, they may have done as much as anyone to further advice on reproductive control. Both appear to have been, for a while, strong-minded women, and their verve comes through in anecdotes. As a young girl Mary Jane Robinson had shown spirited independence in an urban milieu. Before her marriage, she had "mastered a trade" (although her husband's biographers do not specify what it was) and attended the lectures of Fanny Wright and other freethought events and debates at the Hall of Science. She had even boldly endorsed *Moral Physiology*,[143] a daring act for any woman, but especially for one young and single. At their marriage ceremony, she, like Owen, wanted no clergyman, and both agreed to a prenuptial contract stating that marriage did not give a husband control over his wife's person or property. On their honeymoon Owen abandoned her for several weeks in Fanny Wright's dispirited household in France, hoping, condescendingly, that his bride (whom he had described earlier to a friend as "neither pretty nor interesting looking") would learn from Wright's intellectual style. Mary Jane had the gumption to leave and, to her husband's surprise, rejoined him in London.

Tabitha Knowlton, in contrast, was retiring early in her young married life—daunted perhaps by the rapid succession of infants, her husband's proclivity for legal transgressions, and their grinding poverty. But in 1845, when her youngest child was four years old and she was forty-one, she boldly became one of the founders of the United Liberals of Franklin County, signing her name "Mrs. Tabitha Knowlton," to the constitution. One of the principles of the new organization was that women members were to be treated equally with men and, of course, that women were equally able to check books out of the lending library of liberal literature which the group established.[144] Nor did Tabitha Knowlton hesitate before the law. After her husband died unexpectedly in 1850, she challenged the way he had disposed of their property in his will. Even though she won the appeal and inherited a larger share of his estimated holdings of $4,400, like many other widows of the period she had to purchase back from the estate her personal property, including her rocking chair, sewing chair, sheets, bedding, plates, and even her cow.[145]

Although both women struck out in small ways for untraditional public roles, they quickly retreated. Mary Jane Owen retreated to the obscurity of rural Indiana shortly before the birth of her first child. She remained there the rest of her life. To what degree this was her decision and to what degree her husband's cannot be gauged. Their marriage was not close or particularly intimate, although the arrangement whereby Owen traveled and lived in Washington, D.C., and elsewhere to pursue his career in politics may have been satisfactory to both of them. Tabitha Knowlton died in poverty in 1882, her estate valued at $157.74.[146] Whatever her earlier sympathy for freethought, neither she nor her surviving children evinced any sympathy for it after Charles's death in 1850. No one in the family even notified the *Boston Investigator*, so the leading freethought journal in the United States did not carry Knowlton's obituary until several months after his

death. Among the few possessions listed in the formal inventory of
Tabitha's estate when she died was only one book—a Bible.

Robert Dale Owen and Charles Knowlton initiated a public consideration of safe and reliable ways for respectable people to control reproduction. Yet, following their precedent, as a public discourse became established in this most compelling of issues for women, women
themselves remained very much in the background. Although there
was as yet no organized movement to support—or oppose—reproductive control, women, individually and in informal groups, were more
and more conscious of the importance of control over pregnancy, even
though generally unwilling to take public stances, and men were more
and more alert to the implications of the issue of reproductive control
in family and gender politics. The new information and the new ways
of ordering it generated changing public responses to the emerging
public debate and stimulated the beginning of a genuine cultural revolution.

5

The Antebellum Public Audience: Who Were They and How Did They Find Out?

Information about fertility control—mixed in reliability, sometimes veiled and obscure, sometimes jumbled and inaccurate—stimulated in its newer written and oral forms the development of an increasingly self-aware constituency in the decades before the Civil War. There was yet no organized movement to support, or to oppose, reproductive control, but the deepening involvement of freethinkers and medical sectarians dispersed it more broadly. So, too, did its increasingly vocal opponents.

Freethinking Printers, Publishers, and Sales Agents: Allies and Advocates

In antebellum America a number of courageous individuals, men and women, abetted the spread of ideas of reproductive freedom. Some were printers and publishers who issued much of the earliest advice literature, offering their printing presses to authors of such reforms and various other "liberal" and "infidel" causes as well. They kept some of the most important books in print for decades.

Abner Kneeland, editor of the freethought *Boston Investigator* in the 1830s, knowing that Charles Knowlton had been indicted for selling the first edition, bravely (although anonymously) published the second and third editions of *Fruits of Philosophy* in 1833 and 1834. He also advertised Robert Dale Owen's *Moral Physiology* in his paper, offering copies for sale at the newspaper office, as well as from agents and through the mail. He put out a pamphlet (a copy cannot be found) called *A Friend to Free Inquiry; A Review of 'Fruits of Philosophy; or, Private Companion of Young Married People.'*[1]

Kneeland encountered legal problems for his pains, in part related to his support of *Fruits of Philosophy* and of reproductive control in general. He had been born in Gardner, Massachusetts, in 1774, and was a carpenter until his late twenties, when he became a Baptist preacher. He converted to Universalism in 1811 and sometime in the 1820s he renounced the Christian faith, later attributing this action to the influence of his wife, and he became active in free enquiry in New York City. In 1831 he became the principal lecturer for freethought in Boston, editor of the *Boston Investigator*, and general organizer of weekly lectures, debates, and dances. He also took an active role publishing and distributing liberal literature, efforts that were to bring him into trouble with the authorities from 1834 to 1839.

Kneeland has the dubious distinction of having been the last person tried in Massachusetts for the crime of blasphemy.[2] He was indicted and tried in Boston Municipal Court in January 1834 for statements in three articles he published in the 20 December 1833 *Boston Investigator*. Two of the articles were inserted by his press foreman while Kneeland was out of town (the foreman was not indicted), and charges pertaining to them were dropped at the trial; one was an extract from Voltaire "ridiculing the miraculous generation of Christ," the other a statement ridiculing the "practice of addressing prayers to God."[3] Kneeland admitted to publishing the third article, a letter to Thomas Whittemore, editor of a Universalist newspaper, the *Trumpet*; in it he stated that "Universalists believe in a god which I do not; but [I] believe that their god, with all his moral attributes (aside from nature itself), is nothing more than a mere chimera of their own imagination."[4] Kneeland was convicted, but spent the next four years in three separate appeals and retrials, some with juries, some not. Finally, in January 1838, four of the five judges hearing his appeal voted to uphold his original conviction (chief justice of the Commonwealth's Supreme Court, Lemuel Shaw, the only holdout), and he was sentenced to two months in prison. Prominent Bostonians William Ellery Channing and Ellis Gray Loring organized a petition for a pardon on grounds of a constitutional guarantee of religious freedom; they obtained 167 signatures, of which Loring said that almost all were "Unitarians of the prosperous class, with a few Baptists."[5] Two Boston newspapers, the *Courier* and the *Daily Advertiser*, and the Rev. S. K. Lothrop of the Brattle Street Meeting House, among others—mounted a counter-petition to sustain Kneeland's conviction. Kneeland, they said, was a publisher of obscenities.[6]

On his release from prison, Kneeland, then sixty-five, his sons and daughters from his several marriages, and his fourth wife—the three previous ones had died, his third after childbirth in the middle of the trial—moved to a frontier community he called Salubria in Iowa Territory (near present-day Farmington, Iowa), where a small band of free enquirers already lived. He died there in 1844.

Kneeland's publication and public defense of Knowlton's *Fruits of Philosophy*, his advertisements for it, and his sale of it as well as of Owen's *Moral Physiology*, and also his ready access to members of the working class had all fueled the hostility of Boston authorities, and these factors figured significantly in his trials and his conviction. Two prosecuting attorneys, James T. Austin and Samuel Dunn Parker, in separate trials brought up the question of Kneeland's association with reproductive control. In his lengthy closing remarks at the trial, Parker himself went through Knowlton's book chapter by chapter quoting to the jury passages he found particularly offensive. Of Chapter 4, "Of the Checks," he said: "[It] shows how the instinct can be gratified and the *natural consequences* prevented; in other words, how lewdness and prostitution may be safely practised and young men and women indulge their passions whenever they please and refrain at will from becoming parents."[7] Parker's closing arguments charged that the "infidelity" of Kneeland, as of Knowlton, Owen, and Fanny Wright, taught the young that "there is no God or religion to restrain their passions and no lawfulness in the institution of marriage. I believe also, it is asserted quite publicly, that some secrets of physiology, said to be worth knowing to persons fond of certain pleasures, some checks to a too great increase of population, are now taught to the initiated in the schools of infidelity." "Blasphemy," he continued, "is but one part of the system of Fanny Wright," and its other aspects were "illicit sexual intercourse to be encouraged by physiological checks upon conception."[8] Thus, although Kneeland's dissemination of information on reproductive control was never part of the formal indictments against him, it was part of every trial and was publicized far beyond the courthouse in an 1834 pamphlet, *Report of the Arguments of the Attorney of the Commonwealth at the Trials of Abner Kneeland, for Blasphemy in the Municipal and Supreme Courts in Boston, Jan. and May 1834* "collected and published at the request of some Christians of various denominations."

In addition to Owen and Frances Wright, who together published the first five editions of Owen's *Moral Physiology* at their New York printing press for their *Free Enquirer*, other freethinkers put out additional editions: George Washington Matsell and Augustus Matsell and Gilbert Vale in New York; Josiah P. Mendum, second editor of the *Boston Investigator*, who put out two editions in the early 1870s in Boston; and an anonymous printer in Chicago, who issued a mail-order subscription edition of Owen's book in 1881 as a monthly selection of the People's Popular Liberal Library. None of them had the legal problems encountered by Kneeland and Knowlton.

Two brothers, Augustus and George Washington Matsell, aided the circulation of ideas about reproductive control in the 1830s and 1840s. Sons of a tailor, apprenticed in adolescence to a dyer, they became printers—Augustus working as an assistant to Owen at the press of the *Free Enquirer* in 1829. By 1832 they were the booksellers and stationers of the Free Enquirers' Reading Room in Manhattan.[9] From 1835 until sometime in the 1840s (exactly when it folded is unknown), they operated a "liberal bookstore" at 94 Chatham Street, offering a list of some sixty-four works including *Moral Physiology* and "several other works on the same subject."[10] In 1835 they published the eighth edition of *Moral Physiology*. In the late 1830s the brothers worked for the U.S. Moral and Philosophical Society for the General Diffusion of Useful Knowledge, whose headquarters were in New York City. Augustus was secretary, George was trustee. Both also worked their way through the ranks of Tammany Hall, Augustus accepting a position as clerk in the Hall of Records in 1841, George, unsuccessfully running for the state assembly in 1836 and for city sheriff in 1837, then in 1843 helping to organize the first municipal police force in the United States. He later served as New York City police chief.[11] George Matsell's dealings with the subject of reproductive control did not end with his death. When he died in 1877, at sixty-six, his reputation was still clouded by a widespread belief that in his years with the police he had been "on the payroll" of Ann Trow Lohman—"Madame Restell"—one of New York's most successful, and notorious, abortionists.[12] One year later Madame Restell committed suicide.

Gilbert Vale is another example of a freethought publisher who disseminated the earliest writings on reproductive control in the United States, often in a distinctly unsystematic way, but sometimes with considerable organization. An immigrant from England, an inventor and teacher, an eccentric and impassioned free inquirer, Vale, according to one brief biographical reference, "had studied for the church but abandoned it" to become a Deist and perhaps, after 1850, an agnostic.[13] He was acquainted with Owen, Knowlton, Kneeland, and the Matsells (he and George Matsell published a compendium of the writings of Thomas Paine in 1837), but quarreled bitterly with other free-thinkers. (Biographers said that he had a "quick" and "impatient" manner and "irritable temperament."[14]) The 1850 Federal Census for New York City listed Vale and his wife, Hepsebah, both aged fifty-eight. Living with them were two young clerks from Germany, as an illustration that at least some in the working class had direct access to birth control information.

Vale certainly published one edition and possibly a total of four editions of Owen's *Moral Physiology*: probably one in 1833 or 1834, possibly one in 1839, definitely one in 1858, and probably another around 1870.[15] At the end of the 1858 edition Vale added advice of his own in the form of publisher's notes. As noted earlier, he included engraved illustrations of sperm and the female uterine system—fallopian tubes, ovaries, uterus, and succinct, useful, contraceptive advice: "Consequently, to avoid impregnation, we must prevent the entrance of the animalcule into the womb when the ovum or egg is present, or destroy it when there. This object can be effected in various ways, any one or all of which it may be desirable to use in different circumstances." He gave unreliable advice on the rhythm method. He recommended douching with cold water and "a little alcohol or common whiskey," adding, "A folded cloth or sheet may be laid under the subject and the remedy applied while in bed with no inconvenience . . . may be relied upon, for the alcohol destroys the animalcules." Partial withdrawal, he advised, "is safe if the semen be removed by a syringe immediately afterwards." He recommended a "French Safe" made of India rubber and gutta percha, more durable and less expensive than regular condoms. He noted, further, that he had for sale Nichols's *Esoteric Anthropology* and Hollick's *The Marriage Guide*.[16]

In 1841, Vale began an ambitious project of printing other literature of free thought, distributed throughout the United States by mail, through "liberal" bookstores, and directly to audiences at free thinkers' lectures. He was spurred to work on the project by a desire to revive the National Tract Society, founded in 1828 to supply low cost "liberal literature" to every family in the state of New York, a society then lapsed. (Antebellum freethought publishers' lists of "liberal literature" included from twenty to forty works of Paine, Voltaire, and other writers of the Enlightenment and now-forgotten, local free enquirers.) He solicited the aid of two Bostonians prominent in freethought, the two editors of the weekly *Boston Investigator*, Horace Seaver and Josiah Mendum. They issued contraceptive and sexual advice tracts also. Vale's publisher's notes in the 1858 edition of *Moral Physiology* stated that its low price "will place it in the hands of the poor as well as the rich, a desirable object for every useful work,"[17] In the 1850s, Vale began to distribute such literature in some of New York's poor neighborhoods. By September 1856 he was operating Vale's Hall in the Bowery, in a building that earlier housed the Mechanics' Institute; it offered not only a free lending library but cheap bed and board, a gymnasium, and a lecture room. Copies of newspapers and liberal books were for sale there, too.[18] No lists of these books are available, but one supposes that Hollick's *The Marriage Guide* and Nichols's *Esoteric Anthropology*, along with Owen's and Knowlton's works, were probably among them because Vale was advertising both Owen's and Knowlton's tracts in the *Beacon*, the newspaper of the Moral and Philosophical Society for the General Diffusion of Useful Knowledge, sold by subscription and on newsstands, but also distributed free in various public places such as on steamboats and in hotels.[19] As editor of the *Beacon* from 1836 to 1850, he sold both books from the newspaper office itself.[20]

Vale had, for years from 1836 and continuing intermittently throughout the next decade, been traveling through New York State and neighboring states as well, organizing lectures and debates and other public events. Sometimes he lectured himself—one favorite topic was physiology (including no doubt, reproductive control)—and he may even have peddled contraceptives there.

These bold professionals who supported such movements of reform were "freethinkers," persons of daring and energy, men and women who became deeply involved with the issue of reproductive control, in particular, though usually not for its own sake but as part of a broader defense of freedom of the press, freedom of speech, and the right to "mental liberty." They identified themselves also sometimes as "free enquirers" and "rationalists." Historians of American freethought note that the fluid movement had different characteristics in different periods and that even in one era it ranged over a wide continuum of beliefs.[21] Nor were freethinkers geographically concentrated or identified principally with either a working class or an upper class in the antebellum United States. Many freethinkers took public stands on religion, ranging from Deism and agnosticism to Universalism and Unitarianism. The mainstream churches castigated them as "atheists" and "infidels," and some adopted the epithets with pride, atheist or not. All did, however, share a pronounced skepticism about orthodox religion, an insistence on the separation of church and state, and an adherence to the secular philosophy that humans should strive to be happy and productive on earth rather than wait for Heaven.[22]

These free enquirers shared no single body of political beliefs either. Many freethinkers resented the accumulation of wealth and power by the few at the expense of the many; they sought greater social and economic justice, equality, and autonomy.[23] Above all, they shared an antagonism to elites, officially trained doctors and lawyers among them, regarding them as selfish monopolists of knowledge who were depriving ordinary citizens of the valuable information that could give them power over their lives. In the early 1830s the *Boston Investigator* proclaimed that its objectives were "to improve the condition of man, by disseminating the knowledge of that which is true and thereby the better enabling him to judge of what is probably false." It supported the abolition of slavery, the abolition of debtors' prisons, the rights of the working class and of women, and the efficacy of Thomsonian medicine.[24] Many, but far from all, were Democrats. Abner Kneeland belonged to a group calling themselves the Tammany Hall Infidels in the late 1820s, but others supported Jackson, some expressed hostility to the Whigs but aligned themselves with no party; some joined workingmen's parties that mushroomed briefly in northeastern cities in the late 1820s and early 1830s; some rationalist radicals (in Philadelphia in the 1830s) regarded themselves as "republicans" and as heirs of the American Revolution.

Freethought was not exclusively an urban phenomenon; it thrived in villages and frontier settlements as well. The *Home Missionary* complained in 1846 that even in the cabins of the newly settled territories "the works of infidels have preceded the Bible."[25] One hundred men and women proposed toasts in honor of Thomas Paine's birthday in Clear Creek Township, Warren County, Ohio, in 1840; a group celebrated his birthday in a log cabin in Salubria, Iowa, in 1841; other men and women formed grassroots societies for "Mental Liberty" in rural hamlets in the 1850s.[26]

An informal but extensive network of individuals committed to freethought and social reform throughout the country arranged events and sold and distributed liberal literature. Most were concentrated in New England and the Middle Atlantic states. Seventeen agents in eleven states (but among the eleven were also Virginia, Tennessee, Georgia, and Louisiana) delivered the first issue of the the *Free Enquirer* in October 1828. One year later thirty-five agents were distributing the weekly paper in nineteen states, from Vermont to Alabama.[27] By 1836 some two hundred agents for the *Boston Investigator* were delivering 3000 subscriptions throughout the settled states and territories, north, east, south, and west. Even in 1840, a year of hard times, there were sixty such agents. Agents also provided a direct mail service of books and pamphlets. Dozens of books were sent out each month, the great majority to rural hamlets without access either to a library or a bookstore. The editors were apparently hesitant to list the contraceptive and sexual advice tracts by title, but they did so occasionally; my searches of various issues of the *Boston Investigator* between 1854 and 1861 turned up references to Owen's *Moral Physiology*, Knowlton's *Fruits of Philosophy*, "the works of Dr. [Frederick] Hollick," and books of Thomas Low Nichols, as sent to customers (referred to by their initials only) living in Massachusetts, New Hampshire, Connecticut, Louisiana, Mississippi, Tennessee, Ohio, Indiana, Michigan, Wisconsin, California, and Canada. Other freethought newspapers listed book purchasers also, some of whom requested literature on reproductive control. The *Cleveland Liberalist* advertised in 1837 that J. Underhill (the newspaper's editor, a "justice of the peace" and a botanical doctor) had for sale *Moral Physiology* and "several other works on the same subject." In 1854 the *Liberalist* regretted to inform subscriber Peter Mulks that they had no copy of Owen's *Moral Physiology* to send to him; they sent other books instead.[28]

A Network of "Irregular" Medical Practitioners: Thomsonians and Water Curists

In the second half of the century, medical professionals were among the most vociferous opponents of reproductive control, though organized medical opposition earlier had been sporadic and individual. But until mid century the medical profession as a whole appears not to have regarded abortion as a social or a moral problem. As a group they were not much concerned with issues of family limitation. If the issue of deliberately induced abortion arose it was usually dealt with matter-of-factly, occasionally with any criticism directed to the abortionist and sympathy expressed for the woman. The concern of medical professionals focused rather on medical procedures for coping with postabortion ailments. In an 1825 article in the *American Medical Recorder*, a "Doctor Baxter" of New York commented on his treatment of a sixteen-year-old girl who was suffering the aftereffects of an "abortion procured by violence" by another physician. There was no criticism of the girl, little outcry against the abortionist (other than the use of the word "violence"), and no moralizing. Baxter did say that ergot (an abortion-inducing substance), which he used to expel the fetus, "may encourage vice and licentiousness," but his principal concern was with the medical difficulties of the case and with his own success in saving the girl's life.[29]

The association that emerged between practitioners of the medical sects and the promotion of fertility control in the decades after 1830 did act to stimulate official medical opposition to contraception and to abortion, but that opposition did not crystalize until mid century (see Chapter 8). Later orthodox medical opposition can be traced to the emergence of the informal network of medical sectarians who were dispersing information on reproductive control in the antebellum decades.

By the 1830s three medical traditions existed side by side in the United States: domestic medicine, official medicine, and "irregular" or sectarian medicine, whose practitioners operated outside professional medical channels.[30] The most common was domestic medicine, which was self-treatment with simple homemade folk remedies made from roots, herbs, and barks, some used for purposes of contraception and abortion. By the the mid eighteenth century, practitioners trained in medical schools and societies had begun to compete with domestic medicine and several colonial legislatures had passed licensing laws to restrict medical practice to those judged by formal procedures to be both trained and competent. The first part of the nineteenth century saw a rapid increase in the number of state-chartered medical schools, dependent for their survival on attracting students and their fees, but with no supervision of curricula, examinations, and licensing. Physicians tried to organize independent licensing and examining boards, but it took years of concerted action by the American Medical Association, newly founded in 1846, to begin to assert professional standards for medicine.

Public attitudes toward physicians underwent changes, too, during this period. Many Americans in the Jacksonian decades resented officially trained physicians, believing them to be an elite group monopolizing knowledge that would be better widely diffused. Some Americans also voiced doubts about the reliance of medical "regulars" on such treatments as bleeding and the use of cathartics and purgatives (what were then known as "heroic" medicine). Such public displeasure led to the rise of a general health reform movement and to the emergence of many popular medical sects.[31]

Among the medical sects that flourished in the nineteenth century were the Thomsonians, the largest of all the "irregulars" in the 1830s; eclectics and homeopaths, dominant in the decades after 1840; and those devoted to the water cure. It is true that the lines between domestic medicine, regular medicine, and the sectarians were not sharply defined, but the medical sects tended to opt for the use of botanical remedies, steam baths, herbal teas, and wines over calomel, mercury, and bleeding. Most emphasized preventive medicine through simple diets, sensible clothing, and exercise. To their critics they were "quacks." Still, their cure rate may well have been high if only because their remedies allowed diseases to heal themselves without seriously weakening the patient as part of the cure.

The Thomsonian system was the brainchild of Samuel Thomson, an itinerant herb and root doctor who was born in New Hampshire in 1769. His theories about disease and health were common variants on regular medical ideas, and most of his remedies were well known in domestic folk medicine. Yet his medical system was novel in two respects. He insisted that the botanical products he prescribed be taken in specific sequences and in precise dosages and that a system of "injections" (enemas and douches) be initiated. He gave detailed instructions on how to obtain the medicines and the douches, mostly through his elaborate network of agents and Thomsonian physicians. Thomsonian practitioners and agents sold douching syringes and spermicides in addition to other products and literature.[32] The Botanical and Thomsonian Depot in Bangor, Maine, in 1844, for example, offered "a large store of medicines," medical books, surgical instruments, syringes, and liquors. Morris Mattson, one of the major manufacturers of douching syringes in the second half of the century and a man whose profit from the sale of syringes and "general rubber goods" was estimated to be $100,000 to $200,000 in 1878, got his start as editor of *Philadelphia, the Botanic Sentinel and Thomsonian Medical Revolutionist.*[33] In Boston in 1835 there was a Thomsonian hospital at 554 Washington Street under the care of a Dr. J. A. Brown, perhaps the same "A. Brown" listed as a Thomsonian agent in Boston that same year and possibly the same man who, four years later, from 481 Washington Street, was advertising Brown's Patent Self-Injecting Apparatus"—a type of douching syringe.[34] Abner Kneeland, also, was a Thomsonian agent in the Boston area in the 1830s. Acting as his family's physician, he credited the Thomsonian regimen with saving his wife's life.[35]

The Thomsonian networks created an efficient communication and distribution system. Thomson organized his followers into Thomsonian societies pledged to his rigorous medical regimen. He published a "medical circular" and franchised his system of sequences and precise dosages to anyone who paid the then steep twenty-dollar fee. Agents sold Thomson's "patents," medical products and literature, including douching syringes, douching substances, and instructions. They wrote and published botanical journals and, between 1825 and 1845, published about forty newspapers, some with extensive circulations. One such paper, the *Independent Botanic Register*, edited by a Thomas Hersey, had three thousand paying subscribers in 1835.

Thomas Hersey is a good example of the Thomsonians' distribution of contraceptive advice. By his own account he had been "a practitioner of the old school" for forty years before becoming a Thomsonian, although he had always had "a predilection for botanic remedies."[36] After a "regular" medical career, after founding the Western Medical Society of Pennsylvania and serving as a U.S. Army surgeon, Hersey had joined the botanic ranks. He served twice as president of the U.S. Botanic Convention. By 1832 he had become a general agent for Thomson, and, from 1832 to 1835, edited in Columbus, Ohio, what became one of the sect's most important journals, the *Thomson Recorder*. He served as secretary at two national Thomsonian conventions, edited the *Independent Botanic Register* from 1835 to 1836, and intermittently lectured on midwifery. He published *The Midwife's Practical Directory; or, Woman's Confidential Friend*, which was so successful that he put out a revised and expanded second edition two years later.[37] It was dedicated to the "Thomsonian brethren" and the "numerous intelligent Thomsonian sisterhood." He particularly wanted midwives to read it, "not only for their own convenience but by becoming familiarly acquainted with a delicate mode of conveying ideas on such matters, we shall be able by a modest example, to afford useful instruction to others, and extend a salutary influence in correcting the taste and improving the habits of conversation in those circles where occasional hints on these subjects appear to be indispensable."[38]

Hersey devoted chapters to menstruation, gestation, the female organs of generation, prenatal development, and the process of conception. In the second edition were eleven engraved plates illustrating female sexual anatomy and the stages of pregnancy. One tinted plate folded out to show a fetus in the womb. The contraceptive advice was direct, explicit, easy to find and to understand. It came directly from Knowlton's *Fruits of Philosophy*.[39] He advised women who missed a period to use a mixture of tansy syrup and rum.[40] He may or may not have intended this prescription to be abortion advice. But even if he did mean it as a straightforward midwifery remedy for amenorrhea (menstruation delayed for reasons other than pregnancy), women probably recognized its other connotations.

Thomsonianism declined in the 1840s, when hydropathy, or the water cure, gained enormous popularity. In its heyday in the 1850s, scores of men and women made a living as water-cure practitioners, writing and lecturing on how their system would prevent disease and regenerate society. Books and newspapers on the water cure sold well; water-cure boardinghouses and hotel resorts attracted a large clientele, and its lecturers attracted wide audiences. The *Water-Cure Journal* was purported to have a circulation of over fifty thousand after 1850.[41] In 1848 the *Water-Cure Journal* counted twenty-one well-known water-cure establishments. including the ones operated by Russell Thacher Trall and Mary Gove in New York. By the mid 1850s an additional twenty-seven hydropathic institutions were in rural areas. There were hydropathic medical schools, among them Trall's and Mary Gove's—which became the Nichols' Medical School in 1851, with a three-month course of lectures, including Mary Gove's lecture on midwifery and gynecology and a first class of twenty women.

The principles and practice of water cure were far older in Europe. The American Hydropathic Society itself was founded in 1849, replaced by the American Hygienic and Hydropathic Association of Physicians and Surgeons the next year. Some water-cure doctors had been trained originally as physicians, but many had not been trained at all. It was their conviction that good health depended on the external and internal use of pure, cold water. They urged Americans to drink more water (thus gaining allies from the temperance movement), to use a variety of sitz baths, full and half baths, and to wrap themselves daily in wet sheets for an hour or two. Followers of hydropathy, like other health reform advocates in Jacksonian America, were convinced that good health lay in the ability to control all the appetites and passions—hence many practiced vegetarianism as well, avoided coffee, tea, and spices, and advocated caution in the expenditure of sexual energy. With the endorsement of Mary Gove Nichols, Thomas Low Nichols, and Russell Thacher Trall, water cure came to be linked to reproductive control in mid century.

Russell Thacher Trall, who was born in 1812 in Connecticut, had received a medical certificate from the Albany Medical College, and in the 1840s opened a water-cure establishment, the Hygienic Institute, at 15 Laight Street in Manhattan. He was a founder, in 1849, of the American Hydropathic Society along with a better-known hydropathist, Joel Shew, who was president of its successor organization, and reform publisher Samuel R. Wells. He organized the American Hydropathic Society Convention in New York City in 1850.[42] Three years later he opened a medical school, the Hygeio-Therapeutic College, designed to teach male and female students the fundamentals of the water cure. Trall's own concern with diet, exercise, dress reform, and control of the passions took him into other reforms, as well, and with Samuel R. Wells, partner in the publishing concern Fowler and Wells, he organized the American Anti-Tobacco Society of New York in 1849, and the next year, with Thomas Low Nichols and William Alcott, the American Vegetarian Society (its annual meetings were held at Trall's water-cure establishment). Trall wrote more than thirty books on medicine and reform, specializing in sexual advice, many published by the press operated by Wood and Holbrook at Trall's Hygienic Institute on Laight Street.

Trall was significant in the dispersal of reproductive control information in the second half of the century for several reasons: because of his contacts with patients as a water-cure practitioner (which included correspondence), because of the forcefulness of his arguments in favor of controlled fertility, and because of both the contents and the wide circulation of his books. Although he was personally ambivalent about contraception, he provided advice about it, especially in his most important work, *Sexual Physiology*, published in 1866 and in print for the next thirty years. Trall wrote in the book, "Let it be distinctly understood that I do not approve any method for preventing pregnancy except that of abstinence nor any means for producing abortion. . . . It is only the least of two evils. When people will live physiologically . . . there will be no need for works of this kind." Elsewhere in the book he wrote, "I am not here advocating the doctrine that sexual intercourse . . . should be limited to reproduction—a mere generative act."[43] However, in chapter twelve, "Regulation of the Number of Offspring," he was recommending a variant of the rhythm method (not a particularly reliable one, for his timing would have women resume sexual intercourse in mid cycle), or the wearing of a vaginal sponge or any other "mechanical obstruction placed against the os uteri which will prevent the seminal fluid from coming in contact with the ovum," ways to cause the uterus "to expel its contents at any period of gestation" by squeezing, exercise, voluntary muscular bearing-down actions, and "the administration of many acrid and narcotic drugs—cayenne pepper, savin, ergot, cotton seed, quinine, etc."[44]

As a water-cure physician, Trall recommended vaginal douching to cure and prevent disease, and in his 1852 *The Hydropathic Encyclopedia* the section "Lavements and Injections" told women when, why, and how to douche and where to buy effective and cheap syringes. Above all, Trall offered justifications for birth control, writing that there were "a thousand reasons for limiting offspring." He said that he was publishing information on the process of conception because it would allow the "legitimate limiting of offspring."[45]

Thomsonians and hydropathists promoted reproductive control in diverse ways. Both groups promoted douching, though primarily for medicinal rather than contraceptive or abortifacient purposes. Women received widespread advice about douching from both regular medical practitioners and from "irregulars," the Thomsonians and hydropathists reinforcing this broad practice among middle class women (it may also have extended into the working classes). In other, less direct, ways, medical sects deepened and widened communication about reproductive control. The information they dispensed about conception, pregnancy, and childbirth carried multifaceted messages: it promoted, even glorified, motherhood and child rearing, elevating pregnancy and childbirth to all but sacred status, and much of their advice sought to help women overcome the problems of sterility. Yet their promotion of motherhood underscored the importance of nurture and the importance of each child. The quality of attention each child received was deemed crucial. Obliquely, such arguments raised important issues about the optimal spacing of children and ideal family size. To sectarians, disease could be prevented by forethought and rational planning, and by care and consistency in regular, preventative practices. Many of their self-help manuals, written for popular audiences, were illustrated, like Hersey's, with tinted engravings and detailed anatomical drawings that rendered gynecologiy and obstetrics less mysterious. They encouraged followers to think ahead, to take daily, even hourly, actions to prevent disease and to foster a sense of well-being. Sectarians sought to inculcate greater individual responsibility for maintaining a healthy life. They encouraged women to understand their bodies, to read and talk freely about menstruation, ovulation, conception, and pregnancy—lessons in active intervention that could transfer readily to other arenas of life, including pregnancy intervention. The emphasis on action and the optimism about human abilities encouraged the belief that pregnancy, too, could be controlled.[46]

The medical sects made special efforts to attract women not only as followers but also as practitioners. Thomsonians, for one, did more than build on the traditional roles of wives and mothers in caring for the sick and preparing medicines: they also respected the tradition of female midwifery at a time when regular physicians were becoming increasingly wary of anyone but regularly trained male physicians who involved themselves in obstetrics. The Thomsonians encouraged women to buy and read medical guides, particularly, of course, their own. Women were encouraged to become practitioners, to establish

Thomsonian societies, to act as agents selling Thomsonian products, to attend lectures, and to participate in the national conventions. The elaborate medical regimens augmented women's sense of power and control, and participating in the sects, in general, gave women recognition in the institutions and rituals of public culture in an era when, without the vote, their influence was predominantly in the private sector. Like their organizational activities in temperance and abolitionism, women's work in health reform was both a result of and a spur to the emergent feminism of the early nineteenth century.[47]

The Opponents: Charges of Obscenity and Sexual Anarchy

The response of the official medical profession to reproductive control, on the other hand, was more restrained, more circumspect, and more conflicted. Medical opinion had already disagreed about withdrawal, douching, and even, after a while, about the rhythm method. Many began to oppose reproductive control altogether. It was a time when physicians (most of them men) were trying to gain control over their ranks and the practices of their profession; when critics of reproductive control in the American Medical Association mounted a campaign of opposition to it in the second half of the century, they naturally sought to win the support of fellow physicians. Still, it was not always easy to do so. Regular doctors continued quietly to teach patients contraceptive methods and many performed abortions as well, and interested themselves in the issue of reproductive control. Some regular physicians wrote books containing contraceptive advice.

It is not only those who favor ideas who help disseminate them. Critics, too, can raise the level of public awareness and stimulate debate and discussion. Garrisonian abolitionists recognized early in the 1830s that hostility and attacks on them worked as effectively at raising public awareness of their stand for the immediate abolition of slavery as did their more peaceful assemblies. Their enemies brought them invaluable publicity. So, too, did the opponents of reproductive control, in spite of themselves, heighten public awareness of methods, of information tracts, and of new possibilities in reproductive autonomy.

Robert Dale Owen had expected intense criticism of his *Moral Physiology*. No stranger to public hostility, he added to an announcement about the book's imminent appearance, "I know the prejudice that exists on the subject; I have had occasion to know it. . . . I have been told my character will suffer by the publication of this book . . .

[but] all I ask for is a careful, dispassionate perusal." He was surprised, in fact, at how little public opposition it aroused; he wrote in an 1831 editorial, "I have been surprised to find it so favorably received, even by many whose approbation I had more than doubted. I expected, and was prepared to meet, ten times the amount of prejudice it has hitherto incurred."[48] Prominent men such as Nicholas Trist, a Virginia diplomat and at one time a private secretary to President Andrew Jackson, praised *Moral Physiology* privately to Owen and quietly distributed it in Washington, D.C., along with other freethought literature.[49] Women liked it too, although some were silenced by the force of public opinion against Owen and by his religious hostility, and some by the topic of reproductive control itself.

In December 1830 Owen published in the *Free Enquirer* a letter he had received from "Mary," who had read *Moral Physiology*—"a bold confession from a woman." She had been married three years to "a young man of good habits, moderate talents and excellent dispositions" and they had one child. Both favored free enquiry, but were quiet and retiring so that they lived secure "from any degree of persecution." She liked the book, but warned Owen: "I do not think that one out of ten women into whose hands your book may fall will, in her heart, disapprove it or condemn you; and yet I almost doubt whether you will find one except myself, to tell you so." She believed him to be ignorant of the weight of public pressure most women felt, but urged:

> Take courage. Do not expect open approval, especially from my sex; I tell you candidly you will not receive it. . . . Are you satisfied to labor without any open reward? are you satisfied to know, that although we say little we think much? are you satisfied to be assured, that almost every one of our sex who reads your book fairly through will in her heart do justice to your motives? and are you satisfied never to hear us—even the most independent among us—admit a syllable of all this? . . . But . . . do you wish oral evidence of our sympathy—you may as well make up your mind at once to be disappointed.[50]

The only open attacks on *Moral Physiology*, indeed, came from those who for other reasons already disliked Owen. By 1831 he had made peace with some of his earliest religious critics, for he noted that he had begun to be treated "with much more consideration . . . by the press and by the pulpit of the more liberal sects, Unitarian and Universalist, and more especially by the Hicksite Quakers."[51] Even so, some Universalists who carried on old animosities against free enquiry used Owen's book as a new weapon. Linus S. Everett, editor of Boston's *Trumpet and Universalist Magazine*, described *Moral Physiology* as "a mean, disgusting and obscene book filled with arguments that would disgrace the tenants of a brothel." And it was Thomas Whittemore, another editor of the same Universalist journal, who carried on a public feud in the mid 1830s with Abner Kneeland, resulting in the most serious of Kneeland's indictments for blasphemy. Owen's rival in New York City's workingmen's politics, Thomas Skidmore, also criticized *Moral Physiology* as part of his more general antagonism toward Owen (developed later in this chapter).

Charles Knowlton's tract aroused more serious ambivalence than Owen's did. As noted earlier, he stood trial four times between 1832 and 1835, charged with publishing and selling an obscene book, a relatively uncommon indictment. A purveyor of an "indecent" engraving had been prosecuted under the common law in Pennsylvania in 1815, and the publisher of a "lewd and obscene book" had been convicted in Massachusetts in 1821, but not until that year was any state law passed against obscenity—Vermont passed one in 1821, followed in 1834 by Connecticut and in 1835 by Massachusetts.

The motivation of the framers of the new obscenity laws appears to have been a general desire to tighten criminal codes rather than any open opposition to birth control. So, too, the obscenity laws stemmed from fears of state authorities that the declining power of the clergy and the rising literacy rates would corrupt the public sexually and morally, especially the lower classes.[52]

Knowlton himself was convinced that the real reason for the legal attacks on him was not the subject of his book as such but the anger of the new Presbyterian minister in town, the Rev. Mason Grosvenor, who, "not liking the smell of materialism before his olfactories . . . did determine and contrive to drive me, a heretic, out of town."[53] Grosvenor and local "partizans" (Knowlton suspected fellow physicians in Ashfield, jealous of his growing practice) succeeded in getting indictments against Knowlton and Shepard. Grosvenor preached sermons against Knowlton and "infidelity" from his pulpit. Once, while Knowlton was away for several weeks, Grosvenor related stories from the pulpit about "infidel doctors"; "and what tended considerably to increase the excitement was that some of these stories were of such a nature as necessarily to involve the character of some as respectable females, for ought I know, as the town of Ashfield can produce." Knowlton wrote a pamphlet, *A History of the Recent Excitement in Ashfield* in 1834, in which he elliptically described aspects of

Grosvenor's attack.[54] What, Knowlton asked, could induce Grosvenor to tell Knowlton's patients "not to employ me?" Furthermore, he said, someone was circulating "false, foul and slanderous reports" about him and even about his wife, Tabitha. Grosvenor's sermons played on a theme that continued to resonate whenever the matter of reproductive self-determination came up, explicitly linking contraception with promotion of uncontrollable sexuality and a consequent loss of a woman's reputation. He warned that the reputation of the entire town of Ashfield, and especially of its female residents, would suffer because of the town's association with *Fruits of Philosophy*.[55] Even the marriageability of the town's young women would be damaged by a link to the book. Even eighty years later, the town historian described Knowlton as the root cause of a schism that had occurred in the church, "for his belief and also because of a book he had published believed to be injurious to the morals of the community."[56]

Ironically, although religious objections were among the earliest to be raised against the emerging public issue of reproductive control in the 1830s, formal religious opposition during the rest of the century was generally muted, unlike the clearcut opposition to birth control mounted in the twentieth century by the Catholic church and fundamentalist Protestants. The only well-known opponent of reproductive control who spoke as a clergyman was the Congregationalist minister, the Rev. John Todd. Born in Vermont in 1800, putting himself through Yale and Andover Theological Seminary, he became a leading spokesman of orthodox Congregationalism and, in that capacity, a popular writer of over fifteen books urging chastity, temperance, and morality on the young.[57] In his 1867 book, *Serpents in the Dove's Nest*, Todd criticized abortion as "fashonable murder," and contraception and family limitation as "the cloud with a dark lining. He advertised his book as calling attention to "child murder" and also to a topic "to which the attention of people is only just beginning to be called— measures to *prevent* having children."[58]

Except for Todd's, few clerical voices appear to have been raised against birth control. In the second half of the century, the physicians and "social purity" forces mounting a campaign to criminalize reproductive control did not view the Protestant clergy as strong allies. Some physicians tried to enlist more active support from the ministry by publicly commending even their slightest efforts. An 1867 editorial in the *Boston Medical and Surgical Journal* mentioned an article in the *Northwestern Christian Advocate*, welcoming it from a religious journal.[59] In his 1876 pamphlet *Criminal Abortion: Its Extent and Prevention*, Pennsylvania physician Andrew Nebinger thanked H.

Cleaveland Cox, the Episcopal bishop of western New York, for an 1869 pastoral letter in which he said, "I have heretofore warned my flock against the blood-guiltiness of ante-natal infanticide."[60] The Old School Presbyterian Assembly of New York tabled a resolution against abortion in 1869, preferring to avoid dealing publicly with the topic.[61] In their effort to involve the clergy some AMA physicians portrayed abortion as a crime practiced particularly by Protestant women; Horatio Storer attributed the large families of immigrants to their religion and commended the Catholic church for its watchfulness concerning birth control, explicitly contrasting it with the silence of the Protestant clergy. He was roundly taken to task for such statements by an elderly physician long sympathetic to reproductive control, Daniel Garrison Brinton, who pointed out that France was the first country to experience declining marital birth rates and that not all the foreigners with large families were Catholics.[62]

Individual clergymen and priests may have preached sermons or spoken less formally against contraception and abortion, but few commentators noted their involvement on one side or the other of these issues. Church leaders may have viewed the subject of reproductive control as unseemly and improper for public discussion in sermons. It may be, too, that the complaints of the physicians in the forefront of the antiabortion campaign did not so much reflect a lack of religious support as the desire of doctors to be in the forefront of a movement to restore morals. If physicians wanted a greater role as moral leaders and if publicizing the evils of abortion was a step toward that goal, then it would be strategically sound to criticize the older arbiters of the community's moral behavior—the clergy.

Grosvenor's own attack continued themes critics had already raised against free enquiry, an attack its new linkage with reproductive control only intensified—the specter of what seemed to contemporaries to be sexual anarchy or, that is, of fundamentally altered relations between the sexes. In articles from his Universalist newspaper, *Trumpet*, Thomas Whittemore in 1831 accused the Boston freethinkers under Kneeland of wanting to loosen all restrictions on marriage, allowing men to take "fifty wives in the course of a year."[63] The skepticism of free enquirers about orthodox religion made it easy for critics to label them political and social revolutionaries, to view them all erroneously as advocates of free love who wanted to abolish monogamy and promote sexual licentiousness, grant women equality with men, and foster discontent among the classes. The power to curtail pregnancies and thus to separate sexual intercourse from reproduction threatened to alter the relations between men and women, to diminish the power of husbands over their wives and of parents over their children, especially over their daughters. Grosvenor's hints from the pulpit were not unique: opponents feared that if fear of pregnancy were removed from sexual intercourse, wives' sexual faithfulness could not be assured, legitimate children might not so easily be distinguished from illegitimate children, and bloodlines and inheritance might, in consequence, be jeopardized. Pregnancy control, by offering women some power over reproduction, raised in some minds the specter of illicit female sexual activity before and during marriage. Robert Dale Owen recognized this at once, for example, in attributing the initial hostile reaction to *Moral Physiology* to men who thought that the pamphlet held out "the inducements and facilities for the prostitution of their daughters, sisters, and wives."[64]

Other early critics of reproductive control feared political and economic anarchy and focused their anxieties on changing class relations. Opposition to reproductive control did come from some of the traditional arbiters of authority, who, faced with the massive social, political, and economic changes of the Jacksonian era, wanted to preserve the status quo.[65] Massachusetts attorney general James T. Austin, longtime Bostonian and Harvard Law School graduate, warned in the trial against Abner Kneeland, "The crime of the defendant is of this deep and deadly character. It strikes at the peace, the security, and existence of society."[66] Some particularly feared the social and economic leveling advocated—and symbolized—by free enquiry. Judge Thacher at Abner Kneeland's trial stated as an aggravation of Kneeland's offense that he circulated his paper "among the poor and laboring classes" and disseminated his sentiments among the "poor and ignorant." Prosecutor Parker said of the *Boston Invesgigator*, "But here is a Journal, a Newspaper, cheap—and sent into a thousand families, etc. Where *one* man would be injured by [reading] Hume, Gibbon, or Volney, a thousand may be injured by this Newspaper, so widely circulated, so easily read—so coarsely expressed—so industriously spread abroad." Parker, nervous about the working class loyalties of the first jury, reminded them to adhere to the "excellent motto" of the Mechanics' Association "to which some of you I know belong" to "Be Just and Fear Not."[67]

Knowlton said that what he called a "Persecution party" had harassed him in Ashfield in 1834; it included the Presbyterian minister Grosvenor (later forced out of his parish because of the Knowlton controversy), a rival physician, and Elijah Paine—a lifelong resident of Ashfield and former judge of the Circuit Court of Common Pleas in Franklin County, who, by the time he helped prosecute Knowlton, was in his seventies and an associate justice of the Court of Sessions of Franklin County.[68] On the other side, Knowlton said, was the "Toleration party" of "Liberals," with his good friend Nelson Gardner, a mechanic, and several farmers. Not all of those who took the lead against the dissemination of information about reproductive control were social and political conservatives; one of Boston's leading liberal reformers, Samuel Gridley Howe, joined the opposition to Kneeland in 1834, expressing concern that "devices of the brothel" were being openly displayed before working class men and women at public lectures.[69] Kneeland suspected Lucius M. Sargent, a temperance tract writer, of being one of the chief agitators securing the indictments against him.

Arguments that the opponents of birth control were motivated chiefly by desires to reassert social control do not always hold, however. Lemuel Shaw, chief justice of the Supreme Judicial Court of Massachusetts, was the only one of the five judges who voted to overturn Kneeland's conviction, and he was also the judge who, in an important ruling for labor, upheld the right of workers to strike, ended imprisonment for debt, secured married women's property laws, and made divorce easier to obtain—not the judgments of a man frightened by social, class, or gender change, although in all respects he was part of Boston's economic, political, and cultural elite.[70] In some cases party politics rather than diffuse fears about "social anarchy" or even reproductive control per se fueled the animosities. Kneeland's defense attorney was Andrew Dunlop, a leading Massachusetts Democrat well known for political opposition to Kneeland's predominantly Whig prosecution.

Nor did the opposition to birth control stem only from men of power. One of the most vociferous critics of Owen's *Moral Physiology* was a workingman, Thomas Skidmore, who considered *Moral Physiology* the meddling of a paternalistic do-gooder in the private lives of independent workers. Skidmore, who died in the cholera epidemic of 1832 at forty-two, had been a teacher at age thirteen, an itinerant tutor up and down the eastern seaboard, then a tinkerer and inventor, and eventually a machinist. His views were those of true radical agrarianism. He rejected the conviction that social change lay in education, maintaining instead that only when property was redistributed equally would justice result. He argued that the poor and "friends of equal rights" should seize the government by elections, not bloodshed, and redistribute all property. A recent biographer calls Skidmore's ideas about property redistribution "an anticapitalist vision of extraordinary boldness," "a breathtaking" and "audacious" analysis.[71] At an early 1829 organizational meeting of the Working Men's party he called for revolution "such as will leave behind it no trace of that government which has denied to every human being an equal amount of property on arriving at the age of maturity, and previous thereto, equal food, clothing and instruction at the public expense."[72]

In the political and electoral skirmishing of the Working Men's party in 1829, Skidmore's faction lost ground to Owen's. One consequence was Skidmore's hostile attack on *Moral Physiology* two years later.[73] He reprinted the fourth edition of Owen's pamphlet with the title *Moral Physiology Exposed and Refuted*, adding a long conclusion lambasting reproductive control as an insult to workers and a ploy to force working families to live on smaller wages.[74] Skidmore viewed family limitation as yet another way by which the elites sought to constrain and reshape the working class, yet another attack on the economic needs of workers who depended on the wages of their many children. He particularly disliked Owen's plan for state education, which, like reproductive control, he considered a way to weaken workers' political and economic power by arranging for fewer workers.

Skidmore called Owen the leader of "the sponge party" in America—a fascinating pun on Owen's contraceptive advice, but Owen never recommended the contraceptive sponge after the first edition's brief mention. Perhaps a dynamic beyond that of class and property motivated Skidmore's hostility to contraception—the politics of gender, inasmuch as the sponge was a female contraceptive. But unfortunately, because we know nothing about Skidmore's private life other than the fact that he was married, this possibility can only be speculative. However, one clue about Skidmore's attitude toward women can be picked up from an 1830 statement when he explained that the only women he expected to attend his agrarian "state auctions" were those who were unmarried or "who have no friends to attend for them, and such married females as have absent or sick husbands and who, besides, have no friends to serve them."[75] Skidmore's opposition does serve as an important reminder that the vocal opposition from the workingmen's movements came from men. The views of their mothers, wives, daughters, and sisters are unknown.

As with other negative publicity, the impact of Skidmore's assault may have had unintended consequences. The publicity he engendered increased the renown of *Moral Physiology* in working class quarters. Owen, no simpleton about the value of publicity, allowed the full title of Skidmore's version to be printed in the *Free Enquirer* and he put the work in his circulating library.[76]

Just how many Americans shared the fears of the relatively few vocal critics is unclear. The critics' views appeared in editorials and other newspaper denunciations, sermons, and other printed materials, but those who attended the public lectures and other freethought events in the 1830s, who bought, read, and circulated the contraceptive advice tracts, have left far fewer records about their response to reproductive control. They may, of course, have agreed with the critics and may have continued to rely on traditional methods or no intervention at all. Yet it is as probable, maybe more so, that many bought eagerly whatever promised to be the newest, most scientific, safest, and most effective information.

The Publics

Which Americans had access to reproductive control information in the nineteenth-century United States? The question is of great importance, but who bought or borrowed the books, went to the lectures, bought the devices and spermicides continues to be unclear. Where were those men and women from? What did they think of what they read and heard? How did they interpret it? The meanings attached to any given "text" are many and varied: our interpretations today may be far removed from the meanings of over a century ago.[77] But some of the assumptions can be shown to be incorrect. Some historians have believed that information and products relating to reproductive control were most available in urban areas and filtered down from the affluent to the middle class and then to the working class. This is not so. Rural communities, too, had access to information, particularly information about withdrawal, douching, and the rhythm method.

Americans in the first half of the century—women and men, urban and rural, middle class and manual workers—were far from being illiterates suspicious of anything but word-of-mouth information about reproductive control. There seems to have been increasingly widespread basic literacy by the 1830s, at least for the native-born whites.[78] Some other traditional assumptions about an illiteracy based on class, regional, and urban/rural differentials seem to have been mistaken. A culture of reading was important not only in urban centers but in hidden byways throughout the states and territories, especially in rural areas. Rural New Englanders, for example, had access to printed materials: there was a relatively high literacy rate in New England and a culture that valued reading, especially after 1815. William J. Gilmore found that the antebellum "lower middle class" residents of Vermont counties had the largest number of books per household, nearly four times as many as were listed in estate inventories of wealthy Vermonters; 46.5 percent of those he defined as "lower middle class" owned books and even 8.5 percent of the "poor" did so.[79] A Boston author in 1835 said that periodicals were taken "well beyond the route of mails or the region of passable roads."[80] In the town of Medbury, Massachusetts, twenty miles beyond Boston, with a population of 892, 168 copies of forty-seven different periodicals circulated in the 1830s.[81]

In the South, traditionally believed to have lagged behind the rest of the antebellum United States in book ownership, book culture flourished in various regions. Rural residents were as likely to have owned books as were city dwellers in Virginia, although perhaps not necessarily in substantial numbers, and throughout the early part of the century some poor and middling people had sizable libraries.[82] In the mill hamlets of Rockdale, Delaware, also, wealthier households read and owned books, but so did workers. In the 1830s there was a steady demand in Rockdale for written guides to all things, though especially useful printed materials on machinery.[83]

Millions had access also to the literature and other wares of those in the health reform networks. By 1840 some three to four million Americans were following the Thomsonian regimen, for example, from New England, where the sect started, down the Atlantic Seaboard into parts of the South, and throughout the frontier areas of the Midwest. In mid century the water cure, too, attracted a huge following, popular in New England and the Middle Atlantic states, but thriving, also, in the old Midwest and in parts of the South. Freethinkers, who often thought of themselves as a small, embattled group, in the antebellum decades had a sizable following. In New York City and Boston, dances and lectures sponsored by freethinkers attracted audiences of one to several hundred.[84] Historian Bruce Laurie estimates that, in Philadelphia, church rolls listed at least two thousand freethinkers and Universalists in the early 1830s.[85]

In antebellum America it is true that women had far less access than men to books and products pertaining to reproductive control. The culture tended to set constraints on reading materials and information for women. Many women therefore had to rely on their husbands for information.[86] Women's economic ability to buy books or commercial reproductive control products was undoubtedly also restricted. If husbands or fathers did not approve of contraceptives or abortives, their wives and daughters, with little discretionary income, would have found it hard to buy them. Even so, many women of the Jacksonian era did have the desire and the ability to buy books and pamphlets and did buy and read birth control literature. Women had ways to secrete small amounts of money, to make purchases of their own. Colonial women sometimes had extensive personal trade networks and retained control over their earnings; by the nineteenth century, as women became increasingly the chief buyers of family products, they had even greater access to pockets of household income. It is difficult to maintain that a woman who wanted to purchase a contraceptive tract or douching syringe would not have found a way to pay for it.

Among the likely audiences for contraceptive advice literature were the women of the managerial class, as for example, in Rockdale, Delaware, in the 1840s. A. F. C. Wallace, who has studied that community more closely than anyone else has, does not document family sizes, child spacing, or any indices of family limitation, but he does note that the women read widely and did not hesitate to express resentment of the restrictions motherhood and housewifery had placed on their intellectual, religious, and artistic interests.

Information on reproductive control was probably most readily available, however, in towns and cities. The flow of information in the early nineteenth century was relatively greater and faster to urban areas than to rural hamlets. Print communications traveled along the same geographical and transportation networks as other goods, by footpaths and roads, rivers and canals, so that communities differed enormously in their access to printed materials before mid-nineteenth century.[87] Mercantile cities in the United States in the 1830s and 1840s were compact areas in which businesses clustered together and information flowed relatively easily between widely different groups.[88] A broad spectrum of New York City's diverse population in the 1830s ebbed and flowed daily around the Hall of Science run by Fanny Wright and Robert Dale Owen. Their bookstore provided ready access to his *Moral Physiology* and, probably, other reproductive control literature as well. Charles Knowlton, complaining that he was uniquely singled out for harassment, noted that *Every Woman's Book* was sold openly without prosecution, as was a book plagiarizing his douching method but written by "a preacher."[89] In Boston, the freethinkers' Hall of Science in the heart of the commercial district housed the press of the *Boston Investigator* and a bookstore selling *Moral Physiology* and *Fruits of Philosophy* and served as the site of weekly lectures, dances, and debates that attracted what Abner Kneeland admiringly called "the producing classes," "mechanics," and the "middle or lower class of society," and what worried authorities referred to as "the poor and laboring classes."[90]

While it is easier to reconstruct the lines of access to printed information about reproductive control in cities and large towns, one very special case may serve as an example of the informal and interwoven strands of communication in the "web of access." Knowlton's Berkshire community of Ashfield with its rural farms and villages illustrates the growing density of such communication and also the range of diverse publics that had begun to try and read such books as *Fruits of Philosophy*.

Of Ashfield, Massachusetts' 1830s population of 1,732,[91] only a few could have remained ignorant of Knowlton's subject matter in view of the notoriety of his trials. Nor was it hard to obtain the pamphlet. Knowlton's medical rounds took him on an eight- to ten-mile circle of the countryside around Ashfield, extending by concentric rings the range of his influence. The affluent in Franklin County, of course, had easy access to his contraceptive advice, but so did his kin, his neighbors, his friends, and his patients, most of them middling farmers, laborers, and mechanics. William Barnard, the secretary of Knowlton's Franklin County group, the Friends of Mental Liberty, was a self-styled "yeoman," as were Knowlton's father and his father-in-law; Seth and Elizabeth Church, friends of the Knowltons, were "laborers"; E. Franklin and Julia A. Goodwin, who witnessed Knowlton's will, were farmers; Nelson Gardner, a close family friend who became guardian of the Knowltons' youngest child, Willis, in 1857, was a mechanic; another friend, Gerald Ranney, kept a tavern.[92] Knowlton dispersed copies of his *Fruits* liberally to friends, though in response to accusations that he gave such literature away too generously, he protested that, except for *Fruits of Philosophy*, "I have not sold, lent or given away liberal publications to more than six or seven persons in town."[93] He said that he had sold his pamphlet only to one man and had let no copies fall into the hands of boys. Still, his many women patients had direct access to his work. He almost certainly carried a copy or two along on his rounds around Ashfield at least once a week. His patients were primarily women and he was not at all averse to discussing gynecological and obstetrical problems with them and the other women who were often present during his ministrations. Once Knowlton asked the female attendants at a birth for their opinions about treatments and about their own histories of conception and pregnancy. These discussions of women's earlier reproductive histories were sometimes carried on in writing—an important point, for the fact that a brash and direct doctor like Knowlton communicated in written notes with his female patients suggests a shift to greater reliance on the written word. If it was becoming easier to communicate on sexual topics in writing, even between a patient and her doctor, then the role of advice literature was bound to be elevated. It may have become much easier for Knowlton to leave copies of his pamphlet with his patients than for him or them to circle the topic in conversation with embarrassed euphemisms. Also, he carried female syringes and taught female patients to use douches for medicinal purposes.[94]

Farmers may have had fewer reasons for wanting smaller families than did urban middle classes, because children's labor was essential on the farm and the economic costs of farm children may have lagged behind those of townspeople. Yet farming women and men were not immune to the broad cultural changes in America which made women concerned about their health and which made having fewer children preferable for economic and personal reasons. Historians who have traced declining child/woman ratios by the mid nineteenth century in certain areas of rural America have concluded that farmers did practice family limitation. They have not been able to find much information on how rural marital fertility was, in fact, reduced, but withdrawal, sexual abstinence, perhaps abortion (although not all mention this) and prolonged lactation seemed the most likely methods. John Mack Faragher notes that the second generation in the Sugar Creek, Illinois, community practiced family limitation by the 1850s. He does not suggest motivation; although he notes earlier that the work of children was important, he mentions that the work of farm wives "made the difference between the success or failure of productive strategies." Changing valuations placed on women's time in productive labor compared to their time spent on and with children may have been a motivation for family limitation.[95]

It is possible, as some historians believe, that rural couples used celibacy as a preventative technique, but no historian has documented any significant differences in sexuality between rural and urban populations. In many parts of the Mississippi and Ohio river valleys, in the frontier areas of the Midwest and upper South, wherever freethinkers or practitioners associated with medical sects created methods of communication and marketing, men and women could obtain books, douching devices, spermicides, condoms, and vaginal sponges. They could also buy materials by mail. In 1849 a mail stage came every day except Sunday to Sugar Creek, Illinois, where, in 1848, the postmaster received a packet of mail twice a day.[96] Except in the frontier South and West, farmers were linked to villages and village culture, but even more isolated families had some links to the outside world. In rural Sugar Creek, from the 1830s through the 1850s, although farmers did not travel much outside of a ten-mile radius, families recorded an average of thirty to fifty visits with neighbors each year. At the general store–post office, their central meeting spot, information was dispersed informally.[97] Nor is there evidence that farmers were less interested in print culture than were town dwellers. In New England and the Midwest, farmers and their wives bought, read, and circulated literature. Literacy was a supplement to word-of-mouth and local networks for American farmers.[98]

Farmers, in addition, had an increasing discretionary income in the antebellum decades. Even rural villagers and farmers were becoming more enmeshed in the market economy. In the 1820s and 1830s so many hundreds of farmers, villagers, and townspeople from New England to the mid-Atlantic states were willing to spend money on portraits, for example—twenty cents for a simple profile, three dollars for a full front view—that dozens of itinerant portraitists could make a living.[99]

Working class men and women had better access to contraceptive and abortion information in the antebellum decades than they would have again for several generations. Both freethinkers and Thomsonians of the period made a direct appeal to the workingmen and women in urban areas—mechanics, small masters, journeymen—and to those Americans in rural farms and villages.[100] Some contemporary critics may have worried about the declining birth rate among middle class families, but others noted that numbers of native-born workers also wanted smaller families. In 1852, Frederick Hollick said that "all classes" wanted information about pregnancy checks, and the pseudonymous "A. M. Mauriceau" claimed to have spoken to forty or fifty "poor women" every month about reproduction.[101] The few existing detailed statistical studies of marital fertility show the same broad class trends. In 1855, across class lines, couples in Erie County, New York, for example, had substantial control over their fertility. Class differences were not significant in this regard.[102]

Class categorizations are difficult for nineteenth-century Americans: definitions are problematic and terminology is slippery. Once we move beyond the two extremes of the rich and the very poorest (the indigent and day laborers), stratification of lower and middling groups varies depending on the date, the region, and the individual scholar doing the labeling. A "middle class" was crystallizing in the first half of the nineteenth century and a "working class" coalesced, too, although historians of this phenomenon in the United States are correctly tentative about the pace of the change and the self-identification of people within one class or another.[103] Many laboring class women and men shared the attitudes and motivations of the middle classes with respect to reproductive control: concern about the health of wives, about the nurture of children already born, about having the power to determine the timing and frequencies of pregnancies. Like farmers and unlike their bourgeois counterparts, however, many working class families continued to need their children's help for economic survival. Even in mid century, families in the Rockdale, Pennsylvania, mills were relying on family wages, including the income brought in by their children. To such men and women, family limitation may have been doubly unwelcome, threatening economic hardship and imposing new necessities for self-control, calculation, and forethought on sexual behavior. For these reasons some male workers took offense when the issue of family size was raised. We have noted Thomas Skidmore's angry reaction to Owen's contraceptive pamphlet. Some workers associated reproductive control with yet another attempt by bosses and other authorities to constrain them.[104] Industrialists, middle class moralists, the evangelical ministry, in their efforts to define the appropriate uses of leisure time for workers and to enact laws to control public behaviors—especially drinking and fighting—were indeed trying to impose self-control, self-discipline, and moderation on workers. Employers, creditors, and moralistic reformers had begun to associate workers with large families as having insufficient self-control. In Lynn, Massachusetts, coalitions of employers and reformers began, in the late 1820s, to try to encourage self-control among workers by curbing their appetites for drink and sex. In Oneida, New York, bank loans appear to have been rejected at times and other forms of pressured applied to encourage family limitation.[105] Owen, in his contraceptive advice, included a letter, purportedly from a mechanic, praising the benefits of family limitation through withdrawal—certainly Owen himself believed that the sexual self-control required by the practice of coitus interruptus was beneficial, and his praise of the method may have raised hackles among artisans who were feeling the pressures of the new industrial morality. When a Lynn manufacturer told workers that poor workmen should not have children, a mechanic replied, "What impudence! Who made them rulers over us?"[106]

Yet to other workers, the new reproductive control methods may have seemed a symbol of and an aid to social aspiration, just as did the restrictions they generally accepted on drinking, leisure activities, and election-day celebrations. Workers obviously cared whether an ideology of self-control was self-imposed or thrust on them, and the origin almost certainly would have made a difference in the effectiveness with which they practiced reproductive control.[107]

Of the 124 men who signed the membership rolls in the American Physiological Society in 1837, Stephen Nissenbaum was able to trace forty-nine, all apparently skilled workers: piano makers, housewrights, and carpenters.[108] And the twenty-five lodgers at Russell Thacher Trall's water-cure boardinghouse in New York in 1850 would have had especially easy access to his ideas about the rhythm method, women's contraceptives, and abortion methods. A broad group occupationally, the lodgers included a printer, a tobacconist, an apprentice, several Irish servant girls, and a pianoforte maker (who had six children).[109] They were essentially the same type of earnest, upwardly mobile young people who embraced temperance and moral reforms as a way of elevating themselves. Paul Faler categorized three groups of workers in Lynn, Massachusetts, in the 1830s: "traditionalists," who ignored preaching about self-control and frugality; "loyalists," who were cowed by their economic and cultural custodians; and "rebel mechanics," who embraced self-control and the new work ethic, not as obeisance to the bosses but as means of achieving new power and control over their lives.[110] Their counterparts in England bought birth control literature; an 1834 study by the Statistical Society of Manchester of the reading habits of the city's working class showed that six hundred copies of *Fruits of Philosophy, Moral Physiology*, and an obscure work called *Bridal Gem* were circulating. Thus one family in twenty owned a copy of a leading contraceptive advice book.[111] Workers in Lynn may have done the same.

In the 1830s workers most attracted to freethought were artisans, mechanics, and struggling journeymen—printers, shoemakers, stonecutters, and watchmakers, among others—and small masters; nearly 77 percent of freethought followers in Philadelphia in the late 1820s were journeymen artisans, 13 percent, master artisans, 7 percent, "lower white collar," 3 percent, professionals.[112] In the factional fighting among the leaders of the workingmen's parties in New York City, 1829–30, the Owenite faction (the group presumably relatively sympathetic to reproductive intervention) consisted of more journeymen than did the followers of Thomas Skidmore.[113]

Fertility control practices and attitudes of young laboring women in antebellum America are even harder to trace than those of their male counterparts, but the growing body of historical literature about working women suggests that in the 1830s and 1840s a number began to demonstrate a more forthright, determined, self-conscious public assertiveness. Women tailors in New York City, who formed a union and went on strike in 1831, exemplified such a new self-reliance.[114] If their determination to have greater control over their work lives was transferable to determination to have reproductive control, they may well have read and used the new information. In the 1850s New York

City's female straw-hat workers, for one group, openly discussed what they learned at public lectures on physiology.[115] Their families worried about their daughters' independence. Christine Stansell notes that "defiant daughters" were even more rebellious than sons in antebellum New York, and they raised among parents and others fears of female passion on the loose and consequent burdensome out-of-wedlock pregnancies.[116]

So, too, the hundreds, if not thousands, of young urban women who eked out a subsistence in lean times through casual prostitution may have learned something about douching and spermicidal sponges as a protection against unwanted pregnancies. The historical record with respect to prostitutes' lives is sparse, however, and there is little evidence about what they did to prevent pregnancy or whether, for example, their principal recourse was to abortion.[117] When aging prostitutes in the late-nineteenth-century American West turned to other work, some became abortionists: perhaps they were already knowledgeable about methods.[118] They may have encouraged clients to use condoms, and, indeed, men were so fearful of venereal diseases that they may have needed little persuasion. Condoms were available in functional styles, sold simply in boxes by the dozen (see Chapter 7), but the availability of "fancy" condoms in colors (pink and white) and rolled into cigars and other fanciful shapes carries playful connotations suggesting that they were used in brothels and casual prostitution. Some prostitutes, perhaps many, douched with spermicides.[119]

It is apparent that at least some wage workers could afford the contraceptives and advice publications offered for sale, but the nineteenth century was a period of wildly fluctuating "boom and bust" cycles, and what was affordable during good times could have been a luxury during hard times. Historical records of incomes, wages, and costs of living are notoriously incomplete, and the relative costs of reproductive control products varied over the course of the nineteenth century. For some Americans, any cost would have been too great; but when farmers' cash crops did well and when workers' wages kept pace with the costs of living, many workers could afford to buy medicinal drugs, to pay doctors' and druggists' fees, to subscribe to newspapers and lending libraries, to procure some luxury goods, and to attend lycea lectures. Reproductive control products were inexpensive compared to the costs of such goods and services.[120]

The Shakers' mail-order business in medicinal plant products, for example, was so lucrative from 1830 through 1860 that it could not have rested solely on the purchases of middle class Americans. In 1830 the Shakers sold four thousand pounds of roots, herbs, and fluid extracts, by 1850 more than seven thousand pounds of fluid extracts alone.[121] Reconstructed budgets for hypothetical working class families in the 1850s estimate that 1.7 percent of annual income would be spent for medical care; in one such budget, a New York City family in 1853 was allotted ten dollars a year for physicians' and druggists' fees.[122] Charles Knowlton noted in 1832 that a female syringe for douching could be bought at any apothecary's shop for a shilling or less, and by mid century druggists obtained syringes in wholesale lots for pennies each but retailed them for a dollar or more. The early diaphragm—"Dr. Cameron's Patent Family Regulator"—peddled by a Boston entrepreneur in 1847, cost five dollars, although diaphragms, too, came down, costing a few dollars in the 1860s and 1870s. Condoms may have cost one dollar each in the 1830s, but after mid century sold for three to five dollars a dozen.[123] At those prices even a working class couple might have been able to buy such products.

In the 1830s and 1840s, however, most contraceptive or abortion-inducing products could be made at home from readily obtainable and relatively inexpensive household and garden products. The spermicides Knowlton recommended in the 1830s—vinegar and baking soda—were cheap and common household ingredients. Other spermicides could be prepared from common roadside plants or grown in gardens. Women in the privacy of their homes could easily cut vaginal sponges to size and attach a ribbon for easy removal.

The contraceptive advice literature, although relatively expensive, was not exorbitant. Owen sold *Moral Physiology* for thirty-seven to forty-four cents in the 1830s; the cost of *Fruits of Philosophy* varied from fifty cents to one dollar. In a budget constructed to illustrate expenditure of a hypothetical Philadelphia working class family in 1853, $6.24 was allotted each year for newspapers; a New York family was allotted ten dollars a year for reading materials.[124] And, as these hypothetical budgets suggest, many American families—workers and farmers alike—placed a high priority on books, pamphlets, and newspapers and were willing to spend precious resources on them.[125] In only one year, 1829–30, Owen reported profits of about two thousand dollars in sales of "liberal" books published by the *Free Enquirer* press.[126]

In 1845 the members of the Friends of Mental Liberty of Franklin County, Massachusetts, who paid two to twelve dollars apiece to join, could borrow any work for three to twelve cents.[127] Among those who joined was the "yeoman" William Barnard. Readers may well have found *Fruits of Philosophy* among the volumes, since Knowlton and his wife were founding members. When Knowlton's friend and fellow freethinker William Russell died and the titles of the seventy books in his library were recorded, the only one on the list whose title was not given, listed simply as "Domestic Manual—seven cents," was probably *Fruits of Philosophy*.[128]

Haphazardly, sometimes even unintentionally, the currents of freethought, Thomsonianism, and hydropathy brought both specific knowledge and transformations in general attitudes to women and men in swirling urban areas and quiet rural backwaters alike. The legal repression and denunciations from pulpit and press suffered by a few of the early promoters did not shift the tide and may even have furthered it. But the metaphor of music may be more apt here. The 1830s saw the first significant American solos on reproductive control, and in the next decades these swelled in number and force. To critics, the resulting crescendo of reproductive control was cacophonous—a threatening assault on the status quo of gender, family, and class relations. The contributions of freethinkers and medical practitioners to the availability of such knowledge did not automatically create harmony, for there was little overall orchestration and much of what circulated was discordant. But the public chorus demanding ever more information and the responsive outpouring continued.

Portrait of Mary Pierce Poor. Carte-de-visite (c. 1865). Reproduced with permission of The Schlesinger Library on the History of Women in America, Radcliffe College.

Portrait of Robert Dale Owen (c. 1847). Daguerreotype by unidentified photographer. Reproduced with permission of the National Portrait Gallery, Smithsonian Institution.

Portrait of Charles Knowlton (n.d.), from Frederick G. Howes, *History of the Town of Ashfield, Massachusetts* (n.p., 1914). Courtesy of the Ashfield town library which owns the unique illustrated copy.

FRUITS

OF PHILOSOPHY,

OR

THE PRIVATE COMPANION

OF

YOUNG MARRIED PEOPLE.

BY CHARLES KNOWLTON, M. D.,
Author of "Modern Materialism."

"Knowledge is Wealth."
Old Saying.

THIRD EDITION, WITH ADDITIONS.

BOSTON:
1834.

Title page of Charles Knowlton's *Fruits of Philosophy* (1834). Note the pocket-size of this essentially miniature book. Reproduced with permission of the History of Medicine Collections, Duke University Medical Center Library, Durham, North Carolina.

Portrait of Abner Kneeland (n.d.) from Samuel Palmer Putnam, *Four Hundred Years of Freethought* (1894). Courtesy of Widener Library, Harvard University.

Portrait of Frances Wright (n.d.). Reproduced with permission of the Boston Athenaeum.

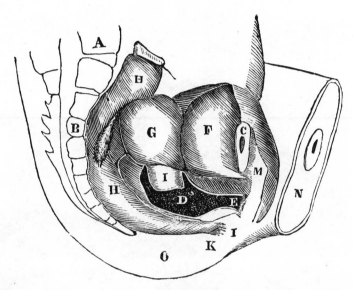

"Female Reproductive Organs," from Thomas Hersey, *The Midwife's Practical Directory* (1836). Reproduced with permission of the Boston Medical Library in the Francis A. Countway Library of Medicine.

Portrait of Frederick Hollick from Hollick, *Outlines of Anatomy & Physiology* (1846). Reproduced with permission of the Boston Medical Library in the Francis A. Countway Library of Medicine.

PLATE IV.

The Internal Organs cut through.

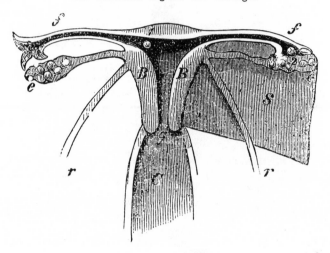

B. The Womb cut through.—C. The Vagina.—g. The Mouth of the
Womb.—f, f. The Fallopian Tubes.—e, e. The Ovaries.—r, r. The
Round Ligaments.—S. One of the Broad Ligaments. On one side,
marked 2, the egg is just entering the Tube from the Ovary, and
on the other at 1, it is just passed into the womb.

"Internal Organs Cut Through," from Frederick Hollick, *The Marriage Guide* (1850).
Reproduced with permission of the Boston Medical Library in the Francis A. Countway Library of Medicine.

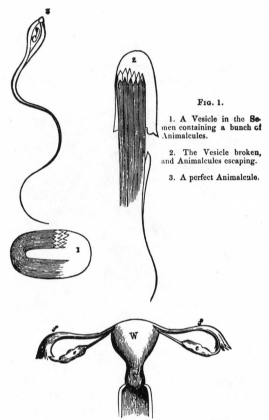

Fig. 1.

1. A Vesicle in the Semen containing a bunch of Animalcules.

2. The Vesicle broken, and Animalcules escaping.

3. A perfect Animalcule.

Fig. 2.—*f, f*, Fallopian Tubes.—*e, e*, Ovaries or Eggs.—*W*, Womb.—*N*, Neck of the Womb.—*C*, Passage into the Womb or Vagina.

"Animalcules" and the Female Reproductive Tract, Fig. 1 and Fig. 2, from Robert Dale Owen, *Moral Physiology*, "Publisher's Notes" [by Gilbert Vale] (1858). Vale added these and other drawings to Owen's text. Reproduced with permission of the Boston Medical Library in the Francis A. Countway Library of Medicine.

Portrait of Mary S. Gove Nichols from *Nichols' Health Manual* (1887). Most likely made when she was in her sixties, this is one of the few known portraits of Nichols. Reproduced with permission of the British Library.

6

The Boom in Self-Help
Literature after 1850

By the mid nineteenth century, women and men whose parents had been persuaded to buy written advice on reproductive control with such titles as *Moral Physiology* and *Fruits of Philosophy* were now being enticed by titles promising *A Confidential Letter to the Married*, *The Wife's Secret of Power*, *Science of Reproduction and Reproductive Control*, *The Marriage Guide, How Not to and Why*, and *Conception: The Process, Method of Prevention without Any Expense or Any Hindrance to Perfect Intercourse*. Dozens of new titles promised information on contraception and abortion; older works were reprinted in new editions; tinted engravings, fold-out illustrations, and illustrated advertisements offered pictorial inducements, and whether at the local newsstand, bookstore, stationers, or from peddlers and agents, or by mail order, the works were widely available.

Medical Guides for Lay Readers: "To the Pure All Things Are Pure"

Much of the newly available literature was pamphlet-sized and focused specifically on contraception or abortion. But unlike the pioneering works of the 1830s, the lines were increasingly blurred between sober advice tracts and lengthy advertising booklets for birth control products or services. Among these are such works as James Ashton's *The Book of Nature*, Annie Besant's *The Law of Population*, Edward Bond Foote's *The Radical Remedy in Social Science; or, Born-*

ing Better Babies. Many of the pamphlets are no longer available and we know of their existence only by their titles in card catalogues or by references to them in court records: Edward Bliss Foote's *Words in Pearl*, Daniel Winder's *A Rational or Private Marriage Chart: For the Use of All Who Wish to Prevent an Increase of Family* (1858), Thomas Low Nichols's "Letter to a Married Woman on the Means and Processes for the Healthy Regulation and Voluntary Control of the Maternal Function" sent sealed in a "prepaid government envelope" for one dollar.[1] But others, the more numerous of the reproductive control publications that soared in mid century, were books and pamphlets of medical self-help which included sections on regulating pregnancy along with longer discussions on reproduction, obstetrics, gynecology, "female complaints," and sexual anatomy. Typical of these popularized medical guides for lay audiences were Thomas Low Nichols's *Esoteric Anthropology*, Frederick Hollick's *The Marriage Guide*, Edward Bliss Foote's *Medical Common Sense*, and Russell Thacher Trall's *Sexual Physiology.*[2]

Some authors were drawn from reform ranks, especially medical sectarians. Others were entrepreneurs hoping to make money out of public demand. The anonymous author of *Reproductive Control*, a booklet published in Cincinnati in 1855, hired agents to sell it along with female douching syringes, the method the author recommended. Its instructions for cold-water douching are among the most explicit, detailed, and clearly written of any in the century's literature.[3]

Some of the authors made a good deal of money. "Dr. J. Soule," who copyrighted *Science of Reproduction and Reproductive Control* in New York, in 1856 was probably the Asa J. Soule whom Anthony Comstock arrested in Rochester, New York, in 1878 for sending contraceptive advertisements through the mails.[4] Soule, a successful businessman, president and major stockholder of the Hop Bitters Manufacturing Company, was estimated to be worth at least fifty thousand dollars in 1874.[5] He pleaded guilty to the charge of circulating obscene literature and was fined one thousand dollars. A second charge of selling drugs to prevent conception was dropped.

In tone and language, this mid-century literature dealt with the subject of reproductive control with less coyness than had earlier literature. Fewer authors presented apologies for broaching the topic. Some works put "To the Pure All Things Are Pure" at the beginning of the text, but even this seemed perfunctory. For every George Napheys, who wrote in the 1869 edition of his book, *The Physical Life of Woman*, that "limitation of offspring" was "the most delicate part" of his book, there were a half-dozen authors who felt no need at all to warn readers against any information provided. Ralph Glover, publishing a pirated edition of Owen's *Moral Physiology* in 1846, believed that Americans had become less prudish about public discussions: "Ten years have elapsed since the publication of the last edition of Mr. Owen's book [*Moral Physiology*], and it is believed that such change of public sentiment has taken place as will render a republication of the work . . . acceptable to the author, his friends, and the public."[6] The new boldness notwithstanding, many works remained small in actual size—soft-cover pocket books whose existence could easily be hidden.[7]

Rationales for "Escaping Pregnancy": A Wife's Health Foremost

Most works continued to provide some rationale for the control of reproduction. James Ashton, on the other hand, declared he would give no reasons but would simply impart to readers "in brief, matter-of-fact form reliable information."[8] Some suggested that audiences no longer required the carefully marshaled arguments of a generation earlier, but pamphlets and the longer medical works typically presented a few matter-of-fact reasons. Brief and cogent, the explanations rarely were a substantial part of the work, as Owen's had been in 1830.

In both the pamphlets and the longer works the single most important rationale offered for family limitation was preservation of a wife's health. Much of the literature noted the importance of preventives for women who could not bear living or healthy children, or for women who had trouble breastfeeding and, by implication, did not have its protection. In a French work attributed to P. C. Dunne and A. F. Derbois in 1854, *The Young Married Lady's Private Medical Guide*, the translator, F. Harrison Doane, said that "women who habitually abort" should use preventives as should "women who cannot nurse . . . [or they] will be pregnant again within three to four months." The author added that children could not have strong constitutions if their mothers gave birth at invervals shorter than two and a half to five years.[9] So, too, the most respectable of the medical practitioners, if they approved of family limitation at all, considered women's health the principal reason for disseminating information on contraception. George Napheys began his eight-page discussion "On the Limitation of Offspring" in the 1872 edition of his *The Physical Life of Woman* by acknowledging that while many "physicians and clergy object to *any* effort to avoid large families" and "numberless married couples" would do anything to "escape pregnancy," "there is definitely such a thing as *over-production*"—having "too many children." He quoted another medical authority, a Dr. Tilt, whose *Handbook of Uterine Therapeutics* claimed that two-thirds of all womb disease were due to "child-bearing in feeble women." Too-frequent pregnancies caused women to bear "idiots," "puny children," or children with rickets.[10] A desire to limit the number of children, Napheys added, was based on the parents' love for the ones already born; he quoted an unnamed writer in the *Nation* who had argued that the desire to limit offspring "is noble," springing from the parents' desire that their living children "can be properly nourished and educated."

Occasionally the arguments touching on women's health veered into what a later generation would call eugenics. Books were more likely to recommend contraception to parents with backgrounds of hereditary disease, insanity, or criminality. Typical was Soule's argument that women who could not bear healthy or living children should have ways to avoid pregnancy and that individuals with hereditary diseases, imbecility, or criminality in their past should avoid having children. Soule also stated that "many, very many, comparatively good men and good women are miserable for life" because unhappily married. If "parents hate each other," their children, Soule warned, will be "hateful, ugly, [and] despondent." His final explanation of why people wanted reproductive control was that newlyweds needed to have time together before incurring the costs of having children.[11]

Economic arguments for reproductive control were, on the other hand, generally sparse. Owen, in the 1830s, had said that *Moral Physiology* would benefit the poor. Annie Besant, writing in the 1870s from Britain, shared the traditional English neo-Malthusian concern with family limitation for the poor. But American literature on reproductive control gave only the most fleeting attention to poverty or class. One exception was the anonymous author of *Reproductive Control*—who said that he had "lived half a century," was the father of a "large family," had "officiated as a minister for over twenty years," and had practiced medicine for five—noted that he was writing for the poor, especially poor women who, without preventives, would spend all their time in pregnancy, nursing, or dreading and hating sexual intercourse. If the poor would limit themselves to one or two children, they would get richer, and if the wealthy would have four, "they would gradually approach the level of their more humble neighbors"—a concept of erasing class distinctions through reproductive control unique in the advice literature. This author dealt no further with economic issues and centered most of his justification on the importance of reproductive control for women's health and, above all, on its importance in enhancing sexual pleasure: "That sexual enjoyment is the chief end of matrimony will be acknowledged by all persons of cool and sober reflection. All other considerations are secondary and merely the consequences." Reproductive control was valuable not only for reasons of health: couples needed to consult "convenience, inclination, and wishes."[12]

Most writers clearly expected women to be their readers, as did, for example, the "private" medical guides for "ladies." The assumption that women had a natural interest in family limitation and ought to study the issue was a far cry from the earlier tentativeness of Owen and Knowlton.

The rationales legitimating reproductive control given by the pseudonymous authors "Madames Beach, Putney and Co." in their circular, *The Habits of a Well-Organized Married Life: By a Married Woman*, published in several editions between 1863 and 1867, are particularly noteworthy in this respect. The author(s), who used the first person singular throughout the pamphlet, called herself an "authoress." But the writer was not necessarily a woman, because it was not uncommon by mid century for reproductive control entrepreneurs to give themselves women's names, especially the names of French women, as a boost to credibility with female customers. The author(s) professed a knowledge of the French methods of reproductive control, but the English is colloquial, so she/he may not have been French at all. The pamphlet was not addressed exclusively to men or to women. The testimonial letters quoted made clear the author's view that reproductive control should be the concern of both sexes. The pamphlet did address women in particular; the authors spoke of a modern couple, and especially of a modern woman concerned about maintaining her health, vigor, and beauty so that she could be a good mother and a good wife. It emphasized that the contraceptives it recommended permitted greater sexual pleasure and greater variety. Readers were told that they needed only to buy one device, but would find greater happiness if they had more than one: "A ship needs but one compass, but may carry two; a family needs but one residence, but many in the city have their summer residence off in the country; a house needs but one clock but may have two . . ."[13]

The Beach Company pamphlet emphasized that the most important reason that a woman should practice fertility control was concern for her health. This was not self-indulgence, it was the *duty* of married couples to regulate their family size—even more important it was a woman's duty. If a woman controlled reproduction, she preserved her health and enhanced her role as mother and wife: "Now it is her privilege and duty, first of all, to preserve her health and to pass through confinement only at such intervals as is advantageous to her health, circumstances and family."[14] The issue of morality was dealt with only cursorily, as were economic concerns.

Ways and Means: Devices, Instructions, and Foldouts in the New Literature

The degree of attention paid to specific methods in this literature varied greatly, as did opinions about their safety, reliability, morality, and practicality. Books for female audiences routinely mentioned condoms and withdrawal. Although the majority of publications listed at least a half dozen methods, if only to disparage most, they recommended only one or two. The problem for readers was that one adviser's favorite method was another's most sharply criticized.

Pamphlets tended to list more methods and to discuss them in greater detail and with less euphemism than did the medical books. One of the most direct discussions of reproductive control in all the nineteenth-century literature was James Ashton's sixty-four-page advice tract, *The Book of Nature*, published in 1860 and reprinted without substantive changes in 1861, 1865 and 1870. In explicit yet proper language, without coyness or romanticism, Ashton advised readers of five of the most reliable contraceptive options of the day: withdrawal, douching, the vaginal sponge, condoms, and the rhythm method (a relatively reliable version). Since he called himself a "lecturer on sexual physiology," Ashton may have given lecture audiences similar advice, or at least sold them the booklet. Recognizing that men and women differed in their needs and desires, he was one of the few advisers to note the advantages and limitations of particular reproductive control methods for each sex. Ashton was unusual, too, in his approbation of withdrawal, in that by the 1860s most authors assumed that readers already knew about it, and although most mentioned it, few devoted much space to explaining it and many disparaged it as unpopular, difficult to use, and unreliable.[15]

Soule's discussion of methods in *Science of Reproduction* was fairly typical. He listed ways to prevent conception: (1) the rhythm method (basically Hollick's view that a woman is rarely fertile after twelve days from menstruation); (2) drugs to prevent the development of ova (a method Soule discouraged as dangerous); (3) prevention of emission of

semen into the female organs by complete withdrawal or use of condoms; (4) expelling the semen by immediate douching, use of the
sponge, or pre- and postcoital douching, and (5) drugs or cold-water
injections to destroy the seminal animalcules. Soule's advice was well
organized, direct, clearly stated, but probably of mixed reliability. His
advice on the rhythm method fell in the mid range of the era: he
believed conception impossible sixteen days after menstruation, but
that a woman was rarely fertile after the twelfth day. A woman who
followed the first recommendation may have been safe; a woman who
followed the latter was probably at risk. His douching advice may have
been useful, especially his recommendation of tannic water, but his
best advice was to use condoms and the vaginal sponge or to practice
withdrawal provided there was "no accidental introduction of the
smallest particle [of semen] into the vagina."[16]

Pamphlets often gave more attention to devices than did longer
works, perhaps because their authors, often entrepreneurs, were eager to promote products. The Beach Company advertising pamphlet,
for example, criticized "solutions of salts, sulphate of zinc, chloride of
zinc, alum, sponges, and compression of the scrotum" as dangerous to
health and ineffectual and recommended several methods, the principal one "the French system," which included choices of five types of
condoms and "the womb guard." There were "Printed Instructions" on
contraception and sexual matters—for example, use of "envelope powders" (the purposes of which were unclear) and information on cures
for painful menstruation. One of the (purported) testimonial letters
makes it clear that the instructions included advice about how to induce abortion. The Beach Company maintained that sexual abstinence
was bad for health and that, anyway, "the masses will not submit to
such a restriction." It criticized "the old system" of limiting reproduction, arging that withdrawal was unhealthy and unsatisfying to both
partners and that the rhythm method ("certain intervals") was ineffective because no woman could count on precise menstrual regularity.

Some works, especially the longer medical books by regular doctors, condemned abortion as a moral evil and physical danger. Some
sought to promote contraception as a way to mitigate what they believed to be the growing problem of abortion among middle class couples, although a few were sympathetic to women who had abortions.
Some provided advice inadvertently through their condemnations of
abortionists and specific means of inducing abortion. Only Ashton's
pamphlet, singular in this as in other ways, provided dispassionate
advice about when and how to bring about miscarriage. He warned
that abortions "should never be resorted to except in extreme cases

and then only under medical advice," yet devoted three pages to information on how to induce abortion. He was not selling anything, so unlike the great majority of writers who discussed abortion techniques, Ashton told readers to avoid buying the drugs from quacks: "There is no doubt that many women can escape child-bearing by the use of ergot but it would be better for any one to get it from her family physician who would know something of her constitution than to pay a hundred times its worth to a quack and perhaps endanger life or health by taking more than is prudent and at an improper time."[17] Abortions and miscarriages, he warned, "are collisions with Nature's laws." They were always dangerous, he added, but some women "get by without suffering or harm."

As with advice on curbing reproduction, information on sexual anatomy and the processes of conception became more voluminous and more widely available in mid century. A number of the new publications on sexual physiology devoted full chapters to subjects rarely touched on in the earlier popular literature, and often not dealt with even in official medical literature. Mid-century publications had extensive treatments of spermatozoa, ova, ovulation, fertilization, and fetal development. In 1859, Seth Pancoast's *The Ladies' Medical Guide*, clearly intended for respectable married women, carried engravings and descriptions of male genitalia and sperm. Pamphlets addressed conception in varying detail, chiefly so that their readers would be better able to practice contraception. Besant deplored "the complete ignorance of their own bodies, which is supposed to be a necessary part of 'female modesty'" and proceded to give a succinct one-paragraph explanation of the vaginal cavity and why "the most reliable checks are those which close the passage into the womb."[18]

The information on sexual physiology and anatomy in the popular literature was sometimes more ample than in official medical textbooks—many gynecology and obstetrics texts treated the subjects briefly, if at all, though official texts on midwifery occasionally had more extensive treatments. William Tyler Smith's *The Modern Practice of Midwifery*, in 1858, had numerous engravings, a chapter on "generation" with two sentences about reproduction of the "higher animals," a chapter on ovulation, another on "the external organs of generation" with two paragraphs on the physiology of coitus, and a lecture on conception which discussed spermatozoa and the development of ova.[19] Early editions of Knowlton's *Fruits of Philosophy*, as noted earlier, had not provided illustrations of male reproductive organs for fear of offending female readers, but an 1839 edition contained engraved plates and a description of the male generative organs.[20]

The advice literature demonstrated a range of attitudes toward sexuality and sexual pleasure for married couples and does not support the arguments that Americans were curtailing their marital fertility by rigorous sexual abstinence.[21] All—books and pamphlets—criticized celibacy outside of and within marriage; celibacy was unnatural, harmful to health, and unpopular. Sexual pleasure was important. They differed in their criteria for sexual moderation. The pamphleteers in particular thought sexuality important to both male and female readers. Contraceptive methods that interfered with sexual pleasure, they reported, were unpopular with the public. The anonymous author of *Reproductive Control* promoted his favorite contraceptive method— douching—in part because it permitted greater sexual pleasure: "It lays no restraints upon the impulses of nature. It requires no caution during the sexual embrace; but leaves the mind free, as it should be, to revel in the abstraction and extacy [sic] of sexual union. . . . As well might we be compelled to eat and drink under the constant apprehension of being poisoned as to be compelled to administer to the sexual appetite under the constant fear of consequences almost as much dreaded."[22] The author did not differentiate male from female sexual pleasure, but his arguments pertained more to men's experiences. Women would not, in fact, necessarily be freed from anxiety and better able to enjoy sex through use of douching. A male partner freed from the obligation of withdrawal, indeed, may have found his sexual pleasure enhanced.

Books and pamphlets began to include drawings as well as words, and the pictures they used may have had far greater impact than any amount of written advice. Colored engravings of male and female reproductive organs, colored fold-out plates illustrating fetal development, black-and-white engravings of sperm, ova, ovaries, and fallopian tubes—although often inexact by twentieth-century standards—may have helped readers overcome inhibitions about contraception. If women gained from such drawings clearer ideas of the vaginal canal and cervix, they may have had fewer fears about inserting diaphragms (which began to be available in limited numbers by the 1840s and in greater variety by the 1860s; see Chapter 7) and contraceptive sponges and less anxiety about losing the devices in an unfamiliar cavity. Drawings of male and female sexual anatomy appeared in the popularized sexual physiology literature even earlier than in much of the official medical textbooks.[23]

In the written instructions that often accompanied purchases of reproductive control devices—especially douches and diaphragms— some instructional brochures offered drawings of female sexual anatomy, showing where the diaphragm or sponge would fit across the cervix, or how the folds of the vagina made thorough douching important. In the 1850s and 1860s the douching syringes sold by the Mattson Company included such instructional pamphlets, with its "Elastic syringe" packaged in 1863 in a box with a "Family Guide," with information about the use of the syringe "so doctors do not have to explain." The Mattson Company in 1869 inserted with their "Vaginal Irrigator"—"a perfect and most desirable Family Instrument . . . purchased by all first-class ladies," a sixty-eight-page anatomical chart "containing much information, with full directions for using the instrument."[24] In 1883, William Rothacker, a pathologist at the Cincinnati Hospital, described the circular that accompanied a soft rubber diaphragm sold by agents and druggists. This circular describing the "French Pessaire Preventif" stated that it was easy, safe, and convenient to use, and reassured customers that it could not possibly get lost in the vagina: "If at any time you cannot readily grasp it with your finger, to remove it, just walk about in your room for a few minutes and it will have fallen so low in the vagina that you can easily reach and withdraw it."[25]

The outpouring of self-help literature after mid century had the important effect of opening the subject of reproductive control to greater public scrutiny. Whether the profusion led to changes in reproductive control practices depended on what one read, "how" one read it, what one retained, and whether and how anything book-learned was translated into practice. Just as in the 1830s, when the superior tracts of Knowlton and Owen competed with unorganized assemblages of prurience and ancient superstitions with occasional useful advice, so good advice disseminated now competed with much that was bad. Thus the useful information in Ashton's *The Book of Nature* was circulated in many of the same places and in the same ways as the useless information in Marcus Lafayette Byrn's *The Physiology of Marriage*, which promised much but delivered nothing.[26] There was also a world of difference between a Harmon Knox Root and a Frederick Hollick, although both published large medical self-help books, advertised their own medical inventions widely, and lived near each other in mid-century Manhattan. Root's medical knowledge was spurious and his advice on all subjects, not just contraception, was little better than useless. Readers would have learned from him where to buy condoms, but that was about all. Hollick, on the other hand, while not above turning a profit at every turn, was abreast of the medical currents of his day and provided sober, responsible advice.[27]

By mid century, readers may well have been mightily confused about the array of advice, for some advised that nothing was as dangerous as method "x", while a competing pamphlet argued that nothing was as effective or as safe as the same "x." Perhaps the most important lesson any reader would have learned from this array of conflicting opinion was that some methods worked and some did not. If this knowledge encouraged experimentation and flexibility, if it encouraged women and men either separately or as couples to study and observe, then the lack of consensus may have had beneficial results.

With sufficient experimentation and confidence that fertility could be curbed, couples or individuals may have hit on something that worked for them. The tone of the flood of publications encouraged optimism that fertility could, indeed, be controlled; it encouraged expectations that methods should be both effective and safe, and thus, irrespective of the quality of their advice, they may have motivated couples to experiment until they found effective methods.

Advertising: "Rubber Devices for Ladies and Gents," "Lydia E. Pinkham's Vegetable Compound and Uterine Tonic"

The advertisements for contraceptive and abortion-inducing services and products in mid century ranged from notices of a few simple words in a newspaper, to broadsides circulated on city streets, to multipage circulars sent through the mail. By the late nineteenth and early twentieth centuries American advertising techniques were changing and many products were being marketed with symbolism and subliminal messages designed to persuade customers that their happiness, their identities, their very personalities were dependent on their ownership of particular goods. Historians usually date these changes in advertising and the simultaneous development of a consumption-oriented culture in the United States to the turn of the nineteenth century, yet with birth control advertising we see some of the earliest roots of this transformation from single factual ads to persuasive copy.

Newspapers were the most common source for the succinct, straightforward birth control advertising most characteristic of the nineteenth-century genre. In the 1830s and 1840s abortion drugs, condoms, cures for venereal disease, aphrodisiacs, and abortions were advertised in major urban newspapers of New England and the Middle Atlantic states. Advertisements for condoms and diaphragms (Chapter 7 discusses these devices) were especially common in the sensational tabloids specializing in sports, theatrical news, murders, police reports, and courtroom dramas; newspapers aimed at an urban class of stable boys, maids, day laborers, upwardly mobile young clerks, and salespeople. It was a genre that Frank L. Mott, historian of American periodicals, calls the "lower class of story papers"—the cheap, spicy periodicals, the penny miscellanies and those "sub rosa periodicals designed for sly circulation in resorts of questionable character."[28] Well into the mid 1870s, at least one-third of all the advertisements in New York City's *Sporting Times and Theatrical News* were for condoms, women's contraceptive devices, and abortions, a typical example being those of "Dr. Elliott" at 77 Gold Street in Manhattan, who advertised "Best protectors against disease and accident. French rubber goods, $6.00/dozen; rubber $4.00/dozen. Sample 30 cents. Trade supplied. Ladies Protectors $3.00."[29]

Magazines and periodicals aiming for gentility carried few if any advertisements of any type, let alone for reproductive control.[30] The *American Agriculturalist*, until the mid 1870s the leading farm journal in the United States in circulation and prestige, did have medical ads, some for douching syringes and various types of unspecified "rubber devices" for "ladies" and "gents," and an occasional advertisement for birth control devices appears to have slipped by even the most watchful editors. Anthony Comstock, enforcing the new federal law he helped secure which forbade mailing information about contraception and abortion, accused the eminently respectable *Waverly Magazine* in 1876 of advertising womb veils, and he arrested an Indiana man, H. Gustavus Farr, for advertising his contraceptive diaphragms in several magazines.[31]

Some health journals, too, carried advertisements for birth control products. The water-cure publication the *Herald of Health*, with one of the largest circulations of any nineteenth-century medical journal, publicized douching syringes, promoted "voluntary motherhood," and argued the need for controlled reproduction. Some entrepreneurs published what purported to be medical newspapers but were actually vehicles to promote the purveyor's products. Harmon Knox Root's newspaper, the *Medical Advertiser*, in the early 1850s included drawings of male and female anatomy; it was principally a series of advertisements for Root's vegetable medicines, for his book *The People's Medical Lighthouse*, and for condoms. Frederick Hollick's *People's Medical Journal and Home Dr.*, published between July 1853 and December 1854, was a similar advertising vehicle.[32]

Advertisements were also often distributed by paid agents who stood on street corners or in railway and steamship depots and handed them to passersby. The young entrepreneur Harmon Knox Root, who advertised extensively to promote his medical consultation services, his books, and his birth control products—including contraceptive condoms, a "French Male Prevention Powder for the Prevention of Conception," and a douching substance, "Dr. Root's Female Wash"— apparently often relied on street promotions. The testimonial letters he published at the end of his 1854 book, *The People's Medical Lighthouse*, refer to his handing out advertisements as he traveled—a British couple stated that they tried his remedies after they "providentially" met him while journeying to Leicester. Root liked to leave circulars in such public places as hotel lobbies and railroad and steamship depots so that people could chance on them; one who did was an Albany, New York, bachelor who noted that he "accidentally saw Dr. Root's notice."[33]

Because increasing numbers of products, lectures, and services— especially those of a dubious nature—were publicized in this way, passersby were wary. By the time Dan Pinkham went to New York in the 1870s to distribute advertising flyers for his mother's product, "Lydia E. Pinkham's Vegetable Compound and Uterine Tonic," men, he said, would accept them but women were embarrassed and "if caught looking at one are apt to tear it up in front of the observer."[34]

Loose advertisements were common in books of the period, and notices were also printed on the inside covers of books or in the bottom margins on inside pages. Home medical manuals were the most obvious sources for birth control ads, especially those for women, as were books of advice about sex and marriage. Hollick advertised a "superior brand of condom" in his 1852 edition of *A Popular Treatise on Venereal Diseases*, but also in a somewhat less obvious place, his 1849 edition of *The Matron's Manual of Midwifery*. Almanacs, joke books, even cookbooks contained advertisements for contraceptives or abortion-inducing agents—advertisements inserted by the author, the publisher, or a bookseller, a druggist, or even a peddler.[35] As late as 1884 a Kansas City physician complained about druggists inserting abortion advertisements into almanacs and cookbooks distributed free to customers.[36]

Critics of family limitation deplored the increasing circulation of advertisements promoting reproductive control, especially appalled that householders received such information in the privacy of their homes. A Congregational minister, John Todd, was distressed that the names and addresses of newly married couples were so easily obtainable from public records and newspapers. In 1867 he wrote in *Serpents in the Dove's Nest*, "No young lady in New England (and probably in the

United States) can have a marriage announced in the papers without receiving in the mail within a week a printed circular offering information and instrumentalities and all needed facilities."[37]

An equally vociferous opponent, Hugh S. Pomeroy, complained in 1888 that even as he was writing a chapter of a book criticizing family limitation someone left an advertisement about controlling reproduction at his door.[38] In 1876, Nicholas Cooke complained in his sex education book *Satan in Society* of a similar incident: he was at work on the preface to the book when he received in the mail a printed circular for a "mechanical device to be worn by women as protection against conception." "The scoundrel who sends this circular ranks as a respectable druggist and boldly signs his name and address in full." Cooke is a good example of how even an opponent of birth control helped disseminate information about where to obtain it in the process of criticizing it. His own book was sold by "all newsdealers, booksellers and on all railway trains," thus affording a broader awareness about the availability of diaphragms at respectable drugstores than if he had kept quiet. The author of the particular advertisement for diaphragms which Cooke found so offensive sent it to physicians, hoping that they would then recommend it to their patients. Cooke believed that "more than one reputable doctor" had supplied "this invention of hell to his female patients."[39] By the 1880s even the staid Pinkham Company had begun to send advertisements directly to private homes to solicit customers. A testimonial letter purportedly written in 1883 by a satisfied woman customer stated, "As I sat in my house Mrs. Pinkham's pamphlet for married women was thrown into my house and I sat right down and read it."[40] The Pinkham Company never directly involved itself in dispersing birth control information, but it indirectly contributed to the flow of knowledge. Lydia E. Pinkham repeatedly sympathized with women worn out from frequent childbearing and advised women to delay pregnancies in order to build up their strength. She did not provide explicit advice about how, and she was decidedly unsympathetic toward abortion—the subjects treated in her publications "may attract the attention of a class of women who may perhaps expect to find here some hints which will aid them in violating the greatest of nature's laws, that of reproduction. *Such hints are not to be found here*" (her italics). Yet immediately after this warning, her text described things she believed would cause sterility in women, including "when the ovule is unhealthy . . . when the vitality of the egg is interfered with . . . when it is impossible for the semen to enter the womb and tubes."[41] Recipients of Pinkham advertisements were told that the Vegetable Compound was an emmenagogue; they were advised to use regularly vaginal douches, vaginal suppositories, vaginal sponges, and electricity for gynecological problems. Among the company's products were douching syringes, a douching solution called "Sanative Wash" (containing sodium salicylate) to be used every night. In spite of company protestations to the contrary, some ads were ambiguous. In the 1890s, for example, the company's "blood purifier" was said to remove stomach and uterine "tumors" in "an early stage of development"—a suggestion that may have carried abortion implications to many readers.[42]

Publishing for Profit or for Reform

From the 1840s on, there was a growing trade in the United States in what critics called "cheap and nasty" publications. Much of this trade consisted of mild erotica with such titles as *Wicked Nell: Girl of the Streets* or foreign imports of the bawdiest passages from Rabelais or Boccaccio. Many publications on reproductive control, though quite different in tone, content, and purpose, were published and distributed along with the sensationalist literature. The book business in real pornography was probably relatively small, but the trade in advice literature on sexual and reproductive control was large. Historians, surprisingly, have paid little attention to the production and distribution of this literature.[43]

Although reproductive control publishing became a significant part of the publishing business in the decades between 1850 and 1875, it was neither openly accepted nor respectable. The most reputable and well-established publishers of the nineteenth century, even those specializing in medical publishing, hesitated to associate themselves openly with any books about sex and reproductive control. Yet the lines between the respectable and the illicit were far from tightly drawn. The *New York Tribune* reported in 1857 that some respectable publishers were heavily involved in the trade in "obscene books and engravings" but that they used aliases. The converse was also true. Publishers of less licit works used as aliases the names of respectable firms. James Bryan, arrested in the early 1870s by Anthony Comstock, published under the name "Dutton & Co."—the name of a reputable printing establishment near his abortion clinic. When he was arrested he had on hand 25,000 pamphlets and three thousand books.[44]

Yet by the second half of the century, fewer people involved in the production and distribution of reproductive control literature felt it necessary to remain anonymous. Printers and publishers put their imprints on title pages. Some of these were pseudonyms, but many connected with birth control publishing in mid century have not proved to be completely elusive. Their names turned up in the voluminous credit-rating reports of the R. G. Dun Company, or their careers had a trajectory in the book world that makes it possible to trace them. Often obscure entrepreneurs printed, published, and distributed the contraceptive and abortifacient advice literature that began to be part of commercial America in the decades from 1850 until the clamp-down of the Comstock laws in the 1870s.[45]

Even in general publishing in the nineteenth century, publishers had functions similar to those of their counterparts today. That is, they functioned as entrepreneurs mediating between the author and the public by orchestrating the wholesale production of literature by contracting the services of printers, lithographers, stereotypers, and bookbinders who "manufactured" the final product from the author's handwritten manuscript, and by advertising and marketing the works they produced. Even some of the largest general publishers often contracted out the printing and binding. In marketing they also dealt with independent book jobbers, retail establishments (chiefly bookstores, stationers, and bookstands). Many hired agents to sell door-to-door. Increasingly, in mid century, publishers shared with the author the responsibility for mail-order sales. The words "publisher" and "bookseller" were often used interchangeably.

In the 1830s both Owen and Knowlton had assumed primary responsibility for getting their works printed, bound, and distributed. This "artisanal system" of publishing declined in general book publishing in the second quarter of the century but continued to be important in birth control publishing itself. A number of contraceptive advice pamphlets came from author-publishers in mid century, probably because the authors wrote from small midwestern and southern towns with access to the local printing press but without ties linking them to larger publishers in New York and Philadelphia or to the newer urban marketing strategies. Such were Dr. Daniel Winder (a possible pseudonymn), who issued *A Rational or Private Marriage Chart: For the Use of All Who Wish to Prevent an Increase of Family* from Mansfield, Ohio, in 1858, and J. W. Luse, B. C. Ross, and W. R. King, from Clyde, Ohio, Independence, Kansas, and Cullman, Alabama. Later in the century, when the Comstock laws made distributors of such advice criminally liable, many more birth control works were issued by author-publishers from out-of-the-way locales.[46]

Another common practice for publishing materials on reproductive control—and other highly specialized literature for a particular public—was subscription publishing, in which a work was published only when enough buyers had paid in advance.[47] It proved to be a safe and profitable strategy in all types of publishing in the second half of the century. John Cowan published his health reform and sexual advice books in the 1870s by subscription under the aegis of his small company.[48] Cowan's *Science of a New Life* criticized the best-known reproductive control methods of the day, but in so doing he provided ample information about what couples were doing to prevent births. Using hired agents to canvass for subscriptions, Cowan claimed to have sold some thirty thousand copies of *Science of a New Life* between 1869 and 1880.

Reformers, too, disseminated advice literature on reproductive control throughout the second half of the century. Water-cure physicians distributed the works of Thomas Low Nichols and Russell Thacher Trall; several editions of Trall's *Sexual Physiology* were published by his friends and colleagues in water cure under the imprint Wood, Holbrook and Co. (Allan E. Wood and Martin L. Holbrook, both active in sectarian medical movements).[49]

Although freethinkers were, generally, a dissident minority social voice in post–Civil War America, their contributions in the printing and distributing of contraceptive advice literature were significant. Some continued to attract special wrath because of their dual association with anticlericalism and reproductive control. DeRobigne Bennett, a leading publisher, was arrested several times between 1877 and 1879, charged with selling an obscene work, Ezra Heywood's anti-marriage tract, *Cupid's Yokes*. At least one case against him never came to trial, but at another he was convicted and sentenced to thirteen months in prison. Judge Samuel Blatchford's use of the British definition of obscenity at that trial, "whether the tendency of the matter charged as obscenity is to deprave and corrupt those whose minds are open to immoral influences, and into whose hands a publication of this sort may fall," became the basis of U.S. obscenity law for the next fifty years.[50] In 1878, Anthony Comstock, in his role as a special postal agent enforcing the obscenity laws, personally arrested and sought indictments against Bennett; he was offended as much by his free-thought views, openly expressed in his newspaper the *Truth Seeker*, as by his support of contraception.[51]

Asa K. Butts, an idealistic young n'er-do-well, published editions of Besant's *The Law of Population* in New York in 1878, 1879, and 1886, advertising it as "a scientific and medical work every way superior to the *Fruits of Philosophy*, or any of its kind. Adapted to the wants of the married poor and to the consideration of all mature persons."[52]

Butts, a personable young man but miserably lacking in business sense, was rated by credit reporters in the early 1870s as "a visionary" who should not be extended credit. In the 1860s he had worked in a small book business, Butts and Kennaday, but that was dissolved in 1868 and he went to work as a traveling agent selling patent medicines, dry goods, and carpets on commission. In the early 1870s he was hired to buy books for county libraries and to solicit book subscriptions. Throughout the 1870s, deeply involved also with selling stock of the Wakefield Earth Closet Company, he met a partner in that company, John P. Jewett, who happened also to be involved in publishing literature on reproductive control.[53]

Jewett had spent most of his life in the publishing business, but he found neither fame nor wealth even though he was the first publisher of *Uncle Tom's Cabin* and, shortly thereafter, of one of the novels of Maria Cummins, a bestselling novelist of the mid-nineteenth century. He published William Alcott's *The Physiology of Marriage* in Boston in 1855, but, in the depression of 1857, left publishing to become a vendor of watches and patent medicines and from 1871 to 1882 a partner in the Wakefield Earth Closet Company.[54] He returned to publishing in the mid 1870s, managing Edward Bliss Foote's Murray Hill Publishing Company; after Foote's trial and conviction in July 1876 for publishing birth control information, he lost his job.[55]

In the second half of the nineteenth century, for a number of earnest, hard-working, upwardly mobile young men the publishing and distributing of literature on reproductive control became a career. Some were financially successful. Some, not all, were considered respectable. Thomas W. Strong of New York City, who published many of Hollick's works between 1847 and 1868, found both considerable pecuniary success and social respectability. He was a publisher, engraver, printer, stationer, and dealer in miscellaneous goods (including contraceptives). Strong took responsibility for the books' engravings and also marketed the books, at his own retail store at 98 Nassau Street in the heart of the print and pictorial trade in Manhattan, through the mails, and through retail booksellers such as G. W. Cottrell in Boston.[56]

Strong began his career as a clerk, and in the 1840s, in his twenties, he made enough of a profit selling valentines (in an era when valentines were often ribald as well as sentimental) to buy a printing and lithographic press. He began to specialize in inexpensive paperbound literature, particularly advice guides on sexuality, marriage, and reproductive control, and he opened a store to sell it along with other cheap books, stationery, engravings, and "notions," which included condoms, douching preparations, cures for venereal disease, aphrodisiacs, and possibly contraceptive pessaries. Many booksellers and stationers sold such wares in the mid-nineteenth century, especially those whose print specialties were gynecological, obstetrical, marital, and sexual advice. B. Leverett Emerson, for example, the Boston publisher of Russell Thacher Trall's *Pathology of the Reproductive Organs* (1862), was the "general agent for the United States" for Davidson's Patent Syringe, which he sold along with other goods at his Washington Street, Boston, store.[57]

Strong and Hollick met and formed a close business relationship. Both were in their early thirties in 1850, a year in which both were benefiting economically from the popularity of Hollick's *The Marriage Guide*. Both had made several career changes in their twenties, but by mid century both were married with growing families; their specialization in birth control advice brought them some financial security. Hollick's medical office was at 599 Broadway, a building owned by Strong, where Strong housed his press and bookstore.[58] Over the years, their relationship deepened, and notices in several of Hollick's books informed readers that they could contact him through Strong.

Publishing of all types was a precarious field at best, with little career stability and often few financial rewards, especially for those involved with birth control publishing. Hiram Rulison, publisher of an 1856 edition of Harmon Knox Root's *The People's Medical Lighthouse* in Cincinnati, had earlier made a modest living peddling books. Rulison saved enough capital to found the Queen City Publishing House, a pioneering independent subscription publishing venture in Cincinnati. Credit-rating reporters noted in 1856 that Rulison had made quite a bit of money selling one or two works; one of which was almost certainly Root's 472-page compendium of medical advice with its belabored discussions of reproductive control and sexual physiology. The Cincinnati public bought enough copies to give Rulison a small measure of financial success, but at the same time disapproved of it loudly enough for credit investigators to note that although Rulison was "hard-working and honestly disposed," his establishment in Cincinnati was "tainted" by his reputation for publishing "obscene works."[59]

In the Panic of 1857, Rulison nearly went bankrupt and was bailed out by his brother, Duane Rulison, who sold similar types of medical advice books, gift books, and jewelry in Philadelphia. He lasted, precariously, in business in Cincinnati until 1861, when he failed and disappeared from the historical records. His brother, however, continued in the Philadelphia book business for twenty-one years. One of his publications was the 1859 edition of Edward Bliss Foote's *Medical*

Common Sense. Credit reporters noted that he "lost heavily" in the South during the Civil War and afterward struggled along with a very small book business until his death in 1882. He was never again judged worthy of credit.[60]

Several advice books on reproductive control were published through a "correspondence system" that flourished from the colonial era through the century. Under this system books were published simultaneously by various publishers in various places, each publisher assuming responsibility for a particular, relatively local market.[61] This system was effective until the railroad revolution in transportation made it possible to ship bulky and heavy objects profitably long distances. Some authors themselves found the booksellers in each location. In other cities publishers or booksellers passed the works on to friends, relatives, or colleagues in the book business in another area. The correspondence system was particularly well suited to birth control publishing for it allowed books to be published by relatively small entrepreneurs, at the same time assuring a wide distribution like that larger commercial ventures were beginning to provide. Thomas W. Strong utilized the correspondence system to get Hollick's works published in Boston by G. W. Cottrell, a young man Strong helped get started in publishing. Cottrell left New York for Boston in 1850, supplied with goods from Strong—including Hollick's *The Marriage Guide.* Credit reporters noted that Cottrell sold "light trash" and that he had "a peculiar trade with [a] provincial business which is profitable." He sold very heavily in the villages and rural areas outside of Boston.[62]

The tenth edition of Root's *The People's Medical Lighthouse* was published in 1854 by the correspondence system. Hiram Rulison had the Cincinnati and Mississippi Valley markets, while Adolphus Ranney published the work in New York. Root probably found his New York publisher by simple proximity, since his office at the time was at 512 Broadway, while Ranney worked out of 195 Broadway selling books, maps, charts, and prints. Ranney, in fact, may have had a minor speciality in popular medical works dealing with women's diseases, sex, and reproductive control, for in 1857, after obtaining the copyright two years earlier, he published Edward Dixon's *Woman and Her Diseases* . . . with the "Appendix on the Propriety of Limiting the Increase of Family" defending the right of people to learn about reproductive control.[63]

In the decades of its greatest commercial expansion, reproductive control literature was distributed in retail establishments, by mail order (discussed in the next chapter), and by agents hired by publishers or acting on their own as independent middlemen. Agents, both male and female, were an important part of the distribution process in all types of publishing operations, from self-publishing and subscription houses to the well-established publishing companies. Agents sometimes worked on commission for the publisher, but just as often they operated as independent jobbers, buying batches of books to sell for their own profit or loss. Male agents peddled copies of Marcus L. Byrn's *The Physiology of Marriage and Philosophy of Generation* door-to-door and at railway stations in New York in the early 1860s.

As agents became a force in the book business, the pattern of dissemination of literature in the United States shifted from the concentric rings emanating from the central cities of the eastern seaboard to a dispersal path that followed the railroad lines. This process brought an even greater access to areas outside the eastern cities while at the same time bringing New York into dominance in the literary market.[64] Agents were an especially important channel for the distribution of literature on reproductive control and other controversies. They could reassure nervous bookstore proprietors and individual customers at their own doorsteps that a work was useful and respectable. The publishers Segner and Condit in Iowa explained in an 1880 preface to John H. Kellogg's sexual advice book *Plain Facts for Old and Young* that they relied on agents because agents used discretion in selecting customers and ensured a "judicious circulation."[65] Some publishers enticed agents with explanations that a book with birth control information would sell well. Asa K. Butts advertised his edition of Besant's *The Law of Population* in 1880 with the promise:

> Agents are informed that the best thing to sell and make money on and also to benefit mankind is this book. It explains and advocates the only harmless and practical means of avoiding the evils of celibacy on the one hand and of overburdened parentage on the other. . . . It contains the latest medical researches and results of science. The medical directions are easy, plain, explicit through chaste and delicate. No married couple should be without it.[66]

If books had a specific identifiable audience, publishers hired special agents. Clergymen were good agents for religious books, women for health advice books, especially books for women on reproduction, marital relations, child rearing, and birth control. Rachel B. Gleason recognized this opportunity when in 1870 she advertised for "Lady agents of good moral character" to sell her book *Talks to My Patients*. Female customers liked to buy goods from women agents. The La

Perle Rubber Company sent advertisements to farm journals soliciting female agents to sell douching syringes. Some of the birth control literature was sold by agents who also sold douches and other products. The anonymously authored advice pamphlet *Reproductive Control* was sold in Cincinnati in 1856 by paid agents who also carried vaginal syringes for contraceptive douches, the chief method the pamphlet recommended.[67]

Circulation—A Wide Outreach

The advice literature on reproductive control circulated in large numbers in the middle decades of the century. Some titles would have qualified as "bestsellers," meaning they had sales reaching 225,000 in the 1850s, 300,000 in the 1860s, 375,000 in the 1870s, 500,000 in the 1880s, and 625,000 in the 1890s.[68] Hollick's *Matron's Manual of Midwifery* went through one hundred editions from 1840 to 1853, while his *The Origin of Life* had ten stereotyped editions in its first year, 1845–1846; his *Diseases of Woman* saw fifty-three editions between 1847 and 1855; and *The Marriage Guide*, two hundred editions from 1850 to 1860, an additional hundred from 1860 to 1877, and two hundred more in the six years after 1877. James Ashton's *The Book of Nature* saw at least four editions, all put out in New York between 1860 and 1870, but it probably had a far greater circulation than this figure suggests because the copyright holder in 1859 was Benjamin H. Day, one of the pioneers of the penny press in the United States. Ashton's booklet was published in 1865 and 1870 from the office of "Brother Jonathan," one of the "mammoth papers" of the mid century—as Frank Luther Mott describes it—a sensationalist, "spicy," weekly newpaper that had a circulation of ten to thirty thousand a week. *The Book of Nature*, therefore, probably had a wide circulation indeed, one that included New York City's laboring women and men.[69]

Other titles also sold well, although the lack of information about edition sizes makes it difficult to judge how many copies were actually in circulation in given periods. Edition sizes were not standardized and could vary greatly, although by mid century it would not have been unusual for a typeset edition of a title on birth control to have at least two thousand, and more probably three to five thousand, copies, and a stereotype edition to have at least ten thousand.[70] Soule's *Science of Reproduction* had a larger circulation than its one edition suggests because it circulated in 1856 in a stereotyped edition simultaneously in New York and Cincinnati. The decade of the 1850s saw rising sales: Larmont's *Medical Adviser and Marriage Guide* had thirty editions from 1854 to 1859 and then another fifty from 1859 to 1864; Root's *The People's Medical Lighthouse* saw four editions from 1852 to 1856; Nichols's *Esoteric Anthropology* had seven editions from 1853 to 1862, and Dunne's *The Young Married Lady's Private Medical Guide* went through four editions in one year from 1853 to 1854. Twenty-five thousand copies of Alcott's *The Physiology of Marriage* were sold by 1860 after its appearance in 1855. The Civil War reduced both publishing and book sales, but several reproductive control works sold well in the late 1860s and early 1870s. Trall's *Sexual Physiology* saw four editions in its first year from 1866 to 1867, then another twenty-three editions before 1877. After Ezra Heywood was sentenced to two years at hard labor for sending it through the mails, booksellers grew wary of handling the book and only one edition was published between 1877 and 1881, although editions were issued later, in 1885, 1895, and 1901. A blurb on the title page of Foote's *Plain Home Talk* in 1887 claimed sales over 500,000, although in a letter to Elizur Wright that same year Foote noted that the book, now out of print, had sold 250,000 copies.[71] The works of George Napheys were especially popular in the 1870s. His *The Physical Life of Woman* saw at least seventeen editions from 1869 to 1890, selling fifty thousand copies its first year, ninety thousand its first three years. It was republished in "new stereotype" editions in 1873 and 1876, and in spite of Napheys's suicide in 1877, his publisher successfully issued further editions in 1878, 1887, 1890, and 1927.

Books, pamphlets, tracts, and booklets ranging from a dozen pages to several hundred, some solely text and others with dozens of engravings or elaborate colored and fold-out illustrations, circulated in the mid nineteenth century. Their effect, however, is less easy to judge. For when we come to a crucial assessment—what impact did this literature have—we reach the limits of historical reconstruction. We have long since learned to beware of assuming that readers followed the advice they received in prescriptive or proscriptive literature. What readers learned from the literature on reproductive control which circulated in such growing numbers and variety, therefore, remains problematic and debatable. Yet a few pieces of evidence are available. Fourteen of the women who answered Dr. Clelia Mosher's questionnaire about their sexual and birth control practices responded to her question "What knowledge of sexual physiology did you have before marriage and how was it obtained?" by citing books. Eight listed specific titles: three women, all born in the 1860s, had read

Alice Stockham's *Tokology* in their twenties; two others had read George Napheys's *The Physical Life of Woman*; two cited John Cowan's *The Science of a New Life*, and one mentioned Russell Trall. They were clearly not always persuaded by what their authors said about contraceptive methods. One woman, born in 1862, who "learned everything I know from good sources and in a good and sacred way," read Cowan's *The Science of a New Life*, Napheys's *The Physical Life of Woman*, and "the best pages of Fowler." Although Cowan disparaged withdrawal as "beastly, and not one iota different in its effects on the mind and body of the man, from self-abuse," and Napheys, too, was critical, withdrawal is what she and her husband had used for birth control in their seven years of marriage.[72] Another woman, born in 1889, learned about sex from her mother and from Cowan's *The Science of a New Life*.[73] She had two children, the first because she was "allured to take a chance," and the second intentionally. She did not believe, as Cowan argued, that she should have intercourse only for reproduction. Nor did she follow his recommendation to avoid douching as unreliable and harmful to a woman's health, for she used a "pastile suppository of cocoa butter" and "alum and a cold water douche." Readers had to make their own judgments, based on already existing values and ideas, but pushed, too, toward independent judgments by the sheer number of works, by new looks of these works, by the diverse channels and people from whom the literature could be obtained, by the very lack of consensus in the advice, by the hostility of the opponents, and by the warmth of the proponents.

7

The "Most Fashionable"
Contraceptive Devices

As reproductive control moved into the public arena, the proliferation of products and growing commercial emphasis on contraceptive
devices helped to depersonalize what had traditionally been intensely,
even embarrassingly, personal and private. There was an abundance
of choices. In 1888 an obscure physician, Dr. David E. Matteson,
reported from the small town of Warsaw, New York, that the three
most "fashionable" methods were the "use of the syringe in some form
or other," "conjugal onanism," and the condom or "veils"—a slight
variation from Mosher's later California study discussed in Chapter 2.
Edward Bond Foote wrote in his 1886 booklet, "Certainly it is that a
very large amount of knowledge as to the physiology of conception and
the means of prevention is already abroad among the people, and the
general complaint is not a lack of knowing some way, but a desire to
know which way is least objectionable." F. Wallace Abbott, an M.D.
in Taunton, Massachusetts, even read his paper "Limitation of the
Family" at the annual meeting of the Massachusetts Medical Society
in 1890, reporting that the most common means of prevention for men
were "premature withdrawal," the condom, and "male continence";
the most common for women were injections of water or medicated
fluids, mechanical devices, and spermicidal injections. A favorite of
couples, he reported, was "abstention except during the safe period."[1]

The anonymous author of "The Fashionable Crime," in 1880, advised gynecologists to question their female patients about their reliance on "every damnable practice that can be imagined to subvert
the natural result of married life." Doctors should ask: "Has the natural process been shortened and the 'seed cast on the ground?' Has she
been accustomed to spring from her couch and douse the engorged

uterus and vagina with cold water? Has she rejected her spouse until within a short period of her menstrual period and then submitted to his approaches when she had not sexual desire? Has she dosed with remedies calculated to do violence to the uterine tissues?"[2] Augustus K. Gardner, a well-known gynecologist and a vociferous critic of family limitation, listed principal "precautionary measures against conception," all in Latin, possibly hoping to keep the information from falling into the wrong hands: "coitus imperfectii, tegumenta extaria, ablutiones gelidae, infusiones astringentes" (withdrawal, condoms, and douches).[3]

Products for reproductive control were widely available from reputable entrepreneurs, but some methods—condoms, for example— never reached wide respectability. Finally, none of the devices was strictly a new invention, especially in Europe, where condoms had been associated with prostitution for centuries and with family limitation since the early nineteenth century. In the United States, however, condoms, douches, vaginal pessaries, and spermicidal preparations all appeared to be novel, given their new packaging and promotion.

Contraceptive Devices for Men: "French Male Safes," "Fish Skin Condoms"

Protective sheaths to cover the penis during intercourse had been used in Europe as prophylactics against venereal diseases at least since the seventeenth century, but chiefly by men frequenting prostitutes. Still, by the early eighteenth century, they appear to have been used also as contraceptives by men of the upper classes of England and France.[4] By the end of the eighteenth century, entrepreneurs were producing and advertising their wares by handbills to working class men in London.[5] In the American colonies men may have used condoms—some may have been imported—but there is no historical record that they were in use here. Possibly colonists fashioned their own for personal use. After all, farmers were butchering animals to eat and it may have occurred to some that those same membranes could be made into condoms—their use in France and England could have been no secret. At least one advice book, published in 1844, *The United States Practical Receipt Book; or, Complete Book of Reference*, provided detailed instructions for making condoms from the caecum of a sheep; such a recipe could have evolved from homemade condoms used in an earlier century.[6]

By the early nineteenth century, newspapers and circulars were occasionally carrying advertisements for condoms, usually for protection against syphilis. In 1819, for example, an advertisement appeared in the *Boston Patriot & Mercantile Advertiser*, placed by the Boston Infirmary, offering to mail condoms anywhere in the country as a preventive against syphilis. Captains of seagoing vessels stocked condoms for the health of their sailors. In 1840 a notice in the *Boston Daily Times* urged seamen, travelers, "and all others who wish to avoid exposure to consult Dr. Dow for his preventative of all private diseases."[7]

In America in the nineteenth century the growing availability of condoms and their use within respectable marriage chambers distressed those who refused to sanction reproductive control. Condoms had been associated only with the brothel, and many saw their use within marriage as defiling the marriage bed. J. H. Kellogg wrote in his *Plain Facts for Old and Young* even as late as 1880 that condoms, like douching, were "crimes against nature similar to pederasty and sodomy."[8] As important as condoms were quickly to become in family limitation, they never quite lost their disreputability. They remained tainted by the old association with prostitution and venereal diseases and disreputable because they were so often sold in shops that also carried pornography and erotica in the seamier areas of American cities. Yet lack of respectability ceased to be sufficient cause to stop their use. By the latter decades of the century questions of effectiveness, reliability, healthfulness, availability, and cost became more important. Condoms were increasingly being used as a means of family limitation: eight of the forty-five women who filled out the Mosher questionnaire between 1890 and 1920 reported that their husbands had used condoms as part of a means of preventing pregnancy.[9] Mary Hallock Foote, who lived in Idaho, wrote a letter in 1878 to a friend in New York City to thank her for advice about childbirth (Foote was pregnant—"the evil day that is coming") and to tell her how she and her husband planned to avoid another pregnancy soon after this one:

> I spoke to you about the advice Mrs. Hague gave me about the future. Of course I know nothing about it practically and it sounds dreadful—but every way is dreadful except the one which it seems cannot be relied on. . . . Mrs. H. said Arthur must go to a physician and get shields of some kind. They are to be had also at some druggists. It sounds perfectly revolting, but one must face anything rather than the inevitable result of Nature's methods. At all events there is nothing injurious about this. Mrs. Hague is a very fastidious woman and I hardly think she would submit to anything very bad. . . . These things are called "cundums" and are made either of rubber or skin—They are to be had at first-class druggists.[10]

By the 1850s condoms could be purchased in several styles and materials. They were known by many names, explicit or euphemistic: "safes," "French Male Safes," "badruches," "baudruches," "the French secret," "the English letter," "cundums," "cundrums," "capotes," "caps," "capotines," "rubbers," "gentlemen's protectors," "skins," "membraneous envelopes," "apex envelopes," and "fibrous envelopes"—the nomenclature was much more diverse for these devices than for any other contraceptive device. Condom names differed by country too. In England in the late nineteenth century they were known as "English overcoats," and "English armour"—two terms not common in the United States. They were available in two basic styles: full-length sheaths and small "caps" that covered only the glans penis. Some "caps" had self-adjusting rings that clamped the open end firmly at the tip of the penis. Caps needed to fit tightly if they were to work. By some nineteenth-century accounts, caps were more popular than full-length condoms, in part because they seemed to permit men greater sexual pleasure. Most important in terms of effectiveness of all condoms and caps was the material they were made from. It was not enough, however, for the device to be well made; the consumer alone could determine effectiveness by regular and careful use.

The cheapest and easiest way to manufacture condoms was from the process of animal membranes. The very crudest, made from unprocessed skins sewn or pasted together to form a sheath, were notoriously unreliable and unaesthetic. An advertising pamphlet for contraceptives in the late 1860s warned that, although such condoms were economical to begin with and although they never wore out, they were liable to be "too heavy to suit a man of nervous temperament."[11] A far superior product was produced by a lengthy and relatively expensive process in which animal intestines were soaked in solutions of lye and acids, stretched and dried, then soaked again. The repetitive process made the skins thin and pliant, delicate yet strong. Made this way, they may have equaled the quality of condoms discovered in 1953 in an English country manor: a packet of condoms manufactured between 1790 and 1810 in Europe from sheeps' intestines and packaged in various sizes and extraordinarily thin, with a texture so fine yet strong that attempts to duplicate the condoms with mid-twentieth-century techniques proved unsuccessful.[12] In 1839 a French work translated into English, Jean Dubois's *Marriage Physiologically Discussed*, recommended the "kundum" as the safest, speediest, least troublesome of all contraceptives. The author explained that it was a "little bag, made of fine prepared silk or bladder and fastened at the head of the penis during the act of copulation."[13] In *Physiological Mysteries*, Eugene Becklard in 1842 recommended as a contraceptive "an oiled silk covering worn by males and sold at most of the [Parisian] toy shops."[14]

The finest of the early condoms were known as goldbeaters' skins, after the ancient art of beating gold into foil or gold leaf, in which animal membranes, taken usually from the external coat of the caecum of cattle, were carefully processed to elasticity. The most famous reference in literary sources to goldbeaters' skins is the scathing comment by Madame de Sévigné in 1671. Writing to warn her daughter against another pregnancy and to advise her on contraception, she called sheaths made of goldbeaters' skins "armor against enjoyment and a spider web against danger."[15] In the nineteenth century these carefully prepared skins were used not only in gold beating but also to stop wounds and to seal perfume bottles. The importation of these processed animal skins into the United States in the second half of the nineteenth century dramatically increased; the only explanation could be their growing use as condoms. There was no separate listing of goldbeaters' skins on import lists until 1868, but in that year $14,741 worth of skins and also molds for their manufacture were imported into the United States. Because items imported in small quantities were not enumerated separately in the lists, the special category given to skins signifies a rise in the number brought in. Also the duty on skins was abolished in 1873, and $36,042 worth were imported. In 1879 only $11,126 in skins came in, but by 1883 the value was up again sharply to $35,979. The Comstock laws that forbade the importation of contraceptives were never enforced against goldbeater's skins or their molds, so that throughout the decades when the laws against reproductive control were most stringently enforced a constant supply of materials ready to be turned into condoms was available.[16] Still, Augustus K. Gardner, in his 1874 book, *Conjugal Sins*, specifically singled out "intermediate tegumentary coverings made of thin rubber or goldbeater's skins, and so often relied upon as absolute preventives" as ineffective, causing lesions, and suggestive of "the brothel."[17]

Most of the druggists who listed condoms at all in their catalogues, as only a few did, offered several varieties, distinguishing "goldbeaters' skins" from "caps," "capotes," and simply, "skins." John H. Nelson's *The Druggists' Cost Book* in 1879—an order book of common druggists'supplies with blank lines left in which individual druggists could write in their choice of brands—allowed eleven lines for "capotes", three for various brands of goldbeaters' skins, three for rubber capotes, two for rubber caps, and two lines for the individual druggist's own types.[18] Entrepreneurs fashioned high quality condoms from delicate fabrics such as silk. They were cut, sewn, oiled, and then packaged. The anonymous *Reproductive Control; or, A Rational Guide to Matrimonial Happiness* noted in 1855 that of the "Preventives in Use; Objections to Them" were coverings of oiled silk "or some other thin, water-proof substance drawn over the male organ during the act of coition."[19] Some nineteenth-century condom entrepreneurs said that their condoms were made from fish membranes, and, as early as 1788, a German physician—author of books on syphilis—described condoms made of fish membranes used to prevent conception, as well as a protection against syphilis; he reported that they were sold openly in London, Paris, Berlin, and St. Petersburg.[20] Despite this history, Edward Bliss Foote claimed that a "membraneous envelope" he was marketing was a new type of condom, made from the membrane of a Rhine fish and superior to those made of animal intestines because it was "flexible, and silky in texture, and a perfect conductor of electricity and magnetism, being entirely free from fatty matter. In consequence . . . its use does not in the least interfere with the pleasure of the act while its susceptibility to electrical influences renders its use entirely *harmless*. It is also more reliable because *stronger*."[21] Fish condoms were apparently still available at the turn of the century; in her contraceptive advice pamphlet *A Talk with Mothers*, the feminist physician Anna Blount recommended "fish skin condoms" as much superior to rubber ones.[22]

In the middle of the century condoms made of rubber—cheaper and simpler to make than those of skin—began to be manufactured on a sufficiently large scale to drive down prices and to stimulate new demand. Other products made of India rubber, or "caoutchouc," had been available in the United States since the 1820s after the Englishman Charles MacKintosh discovered that waterproof garments could be created by sandwiching between two fabrics a layer of rubber dissolved in coal naptha. Using this process, English and American manufacturers produced waterproof clothing and also mattresses, carriage tires, and boots. All these products, however, became sticky or even melted in warm weather and impossibly brittle in cold weather. Then, between 1839 and 1844, a Massachusetts inventor named Charles Goodyear, experimenting with ways to make rubber impervious to temperature changes and to keep it permanently flexible yet firm, elastic, and resilient, invented "vulcanization." The new process involved heating a mixture of rubber, white lead, and sulphur to a specific high temperature and then cooling it. Goodyear quickly patented his invention and sold licenses to selected manufacturers to produce articles of vulcanized caoutchouc.[23] Even more important for the manufacture of thin, delicate rubber contraceptives was the invention of a cold vulcanization process by a British chemist, Alexander Parkes, in 1846.[24] Even though these processes greatly improved rubber products, they did not guarantee consistently superior results. Individual manufacturers of rubber condoms, especially, insufficiently trained or working too quickly and overly concerned with secrecy and profits, were often indifferent about quality.

Although rubber douching syringes and rubber diaphragms were available from retail and wholesale outlets by the 1840s, rubber condoms were on sale only in the 1850s. In his "Notes by the Publisher," as noted earlier, Gilbert Vale reported enthusiastically in 1858 on "a new article, called 'The French Safe,' made of India rubber and gutta percha. . . . It is more durable and less expensive [than other condoms]."[25] The quality of the earliest rubber condoms, even those made from vulcanized rubber, was unpredictable. Rubber was weak in spots and broke easily; some condoms offered no real protection because they were so poorly made that they had visible holes. Also, they were thicker than skin condoms and dulled a man's sensation of sexual pleasure. James Ashton, in 1861, noted that "penis coverings" available included those "beautifully made from preparations of india-rubber." He praised them as effective but admitted that because they lessened a man's sexual pleasure they were not very popular.[26] The only advantage of the early rubber condoms was their price: rubber capotes cost one-half what the finest goldbeaters' skins cost.

The price of condoms dropped steadily. In the 1830s, when most were imported from Europe, costs went as high as one dollar a condom, a price that kept them from all but the very rich; but by 1847 even condoms imported from Paris cost only five dollars a dozen.[27] By mid century, prices dropped sufficiently that the middle class could buy them quite easily; in the 1850s and 1860s condoms were three to six dollars a dozen.[28] A pamphlet of advertisements for items in the "oldest drug house on Broadway" listed "French condoms or Male Safes" for six dollars a dozen, sent through the mail.[29] Many workers would still have been hard-pressed to afford any, but by the 1870s wholesale druggists were selling rubber, skin, and imported condoms at six to sixteen cents each, and in retail outlets or from peddlers they were one to four dollars a dozen. The Chicago druggist W. A. Week & Co. carried nine types of capotes for one to two dollars a dozen in 1872.[30] Customers expected to reuse their product; in advertisements for his brand of "Male Safes," Harmon Knox Root quoted satisfied customers who lauded the durability and thinness of his condoms, making it clear that they were reusable.[31]

Unlike the objections that critics leveled against other types of birth control, very few such objections were raised about the harm condoms might do.[32] Root went farther than most, writing in his 1854 *The People's Medical Lighthouse* that the "French Male Safe" was "an invaluable and indispensable assistant in the maintenance of health": "The gentleman should use it," he said, "in all cases where the wife is laboring under poisonous mucus discharges from the uterus, or ovaries, produced by cancers, ulcerated tumors, venereal or leucorrheal poisons, or menstruation."[33]

Root also argued that condoms should be worn if either man or woman was intoxicated at the time of intercourse, if women were still nursing an infant and did not want to be forced to wean it by another pregnancy, or if men had diseases of the genitalia. Even in the late nineteenth century, when the ranks of the American Medical Association began to close against contraception as a consequence of their campaign against abortion and when the health dangers of many methods came under review, few doctors considered condoms medically harmful.[34]

Condoms offered enormous scope for individual variation in responses to their use. Some men criticized them for interfering with sexual pleasure. Hollick, who advertised condoms in *The Marriage Guide* for nine dollars a package, "which will last a long time," nevertheless in a chapter called "The Prevention of Conception" disparaged condoms as not giving "gratification" to men or women and as turning intercourse into an experience "like masturbation."[35] Besant disliked condoms, too, describing them in her 1878 book, *The Law of Population*, as critics had much earlier, as a "covering used by men of loose character as a guard against syphilitic diseases." She said that they were distasteful as a matter of both "taste and feeling." Nevertheless, in an 1889 edition (probably unauthorized) of her book put out in New York, Henry Sumner, the publisher, added five paragraphs to her text, recommending three "reliable checks," the first of which was "Patent Circular Protectors," a "very thin sheath to be worn by the husband," which did not interfere "with the natural pleasure of the husband or wife [and] it is warranted not to break, or to become unfit for use in any climate." It caused no health problems, especially no irritation of the vagina as douching did. "The sale of them is now enormous both in America and Europe," Sumner said, "it being generally recommended by the medical profession in all cases where it is dangerous for a wife to conceive on account of the state of her health."[36] The "protectors" could be bought for $1.25 a dozen from agents Sumner named in Brooklyn.

Contraceptive Devices for Women: The "Womb Veil," "French Shield for Women," "Wife's Protector"

In 1885, Rose Williams wrote from the Dakota Territory to answer a question put to her by an Ohio friend, Allettie Mosher: how to prevent pregnancy.

> You want to know of a sure prevenative [*sic*]. Well plague take it. The best way is for you to sleep in one bed and your Man in another & bet you will laugh and say "You goose you think I am going to do that" no and I bet you would for I don't see any one that does. Well now the thing we [use] (when I say *we* I mean us girls) is a thing: but it hasn't always been *sure* as you know but that was our own carelessness for it is we have been sure. I do not know whether you can get them out there. They are called Pessairre [*sic*] or female prevenative if you don't want to ask for a "pisser" just ask for a female prevenative. They cost one collar when Sis got hers it was before any of us went to Dak. She paid five dollars for it. The Directions are with it.[37]

Several things are noteworthy about this letter: the jocularity with which Rose Williams described the contraceptive diaphragm, her sarcasm about sexual abstinence as a contraceptive method, the—one assumes—ready availability of the pessary even in the wilds of Dakota. Yet this last should not be startling, for the most significant part of the commercial explosion in reproductive control products involved the variety of devices for women.

Vaginal contraceptive devices had been known and used since antiquity, but were never publicized in America until the 1840s. The contraceptive sponge was one of the first methods for women recommended in printed advice tracts, mentioned as early as 1797 by Jeremy Bentham as a means of lowering birth rates among the poor in England and by the English reformer Richard Carlile in his 1826 *Every Woman's Book; or, What Is Love? Containing Most Important Instructions for the Prudent Regulation of the Principle of Love and the Number of the Family.* Copies of Carlile's book, which, after women's use of the sponge, recommended the use of the "baudruche or 'glove'" and partial or complete withdrawal, circulated quietly in the United States in the late 1820s. Although there were rumors of an edition coming from the press at New Harmony in 1828, no American edition appears to have been published.

In the 1840s, for the first time, the vaginal sponge became an important contraceptive method for women, increasingly accessible and, because of new knowledge about spermicides, increasingly reliable. The anonymous author of *Reproductive Control*, who rated the vaginal sponge as one of the era's most common contraceptive methods, said that he disliked most methods—except douching—but the sponge most of all: "[It] is in itself so repulsive that I merely mention it as a matter of curiosity and to illustrate the strength of the desire among females to control, by some means, their reproductive faculties." Women placed a sponge in the vagina before intercourse "for the purpose of absorbing the male fluid." After intercourse it was withdrawn "by means of a small cord and after being washed, the operation is repeated until it is supposed the fluid is all absorbed." The author reported that it was not only repulsive but also irritated women's "tender organs" and "renders sex less enjoyable to both men and women."[38]

In the literature on reproductive control and sexual physiology published in America through the century, opinions on the contraceptive sponge ranged widely. Owen changed his mind about its effectiveness. Knowlton, who gave detailed directions (use a "fine sponge," spherical, never less than 1 3/4 inches in diameter, moistened with chloride of soda, withdrawn immediately after intercourse by a narrow ribbon) still criticized the sponge as occasionally unreliable, especially if moistened only with water, which "does not act chemically to destroy the fecundating property of semen."[39] The English translations of Becklard's *Physiological Mysteries* and Dubois's *Marriage Physiologically Discussed*, both popular in the 1840s, recommended it without much further comment (a small sponge about 1 1/4 inches in diameter, soaked in water); but other advisers tended to denigrate it.[40] Hollick merely cited the sponge as a well-known family-limitation method of dubious reliability.[41] Besant lavished the most praise, recommending the sponge above all other methods in *The Law of Population*: "The check which appears to us preferable, as at once certain and in no sense grating on any feeling of affection or of delicacy, is that recommended by Carlile many years ago in his *Every Woman's Book*." Besant favored the sponge method because it gave women responsibility and because it was "unobtrusive."[42]

Contraceptive vaginal sponges became increasingly available commercially by mid century. James Ashton protested in the 1860s that "quacks" charged five dollars for contraceptive sponges with silk threads attached when all women needed to do was go to a nearby druggist, buy a sponge "about the size of a walnut," twist together silk threads to make a fine string, wet it in a weak solution of sulphate of iron, and "before connection" insert the sponge "far up into your person": "You can place it entirely out of the way by the use of a smooth stick of the proper size and shape. The string will hang out but will be no obstacle." After intercourse, "you withdraw the sponge and if you have a syringe, use that also."[43] Druggists sold vaginal sponges in a variety of styles and sizes; New York druggists in 1872 offered twenty-nine styles of "Mediterranean toilet sponges," from large to very small. Their "finest, very small Ladies' toilet sponges" sold from twelve to twenty-one cents each in wholesale lots. A Chicago druggist in 1872 offered fifteen types of sponges including six styles of "sponge balls" from 1 1/8 to 2 7/8 inches in diameter.[44]

Physicians who encouraged their patients to use vaginal devices also taught them to insert and remove sponges, tampons, and pessaries and to use vaginal drugs as suppositories and douches. Although many physicians opposed their use for contraceptive purposes, some of their patients may have put their doctors' lessons to work for purposes their doctors would have frowned on. A Tuscaloosa, Alabama, physician noted in 1838 that in his nineteen years in medical practice in that city he had taught more than two hundred women how to insert and remove "sponge pessaries" and how to apply astringent medicines to the pessaries before use. He said that most of the practicing physicians he knew did recommend pessaries and taught their patients how to use them. Gynecologist J. Marion Sims sometimes prescribed "a small wad of cotton not more than an inch in diameter . . . secured with a string for its removal." He believed that a woman using pessaries should be able to "remove and replace it with the same facility that she would put on and pull off an old slipper."[45]

Lydia E. Pinkham, famous for her "Vegetable Compound and Uterine Tonic," gave just such advice on the use of vaginal devices and medications to her women customers. She urged them not only in published pamphlets and advertising circulars but in the letters she wrote in reply to women who had asked for her help. To an Ohio woman who complained of "hemorrhaging every twenty-three days" (which sounds like a short menstrual cycle) Pinkham advised: "Take daily injections of warm water and wear a small sponge pressed as far up the vaginal passage as can be comfortable. Moisten the sponge frequently with a solution of carbolic acid, 1/2 oz. tannic acid 2 drams, glycerin 4 oz., water 4 oz. or 8 Tbsp. Take the [Vegetable] Compound according to directions and let the doctors alone."[46] The company's advertising campaign urged women to write to Pinkham and promised them complete anonymity. The letters from customers, if any ever came in, were not donated as part of the Pinkham collection when it was given to the Schlesinger Library.

Many of the commercial sponges were already saturated with chemicals, some of which were spermicides. In 1899 the H. K. Mulford Company of Philadelphia sold ten types of "antiseptic vaginal tampons" one-half to one inch by 2 1/8 or 2 3/4 inches in size, made of wool "packed in gelatin capsules" of boric acid, tannic acid, or alum, as well as other less spermicidal ingredients. The Mulford Company headquarters did a retail trade in many states and had stores also in New York, Chicago, Boston, and Dallas.[47] Women could also get contraceptive sponges through the mails, both from druggists and from sales agents. The 1889 edition of Besant's *The Law of Population* included advice about buying saturated "Antiseptic Sponges." They were sold in New York and by mail for twenty-five cents a box; for an additional fifty cents customers could purchase a box of twelve spermicidal powders for use in soaking the sponges.[48]

Medical journal articles occasionally explained how to make spermicidal vaginal tampons, presumably so that physicians could instruct their patients. Many women probably continued to moisten contraceptive sponges with water but without spermicides, and certainly much of the literature on reproductive control did recommend only water. But once the principles of spermicidal douching were known, the use of spermicides with vaginal sponges must surely have increased.

By today's estimates, the contraceptive vaginal sponge can be an effective birth control method if it is large enough (at least two or two and a half inches in diameter), moistened with a spermicide, and left in long enough (at least six hours after intercourse).[49] A 1966 investigation of popular contemporary contraceptive methods found a range of twenty-eight to thirty-five pregnancies resulting for every hundred "woman years" of reliance solely on the sponge and contraceptive foam. (This is a standard measure of contraceptive effectiveness: how many pregnancies would result if one hundred women used only the given method for one year. Without any contraception an estimated eighty to ninety pregnancies would result within three to four months.)[50] In the first half of the nineteenth century the available sponges were not always large enough or thick enough to form a sufficient barrier to sperm, and many were moistened with water, not spermicides. A more serious problem was that women may not have left sponges in place long enough—some advice literature urged removal of a sponge immediately after intercourse and, as in the pamphlet *Reproductive Control*, rinsing repeatedly and reinserting the sponge until they believed that all the sperm were removed. Although all of these practices would have reduced the effectiveness of the vaginal sponge, early-twentieth-century studies of contraceptive effectiveness conducted by the Woman's Bureau found that women who used the vaginal sponge, even without such precautions, still had a 50-percent success rate in preventing pregnancy.[51] Half, therefore, failed.

Over the course of the century, advice about using the sponges became more detailed and reliable. Physician David Matteson of Warsaw, New York, told medical colleagues that the best control method he knew was for women to use a silk or sheep's wool sponge shaped into a small ball, through which a ten- to twelve-inch silk thread had been passed. A wife should wear this as as much a part of her night attire as her nightgown. He advised women to dampen it with water and leave it in place all night to act as a cervical barrier. Besant also advised that the sponge not be removed until morning.[52]

American women also had access, in the decades after 1840, to rubber devices designed to occlude the cervix from sperm. Some of these were early versions of what was later called the diaphragm; others were small "cervical caps" designed to fit snugly around the cervix. A diaphragm is designed to fit longitudinally in the vagina with the forward end under the pubic bone, the back end in the posterior fornix. It is difficult to distinguish between references to cervical caps and diaphragms in the nineteenth-century literature because the terms were often used interchangeably. The most common term for contraceptive pessaries was "womb veil." One Taunton, Massachusetts, physician in 1890 defined womb veils as "like a ring pessary covered by a membraneous envelope," but the term generally referred either to diaphragms or to cervical caps.[53] Norman E. Himes, in his *Medical History of Contraception*, believed that the term referred either to cervical caps or to diaphragms and that it may have occasionally been used to refer to a type of female condom.[54] Other terms used were "check pessary," "womb guard," "mechanical shield for ladies," "French shields for women," "preventive pessaries," "vaginal shields," and "closed-ring pessaries." In 1883 a Cincinnati physician, William Rothacker, described the "pessaire preventif" as only one model of a large variety of appliances whose function was to cover the mouth of the womb and prevent the passage of spermatozoa into the uterine cavity. Rothacker said that these were the "goods for ladies" that advertisements were referring to. It is obvious from other sources that advertisements for "Ladies' rubber protectors" meant contraceptive pessaries and also douching syringes."[55]

Although a German physician, Wilhelm Peter Mensinga, is usually credited with inventing the first actual diaphragm in 1882,[56] American inventions designed on essentially the same principle had been patented in the 1840s and were circulating by mid century. Mensinga published news of his invention, which he called by the common medical term of "pessary" in several German publications in 1882, and knowledge of it spread quickly to Holland, where a Dutch physician, Dr. Aletta Jacobs, came across Mensinga's articles while researching the written material on cervical caps. The early Dutch birth control clinics prescribed the Mensinga pessary freely. Within two years of Mensinga's publication, the diaphragm was mentioned in Henry Allbutt, *The Wife's Handbook*, a birth control tract written by a Leeds physician. Himes wrote in *Medical History of Contraception* that it took several decades for knowledge of the diaphragm to spread to England and that it was not known in the United States until the 1920s "but for random exceptions," but he overlooked his own evidence on Albutt and much evidence about the United States.[57] In 1846 a John B. Beers of Rochester, New York, requested a patent on a "'wife's protector,' the design of which is to Prevent conception."[58] It was a hoop one and a half inches in diameter covered with "oil-silk or some other membranous substance" attached to a thin eight-inch metal handle, perhaps because women would prefer not to insert the hoop into the vagina manually, or perhaps because women (or Beers) feared that the hoop would otherwise be irretrievable. During insertion the hoop could be pressed against the handle edgewise, but like the modern flexible diaphragm, once past the bones of the pelvis it could be extended to a position totally covering the os uteri with only a slight turn of the handle. Beers recommended removing the "wife's protector" after intercourse rather than leaving it in, and so may have reduced its effectiveness. There is no evidence that Beers ever marketed his diaphragm widely, although he may have sold it quietly in the Rochester area, perhaps with the help of peddler-author-botanic physician Alfred G. Hall. One testimonial at the back of Hall's *Womanhood* in 1844, asserting the book worthy of the "confidence of females and mothers," was from a J. B. Beers, a dentist in Rochester. The two men may have influenced each other, for an "A. G. Hull" received a patent in 1835 on a pessary "designed to be supported outside the body."[59]

Within one year of Beers's patent a Boston physician was indicted for distributing advertisements for a similar occlusive pessary. In 1847, Dr. Walter Scott Tarbox was tried in Boston for transgressing the obscenity act by printing and circulating to more than one hundred households in Suffolk County, Massachusetts, a circular for "Dr. Cameron's Patent Family Regulator or Wife's Protector." It boasted that the device had a "safe, sure and easy application" and "is easily introduced by the female and does not diminish in the least the enjoyment, and would not be discovered by the male, were he not apprised of it. . . . It is easily withdrawn, bringing with it every particle of semen, rendering its effects positive; and as it absorbs nothing, can be cleansed in a moment, even without wetting the fingers—can never get out of order, and will last for life. Five dollars." Tarbox was found guilty of a misdemeanor but the state Supreme Court overturned the conviction on a technicality.[60]

By the 1850s dozens of patents for rubber pessaries "inflated to hold them in place" were listed in U.S. Patent Office records. Most were intended not as contraceptive diaphragms but as supports to a prolapsed uterus or as adjustments to a malpositioned one (a problem nineteenth-century physicians believed common); they were open-ring pessaries, devices shaped like a doughnut with a hole in the middle to allow the cervical os to protrude through. They were clearly designed so that women could insert and remove them easily at home without the aid of a doctor. It was only a short step from the open-ring to the closed-ring pessary. In 1864, Edward Bliss Foote advertised his "Womb Veil," an "India-rubber contrivance" to be placed in the vagina "before copulation and which spreads a thin tissue of rubber before the mouth of the womb so as to prevent the seminal aura from entering." Foote added:

> Conception cannot possibly take place when it is used. The full enjoyment of the conjugal embrace can be indulged in during coition. The husband would hardly be likely to know that it was being used, unless told by the wife. Its application is easy and accomplished in a moment without the aid of a light. It places conception entirely under the control of the wife, to whom it naturally belongs for it is for her to say at what time and under what circumstances, she will become the mother and the moral, religious, and physical instructress of offspring. . . . It is durable and will last a great many years.

Foote said that he had "introduced it quite extensively and to all it appears to give the highest satisfaction."[61]

Foote, who was fluent in German as well as English, may have discovered an obscure 1838 treatise on cervical caps written by the German Friedrich Adolph Wilde.[62] It is even more probable that his familiarity with ethnic Germans in the United States had acquainted him with the German midwifery tradition of contraceptive pessaries.

In the 1860s and 1870s contraceptive pessaries, whether true diaphragms or cervical caps, were well advertised under a variety of names in urban areas and available from diverse sources at two to six dollars each. An "M. Larmont and E. Bannister" (probably aliases inasmuch as there is no information on them other than that in their own book) dispensed contraceptives, abortion-inducing products, and possibly performed abortions from their "medical institute" in New York City. Although their book *Medical Adviser and Marriage Guide* (with editions from 1854 to 1870) disparaged the contraceptive sponge and douche, they offered such devices for sale anyway, emphasizing that the occlusive pessary was "so secret that it cannot be known by the husband. . . . It cannot cause the male or female the slightest injury, or interfere in the least with the fullest sexual enjoyment."[63] Russell Thacher Trall wrote in *Sexual Physiology* in 1867 that "it may be proper to suggest that any mechanical obstruction placed against the os uteri which will prevent the seminal fluid from coming in contact with the ovum will be an infallible preventive. A medical friend of mine labored for a year or two on an invention for plugging the os uteri and although it answered admirably in some cases, it was not adapted to all without a degree of trouble and inconvenience fatal to its general introduction."[64] Trall, however, went on to recommend the use of soft sponges "introduced high up the vaginal canal" or other types of occlusive pessaries.

Contraceptive entrepreneurs' emphasis on the secrecy with which these vaginal devices could be worn is striking. Gynecologist J. Marion Sims wrote in 1873 that some of his women patients did not want their husbands to know that they were wearing a pessary (although his were decidedly not contraceptive devices). Why the appeal to the device's secrecy? Sims's explanation was that a wife feared that her husband would feel sexually constrained: "so far as our sex is concerned the knowledge of the presence of a vaginal support might be an unpoetical association." Sims assured patients that if the pessary were "properly adjusted, it is not at all in the way [of sexual intercourse]."[65] His may have been an apt reading of his patients' objections, for he specialized in cases of sterility and had invented a pessary that would not preclude coitus. His patients did not want to find ways to reduce sexual intercourse or to protect themselves from pregnancy, at least according to what he emphasized in his writings. Rather, they wanted to become fertile.

The emphasis on secrecy in the discussions of women's vaginal devices can only have exacerbated the fear that separating sexual intercourse from reproduction would destroy the virtue of wives and daughters, making illicit sexuality possible by removing fears of pregnancy. But a woman had other reasons to want to keep a contraceptive device secret from a husband, because not all men practiced withdrawal reliably or wore a condom consistently. Nor did all men respect the boundaries of women's calculations for the rhythm method. Some men were not merely unsympathetic but were actually hostile to their wife's desire for reproductive control. Ashton said that for such reasons "the wife needs other plans to give her confidence":[66] a contraceptive device that women could wear secretly as an added precaution, a backup measure in case of the failure of methods that imposed sexual abstinence, such as the rhythm method, or that required changes in male sexual behavior, such as coitus interruptus. Women who feared that their refusals of sex would not be consistently respected would have found a secret diaphragm reassuring.

Some historians have minimized the significance of vaginal sponges and diaphragms as pregnancy control devices either as not accessible or as unacceptable to genteel women. In her social history of American birth control, *Woman's Body, Woman's Right*, Linda Gordon argues that for a woman to insert a vaginal pessary may have been too difficult emotionally: "Even the limited ingenuity and basic common sense required for developing home-remedy birth control techniques may have been blocked by deep psychological fears of thinking about sexual matters."[67] Gordon notes the irony that middle class women, who would have had the greatest access to vaginal devices, may have been less willing to use them than working class women who lacked money and access. Her point is important, for even today the diaphragm, one of the few effective contraceptives for use by women, one that has no medical contraindications, is impossible for some to use because it requires preparation for anticipated sexual activity and requires a woman to handle her genitals. Lee Rainwater found in the 1960s that some working class women in Chicago and Cincinnati refused to use vaginal contraceptives because they feared the devices would become irretrievably lost in the vagina.[68] If these anxieties existed in the mid-twentieth century, the argument goes, how could women a hundred years earlier, in an era far more circumspect about sexuality, have overcome such anxieties?

Doubtless there were nineteenth-century women, just as there are twentieth-century women, whose desperation to control reproduction was insufficiently strong to overcome repugnance toward such contraceptive devices. Some may have been inhibited by prudery or by an anatomical ignorance that made them fear losing the device in their vaginal tract. Yet there is considerable evidence that women—many women—learned to insert and to remove vaginal pessaries, to use vaginal drugs, tampons, and sponges for medical and for contraceptive reasons. That the same vaginal drugs and devices were used for contraception gave them alegitimacy that cannot be overstated when we try to assess their psychological availability for reproductive control.

Indeed, pessaries were a fad of American gynecology in the nineteenth century. By 1887 the president of the Illinois State Medical Society earnestly hoped that the vogue for medical use of pessaries had abated: "You all know what a craze invaded our ranks a few years ago. Many of our over-zealous and enthusiastic brethren seemed to think that the surest and quickest way to reach a topmost round in the professional ladder would be to invent a pessary, and such a display of rings, oblongs, circles, semi-circles, curves, twists, turns, contortions and wind-bags was never witnessed before."[69] Elizabeth Blackwell, beginning medical practice in New York in the 1850s after training in Britain, was surprised by this latest trend in American gynecology, for it had not been part of her training in Britain, and she wrote mockingly about American women who demanded pessaries.[70]

Pessaries, as I have noted, were prescribed to correct asymmetry of the uterus (called uterine retroversions, anteversions, retroflexions and anteflexions and considered at that time to be a serious malady), prolapsed uteruses, and cervical problems: there were diverse styles— open and closed ring, open and closed lever, T-shaped, watch-spring, and cup. Some were vaginal; other "stem" pessories were intrauterine or intracervical. Dozens of pessaries were named for their inventors, such as "Thomas's Modification of Smith's Retroversion." Many retail druggists between 1870 and 1900 stocked a dozen different styles.[71] In 1872, McKesson & Robbins in New York offered forty-two, W. H. Schieffelin & Co. of New York twenty-four (two of glass, three of hard rubber, two of gutta percha in different sizes, three brand-name pessaries, seven of soft rubber or "French elastic," and a watch-spring model for four dollars.)[72]

Case histories discussed by doctors in medical journal articles contain references to the use of pessaries, illustrating that American women did wear them, often for long periods of time. A Fort Wayne, Indiana, physician reported in 1883 that a woman patient of his had worn a "pessaire preventif" for two to three years, often not removing it for months at a time. At thirty years of age, she had three children and was so anxious not to have more that she had already given herself three abortions. When she consulted a doctor about pain and paralysis in her lower back he advised her to stop using the contraceptive pessary.[73]

Other medical case histories document pessary use although not necessarily deliberate contraceptive intent. The sample below indicates not only how long women wore such pessaries (the date indicates when the pessary was first inserted), but also the geographic extent of their availability:

1811. Removal of a pessary after 41 years. *Ohio Medical and Surgical Journal* 4 (1851–52): 385.

1847. Globe pessary in vagina for 35 years. *Independent Practitioner* (New York) 3 (1882): 83.

1851. Glass pessary in vagina for 15 years. *Boston Medical and Surgical Journal* 73 (1886): 201.

1853. Pessary removed 25 years "after its unsuspected introduction." *American Journal of Obstetrics* (New York) 11 (1878): 569–71.

1854. Globe pessary retained for 17 years. *American Journal of Obstetrics* (New York) 4 (1871–72): 729.

1855. Pessary worn for 24 years in the vagina. *Transactions of the Minnesota Medical Society* (St. Paul) (1879): 103.

1863. Retention of a glass pessary in vagina for 21 years. *Peoria [Ill.] Medical Monthly* 5 (1884): 20.

1870. Hodge pessary worn for 13 years. *Texas Courier-Record of Medicine* (Fort Worth) 1883.

1875. Pessary in vagina for six years. *Atlanta Medical Register* 1881.

In the last third of the nineteenth century, intrauterine and intracervical pessaries were used extensively in American gynecological practice. The fact that American women in the nineteenth century used these devices, including the most difficult, painful, and dangerous of all the models, is further proof that the number of women unable to use contraceptive devices because of fear or modesty may have been quite small.

These intrauterine and intracervical "stem pessaries" consisted of a stem, usually made of hard or flexible rubber (although some models were also made of metal or glass), with a small cup or button at the bottom of the stem to hold the pessary in place at the cervical opening and to prevent it from disappearing into the uterus. Their most common use was as a type of splint, designed to be inserted through the cervix and into the uterus to straighten asymmetry. They were also recommended in official American medicine to stimulate menstruation in cases of amenorrhea and to alleviate menorrhagia (excessive menstruation) and severe menstrual cramps.[74] The eminent gynecologist William Goodell believed the intrauterine pessary to be one of gynecology's most valuable remedies. Because Goodell was president of the American Gynecological Society in 1878, his opinions had a wide influence. Ironically, his only objection to widespread use of intrauterine pessaries was that they prevented conception.

As early as 1854 the notable physician Charles Meigs had tried to correct a common belief of his students by warning that "the pessary does not put a bar either to gestation or to conception," although he warned that pessaries caused miscarriages.[75] Although a number of physicians recommended the intrauterine-stem pessary as a cure for sterility on the theory that its use would stimulate menstruation and thereby ovulation, it is clear that the contraceptive uses of the device seeped into American (and British) culture. A prominent English physician informed the Obstetrical Section of the British Medical Association in 1878 that in Britain women of high society were wearing intrauterine stem pessaries to prevent pregnancies. And, in an article that cited in great detail instances of the use of douches and womb veils to prevent conception, the pathologist of the Cincinnati Hospital wrote in 1883: "Besides syringes, pessaries, etc. there is an instrument consisting of a short rod of metal with a button-shaped head. The rod is to be slipped into the cervix, the button being intended to keep the entire concern from passing into the cavity of the body of the uterus."[76]

It is difficult to believe that intrauterine pessaries had any widespread use as birth control devices, for foreign objects in the cervix or uterus can cause severe pain and cramping. Even Goodell noted that an important drawback of the intrauterine pessary was the pain that made insertion by the physician difficult. He recommended using a uterine dilator and added that he always inserted stem pessaries at the patient's home, leaving a thread attached to the bottom so that the patient herself could remove it if the pain became unbearable. Goodell reported a case of a woman who had tried to give herself an abortion with bent wire that broke off in her womb. Part of it remained firmly embedded in the os uteri; six years later it was still there and she had not conceived again.[77]

The conspicuous dangers of stem pessaries also make it hard to believe that they were popular. Goodell advised as late as 1879, when rubber was readily available, that doctors should use only glass or hard-rubber pessaries and avoid metal. Some doctors found it necessary to warn their colleagues against pessaries with a stem longer than the body of a woman's uterus. Ely Van de Warker, a gynecologist best known for his treatises on the detection of criminal abortion and for his gynecological investigation of the women at the Oneida Community of Perfectionists, invented a number of intrauterine stem pessaries. He gave as the first "inalterable principle" of their use that the "stem must be shorter than the cavity of the uterus and so small in diameter that neither the outer nor inner os is stretched or occluded."[78]

Yet despite these difficulties and dangers, the supply of such pessaries in the second half of the century suggests a considerable demand for them. Nearly all wholesale druggists' catalogues advertised pessaries with long or short rubber stems, in addition to brand-name models. The 1889 catalogue of George Tiemann and Sons, one of New York's largest suppliers of medical and surgical instruments, included illustrations for twenty-two intrauterine stem pessaries.[79] John H. Nelson's *The Druggists' Cost Book* (Cleveland, 1879), a good indicator of the most popular and essential druggists' supplies, listed twenty-seven types of pessaries, five of which were intrauterine models.[80] In the 1870s and 1880s at least thirty-seven models of intrauterine pessaries were available from druggists in New York, Boston, Chicago, and Cleveland. Prices ranged from $1.50 to seven dollars each. George C. Goodwin's New England Patent Medicine Warehouse sold an oval, pure gum-stem model in 1880 for five dollars a dozen.[81]

Even intrauterine stem pessaries were designed so that wearers could insert and remove them without a doctor's aid. George Gladman of Syracuse, New York, patented a stem pessary in 1895 which could be "readily inserted with a minimum degree of skill [and] can be worn continuously." It would not stop menstruation and it could be cleansed without removal by a hot-water douche. Charles S. W. Hinckley of San Antonio, Texas, included as part of his patent application in 1894 a self-insertion device and the string for easy removal of the pessary.[82]

With such encouragement from the regular and the sectarian medical professionals for the use of vaginal pessaries, and even intracervical and intrauterine devices, it is difficult to sustain the argument that Victorian women found it impossible to go one step further and use the devices for birth control.

Abortion as a Business

Folk remedies for abortion and superstitions about abortion survived essentially unchanged over many centuries. Older abortion methods continued to be available throughout the nineteenth century, but practices were changing. From the 1840s on, the selling of abortive products became a commercial business. Abortion was more openly discussed and increasingly available from sources that seemed scientific, modern, and professional.

Many women continued in the decades after 1840 to bring about abortion in their homes through use of the pills, fluid extracts, and medicinal oils that were nonpublicly marketed with such suggestive names as the "Female Regulator," "Periodical Drops," "Uterine regulator," and "Woman's Friend." Ely Van de Warker, a Syracuse, New York, gynecologist who studied American abortion methods, noted that "every schoolgirl knows the meaning of these terms." Anyone who did not could have learned others from the printed labels on the drug containers. The label on Graves Pills for Amenorrhea was typical: "These pills have been approved by the Ecole de Medecine, fully sanctioned by the M.R.C.S. of London, Edinburgh, Dublin, as a never-failing remedy for producing the catamenial or monthly flow. Though perfectly harmless to the most delicate, yet ladies are earnestly requested not to mistake their condition [if pregnant] as MISCARRIAGE WOULD CERTAINLY ENSUE."[83]

The Boston drug firm Goodwin and Company offered seven brands of female pills in 1874, as well as "Belcher's Female Cure," "Hardy's Woman's Friend," "The Samaritan's Gift for Females," and "Lyons's Periodical Drops." Even as late as 1885, Chicago's Fuller and Fuller Drug Company was still advertising "Dr. Caton's Tansy Regulator," "Chichester's Pennyroyal Pills," "Colchester's Pennyroyal and Tansy Pills," and "Cook's Cotton Root Compound"—all botanicals long associated in folk medicine with inducing menstruation and causing abortion.[84] So prevalent was the association between abortion and women's medicines that some advertisers took special pains to protest that their product was not related. "Dr. Champlin's Red Woman's Relief" was described in 1880 as having "no equal in female weakness and irregularities; not for the destruction nor perversion of ANY OF NATURE'S LAWS and purposes but for their fulfillment."[85]

The preparations that sold widely at mid century contained common botanical emmenagogues. Most abortifacients were sold as pills or as fluid extracts in which one ingredient predominated, usually aloes or black hellebore. The pills often were combinations of aloes, hellebore, powdered savin, ergot, iron, and solid extracts of tansy and rue. The instructions on the pill bottles told women to supplement the doses by drinking tansy tea twice daily until the "obstruction" was removed. The fluid extracts were most commonly oils of savin, tansy, or rue dissolved in alcohol and improved in taste by wintergreen.[86] The E. L. Patch Company in Boston, Massachusetts, listed several emmenagogues in their 1900 catalogue, including their No. Two: "Chocolate covered, 5 1/4 grain tablets with one grain each cottonroot, iron sulphate, aloes, ergotin, black hellebore, and 1/4 min. oil of savin." As late as 1939 the Federal Trade Commission forbade the sale and advertisement of a number of medicines designed to induce a delayed menstruation because they were serious health hazards. The contents of several of the banned medicines included aloes, oil of savin, cotton root bark, ergotin, black hellebore, apiol, and iron sulphate.[87]

These medicines were often effective, though they also posed considerable risk and, at times, acute danger to a woman's life.[88] Ely Van de Warker concluded that "female pills" often worked as abortives because women took them in dangerously copious amounts without regard for their general health. He believed that the extensiveness of the trade in commercial abortion drugs and the relative rarity of publicized fatalities indicated a degree of effectiveness: "I know many married women who have gone years without the birth of mature children, who resort habitually to some one of the many advertised nostrums with as much confidence of 'coming around' as if they repaired to the shop of the professional abortionist."[89] In addition to using drugs, women could induce abortion with instruments. An 1863 article, "Instruments of a Notorious Abortionist," in the *American Medical Times* described forty simple instruments abortionists employed, conveniently providing for interested readers illustrations of fifteen especially simple ones such as spoon handles bent in various shapes, pen holders with attached wires, long-handled mustard spoons, and placenta forceps.[90] In his erotic autobiography, *My Life and Loves*, Frank Harris described how he and a lover made a pencil of ingredients which swelled slowly with body heat so that once inserted into the cervix, it caused an abortion. Harris described this as "Nature" making its own effort to get "rid of the intruding semen."[91]

In medical journals of the second half of the nineteenth century, physicians discussed the uses patients had made of catheters, speculua, and uterine sounds (a type of uterine probe).[92] The president of the Gynaecological Society of Boston said, in 1871, that "the populace seem to have the idea that Simpson's sound was designed to produce abortion," and in the 1890s a physician in the middle of a discussion with his medical peers about the dangers of coitus interruptus observed that he had advised a male patient who did not want additional children to stop using withdrawal because it was affecting his health; the patient managed to avoid an increase in his family because, the doctor implied, his wife was handy in the "occasional passing of a sound."[93] James S. Whitmire, a physician in the small town of Meta-mora, Illinois, wrote in 1874 that he knew of women who produced abortion by taking drugs, by engaging in exercises such as "lifting and jumping," and by using instruments such as "the blunt probe or uter-ine sound," which he believed they learned how to use "by reading obscene books published expressly to impart such information."[94]

Abortion instruments, like drugs, were readily available through the mails or from a variety of retail establishments, particularly drug-stores, and wholesale druggists' catalogues carried a considerable vari-ety of styles and models in uterine sounds and dilators. Newspapers regularly carried advertisements for abortion-inducing drugs. An issue in the *New York Herald Tribune* on 15 July 1841, to pick one at ran-dom, advertised "Dr. Van Hambert's Female Renovating Pills from Germany, a certain remedy for suppression, irregularity, and all cases where nature has stopped from any cause whatsoever."[95] In June 1870, Frank Leslie's *Day's Doings*, a racy New York newspaper carrying sensationalist articles and theatrical and sporting news, carried adver-tisements for seven medicines with language some women no doubt associated with abortion, including "Madame Van Buskirk's Regulating Medicine," "Dr. Richau's Female Remedy," and "Dr. Harrison's Fe-male Antidote . . . certain to have the desired effect in twenty-four hours without any injurious results." By mid century there was a growing number of "professional" abortionists, and not only in large cities, as W.M. Smith, a physician in the small farming town of Atkin-son, Illinois (population 300), noted in 1874:

> I know three married women, respectable ones, who are notorious for giving instructions to their younger sisters as to the modus ope-randi of 'coming around.' After the failure of tansy, savin, ergot, cotton root, lifting, rough trotting horses, etc., a knitting needle is the stand by. One old doctor near here was so obliging as to furnish a wire with a handle, to one of his patients, which did the work for her, after which she passed it to one of her neighbors, who suc-ceeded in destroying the foetus and nearly so herself.[96]

Smith estimated that his town had one abortion for every ten live births. He was opposed to abortion but expressed sympathy for women who needed some means of controlling reproduction, suggest-ing, ambiguously, that women use "bromide of potassium"—probably meaning a douche.

Urban women, in particular, and those with access to transportation to urban areas found highly desirable anonymity and the comfort of a supposedly safer, more modern abortion from the services of a newly visible entrepreneur: the "professional" abortionist.

The term "female physician" was frequently a euphemism for abortionist by mid century, a time when respectable women midwives found their role and power increasingly circumscribed by a medical profession intent on establishing its own professional identity. When Elizabeth Blackwell first tried to establish a medical practice in New York City in the 1850s she was denied rental at the first few boarding-houses she approached because landlords mistook her for an abortionist. This assumption was particularly galling to Blackwell, who abhorred abortion, and she described with scorn the flags midwives hung from their windows as wordless advertisements of their services.[97] Another early woman physician and equally vehement critic of abortion, Rachel B. Gleason, wrote in 1870 that in her early practice she "was often asked to induce abortions, for the impression seemed to prevail then that the important part of woman's work in the medical profession was to prevent pregnancy or procure abortion."[98]

In the cities of New England and of the Middle Atlantic states women could find a variety of offices, clinics, and boardinghouses offering lying-in services and illicit abortions. Although we do not know with any certainty who operated these establishments or even how many there were, contemporary observers believed that many were operated by women who had been trained as midwives in Europe.[99] In Australia, government officials worried about declining birth rates recommended that laws be strengthened against small private lying-in hospitals because they were so frequently abortion mills.[100] In the early 1860s the Lying-In Institute at 6 Amity Place in New York City was operated by H. D. and Julia Grindle, while H. D. Grindle's book *The Female Sexual System; or The Ladies' Medical Guide* provided detailed advice about sexual anatomy, reproduction, and reproductive control; it did not promote abortion, but it did advocate his douching powders and a vaginal syringe.[101] However, the Grindles offered rooms for nursing mothers and unwed mothers and their advertising circulars made it clear that abortion facilities were available. Newspaper notices promised "certain relief to ladies at one interview, with or without medication."[102] For two dollars a bottle, the Grindles would send through the mail a remedy, "which when taken according to directions will remove all obstructions of the womb and bring on the menstrual periods, from whatever cause produced . . . caution: If this medicine is taken during the early months of pregnancy it will be sure to produce a miscarriage. However, if any should make a mistake and a miscarriage be the result, it will not in the least injure their health."[103]

In 1868, Grindle was indicted for performing an abortion on a woman who subsequently died. The trial ended in his acquittal with only a censure from the judge because the prosecution proved only that the woman died at his institute during childbirth and not during or because of an abortion. In 1872 both Grindles were indicted in New York for abortion, but they were found not guilty because the young woman who charged them with selling her a twenty-dollar bottle of medicine to procure abortion admitted that she had not told the couple she was pregnant.[104]

Of all the nineteenth-century abortionists, Ann Trow Lohman (1812–1877) is the best documented. Better known as "Madame Restell," she ran a lucrative mail-order business and abortion service in New York City from the 1840s through the 1870s.[105] She was born in England in 1812 and at about sixteen years old married Henry Summers, a widowed tailor. The Summers emigrated to New York City in 1831; Henry died two years later. Ann Trow Summers probably earned a living as a seamstress for a few years and then in 1836 she married Charles R. Lohman, an experienced newspaper compositor who also considered himself a physician. Shortly after her marriage, Ann Trow Lohman adopted the alias "Madame Restell" and went into the abortion and contraceptives business, advertising her services and products in newspapers and hiring agents to distribute circulars along the eastern seaboard. Historian James C. Mohr notes that she had branch agencies in Boston and Philadelphia in the 1840s, and an 1846 article in the *Police Gazette* suggested that "Madame Costello," another female physician advertising abortifacient pills, was an agent of Restell's.[106] James Gordon Bennett, editor of the *New York Herald*, gave her invaluable publicity through his critical editorials while the paper simultaneously ran her advertisements. She operated an establishment at 148 Greenwich Street in Manhattan from 1839 through 1847 and one on Chambers Street from 1848 until the 1860s, while she was also in business with her husband at 129 Liberty Street.

It did not take "Madame Restell" long to gain notoriety and a fortune. She appeared in the 1844 novel by Thomas Low Nichols, *The Lady in Black: A Story of New York Life, Morals, and Manners*, about the "tangled mass of vice and virtue" in New York City. At a public ball the hero points her out to a friend, "Do you see that lady . . . the one smiling in such a sweet motherly way . . . one of the prettiest and most amiable looking women in the room. That is the famous Madame Restell, or rather Mrs. L."

A few years ago she was a seamstress. . . . Now they ride in a carriage. You are doubtless aware of the means. She never wants for money or influence, as her style of living and the manner in which she has slipped out of the feeble fingers of justice show. Her trade is too lucrative and there are too many wealthy and *respectable* people in her power. . . . In less *moral* cities they have foundling hospitals and lying-in asylums—in this virtuous New York we have Restell and others of the same calling. I have watched her tonight and have seen more than one cheek turn pale as death as she passed smilingly around the room.[107]

Lohman (Restell) was indicted and tried a number of times between 1841 and 1878, charged variously with performing abortions, manslaughter, and with running illegal adoption services for infants born in her establishment. One 1847 case tells a good deal about her practice: she was charged with second-degree manslaughter for producing an abortion on one Maria Bodine after quickening of the fetus. After a seventeen-day trial, reported in the sensationalist New York press with verbatim testimony and the names, addresses, and occupations of the jurors, Restell was convicted and sentenced to a year in prison on Blackwell's Island. The young woman obtaining the abortion was an unmarried servant who had been having regular sexual relations for two years with her employer, a widowed cotton manufacturer in Walden, New York. When she found herself pregnant in the spring of 1846, she took a boat down the Hudson to New York to stay with a married sister, and when she was nearly six months pregnant she called on Madame Restell. The price was five dollars for an examination, from one to five dollars for a box of pills, and one hundred dollars for "operating." Restell asked her whether her "beau" were employed and would help pay for the operation. When the girl returned several weeks later with seventy-five dollars from her lover, Restell induced an abortion by rupturing the amniotic sac and prescribing pills to cause uterine contractions. After several days in bed in a private room, the girl went home. Restell gave her money for the boat fare, told her how to alleviate her milk-swollen breasts, and advised her to come back for a private carriage if approached by the police. Although contemporary critics saw Restell as an avaricious quack, such details of her practice, ironically brought out at the trial by the prosecution, suggest compassion and competence as well as business shrewdness.

Several sources note that Restell did not like to perform abortions after four months, preferring to charge room and board and, when the baby was born, arrange for adoption.[108] In 1847, while Restell was in prison, either her husband or Joseph F. Trow, her brother, or both went into the reproductive control business using the alias "Dr. A. M. Mauriceau." "Mauriceau" wrote *The Married Woman's Private Medical Companion*, which went through at least nine editions between 1847 and 1860. (The 1847 edition was copyrighted by Joseph Trow.) Primarily an inducement to readers to send money for secret remedies and to come to the Liberty Street address for abortions, it offered remedies through the mail or in person, among them a douching solution, "De Someaux's Preventive to Conception" at ten dollars a package (which Hollick warned was simply alum), condoms (referred to as "baudruches to prevent pregnancy") for five dollars a dozen, an abortion-inducing drug, and an "elixir for barrenness." Readers would have found clearly marked sections of advice on the "prevention of pregnancy." In addition, "Mauriceau" recommended that women use astringent vaginal douches for uterine problems or wear a vaginal sponge soaked in alum water as a uterine support; either might have helped reduce the probabilities of conceiving whether used for that purpose or not.[109]

Mail or Plain Wrapper: Confidential Purchases

Although the demand for information and devices was met through an unprecedented number of channels and with a previously unimaginable abundance of options and choices in the decades from 1850 through the 1870s, few historians have studied how such products got to consumers. We know little about the manufacturers and retailers or even about the agents and peddlers of contraceptive and abortive products.

Books, devices, and medical products could be ordered and received by mid century through the post. Edward W. Baxter was arrested in 1878 for selling "articles to prevent conception or procure abortion." Baxter had gone into the birth control business after failing as a furniture dealer. He had an office in Jersey City where he received his mail and stored his stock and advertising circulars. He specialized in business through the mails and express companies, and he had eight hundred circulars on hand when he was arrested.[110]

The invention of mail-order catalogues in the later years of the century boosted the development of a consumer culture. Birth control entrepreneurs and customers were in the vanguard of this trend. In this, as in other ways, Victorian American desire for reproductive con-

trol eased a transition into the consumer culture that is usually identified with a later period. Because the demand for contraceptives and
abortives was more covert than the demand for other consumer goods
it has been overlooked by historians; yet this demand helped introduce female and male consumers to the subliminal persuasions of advertising and to the benefits of anonymity in mail-order shopping.

The advertising pamphlet put out by the Beach Company in the
1860s, *Habits of a Well-Organized Life*, explained how to cope with
the intricate process of a mail transaction. The circular gave detailed
directions about how to order and pay for the products, how to contact
the nearest express company office or post office to place an order
through the mail, how to use a C.O.D. express, how to get a money
order, how to endorse it so that no one would know to whom it was
sent, how to involve a third person in the transaction. The Beach
Company's solicitude suggests that they expected their customers to
be novices in monetary transactions of this type or at least to be new-
comers to ordering goods secretly. The advice told readers what to say
to a postal clerk or to the express company's deliveryman when pick-
ing up the package. Edward Bliss Foote told his customers exactly
what public transportation to take to get to his office in Manhattan,
and what hotels were nearby, though when it came to advice about
ordering and paying for goods by mail he seems to have assumed that
his customers were well informed, for he gave no additional explanations about using the express companies or writing checks.[111] He regularly mailed his contraceptive devices to customers—sending condoms
in letters and shipping his electromagnetic preventive machine and
diaphragms by express companies.

Customers for any of a score of books, including Hersey's *Midwife's
Practical Directory* in 1836, Nichols's *Esoteric Anthropology* in 1853,
and Trall's *Sexual Physiology* in 1866, needed only to write the author,
the publisher, or any of a number of booksellers listed on the title
page to get a mail-order copy.[112] So, too, by mid century, purchasers of
condoms, diaphragms, prevention powders, and abortives relied on
the anonymity of transactions by mail. Indeed, some birth control
products were relatively easy to mail. Pamphlets, folded condoms,
and certain kinds of powdered spermicides and abortives could fit into
letter-sized envelopes. Bulkier items—books, diaphragms, syringes,
suppositories, sponges, and many drugs—were sent as parcels. Then
customers might face the sly glances and knowing winks of an express
deliverer or, even worse, the postal clerk, almost certainly a neighbor.
Wherever folk came to pick up their mail they also congregated to
gossip. Suppliers, recognizing the public culture of the post office,
often promised that their products would be sent in plain, unmarked

envelopes with no revealing outside clues. The Beach Company's advertising pamphlet, for example, sought to assure customers that their purchases would not become public knowledge. It promised that no one would ever know what the customer had bought because no postmaster or delivery man would associate the name "Putney, Beach & Co." with reproductive control. It promised to send all products in plain unmarked packages. The agents of the wholesale drug houses and the express companies with whom the company did business "have no such knowledge of the nature of our business, or goods shipped by us, to enable them to know the character of our calling or contents of our packages, so that our patrons may be confident of the utmost secrecy in obtaining their packages by Express throughout the U.S. and Canada."[113]

In spite of all such difficulties, the use of the mails for delivery of reproductive control products held indisputable advantages. To face a bookseller and request *Sexual Physiology* or *A Married Lady's Private Medical Guide* may have been beyond the emotional capabilities of even the bravest men and women in the nineteenth century. How much better to request and later to receive one's order through the mail, enclosed in a plain wrapper.

Peddlers, Drummers, and Entrepreneurs: The Network of Marketeers

Independent middlemen began to play a new and significant role at mid century as processors, promoters, and distributors in the contraceptive and abortive goods trade.[114] Agents or jobbers, coordinating diffuse markets and creating distribution networks, could be found in all arenas of the wholesale and retail distribution of reproductive control materials. Many bought goods in wholesale batches from producers (often extending credit to enable the goods to be produced) and distributing them in a variety of ways, to other wholesale establishments, to small retail establishments, and to individual agents who hawked them door-to-door.

After the Civil War, the influence of peddling declined in general marketing, although in trashy, ephemeral, or "gray-market" goods it may have been important well into the second half of the nineteenth century. As late as the 1920s and 1930s peddlers were still selling condoms and rubber diaphragms, despite their increasing availability from gas stations, barber shops, beauty salons, bowling alleys, and taverns.[115]

The agents involved in this distribution were often mistaken for traditional peddlers, but they used modern methods, relying on mails more than peddlers did: they mastered advertising (their seized stock included advertising circulars), and they rented offices—usually small and cheap storefronts—for storage, for post office addresses, and for the collection of mail to avoid carrying all their wares about with them. Like independent entrepreneurs vending more respectable wares, most reproductive control agents were young, upwardly mobile men striving for professional status and economic leverage in the fluid mid-century economy. But those whom Anthony Comstock arrested in the 1870s do not appear to have been financially successful, however. There were a few exceptions. When Francis E. Andrews, of Albany, New York, and Ontario, Canada, was arrested in Manhattan in 1871, Comstock seized 1,500 books, 2,000 circulars, 5,000 condoms, and estimated his worth at $400,000. Moses Jacobi, a German- or Polish-Jewish immigrant, who started out as a barber and then worked with an abortionist, in the early 1870s set himself up as "Dr. Franklin, Prussian Doctor," selling contraceptives and abortion services. When he was arrested in 1871, at forty-nine, he was earning two thousand dollars a month according to Comstock, who claimed to have seen Jacobi's accounts.[116]

More typical was Morris Glattstine (also spelled Glattsteine in the sources), twenty-six, single, a Polish Jew, arrested in New York in 1877 on charges of dealing in rubber articles intended to prevent conception. Glattstine bought condoms and diaphragms from the Stuart Rubber Company in Milwaukee, Wisconsin, and sold the goods at a small store at 77 East Broadway in New York. He employed an even younger clerk and peddled the rest of the stock to outlying stores himself. Comstock came into the store and bought a contraceptive, then arrested the clerk. The young man agreed to testify against his boss. Whether Glattstine actually stood trial cannot be learned, but in 1881 he was back in business and doing sufficiently well for credit-rating reporters to file a report on him. They called him a dealer in "fancy goods," operating out of one room with a "nice little stock" and "supplying stores out of town." Glattstine had four different addresses between January 1881 and September 1883, but the credit-rating reporters consistently noted, "Does a moderate business in Druggists Sundries and Rubber Goods. Travels through the country selling to out of town stores. Has moderate credit with a few partners who speak very well of him. Pays promptly, is considered honest and economical." They said he was worth from three to four thousand dollars.[117]

Richard Brogan was more financially marginal. The single, young Irishman was arrested in 1881 for selling contraceptives to other peddlers from a one-room store at 489 Grand Street in New York. Among the stock seized were eleven womb veils, forty dozen "caps," and ten dozen capotes.[118]

Rubber companies themselves sometimes hired agents to sell the goods for them, but often agents bought large batches of goods from them on their own. In 1874, Anthony Comstock arrested one Morris Bass, a forty-one-year-old German Jew who called himself a "Yankee Notions dealer." When he was arrested he was acting as the agent of a Detroit manufacturer of rubber contraceptives. His stock, seized and catalogued at the time of his arrest, included twelve dozen "capotines," two hundred dozen condums, twelve dozen womb veils, two syringes for abortion, one vaginal syringe, and ten dozen "ticklers."[119]

A legion of retail establishments also sold contraceptive and abortive products and advice literature. Reproductive control items were available from tobacconists' stalls, cheap book- and newsstands, stationers' shops, dealers in rubber goods, dealers in "fancy goods," and druggists. Some of the stores that specialized in India rubber goods, especially those advertising "fancy" or "imported" rubber goods, sold condoms and diaphragms along with their more licit luxury stocks. "Fancy" imported articles could mean perfume, ornaments, or combs, but also could mean condoms.[120] William D. Russell's India Rubber Warehouse may have been typical in advertising a full assortment of rubber goods, specifying the respectable "clothing, toys, boots" and perhaps hinting at the less licit, "To druggists—a more full and complete assortment of articles in their line than anywhere else—articles of American, English, French manufacture."[121]

Condoms and rubber "ladies' protectors" were still available in the late nineteenth century even after the Comstock laws had clamped down on such marketing, for though some sources refused to carry advertisements for such products, entrepreneurs continued to try to publicize them through the mail and from rubber-goods stores.[122]

Rubber manufacturers contracted with retail establishments and agents to sell their goods, with an overlapping of economic functions which could become complicated. The Essex Syringe Manufacturing Company in Newport, Rhode Island, for example, produced several models of vaginal and uterine syringes and pessaries, clearly useful for contraceptive douching. They sold their syringes in 1860 to two "general depots" in New York City and Chicago, as well as to five "agents" in Philadelphia, Boston, and in Manhattan. Henry G. Norton, one of their New York agents, was himself a dealer in India rubber goods and druggists' sundries, doing a large business in other cities in western New York State, where he had set up branch offices. He was involved in a factory manufacturing white metal goods (at the same address where, three years earlier, the New Brunswick Rubber Company had sold its twenty-four styles of douching syringes), and he was a stockholder in the Bristol Manufacturing Company. Credit reporters throughout the 1860s considered his to be an "old, well-established house with ample means and unquestioned credit."[123] The Essex Company's other New York agent, Shepard and Dudley, sold rubber goods in one office and in another location ran a branch operation, the Goodyear Rubber Company and India Rubber Clothing Company (two doors down from Henry G. Norton's rubber goods store).[124] The Boston retailer for the Essex Company's goods was George C. Goodwin, who ran a wholesale drugstore with a wide assortment of patent medicines and druggists' goods. He sold many goods associated with birth control: abortion-inducing products, douching syringes, vaginal sponges, and, in 1865, condoms. His business was "large and remunerative," and credit reporters gave him a "first rate credit" in 1873. In 1882 the business was worth $100,000, two-thirds of which belonged to Goodwin, one-third to his wife (who remained unnamed by the credit reporters).[125]

Even early in the nineteenth century, apothecaries' shops had been a place to buy douching syringes and drugs associated with inducing abortion. Mid-century drugstores were a principal source of reproductive control products. Russell Thacher Trall commented in 1895 on the large number of "empirics in every city who sell useless or injurious specifics for the prevention of conception."[126] McKesson and Robbins, a New York drug company whose factory took up five consecutive addresses in Williamsburgh, New York, manufactured many but not all of their own medicines, taking special pride in their ergot preparations. Like many other druggists they stocked products for abortion, both the brand-name variety and the generics (ergot preparations, black cohosh pills, extracts of cotton root). They carried douching syringes and spermicides; frequently, vaginal sponges, condoms, and pessaries that might have been diaphragms. They were also wholesalers of a wide variety of druggists' sundries, shipping batches to retailers, and also conducted a retail business, especially through the mail. Their drughouse carried hundreds of other products that they bought in bulk from manufacturers, including birth control products: pessaries, very small toilet sponges on strings for ladies, douching syringes, and even rubber uterine probes. Unlike competitors, they did not sell condoms.[127] In 1877, A. A. Mellier & Co. in St. Louis sold four kinds of condoms, pessaries, sponges on strings, syringes, and abortives. The drug company Troth & Co. in Philadelphia, wholesale jobbers, kept a large inventory obtained from other jobbers and shipped small lots to wholesalers, retailers, and individual artisans in urban, rural, and frontier areas. They sent their own agents—"drummers"—to drum up business throughout the countryside and dealt with rural retailers who came periodically to the city store to buy goods. Not only in large cities were such products available; Downing's drugstore in Hanover, N.H., for one, carried products that could have been used as contraceptives or abortives. The record of their sales in 1883–84 show that they sold at least thirty douching syringes and at least nineteen pessaries. They bought more than three thousand dollars' worth of drugs over the course of the year, including numerous ergot preparations, "Woman's Friend," bottles of "Pierce's Douche," tannic acid troches, and toilet vinegars.[128]

Druggists were also becoming skilled at mail-order advertising and distribution. Chapman's Old Established Drug House in New York, whose goods included abortifacient pills, condoms, female syringes, and written advice called *A Confidential Circular for the Married*, did most of its trade by mail in the 1860s, although customers were also encouraged to come in person for goods and consultations.[129]

One person, in particular, symbolizes more than any other the changes occurring in the mid-nineteenth-century production and dispersal of reproductive control products and literature. This was Edward Bliss Foote, ideologue and entrepreneur, author and publisher, legitimate inventor and humbug.

Edward Bliss Foote and His Female Customers

Born in a village near Cleveland in 1829, Foote was a printer's apprentice at age fifteen, a compositor with the New Haven *Journal* at eighteen, and an associate editor of the *Brooklyn Morning Journal* while still in his twenties. Foote married a Massachusetts woman, Catherine Goodenough Bond, in 1852; one of their three sons, Edward Bond Foote, later wrote his own booklet of contraceptive advice, *The Radical Remedy in Social Science; or, Borning Better Babies through Regulating Reproduction by Controlling Conception*, and another, Hubert Foote, managed his father's Sanitary Bureau for many years.[130] Raised as a Presbyterian, Foote became a Unitarian while living in New England and attended O. B. Frothingham's church in New York City. Later he became an agnostic and supporter of freethought (joining and donating generously to the Federation of Freethought, the Secular Union, the Manhattan Liberal Club, and the National Defense Association, which was founded to fight the Comstock laws). He was graduated in 1860 from the Pennsylvania Medical University; starting medical practice in Saratoga Springs he called himself a "medical and electrical therapeutist." By 1864 he had opened a medical practice in New York City which continued to be an amalgam of official and unofficial medicine because, as a later biographer explained, he believed that doctors "should be able to relieve illness in any way, not necessarily those ways approved by the medical profession."[131] Unlike some antebellum reformers, Foote remained proud to be associated with "liberalism" even in the second half of the century, although his engraved portrait in the frontispiece of the 1858 *Medical Common Sense* showed an eccentric with unkempt hair, goatee, and unbuttoned coat; the 1864 edition showed a respectable gentleman with white shirt amd collar, tie, vest, and carefully buttoned jacket. The goatee, with its reminders of Foote's German background and youthful reformism, was now gone, replaced by a well-trimmed mustache.[132]

In his first important book, *Medical Common Sense*, in 1858, Foote raised the subject of the "best ways to control reproduction" but refused to discuss them in such a public manner; he informed interested readers that he would, however, sell his advice to married couples if they wrote, enclosing one dollar and both of their signatures, and information on their "temperaments." He criticized many methods as injurious and unreliable, especially abortion, withdrawal, "prevention pills," "caustic washes" used as injections, and douching with water.[133] But over the next five years, Foote had a noteworthy change of heart, although it is not clear what caused the change. He may have come to a clearer understanding of what his patients wanted, or he may have become bolder about public discussion of reproductive control. Samuel Palmer Putnam, in his brief biography of Foote in his 1894 *Four Hundred Years of Freethought*, wrote that Foote was still "pious" in 1858, only losing his religion later.[134] In his 1864 expanded and revised edition of *Medical Common Sense* Foote added more than one hundred pages devoted primarily to reproductive control and sexual physiology. Whereas earlier he had written that fertility intervention could be as injurious as "excessive childbearing" to female health, by 1864 he was calling "excessive childbearing" "the bane of society" because it destroyed women's health and brought into the world "deformed" children who then contributed to the degeneracy of civilization. Readers of the 1864 edition found lengthy descriptions of four contraceptives that he, so he said, had invented: his "membraneous envelope"—a type of condom made from fish bladders, the "apex envelope"—a rubber glans penis cap ("There can be no question as to its safety, if properly adjusted"), "the womb veil"—a rubber diaphragm (all of which would have provided relatively effective contraception, although they were costly), and an "electro-magnetic preventive machine" Foote said prevented conception by altering the partners' "electrical conditions" during sexual intercourse, but this one would have been worthless. The condoms cost three to five dollars a dozen, the "womb veil" cost six dollars, and the "electro-magnetic preventive machine" fifteen dollars.[135]

In the 1870s, concerned about transgressing the new laws against mailing birth control information but desiring to help the desperate people who wrote to him begging for information, Foote published a small, letter-sized pamphlet, *Confidential Pamphlet for the Married* (later retitled *Words in Pearl*). He continued to publish a longer medical advice book, now called *Plain Home Talk* (although the first part was a reprint of most of *Medical Common Sense*), but refused to discuss the prevention of conception. Instead, he told interested married people that they could obtain an important pamphlet "on the subject" for ten cents either in person at his office or through the mail. It "should," he said "be in the hands of every married lady."[136] He mailed the pamphlet widely, even including it in his "Sexual-Science" series of dime pamphlets.[137] He sent a copy to the former abolitionist Elizur Wright in 1876, explaining, "I . . . imagine that I am engaged in a physiological reform. . . . As I state in my little introductory paragraph it was simply scratched out in great haste and intended mainly to convey answers to questions which were almost daily asked me. Was indeed put in the miniature form in which you will find it for the purpose of enabling me to send it in letter form, sealed.[138] What Wright (who eventually had eighteen children) thought of the pamphlet is unknown.

Words in Pearl led to Foote's conviction for breaking the Comstock laws. Foote was arrested in 1874 for sending the pamphlet through the mail in a sealed envelope. To him it was "a purely medical work" but to Comstock it was an advertisement "for an infamous article—an incentive to crime to young girls and women."[139] Foote was found guilty and the judge levied a fine and court costs amounting to five thousand dollars.

Foote had become involved with reproductive control because he recognized the public demand, and throughout his career he missed few opportunities to cash in on that demand, especially if such businesses simultaneously promoted his reform beliefs, as for example his conviction that contraception was not only a health reform measure, but also a way to give women essential power where they were vulnerable and as a way to promote broader social reform through the birth of fewer but healthier and happier children. The censorship of the Comstock laws offended his freethought principles. Foote paid the legal fees of more than one of his liberal colleagues—DeRobigne Bennett, for one—who ran afoul of the censors, in addition to his own.

Foote epitomizes the growing commercialization of birth control in many ways. He was the most successful self-publisher of those involved in reform or reproductive control in the nineteenth century. In 1872 he founded the Murray Hill Publishing Company and under its imprint published more than sixty of his own works, including his pamphlets and books on reproductive control and other literature on health reform and freethought.[140] He became a consummate entrepreneur, selling his own medical devices and medicines through an extensive mail-order practice and a network of agents. Credit raters in 1861 called him a "splendid specimen of the genus humbug," adding that he did a "first rate business" making money from extensive advertising and mail-order sales.[141] Later, New York City credit reporters rated him "fairly well off, though spread out" and heavily mortgaged. When he retired he moved into a large house on the sound in Larchmont Manor, New York.

In the 1880s Foote operated a "Sanitary Bureau" at the same address as the Murray Hill Publishing Company. This became the distribution center for an extensive mail-order and advertising business, which, in spite of the Comstock laws, included "household remedies," several varieties of syringes, electrical machines, "soluble sanitary tampons," and other supplies advertised as "not to be found in every respectable drug-store."[142]

Foote became especially skillful in the developing art of advertising. When he mailed books to customers he included extra advertising circulars to be distributed to friends and acquaintances. Some advertised his contraceptives.[143] Although forced to remove his literature, Foote continued to advertise contraceptive devices suggestively, offering an "impregnating syringe," and a well-known abortion implement as an "impregnating speculum." He carefully described his "sanitary syringes" as adapted for "married women only," to be used for "thorough cleansing and the application of medicinal washes without waste and very simple in their action."[144]

Finally, and perhaps most important, Foote's career illustrates the conjunction of commercialized birth control with female consumerism in the mid-century United States. He aimed his contraceptive products and information at diverse publics, but he quickly recognized the new and growing importance of women as customers. He emphasized in publications both the ease with which women customers could obtain his products and the secrecy with which they could use them. Understanding women's hesitancy about visiting him in person (although he provided careful instructions about streetcars and walking routes to his office), he carefully explained the options of using the mails or frequenting retail establishments.

The growing abundance in reproductive control products and information for men and women alike was not an isolated phenomenon, for by mid century American society was being transformed by, in the phrases of historian Neil Harris, "a system of American consumption," a "national style of purchasing," and "American object consciousness."[145] Many Americans faced the unprecedented difficulty of an overabundance of information—historian Richard Brown notes that Victorian Americans found it increasingly difficult to "achieve a sense of mastery and control of information in an economy of abundance."[146] The very success of the commercialization process enhanced other problems, too. By bringing semirespectable and gray-market products into more prominent public visibility, the radical implications for women and men of separating sexuality from reproduction embedded in reproductive control became more visible, and this visibility in turn generated greater public opposition. One result of the commercial explosion in contraception and abortion was, in the last third of the century, Comstockery.

THE PEOPLE'S
MEDICAL LIGHTHOUSE;

A SERIES OF

POPULAR AND SCIENTIFIC ESSAYS

ON THE

NATURE, USES, AND DISEASES OF THE LUNGS, HEART, LIVER, STOMACH, KIDNEYS, WOMB AND BLOOD;

ALSO,

A KEY TO THE CAUSES, PREVENTION, REMEDIES, AND CURE OF PULMONARY AND OTHER KINDS OF

CONSUMPTION;

ASTHMA,	DEAFNESS,	GRUB AND WORMS,
BRONCHITIS,	BLINDNESS,	PILES AND FISTULA,
HEART DISEASES,	HEAD ACHES,	MISCARRIAGE,
DYSPEPSIA,	CATARRH,	FEMALE DISEASES,
LIVER COMPLAINT,	COSTIVENESS,	CANCERS AND TUMORS,
AGUE AND FEVER,	DIARRHŒA,	FALLING OF THE WOMB,
BALDNESS,	DYSENTERY,	ETC., ETC.

MARRIAGE GUIDE,

On Early Marriage; Pure Love a Stimulator of Mankind, and its Power to Banish Disease; the Magnetism of Love; Theory of Gaining the Affections of the Opposite Sex; Wedded Love to Prevent Consumption; Growth of the Fœtus; Organs of Generation; Prevention of Conception; Impressions on the Female Organs on the Unborn Child; Art of Procreating the Sexes at Will, and how to render Childbirth Easy and Safe; and Directions by which the Vigor, Beauty, and Elasticity of both Mind and Body may be retained from Childhood to a Ripe Old Age.

BY HARMON KNOX ROOT, A.M., M.D.,

AUTHOR OF A SERIES OF LECTURES ON HEALTH, AND INVENTOR OF THE INFALLIBLE LUNG BAROMETER.

ILLUSTRATED WITH 65 RARE AND INTERESTING ENGRAVINGS.

"Blessed is he that readeth, and they that keep those things that are written therein," [*St. John,*] for "It is better to hear the rebuke of the wise, than for a man to hear the song of fools." [*Solomon.*]

TENTH EDITION—REVISED.

NEW YORK:
PUBLISHED BY ADOLPHUS RANNEY, 195 BROADWAY.
CINCINNATI: H. M. RULISON, 115½ MAIN ST., BETWEEN 3D AND 4TH STS.

1854.

Title page of Harmon Knox Root's *The People's Medical Lighthouse* (1854). The lengthy subtitle with its enticing promises of marital information and "rare & interesting engravings" is typical of midcentury literature. Reproduced with permission of the Prints and Photographs Collection, History of Medicine Division of the National Library of Medicine.

Portrait of Harmon Knox Root, from Root, *The People's Medical Lighthouse* (1854). Reproduced with permission of the Prints and Photographs Collection, History of Medicine Division of the National Library of Medicine.

Portrait of Russell Thacher Trall, from Trall, *Pathology of the Reproductive Organs, Embracing all Forms of Sexual Disorder* (1862). Reproduced with permission of the Boston Medical Library in the Francis A. Countway Library of Medicine.

Portrait of Edward Bliss Foote, from Foote, *Medical Common Sense* (1864). Foote had made changes in his appearance as he sought greater respectability (see p. 238). Reproduced with permission of the Boston Medical Library in the Francis A. Countway Library of Medicine.

IMPORTANT DISCOVERY!

TO PREVENT CONCEPTION.

TO THE MARRIED AND THOSE CONTEMPLATING MARRIAGE.

After long reflection, and from consideration of true humanity, we have concluded to place before our readers our physiological discovery of the only reliable and harmless method yet known for the prevention of conception. These discoveries unfold an entirely new principle governing the laws of Procreation, and enable either sex to control an increase of family at will. That the female was designed by the Creator to bear offspring is not denied; but there are circumstances under which she should not have children.

Every physician knows that there are many women so constituted, that they cannot give birth to offspring. They also know that some cannot become mothers without fearful peril. Some cannot give birth to living children. Others should not become parents, because, if they do, they transmit confirmed diseases, as Consumption, Syphilis, Scrofula, etc., and their hapless progeny are doomed to a life of misery, and premature death. Again, too rapid increase of family not only breaks down the mother, but is a cause of great anxiety, especially to those in moderate circumstances.

What woman wishes to be kept in a state of continual pregnancy? How often do we hear a lady exclaim: "I have all the children I want, and am determined to have no more, if I can help it." But, alas! she is unable to escape. We ask any parent if the control of reproduction would not be an inestimable blessing? Every one will say: "Let my wife and self have this ability, whether we chose to exercise it or not." Our discovery gives this power, and imposes no restraint upon the sexual act, while, at the same time, it strengthens all the organs or parts. TO PREVENT CONCEPTION BY THIS MEANS IS ABSOLUTELY FREE FROM DANGER.

This discovery will do more for Virtue, Morality and Humanity, than all the reformers combined. Many a poor soul will be saved from sin; the awful crimes of abortion and child-murder will cease; and disease and crime will be lessened in a vast degree. Multitudes who have used it, are astonished and gratified, beyond measure, at its marvellous effects. As society is constituted, this subject is too delicate to give the testimony of any lady. Suffice it to say, that we have hundreds of letters testifying to the success of the solution.

Woman's Friend.--Anti-Conception Solution.

This beautiful chemical preparation places the control of child bearing directly in the power of the mother, where it properly belongs. A small quantity used before the sexual act will invariably obviate pregnancy. It tones up the system and counteracts the relaxation of the organs incident to child-birth affording renewed pleasure to both husband and wife. The application is simple, causes little or no inconvenience to the most fastidious, may be carried about the person, is certain to accomplish the desired object, and produces no pain or any unpleasantness.

Twenty years' experience enables us to assure ladies, that our discovery not only prevents pregnancy, but also cures falling of the womb, Leucorrhœa, acrid discharges, and inflammation of the vagina and neck of the womb, and all womb complaints.

PRICE:—FEMALE ANTI-CONCEPTION SOLUTION, $3 PER BOTTLE, OR 2 BOTTLES FOR $5.

Prepared by Dr. McTAGGART.

"Important Discovery to Prevent Conception," broadside (n.d., c. 1860s?). This is an advertisement for a douching solution. Although it is called a remedy for women, the author makes the unusual claim that the method permits "either sex to control an increase of family at will." Note, too, the rationales for using reproductive control. Reproduced with permission of the Boston Medical Library in the Francis A. Countway Library of Medicine.

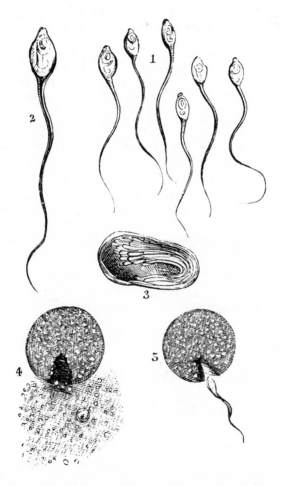

1. Zoosperme magnified.   2. Highly magnified.
3. Undeveloped Zoospermes in the Semen.
4. Female Ovum burst open for impregnation.
5. Zoospermes darting in to impregnate the Ovum.

"Zoospermes," from James Ashton, *The Book of Nature* (1861). Like many contemporaries, Ashton believed that sperm had animal characteristics and that, in addition to moving quickly, they even fought with one another. Reproduced with permission of the Boston Medical Library in the Francis A. Countway Library of Medicine.

DR. BRONSON'S
FEMALE PILLS

Have never yet failed, when the directions have been strictly followed, in removing difficulties arising from Obstruction, or Stoppage of Nature, or in restoring the system to perfect health when suffering from Spinal Affections, Prolapsus Uteri, the Whites, or other weakness of the uterine organs. Also, in all cases of Debility, or Nervous Frostration, Hysterics, Palpitations, &c., &c., which are the forerunners of more serious diseases. ☞ These Pills are perfectly harmless on the constitution, and may be taken by the most delicate female without causing distress ; at the same time they act like a charm by strengthening, invigorating, and restoring the system to a healthy condition, and by bringing on the monthly period with regularity, no matter from what cause the obstructions may arise. They should, however, NOT be taken during the first three or four months of pregnancy, though safe at any other time, as miscarriage would be the result in most cases. Sold in boxes containing 60 Pills. Price One Dollar. Post paid to any address, and sent secure from observation.

SPECIAL NOTICE.

In obstinate and old standing cases of Obstructions that have failed to find the desired relief by the use of the above Pills,

DR. BRONSON'S INFALLIBLE PILL NO. 2

are recommended, being four degrees stronger than the Female Pill No. 1, and are expressly prepared for such cases. They can never fail, and are safe, sure, prompt, and healthy. No female who values health and happiness with married life should be without these Pills. Price $5 per box, with full and explicit directions for use. Sent post paid, and free from observation, by mail.

THOS. F. CHAPMAN,
SOLE IMPORTER,
831 BROADWAY, NEW YORK.

"Dr. Bronson's Female Pills," advertising handbill (n.d.). This was included among the many advertisements in the circular *Chapman's Old Fashioned Cash Drug House* (New York, 186[?]). Reproduced with permission of the Boston Medical Library in the Francis A. Countway Library of Medicine.

HENRY C. NORTON & CO.

SOLE PROPRIETORS OF

DR. DE HENRIE SYRINGES AND ATOMIZERS

MANUFACTURERS OF ALL KINDS OF WHITE METAL GOODS,

Factory and Office, 24 BARCLAY STREET, NEW YORK.

THE SYPHON.

THE De HENRIE SYPHON SYRINGE

Acts automatically, dispensing with the pumping attendant upon the use of other syringes. A decided improvement upon the "Water Bag" or Fountain Syringes, as it combines a "Davidson Style," Syphon or Water Bag in one instrument; invaluable for invalids; unequaled as a nasal douche. Complete set of tubes for male, female, infant, ear, spray, and nose. In polished patent walnut case.

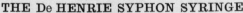

IMPROVED VAGINAL SPRAY.

This useful little instrument is destined to work a revolution in the treatment of Leucorrhœa, Catarrh of the Womb, and Ulceration of the Cervix Uteri, in the cure of which injections of liquid substances have formerly been so unsatisfactory on account of the difficulty of applying the fluid to the deep sulci of the vaginal folds.

The paramount advantages it possesses over any other heretofore used is that it *dilates* the *vagina*, thus expanding and exposing every part of its surface to the immediate action of the injected fluid, which at the same time flows out through perforations at the bottom of the spray. This is a *desideratum* which all Physicians who have had much experience in Gynæcology will at once appreciate.

Another advantage it possesses is the readiness with which it is applied, and the ease with which it is kept clean, and so finished that there are no sharp edges calculated to puncture or inflame.

Another advantage it possesses is that of being flexible; it accommodates itself to the form of the passage.

The spray is so constructed as to be applied to any of the syringes in general use.

The cut shows the instrument about two-thirds its size.

FOR SALE BY MORRISSON, PLUMMER & CO., CHICAGO, ILL.

"Dr. De Henrie Syringes and Atomizers," advertisement for douching syringes from Morrisson, Plummer & Co., *Druggists' Ready Reference* (1880). Minnesota Historical Society Collections.

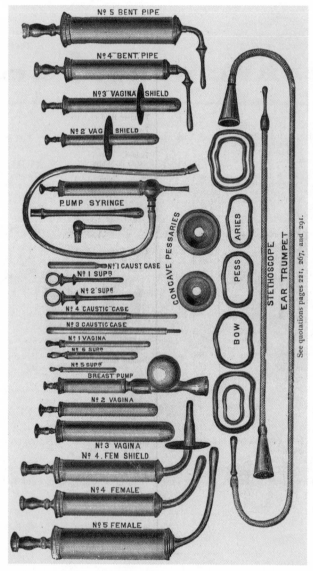

Varieties of "Female Syringes" from Morrisson, Plummer & Co., *The Druggists' Ready Reference* (Chicago, 1880). Minnesota Historical Society Collections.

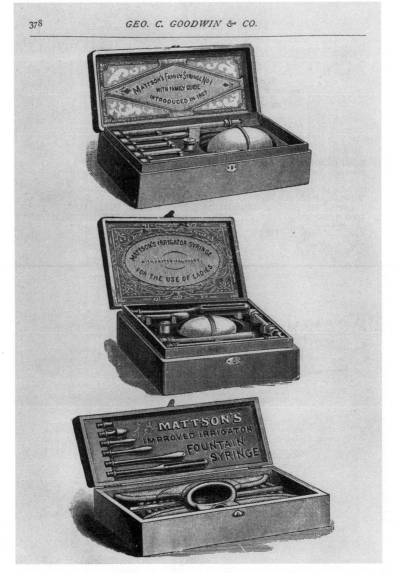

Mattson's Female and Family Douching Syringes in Packing Cases, from George C. Goodwin & Co., *Trade Catalogue* (1885). Note the printed guide. Reproduced with permission of the Baker Library, Harvard University Graduate School of Business Administration.

"National Syringes," advertisement from George C. Goodwin & Co., *Trade Catalogue* (1885). Reproduced with permission of the Baker Library, Harvard University Graduate School of Business Administration.

8

Criminalizing Reproductive Control: The End-of-Century Campaigns to Disempower Women

As reproductive control became commercialized after 1850, and as some women became increasingly able to assert a degree of independent control over their fertility through contraception and abortion, the deep ambivalences with which many Americans regarded such changes came increasingly into play. In the second half of the nineteenth century diverse groups emerged to try to restore American "social purity," and one of the issues they focused on was restricting sexual freedom and control of reproduction. Often historians have studied the campaigns against abortion and contraception as separate phenomena,[1] but the two movements shared important similarities in the opponents' motivations, in the imagery and symbolism of their public campaigns, and in the consequences. Both crusades were led by energetic, driven men; both were backed by professional organizations of white, middle class, native-born men—and women, as well —who had assumed the role of custodians of the public good. All branches of government were their allies; their goals were won through enactments of federal and state legislation and sustained by judicial decisions that criminalized contraception and abortion, both of which had in earlier decades been legal.

After Two Centuries of Legality, Reproductive Control Becomes a Felony

In the second half of the nineteenth century, state laws altered two hundred years of American custom and public policy toward abortion.

In some states it became illegal to obtain an abortion at any stage of pregnancy: abortionists began to face charges of second-degree homicide or manslaughter and women seeking abortions faced criminal prosecution.[2] Some but not all states made an exception if an official physician performed the abortion to save a woman's life.

For two centuries in America, abortion had been treated according to common law tradition in which abortions before "quickening"—fetal movement—were not punishable, and those procured later, after quickening, might be high misdemeanors if the woman died, but not felonies.[3] Some states began criminal code revisions in the 1830s and 1840s and included in those revisions statutes against abortion. The thrust of the new laws was twofold: to regulate those who could legally give abortions and to punish unlawful abortionists. In some states— Connecticut, Missouri, Illinois—abortion restrictions came in the form of tighter laws against the use of poisons. Only in New York was there a foretaste of the more stringent antiabortion laws to come. The New York law, passed in 1829, prohibited anyone, including a doctor, from attempting abortion at any period of pregnancy except to save a woman's life.

Between 1840 and 1860 the new statutory restrictions on abortion were challenged in nine state supreme courts, seven of which had upheld the common law tradition and ruled that an abortion before quickening was not a criminal offense.[4] Even after 1860 abortion cases were hard to prosecute: prosecutors found it difficult to obtain convictions, especially if there was any doubt about whether quickening of the fetus had occurred, or if common law traditions covering evidence and criminal defendants' rights appeared to have been violated by the prosecution or the police.[5] Juries continued to treat the prequickening distinction as significant, and of course it was difficult to prove that quickening had or had not occurred. Horatio Robinson Storer, a leader in the antiabortion campaign, noted disapprovingly in his 1860 book *On Criminal Abortion in America* that between 1849 and 1858 Massachusetts had prosecuted thirty-two trials concerning abortion but won not a single conviction.[6] The Iowa Supreme Court ruled in 1863 that the state law regulating abortion did not apply to self-induced abortions.[7] Historian Roger Lane estimates that of 151 indictments for abortion in postbellum Philadelphia, 127 came to verdict, 22 were found guilty, and 25 resulted in convictions.[8]

From the 1860s through the 1880s, however, states passed a new wave of restrictive abortion legislation.[9] Hugh S. Pomeroy, a Boston physician opposed to reproductive control, compiled information in 1888 about state laws on the subject. He concluded that there was still considerable confusion over whether "destruction of the infant" before quickening was a common law offense, although he cited two states—Pennsylvania and North Carolina—which unambiguously declared it a misdemeanor, eight states—California, Connecticut, Indiana, New Hampshire, New York, Wisconsin, Wyoming, and the Dakota Territory—which made the abortion-seeking woman criminally liable, and five states—Kentucky, New Jersey, Oregon, South Carolina, Texas—and the District of Columbia which had not yet passed any law regulating abortion. Laws in eight states—California, Indiana, Kansas, Massachusetts, Michigan, Nebraska, New York, and Ohio—forbade the advertisement of abortion-inducing drugs, and Illinois, Indiana, and Michigan outlawed advertisements for medicines for women if the language was ambiguous, such as "caution to the married."[10] Loopholes in earlier laws were now gradually eliminated so that, for example, individuals charged with violating the law could no longer claim that the medicine would not have induced abortion.

The most general result of this welter of conflicting and confusing state statutes was to drive abortion underground, making it far more difficult, expensive, and dangerous to obtain—a criminalization that lasted until the 1960s, when sixteen states liberalized their laws, and until 1973, when the U.S. Supreme Court ruled in *Roe v. Wade* that a woman has a fundamental right to decide, without governmental interference, whether to have an abortion in the first three months. Even in the *Roe* decision, however, the Court upheld the right of the state to restrict abortion once fetal viability was determined, unless a woman's life was at stake.

In addition to the changing legal status of abortion, federal and state laws passed in the 1870s and 1880s made it a felony to mail any products or information about contraception or abortion. Between the 1860s and the 1880s activist opponents secured legislation that made contraceptive literature "obscene" and attempts to disseminate information about contraception felonies. In the closing days of its third session in March 1873, the forty-second Congress, embattled and excoriated by the Credit Mobilier scandal (Union Pacific Railroad executives diverted funds into a separate company and bribed investigating congressmen and other politicians) passed what came to be called "the Comstock Law"—named for Anthony Comstock, a self-appointed vice hunter, a sponsor of the bill, and its zealous enforcer in the following decades. The stated purpose of the new law was to tighten loopholes in earlier legislation prohibiting the interstate trade in obscene literature and materials. But in one crucial departure from earlier laws, the long list of items prohibited from the mail, from private mail carriers, and from importation included "any article whatever for the prevention of conception, or for causing unlawful abortion." For the first time in U.S. history the federal government declared the dissemination of information about contraception and abortion to be illegal. State laws that followed went beyond the federal statute, punishing the receivers as well as the senders of information and in some cases making the actual practices of contraception and abortion illegal. Control of women's reproductive behavior now had the force of law.

The Comstock Law, officially the Act for the Suppression of Trade in, and Circulation of Obscene Literature and Articles of Immoral Use, contained five sections. Two dealt with enforcement and one prohibited any of the listed prohibited items from being imported into the United States. Of the two other sections, one, although technically applicable only to the District of Columbia and the U.S. territories, actually had a far wider impact because of its influence on state laws: soon after it passed, several states used it as a model. It was now a misdemeanor, punishable by six months to five years of hard labor or a fine of one hundred to two thousand dollars, for any person: to

> sell, or lend, or give away, or in any manner exhibit, or . . . offer to sell, or to lend, or to give away, or in any manner to exhibit, or [to] otherwise publish or offer to publish in any manner, or [to] have in his possession for any such purposes . . . or [to] advertize the same for sale, or [to] write or print, or cause to be written or printed any card, circular, book, pamphlet, advertisement, or notice of any kind stating when, where, how, or of whom, or by what means any of the articles in this section can be purchased or obtained, or shall manufacture, draw, or print, or in any wise make any of such articles.

The forbidden articles included, along with "any obscene book, pamphlet, paper, writing, advertisement . . . or any drug or medicine," "any article whatever for the prevention of conception, or for causing unlawful abortion."[11]

The last section of the new law, which applied to the entire United States, listed "obscene" materials that could not be sent through the the U.S. mails, including for the first time among the prohibited items "any article or thing designed or intended for the prevention of conception or procuring of abortion." It was now illegal to mail such items, to send out information about where such items could be obtained or were made, or to mail advertisements about them. It was forbidden as well to cause someone else to mail, or to take from the mails any of the above items "in pursuance of any plan or scheme for disposing of any of the hereinbefore-mentioned articles." Transgressing the statute was a misdemeanor punishable by one to ten years at hard labor for each offense and/or a fine of one hundred to five thousand dollars.[12]

By 1885 twenty-four state legislatures had passed "little Comstock laws" modeled on the federal statute or on a more stringent New York obscenity law passed shortly after the federal statute. Because of the federal precedent, the existing obscenity laws of the other states had begun to be interpreted as prohibiting reproductive control itself.[13] Some state laws went considerably further than the federal law. Fourteen—Colorado, Indiana, Iowa, Massachusetts, Minnesota, Mississippi, Missouri, Montana, Nevada, New Jersey, New York, Pennsylvania, Washington, and Wyoming—sought to make even private conversations illegal by prohibiting the verbal transmission of information about contraception or abortion; eleven states—Colorado, Indiana, Iowa, Minnesota, Mississippi, New Jersey, New York, North Dakota, Ohio, Pennyslvania, and Wyoming—made it a criminal offense to possess instructions for the prevention of conception; the state of Colorado forbade anyone to bring contraceptive knowledge into the state; four states—Colorado, Idaho, Iowa, and Oklahoma—authorized the search for and seizure of contraceptive instructions. Connecticut—and only Connecticut—outlawed the act itself of controlling conception; this is why, in 1965, the Griswold case was brought in Connecticut: defense lawyers chose its law as the most extreme violation of women's sexual freedom.[14]

Some states allowed exemptions not in the federal statute. Seven—Colorado, Indiana, Missouri, Nebraska, Ohio, Pennsylvania, and Wyoming—exempted medical colleges from prosecution; eight—Colorado, Indiana, Kansas, Missouri, Nebraska, Ohio, Pennsylvania, and Wyoming—exempted medical books, six exempted doctors—Colorado, Indiana, Nevada, New York, Ohio, and Wyoming—and four—Colorado, Indiana, Ohio, and Wyoming—exempted druggists. What physicians could legally say on the subject of reproductive control was not clear. In seventeen states and in the District of Columbia no doctor was permitted to instruct a patient on contraception even in the privacy of a medical office.[15]

The laws were upheld and even strengthened by court cases. In *U.S. v. Foote* in 1876 the court ruled that "a written slip of paper" giving prohibited information about contraception was a "notice" within the meaning of the law even if it had been sent in reply to a letter asking for information. In *U.S. v. Bott* in 1873 the defendant was found guilty of sending an advertisement even though the prohibited article was not at the designated place. In *Bates v. U.S.* in 1881 the defendant was guilty even though he had not actually deposited the pills in the mail himself and even though they "would not *alone* prevent conception or procure abortion."[16] Although in an 1892 case a Milwaukee judge chastized Comstock for his entrapment methods and in an 1897 case a judge ruled that a whole book and not just the passages deemed obscene had to be admitted as evidence, the Comstock laws were not mitigated by court decisions until the 1930s and were not overturned until a series of U.S. Supreme Court decisions in the 1960s and 1970s.

The Supreme Court ruled in *Griswold v. Connecticut* in 1965 that a state law prohibiting the use of contraceptive devices by anyone, married or single, was invalid and that people who operated birth control clinics were not "aiders and abettors" of criminal acts. The court asked, "Would we allow the police to search the sacred precincts of marital bedrooms for telltale signs of the use of contraceptives?" and responded, "The very idea is repulsive to the notions of privacy surrounding the marriage relationship."[17] In 1971 the prohibition against mailing information on contraception was deleted from postal laws, although the ban on mailing information about abortion was not. In the 1972 *Eisenstadt v. Baird* decision the Supreme Court said that if married couples were not legally barred from getting contraceptives through a physician, a state law forbidding them to single individuals violated the equal protection clause of the Fourteenth Amendment: "[T]he marital couple is not an independent entity . . . but an association of two individuals each with a separate intellectual and emotional makeup. If the right of privacy means anything, it is the right of the *individual*, married or single, to be free from unwarranted governmental intrusion into matters so fundamentally affecting a person as the decision whether to bear or beget a child."[18] A 1977 Supreme Court case, *Carey v. Population Services International*, struck down a state law prohibiting the sale of contraceptives to minors under sixteen, prohibiting the distribution of contraceptives by anyone except licensed pharmacists, and the prohibiting of advertisements for or display of contraceptives.

The stronger antiabortion legislation of the second half of the nineteenth century was the result of a carefully orchestrated campaign organized and led by a few physicians in the nascent American Medical Association. Behind the obscenity laws were "social purity" reformers and their organizers. In the drives against both contraception and abortion, the determined will of zealous individuals gave focus and energy to large public crusades.

Anthony Comstock and the AMA: The "Social Purity" Crusades

Comstock was the most colorful figure associated with the disempowerment of women and men in the practice of reproductive control in the second half of the nineteenth century. Easily lampooned and caricatured from his day to ours as a mutton-chopped buffoon, a fanatical puritan with a horror of sex, he was, nevertheless, a tireless and even formidable foe of those he defined as enemies for corrupting the morals of youth, and he proved to be a wily lobbyist for legislation and a staunch prosecutor of wrongdoing. Sympathetic biographers portrayed him battling "the hydra-headed monster" of obscenity, dangerous patent medicines and "quack" medical practices, dishonest gambling, and lottery schemes.[19]

Comstock was born in 1844 in New Canaan, Connecticut, one of seven surviving children of a farmer and sawmill-owner father and a devout Congregationalist mother who died when he was ten.[20] Educated in local schools, fervently attending the Congregational church and Sunday school, he joined the Union army in December 1863 after the death of his older brother, Samuel, from wounds suffered at Gettysburg. He joined the Christian Commission, volunteering, like others, to visit soldiers to distribute temperance and religious tracts and to write letters home for the dying. Comstock also organized and conducted regular prayer meetings for his regiment, a service that brought him the gratitude of "a little group of twenty or thirty men" and the scorn and ridicule of scores more who hazed Comstock for his intolerance of drink, gambling, and profanity.[21] After the war he worked in low-level positions in dry goods stores in New Haven, where he boarded with the widow and sons of a missionary, and in New York City, where he lived in cheap boardinghouses with other young clerks whose habits of spending evenings in saloons—or brothels—and whose taste for sensationalist literature shocked him. At twenty-seven he had saved enough to buy a small house in Brooklyn and to marry Margaret Hamilton, daughter of a New York merchant and Presbyterian elder, a woman ten years Comstock's senior. His jobs and lodgings in New York in the area around Pearl, Broadway, Nassau, and Grand streets took him into the heart of the district where respectable publishing and mixed commerce coexisted with establishments that sold inexpensive literature and prints, erotica, and contraceptive products and where abortionists' offices thrived. Horrified by this trade in sexual goods and literature, he tried, mostly in vain, to get the police to stop it, then began to chase wrongdoers himself, filing formal legal complaints as a citizen against them. His zealous exertions brought him to the attention of Morris Ketchum Jesup, who became Comstock's chief financial backer and a powerful supporter of his activities for the next thirty years.

Jesup, then in his early thirties, must have seen Comstock as a kindred soul, for he, too, had been raised in a devoutly Congregationalist home in small-town (in Westport) Connecticut and had lost a parent— his father—when he was twelve. His family lost its money in the Panic of 1837 and young Jesup worked from age twelve, but by the time he met Comstock he was a wealthy New York City merchant, banker, and railroad financier, well on his way to becoming a multi-millionaire.[22] He was also a philanthropist, a founder of the New York Young Men's Christian Association, a conservationist working to preserve the Adirondacks, and the founder and million-dollar benefactor of the Museum of Natural History. Jesup introduced Comstock to other influential men in New York and to the officers of the YMCA. Within two months of making these valuable contacts, Comstock had been given the financial and political backing of an offshoot of the YMCA, the newly created New York Committee for the Suppression of Vice. He became their salaried special agent. When the Committee for the Suppression of Vice was granted incorporation in May 1873, two months after the passage of the federal Comstock Law, their charter explicitly granted them the right to help the police in law enforcement, to appoint special agents with the power to arrest suspected wrongdoers, and to search and seize evidence. Their money came from private donations but also from their charter-granted right to retain 50 percent of the fines levied against those transgressors they brought to trial and convicted.[23]

Comstock began his personal campaign against vice in earnest in 1871, a year when he might have been expected to be diverted from his growing preoccupation with wrongdoers (he was especially distraught over purveyors of obscene literature), because he was newly married, the proud owner of a new house, and a pleased father-to-be. Instead, his diary for that year was full of "unrest and dissatisfaction."[24] The next year, however, was transformative, for Comstock met Jesup in March, began to work for the Committee for the Suppression of Vice in May, began an ambitious legal case against Victoria Woodhull in November, and in December began his campaign before Congress for the stronger antiobscenity/antireproductive control law. The financial support of Jesup and his friends gave Comstock the necessary economic freedom to devote all his energies against vice, and he became an effective lobbyist, securing, in March 1873, his major triumph, the passage of the federal obscenity statute that criminalized reproductive control. When it was signed into law he was appointed a special agent for the U.S. Post Office, with power to inspect and seize illegally mailed materials, a position he held until he died in 1915.

Behind Comstock stood the men in the various committees for the suppression of vice and the women and men in the broader "social purity" movement of the late nineteenth century, of which the vice committees were only one part.[25] The founders and leading members of the vice societies that, following New York's lead, were organized in Boston, St. Louis, Chicago, Louisville, Cincinnati, and San Francisco in the 1870s were men raised in small towns and farms, often in deeply religious families "dominated by the ministerial strain." These men, in their thirties and forties, some having amassed large fortunes, found the postwar urban scene alarming. Although they had personally profited economically from the ongoing transformations in American life, they feared the loss of the certainties, the seeming homogeneity and traditional pieties, of the world of their youth. Samuel Colgate, head of his family's soap business, served as the first president of the New York Society for the Suppression of Vice for three decades; William J. Breed came from a Massachusetts fishing village to Cincinnati, where he made a fortune manufacturing undertakers' supplies and where he founded the city's Society for the Suppression of Vice; Boston's Watch and Ward Society was dominated by Frederick Baylies Allen, the highly respected assistant Episcopal minister at Trinity Church.[26] In 1912, Josiah Strong, one of the officers of the New York society, signed a written expression of appreciation for the help Comstock had given the group over the decades. Strong was well known as the author of *Our Country*, a bestseller in 1888, expressing, among other things, his fears of national decline because the superior white races were not reproducing and the less fit races were. His "race suicide" ideas were taken up by other prominent Americans in the early twentieth century, including Theodore Roosevelt. Another member of the New York Society for the Suppression of Vice who stood by Comstock for forty years was William Ives Buddington, pastor of the Congregational church in Brooklyn which Comstock and his wife attended.

The men who created and sustained the country's burgeoning YMCA organizations and committees for the suppression of vice were part of a larger, broadly based "social purity" reform movement that coalesced in the decades after the Civil War. Working at the state and local levels, dozens of organizations of women and men sought to promote temperance and Sunday closing laws, to control prostitution, to end the "white slave traffic," and to suppress obscenity. In David Pivar's analysis of those in the social purity "elite," the greatest number listed their occupation simply as "reformer," but the second largest vocation among the men was that of minister, followed by physician.[27] These reformers shared the impulses of the northern intellectuals analyzed by historian George Fredrickson, whose major lesson from the Civil War was their new willingness to turn the powers of the state to harnessing individual actions and private behaviors.[28] Many people in the decades after the war turned their reform energies to securing changes in laws so as to give the state greater power over areas of life once considered private, as the state began to regulate or restrict gambling, drinking, lotteries, narcotics, child labor, and reproductive control.[29]

One of the underlying issues in almost all of the social purity campaigns was the restriction of sexuality itself. Many reformers saw the growing commerce in cheap literature as inciting unhealthy passions in the young, as leading them to corruption and depravity. Particularly offensive was the flood of sensationalist paperbound literature and illustrations hawked at railroad stations, steamship depots, and through the mails. But others wanted to leash the sexuality of middle class men. As historian William Leach has pointed out, feminists of all types in the second half of the century wanted to harness male sexuality and to give women greater sexual "self-ownership." It was their shared concerns about the dangers of sexuality that gave many reformers a concern about reproductive control. Some of the feminists who talked about reproductive control in terms of "voluntary motherhood" disliked contraceptives because they did not restrict male sexuality, but others were hostile to contraception and abortion when they were used by "fashionable" women who were too frivolous and pleasure-loving.[30] Yet there is little concrete evidence to suggest who and how many among the purity reformers and members of the vice societies specifically wanted reproductive control criminalized. It was not an openly expressed concern. While some certainly took public stands against abortion and opposed obscenity in vague and general ways, it is not at all clear that they were caught up in the specifics of a campaign to restrict access to contraception. They supported the Comstock laws and the work of the vice societies, not because they had a particular antagonism to birth control but because it was vaguely associated with indecent literature and improper devices. The Women's Christian Temperance Union established a department for the suppression of impure literature in 1883, and the National Mothers Congress listened to a speech of Comstock's in 1897. But if they agreed with Comstock's focused attack on reproductive control itself, they did so quietly without leaving much documentation about their specific worries about contraception and abortion.

Comstock himself, on the other hand, was hostile to abortion and the prevention of conception, and it was largely his focused energy that secured the criminalization of reproductive control in the federal and state antiobscenity laws. It was Comstock's doing, for example, that caused the key words "for the prevention of conception and procuring of abortion" to be inserted into the federal legislation of 1873. He may have first gotten the idea from the wording of a New York bill the YMCA drafted in 1866 when it sent two trusted members, Charles F. Whitehead and Cephas Brainerd, to Albany to get a state law suppressing obscene literature. The law Brainerd and Whitehead obtained in 1868 actually included a brief reference to the prevention of conception and the procuring of abortion in its list of obscenities. The brief reference was deleted when the New York law was amended in 1872. At the federal level, when an earlier Post Office regulation against obscenity was amended in 1872 it forbade mailing obscene books and pictures but did not include advertisements or newspapers. Nor did it prohibit the advertisement, mailing, or sale of reproductive control items. Purity reformers were dissatisfied with that law, however, and Comstock wanted to lobby Congress for a stronger law. Once he obtained Jesup's promise of financial support, he went to Washington, D.C., in November 1872 to lobby, taking his own version of a bill. This version included the prohibition on birth control.

It is worth looking in some detail at the way the Comstock bill was handled in Congress from December 1872 until it passed in March 1873, not only because there are few records of the legislative phase of any of the Comstock laws but also because the records underscore the point made above: that there is some ambiguity about the centrality of reproductive control per se in the campaigns against obscenity.

Comstock drafted his own bill, but he solicited the advice of two people before turning it over to the congressional sponsors: a lawyer, Benjamin Vaughan Abbott (Abbott's brother, Francis Ellingwood Abbott, was later responsible for a schism in the National Liberal League in 1878 when, as president, he refused to fight to repeal the Comstock laws) and Supreme Court Justice William Strong. Abbott helped Comstock in one further way: he took three bills against obscenity already before the House (one concerning Washington, D.C., one changing the penalties of the 1872 law without broadening its scope, and one forbidding the transmission of obscene materials by carrier) and combined them with Comstock's. Introduced into the House in early February, the combined bill went before Lowell, Massachusetts, Democrat Benjamin Butler's Judiciary Committee. Butler altered the bill radically (although no sources say what he did to it) and it had to be referred back to committee and to be reprinted.

Comstock persuaded Republican congressman Clinton L. Merriam, from Locust Grove, New York (who had shepherded the 1872 obscenity bill through), and Republican senator William Windom from Winona, Minnesota, to introduce his bill into their respective chambers. There was so little debate on the bill in either the House or the Senate that most legislators probably did not know much about its provisions except, in general, that it tried to reduce the trade in "obscenity." Washington was mired in scandals—the Credit Mobilier affair and in an uproar involving customhouse officers and bribes—which distracted attention from issues on the floor, but possibly even if congressmen had been less preoccupied they might have passed the Comstock bill without much scrutiny because it was politically hazardous not to oppose obscenity.

The only serious issue raised in either house came from forty-five-year-old Republican senator George F. Edmunds of Burlington, Vermont, who wanted to add, after the prohibition on anyone's selling or giving away "any article or medicines for the prevention of conception or for causing abortion" an exemption "except on a prescription of a physician in good standing, given in good faith."[31] When the bill came out of committee on 15 February and Comstock noted Edmunds's amendment, he complained in his diary, "Has he friends in this business that he desires to shield?"[32] Edmunds's amendment was quietly quashed and never reached debate. The senator most responsible for eliminating it and for securing the bill's passage was sixty-nine-year-old Republican William A. Buckingham from Norwich, Connecticut. Buckingham's motivations are unclear, although they may have been as simple as political antagonism to the junior senator from his state, or they may have derived from his background, for like the men of the YMCA, his were the values of an earlier era. He had been a farmer and then a small-town merchant before becoming the war governor of Connecticut. Buckingham was aided in deleting the Edmunds amendment by San Francisco Democrat Eugene Casserly, whose parents had immigrated from Ireland to New York when he was four. Casserly's Catholic background may have made him particularly interested in curbing reproductive control, but there is no proof.

Buckingham removed Edmunds's amendment from the bill but hid the change in deliberately obscure language, proposing to "amend the amendment by striking out the first section and inserting the following." When Roscoe Conkling, Republican from Utica, New York, objected that no one knew what was being substituted, Buckingham replied, "There is no material alteration in the section. It is rather to strengthen it than otherwise."

Conkling complained several times about not knowing exactly what he was being asked to vote on, for the senators did not have legible copies of the bill or of any proposed changes before them: "For one, although I have tried to acquaint myself with it, I have not been able to tell, either from the reading of [the] apparently illegible manuscript in some cases by the Secretary, or from private information gathered at the moment, and if I were to be questioned now as to what this bill contains, I could not aver anything certain in regard to it."[33] But the bill passed, without any exemptions for physicians to distribute birth control information or products.

The only place in the entire legislative record of this bill where contraception itself was even referred to was in a speech published in the *Congressional Record* by Representative Merriam after the bill was passed. Merriam quoted a letter from Comstock which included these words:

> In the same way, by advertising beautiful views or pictures of some celebrated place or person these men receive answers from innocent persons for these pictures, and among the pictures sent will be one or more of these obscene pictures and catalogues of these vile books and rubber goods. For be it known that wherever these books go, or catalogues of these books, there you will ever find, as almost indispensable, a complete list of rubber articles for masturbation or for the professed prevention of conception.[34]

Conkling warned his colleagues: "The indignation and disgust which everybody feels in reference to the acts which are here aimed at may possibly lead us to do something which, when we come to see it in print, will not be the thing we would have done if we had understood it and were more deliberate about it."[35] His warning was prescient: the implications of the new legislation did reach far beyond what most legislators, presumably, wanted, although, on the other hand, there is nothing in the congressional evidence to suggest that the legislators would have defended the public's right to birth control information. When the bill came to a vote on 2 March there was no quorum, so that tellers were appointed, the rules were suspended, and the bill passed in the House 100 to 37. (There is no record identifying the 37.)

In the Senate it was adopted without a recorded vote. It became law on 3 March. Three days later Comstock was commissioned a Special Agent of the U.S. Post Office, empowered to search, seize, and destroy illegal mail.

Of all the aspects of the antiabortion and anticontraception campaigns of the nineteenth century, we know the least about the actual movement of the bills through the state and federal legislatures. Historians have assumed that committees of the AMA and social purity committees were in collusion with the politicians, but little concrete evidence has been adduced about who exactly was involved, what arguments were used, which legislators supported and which objected to the legislation and why. There is some evidence that Comstock himself lobbied for the New York, Massachusetts, and Connecticut laws. Legal historian C. Thomas Dienes writes that "there is no doubt that Anthony Comstock and the vice societies were instrumental" in the passage of those three state laws, but Dienes provides little corroborative evidence.[36] If there were hearings on the state bills, they were not published.[37]

Medical Professionals Struggle for Power and Control of Reproduction

In 1839, Hugh Lenox Hodge, chair of obstetrics at the University of Pennsylvania Medical School and the inventor of numerous pessaries for female uterine complaints, published as a pamphlet the text of a lecture to his medical students, *An Introductory Lecture to a Course on Obstetrics.* The historian John Paull Harper calls it "the first major American polemic on the moral implications of abortion," for in it Hodge criticized abortion on the grounds that embryos could think and perceive right and wrong. Thirty years later Hodge republished the pamphlet with the far less euphemistic title, *Foeticide, or Criminal Abortion.*[38]

Other than Hodge, none of the doyens of obstetrics and gynecology evinced much concern about abortion until 1855, when David Humphreys Storer, the first professor of obstetrics at Harvard Medical School and a specialist also on the diseases of women, brought it up in an introductory lecture to his medical class at Harvard. In his lecture he said that abortion and the prevention of conception, as well, were the principal causes of what he believed to be dangerously increasing rates of uterine disease in the United States. They were also responsible for the "comparative smallness of the families of the present day."[39]

Storer blamed "fashion" for young brides' anxiety about early pregnancy: "She will not endure the seclusion and deprivations necessarily connected with the pregnant condition, but resorts to means, readily procurable, to destroy the life within her."[40] He blamed mothers for wanting to limit family size, and this he attributed to being "pecuniarily unable to have her family provided for in the manner in which they have been accustomed to live." He countered feminist arguments that women are "born for higher purposes than propagation of the species" and criticized as false any medical ideas leading women to believe that childbirth was dangerous.

Although women's willingness to prevent or abort pregnancies horrified Storer, he was equally intent on elevating the moral and medical authority of physicians. Doctors had the responsibility to discourage family limitation practices; the public, on the other hand, could not be allowed to think for itself or to judge the morality of the issue, for prescribing morality was the duty of the physician.

Storer's attempt to publish his lecture caused dissension among the medical faculty at Harvard, some of whom questioned his facts about the increase in uterine diseases, disagreed with his interpretation of the dangers of family limitation, and feared that the publicity "might prejudice the school in the eyes of the community." The article was suppressed until 1872, when Storer's son, Horatio Robinson Storer, himself prominently involved in the antiabortion campaign and the editor of the *Journal of the Gynaecological Society of Boston*, had it published with a brief explanation of its earlier suppression.[41] He said that the lecture had been suppressed by H. J. Bigelow, a prominent Boston physician who, along with Storer, Senior, had been cofounder of the Tremont Medical School and a Harvard colleague. Both men were cantankerous and proud, so personality clashes and ideological differences were unsurprising. Also probably involved in the suppression of Storer's lecture was Edward H. Clarke, professor of materia medica at Harvard, who, at an 1871 meeting of the Boston Obstetrical Society, pronounced "praiseworthy" the effort of women "to regulate the size of their families" ("The endeavor to regulate the birth of children, with the object of producing the most perfect offspring is as commendable in the case of man as in that of the lower animals").[42]

Only when the junior Storer, casting about for a way to gain recognition and to make his own mark, preempted abortion as a target did a full-fledged medical crusade against abortion and, secondarily, against contraception get under way. For the rest of the century, under the aegis of the AMA, physicians became the most visible single group seeking to tighten the laws against abortion.[43]

For Horatio Robinson Storer, an ambitious son following in the foot-
steps of a famous father, his early career was auspicious: Harvard, the
Harvard Medical School, then medical study in London, Paris, and
Edinburgh, where by dint of family connections he was the private
assistant to one of the most renowned physicians in Britain, Sir James
Simpson. He returned to Boston in 1855 at the age of twenty-five, and
within two years his investigation of "criminal abortion" had propelled
him into the leadership of the gathering crusade. Storer may have
been influenced in his purpose by his stay in England and Scotland,
where British physicians were beginning to seek more restrictive
abortion legislation.

Young Storer began by gathering data on abortion and statistics on
stillbirths and maternal deaths from colleagues all over the country,
from Connecticut, Virginia, Tennessee, Ohio, Washington, D.C., Delaware, and even from the Minnesota Territory, from which C. W. Le
Boutillier wrote back: "The practice of producing abortion is frequently resorted to in our vicinity and it is not infrequent for married
women of high social position to apply for medicines which will produce abortion—and it is with regret that I say that Regular physicians
have in many instances [participated] in these damnable practices."[44]
In Massachusetts, Storer persuaded the Suffolk District Medical Society and the Massachusetts Medical Committee each to appoint an in-
vestigative committee with himself as chair of each. In May 1857, at
the annual meeting of the AMA in Nashville, he was appointed chair
of a committee to investigate criminal abortion and shrewdly selected
as the seven other members men whose views he knew from earlier
correspondence agreed with his own but who were broadly representative in geography and age.[45] Storer wrote the final report, but, always the tactician, he sent copies to eminent colleagues to enlist their
moral support. He asked Hugh Lenox Hodge to cosign with him, and
Hodge agreed to do so.[46]

At its annual meeting the AMA accepted the committee's report,
published it in the association's journal, and accepted the committee's
urging that state legislatures and state medical societies be urged to
make abortion more difficult.[47] Storer did not have equally satisfactory
results with the Massachusetts Medical Society, whose report concluded that the laws of the Commonwealth on criminal abortion "are
sufficiently stringent provided they are executed." Storer protested
that he had been "absent from this part of the country" when that
report was accepted and pleaded to be allowed to file a minority report at the next meeting. Whether he was allowed to do so is uncertain, but his relations with the Massachusetts Medical Society, in any

case, deteriorated steadily until, in 1870, he objected to the admission of its delegates into the larger AMA.[48] The quarrel between the Massachusetts Medical Society and the AMA revolved around more than one issue, but the dispute that particularly angered Storer was the tolerance the Massachusetts group displayed for irregular doctors. Although the Massachusetts Medical Society did not allow Thomsonians, homeopaths, or spiritualists to join, a physician, once admitted to the society could not be expelled if he then began irregular practices. This, and their unreceptivity to the abortion campaign, turned Storer sour. He was also caught up in another controversy over reproductive control when the journal he coedited and financed, the *Journal of the Gynaecological Society of Boston*, became a vehicle in the 1870s for articles opposing abortion and contraception, while the rival *Boston Medical and Surgical Journal* published several articles that supported family limitation and refused, in 1865, to publish Storer's article on abortion, explaining that "enough space had already been given to ["this discussion"]" and that the editors "would decline any further communication on the subject."[49]

Storer published the committee's report as his own book, *On Criminal Abortion in America*, in 1860, and persuading the AMA in 1864 to sponsor a contest for a "short and comprehensive tract for circulation among females for the purpose of enlightening them upon the criminality and physical evils of forced abortions." Storer anonymously submitted an essay with that title, "The Criminality and Physical Evils of Forced Abortion," and won the one-hundred-dollar prize and gold medal. (It surely did not hurt his chances that his father was one of the four judges.) This he published in 1866 for general circulation as *Why Not? A Book for Everywoman*.[50]

Storer's efforts shaped the campaign against abortion and, increasingly also by the last third of the century, affected the effort to ensure that contraception be seen as medically dangerous and criminal. Several state medical committee reports issued on abortion quoted Storer, used his statistics, and accepted his basic premises. In addition, as editor of the Boston Gynaecological Society's journal, he was in a position to solicit and select articles favorable to his own views.[51]

The AMA and the social purity reformers worked for the new laws as part of their efforts to gain greater control over key aspects of American life. The physicians wanted broader public respect for medicine, tighter control over who was to be allowed into the profession and what therapies they could practice. They wanted to drive out irregulars and sectarians, "quacks" and abortionists. They sought also an expanded role for physicians as moral arbiters, a role some of the regular medical professionals had aspired to since the days of Benjamin Rush, who, interested in promoting virtue in the newly created republic, envisioned physicians in the role priests held in the Old World.[52] One result of the new antiabortion legislation was an increase in the AMA's control over its own profession. The campaign against abortion was seen as a way to elevate their status among the general public by emphasizing their medical and scientific expertise in obstetrics and gynecology.

Regularly trained physicians in the early nineteenth century had, to the contrary, received little respect from the public and they had little control over the practice of medicine. By the Jacksonian era, with licensing laws under attack in many states, with growing numbers of unregulated medical schools turning out doctors, with the ranks of sectarians and irregulars swelling by the year, the medical "establishment" was embattled. Physicians wanting greater professionalism were caught in a bind. To persuade hesitant state legislatures to reinstitute licensing laws, they needed to persuade the public of their expertise; to raise public esteem they had to be able to control decisions on who entered the profession and what they practiced.[53] The growing public concern with women's health and the increasingly open reliance of middle class, married couples on abortion as a family limitation practice provided a focal issue. Some physicians in the ranks of the AMA began to voice grave anxiety about the evils of what they labeled "criminal abortion," "antenatal infanticide," and "feticide." They gathered statistics, issued reports, and then turned to the legislative process to pass the new and punitive laws against abortion.

The social purity reformers, for their part, sought expanded power over women and the young (what some reformers called America's "dependent groups"), explaining their own aggrandizement as an effort to protect the easily corrupted, innocent, and naive. "Committees for the Suppression of Vice" aimed to eliminate what Comstock called "traps for the young" by undoing the "hydra-headed monster," obscenity. To Comstock, obscenity was anything that created impure thoughts in otherwise innocent minds. He wanted to forbid the public access to literature and pictures capable of creating "impure thoughts." At times he focused on keeping such material from the young, and at other times from a generalized "public."

Comstock not only made no distinction between preventing conception and procuring abortion, he made no distinction between them and obscenity. His writings indicate no awareness that there might be a difference between a contraceptive diaphragm and a "French tickler," a condom and a dildo, a book such as Trall's *Sexual Physiology* and *Nell, Wicked Girl of the Streets*. And, in fact, contraceptives and staid advice literature were often sold together in the areas of town already associated with vice. Comstock's public and private writings are permeated by a concern with tamping down appetites of all types, but his horror of sex especially stands out. Two perceptive biographers have described him as "engaged in his own Civil War, a war which never came to any Appomattox. . . . [He] was a conscript in the enduring fight between Flesh and Spirit."[54]

Horatio Robinson Storer, who came to the fore with his campaign against abortion, considered the prevention of conception to be nearly as pernicious as abortion. He linked the two practices in their effects on women's health: "The demands of fashion shorten or prevent nursing, the demands of fashion often forbid a woman from bearing children; but whether this is attained by the prevention of impregnation, or by the induction of miscarriage, it is almost inevitably attended . . . by a grievous shock to the mother's system, that sooner or later undermines her health if even it does not directly induce her death." And abortions caused many ills in women: "lame backs," "neuralgic breasts," "obscure abdominal aches and pains," "severe and intractable headaches," "disabled limbs," "cramp and paralysis," "impatient bladders," "easily deranged stomachs." Also, much "of the general hypochondria and despondency, that of the most gentle, even almost angelic dispositions made the shrew and virago, and of the purest and most innocent produce . . . the worst of sinners, even at times effecting suicide." Women, Storer continued, tried to prevent pregnancy—"by cold vaginal injections or by incomplete or impeded sexual intercourse"—and those practices, too, "destroyed sensual enjoyment," threatened the physical health of both men and women, and led both women and men to "all the evils and dangers, mental and physical, of self-abuse." The only safeguard was to "restrict approach to a portion of the menstrual interval," or total abstinence.[55] In an article written for medical colleagues he warned that the numerous instances of nervous disease and uterine problems in the United States were caused by abortion and the "systemic prevention of conception." He warned that it was dangerous for men's health to use "capotes" [condoms] or "untimely withdrawal." Men could become impotent from such practices.[56] Storer wrote to Burt Green Wilder privately, "Whatever may be said to the contrary by superficial observers, there can be no doubt that intercourse, unless *complete*, is prejudicial to the health of both parties."[57]

Other leading gynecologists spoke out against the prevention of conception almost as forcefully as they spoke out against abortion. William Goodell, in his article "Conjugal Onanism and Kindred Sins," listed the "unwillingness of our women to become mothers" as one of the "dangers of the hour" (the title of a lecture at the eighty-third annual session of the Maryland State Medical and Chirurgical Faculty). Augustus K. Gardner, a Harvard Medical School graduate, professor of the "Diseases of Females and Clinical Midwifery" at the New York Medical College and an outspoken critic of reproductive control, blamed "preventives" for the declining health of the American woman and called his book opposed to reproductive control *Conjugal Sins*.[58]

Sexual Connotations of the Restrictive Efforts

Both the AMA's antiabortion campaign and the social purity reformers' antiobscenity, anticontraception campaign were hostile to women and to the power that control of reproduction promised (or threatened) to give to them. Other historians, too, have noted the antifeminist rhetoric and arguments of many of the opponents of reproductive control. Carroll Smith-Rosenberg analyzes this hostility brilliantly by examining the symbolic and metaphorical language used by the AMA physicians, who associated abortion not with all women, not with the poor and single, not with seduced servant girls, but with "strong-minded" married women of the new middle class who shirked their natural roles as wives and mothers. Such women they associated with the new "labile" commercial cities where traditional authority was in the process of being challenged and undermined on many fronts. Smith-Rosenberg points to the language: the scarcely veiled anger about women's "unnatural" rejection of men's seed, the punishments (largely ill health) that would befall such females.[59] What Smith-Rosenberg perceives in the writings of the AMA physicians is also illuminating when applied to the responses of the antiobscenity crusaders.

One of the significant themes in Comstock's own career was his outrage at women who stepped out of the roles of quiet wife and mother, no doubt one of the reasons he pursued purveyors of contraception and abortion so zealously. Comstock found women who did not meet his definition of "modest ladies" disgusting. Invited to a White House function during the Grant administration, he was scandalized by the fashionable Washington women who "were almost caricatures of everything but what a modest lady ought not [sic] to be." "They were brazen—dressed extremely silly—enamaled [sic] faces and powdered hair—low dresses—hair most ridiculous and altogether most extremely disgusting to every lover of pure, noble, modest woman. What are they? Who do they belong to? How can we respect them? They disgrace our land and yet consider themselves ladies."[60] It was the women's sexuality that upset him, their "brazenness"—their public display. He could not fit them easily into the only roles he deemed appropriate to women. They appeared too independent, not "belonging" to any man.

It is surely no coincidence that Comstock became embroiled in the campaign against fertility control just as he became simultaneously enmeshed in a humiliating fray with Victoria Woodhull and her sister, Tennessee C. Claflin. Comstock had arrested the two in November 1872 for publishing allegations in their newspaper, *Woodhull and Claflin's Weekly*, that Henry Ward Beecher, pastor of Brooklyn's Plymouth Church and one of America's best-known clergymen, was involved in a longstanding love affair with Elizabeth Tilton, the wife of one of his leading parishioners. By 1872, Victoria Woodhull had outspokenly embraced everything Comstock most feared and detested: free love, spiritualism, radical labor politics, suffragism, and free speech. She had served as the first woman stockbroker on Wall Street. She and Stephen Pearl Andrews, a colleague in free-love agitation, published in her newspaper in December 1871 the first American edition of the English translation of *The Communist Manifesto*. She had addressed, in January 1870, the House Judiciary Committee in Washington, D.C., arguing that under the Fourteenth and Fifteenth amendments women already had the right to vote. In May 1872 she helped organize the People's party, and, with renowned black abolitionist Frederick Douglass as her vice-presidential running mate, campaigned to be president of the United States.[61] At Comstock's instigation, in November 1872, the sisters were charged with violating the federal obscenity law passed earlier that year. Comstock claimed that the article about Beecher's affair was obscene, although he apparently also tried to have some advertisements in the newspaper declared obscene. In the trial, held the following spring, the prosecution and defense seemed somewhat confused about precisely what the sisters had been indicted for. They were held without bail for four weeks in the Ludlow Street Jail in New York City, released in early December, just as Comstock began his intensive lobbying for his stronger law.

The sensational publicity that the flamboyant sisters often generated, the newspaper lampooons of Comstock—for there was considerable ridicule of him and sympathy for the two women—the stony disapproval of his supporters at the YMCA for the publicity (their annual record passed over the Woodhull episode without mention, as did

Comstock's sympathetic biographer, Trumbull), his humiliation when the case finally came before a judge only to be dismissed on a ruling that the law could not be applied to newspapers—all of these fed into Comstock's long disquiet with strong-minded, independent women. It suggests that this, rather than the corruption of the young, which he cited, or the race-suicide fears, which historians occasionally cite as the motivation for much late-nineteenth-century opposition to reproductive control, was the principal basis for his involvement in restricting contraception and abortion—the means by which women could avoid childbearing and domesticity if they chose. Biographers claim that he idolized his own wife, Maggie, and that she—faded, shy, sweet, self-effacing—was his ideal. They had one child, a daughter, born in their first year of marriage, who died before her second birthday. It is not known why they had no other children, but they may have wanted them, for Comstock later adopted a young girl who was raised as their child. This, too, is highly symbolic, for he arranged the adoption without telling Maggie: appropriating solely to himself the decision to have a child.[62]

Left undiscussed in the approach I am taking and in the approach of many other historians is the very real possibility that key antiabortion activists were driven by intensely personal psychodynamic factors. It is worth speculating, for example, not only on Comstock's life but on the fact that Storer and his first wife (who died in 1885) had no children, yet he had four with his second wife. If Storer and his first wife were unwillingly sterile, that condition may have added—unconsciously or otherwise—to his hostility toward women who could bear children but chose not to. It is also possible that Storer was initially influenced by a campaign mounted in the 1850s by British physicians against "the great social evil of the day"—infanticide. (A Dr. William Burke Ryan won the London Medical Society's Fothergillian Gold Medal in 1856 for an essay on infanticide. He published it in 1862 as a book.) Infanticide was not an overt issue in the United States. Storer found in abortion, instead, a cause that brought him a similar gold medal, publications, and renown.[63]

No campaign that succeeds in changing the laws of almost every state in the union can be attributed solely to one individual. Clearly a considerable number of individuals and groups worked hard to bring about the legal changes that criminalized contraception and abortion. Physicians and social purity reformers won support from legislators, judges, government officials, academics, and the public. But it is also a serious misreading of history to underestimate the degree to which only a few driven and energetic people—fanatical is not too strong a word—have been able to shape the nation's reproductive policies with such far-reaching results for so many and for so long.

Counterefforts (Often Ambivalent) for Choice

There was little public outcry against the restrictive reproductive control legislation. Almost no groups or individuals organized to oppose the passage of the Comstock and antiabortion laws. Physicians who disagreed with both the Comstock laws and the antiabortion stance of the AMA, did so as individuals, not as organized groups, and they did so for varied reasons—some because they disapproved of legislators' telling physicians what to do, not because they disapproved of keeping abortion decisions out of the hands of women. Some in the medical community objected to the infusion of moral judgments into the issue of reproductive control. D. G. Brinton, editor of Philadelphia's *Medical and Surgical Reporter*, charged in 1881 that "any man who thinks the morals of himself or his community cannot stand the truth, had better kick such morals out of doors and go in for truth instead." Brinton challenged the reports that preventatives damaged women's health and called for more open discussion of the entire issue.[64] The *Leavenworth Medical Herald*, reviewing Storer's *Is It I? A Book for Every Man*, commented that "of modern medical authors we know of none who is as once so happily gifted in the art of euphemism and the hurling of invective."[65]

The conflicting testimony from experts in a Chicago abortion case in 1858 illustrates the lack of consensus within the medical community on the dangers of abortion. A physician and medical professor, D. Brainard, testified that "the production of abortion by mechanical means which rupture the membranes was not at all dangerous or injurious to life, if proper care were taken of the person subsequently." If performed in the first three months of pregnancy, an abortion was no more dangerous than childbirth. This view was hotly disputed by Professor N. S. Davis at the trial and by E. P. Christian in a review of medical authorities' thinking on the dangers of abortion.[66] A number of physicians who accepted the AMA position against abortion nevertheless rejected its general disparagement of family limitation. William Pawson Chunn told the Gynecological and Obstetrical Society of Baltimore that physicians must provide family limitation advice. He commented scathingly, "If it is admitted that Providence intended some women to conceive and others to be barren, it is certainly just as immoral to force a barren woman to become pregnant as it is to prevent a fertile woman from conceiving."[67] Orris E. Herrick, physician and medical inventor in Michigan, stimulated a debate in the *Michigan Medical News* in 1881 and 1882 with his forceful arguments that women had the right "morally, lawfully, and physically" to prevent pregnancy, "and all this mawkish sentiment about its being wrong or about its doing damage to the health is simply bosh and thousands of people know it from experience."[68]

Herrick's articles elicited both support and disapproval from small-town doctors all over the United States. The editors of the *Michigan Medical News* agreed with his "bold stand," noting that doctors were in daily contact with demands for birth control, though they rarely discussed the matter publicly. The editors said that the medical profession in general "does *not* discountenance most of the devices referred to."[69] A Boulder, Colorado, doctor, Charles Ambrook, wrote to say that he liked the Herrick article and added his own contraceptive advice that douching sometimes failed, the rhythm method was unreliable; the best protections, he said, were a "skin covering worn by the man" and the "Molesworth syringe" for douching.[70]

An 1871 paper by James T. Whittaker, a regular physician and professor of physiology in the Medical College of Ohio, illuminates the mixture of interest in and ambivalence and reticence about birth control which seems to have been widespread among the medical profession. It discussed some of his own "experiments in reproduction." He was particularly concerned with sperm viability and spermicides. Women frequently conceived "in spite of cold and acid injections, tampons, cundums, premature withdrawal, coition at intervals of menstruation, and all the other means resorted to, usually with sinister design," all of which methods he considered dangerous to women, "though scarcely with the absurdly exaggerated consequences so unctuously detailed in our flood of recent literature upon this subject." He went on to explain how carbolic acid would kill sperm almost instantaneously, concluding several pages of explicit details with the note, "I forbear from making any practical applications of this discovery. The question of the limitation of offspring is a question of sociology and political economy. I am content to present the bare scientific fact."[71]

Even in the late 1880s physicians from Pennsylvania to Texas continued to debate in the pages of medical journals the merits of birth control and the best methods to use. From the small town of Eschbach, Pennsylvania, Dr. F. R. Brunner wrote that preventing conception, even by use of the condom or "onanism," was much preferable to abortion. Women "are generally well-informed on matters of this nature," and besides, people should be able to be the judges of their own household affairs.[72] From Cameron, Texas, Thomas A. Pope, M.D., noting that the subject of the prevention of conception "is one that comes almost daily before every physician," urged open discussion about the best methods because "the rich, in town and country, already limit the number of their offspring," and the poor suffered from too many children and too-frequent abortions.[73]

In 1890 the *Cincinnati Medical News* printed a discussion among fifteen physicians (two of them women) on the question "Is the prevention of conception justifiable?" Twelve of the fifteen agreed that it was. Dr. C. B. Gilbert said that the subject was much discussed "in private life and in private practice," and it was his opinion that preventing conception was not "injurious to the organism" (as was abortion) and was not against "moral law." It did not threaten civilization or christianity. Dr. Frank W. Brown agreed, favoring both "moral" and "mechanical means" because "It must not be forgotten that in the majority of cases some means will be employed, perhaps more harmful than those recommended by a physician. The facts of everyday life show us that a majority of people practice these methods and that among educated classes population is regulated." Dr. Helen Warner expressed surprise to hear "such radical sentiments," although she acknowledged that she "did occasionally advise the prevention of conception," especially if a woman could not bear a living child, if pregnancy would endanger a woman's life, or if the woman was insane. Dr. Mulheron believed prevention wrong and not a private matter but a "society matter." When a "man and woman entered the marital relation, they assumed certain duties to society." Furthermore, if a woman "considered she had a right to prevent conception, she would also have the right to empty the pregnant uterus." Dr. A. L. Worden advised doctors not to be too lenient, because it "is not the poverty-stricken people" who asked such advice but those "who are able to support a family . . . but who from society reasons desire to be without children." Dr. Gibson said that prevention of conception was wrong and if it was seen as right "than abortion is right [and] [i]t is homicide." Dr. Devendorf disagreed; "Dr. Gibson," he noted sarcastically, would "go in mourning after an erotic dream." The issue was not a moral one; after all, nine-tenths of the educated classes "use some means to prevent conception." The second woman physician, a Dr. Banks, criticized a colleague's statement that preventing conception was harmful because the ovaries needed the rest brought by pregnancy. To Banks the "natural" period of rest for the ovaries was the time between menstruation, and she believed that in "some cases it is right to prevent conception." Dr. Gilbert concluded with an anecdote about a young man who visited a brothel. His wife wanted no more than their two children, and if they had known preventive methods, Gilbert stated, her husband would have been able to stay at home.[74]

Discussions in American medical journals in the last half of the nineteenth century suggest that physicians' dilemmas over contraception and abortion mirrored those of American society as a whole and that few shared the unequivocal position of the AMA-Storer group. Some quietly gave contraceptive advice to patients who asked for it; some performed abortions for favored patients; others tried to extricate themselves from the entire business—often without success.[75] Homeopaths accepted the position of the AMA with respect to abortion, but with demonstrable ambivalence. Edwin M. Hale, professor of materia medica and therapeutics at Hahnemann Medical College, then one of the leading homeopathic medical schools in the United States, openly differed with Storer. Hale opposed abortion in principle, in his book *On the Homeopathic Treatment of Abortion*, and, in addition, abortion advertisements, women doctors, and "feminists who advocated abortion." Still, he disagreed with Storer about abortion's risks: if abortions were performed by skillful doctors, fatalities were rare.[76] (He listed emmenagogues and oxytoxics that in some circumstances would cause abortion.)[77]

Only two groups as groups openly opposed the Comstock laws and, though more reluctantly, supported reproductive control: the freethinkers (who now rarely used either that term or the earlier "free enquirer," but instead referred to themselves simply as "liberals") and the advocates of free love, individual anarchism, and far-reaching reforms in gender relations whom historians today refer to simply as "sex radicals."

The leading national freethought organization, the National Liberal League, fought the Comstock laws, the final wedge in forcing an open schism in the league. The league was founded in 1870 by women and men who wanted a national organization that would work for secularism in the United States, for the repeal of Sunday laws, for abolition of official religious holidays, and, in general, for reinforcing the separation of church and state. Other than secularism, little united the "capitalists and anarchists, unitarians and atheists, materialists and spiritualists" who were its members.[78] From the first, the league was divided into a minority "conservative" faction under Francis E. Abbott, the league's president, and a more "liberal" faction under DeRobigne

Bennett, editor of the freethought journal, the *Truth Seeker*. A majority of the members at the National Liberal League convention in 1876 voted to seek repeal of the Comstock laws, not on the grounds that the specific right to communicate about reproductive control should be defended, but on the grounds that freedom of speech and freedom of the press should not be restricted. At the Syracuse convention in 1878 (held, ironically, at the opera house built by John Wieting with the profits from his lucrative lecture tours on reproductive control and sexual physiology), the issue of repeal came up again and a majority of the league sought repeal of the Comstock laws. Two minority factions disagreed, one because they supported the laws and the other, led by Abbott and Robert G. Ingersoll, the league's vice president (one of the most venerated—in some quarters notorious—freethinkers of the era) because they feared that the league would sully its reputation if it opposed obscenity laws and appeared to be dominated by free lovers and other sex radicals. Abbott resigned the presidency over the issue in 1878, and two years later Ingersoll resigned the vice presidency, similarly angered by the league's insistence on full repeal. The new president, Elizur Wright, in 1878, sent Congress a petition with seventy thousand names protesting the Comstock laws and seeking repeal.[79]

Elizabeth Cady Stanton was one of the honorary vice presidents (along with Robert Dale Owen) in 1876, but her role and the role of other women deserves fuller treatment. William Leach, one of the few historians to consider women in the Liberal League, traces its origins to the radical clubs that grew up in the early 1870s, inspired by the Boston Radical Club. Leach suggests that the radical clubs displaced suffrage societies as places where feminists met to discuss controversial subjects, including sexual hygiene, abortion, and marriage reform.[80]

Although sex radicals and individualist anarchists joined forces with the league to combat the restrictiveness of the Comstock laws, some members of the National Liberal League were unhappy with that association. The late-nineteenth-century sex radicals, like the earlier freethinkers, promoted reproductive control not for its own sake but as part of a broad campaign to defend their right to publish and to speak their views publicly, particularly on marriage and sexuality. Although their critics mistakenly assumed that free lovers advocated unrestricted sexuality, both groups feared the power of unleashed sexuality and sought ways to harness and restrict it. Free lovers, to whom marriage was simply legalized prostitution, wanted greater abstinence from sex even within marriage. Most agreed with Ezra Heywood that when marriage was reformed and when men had learned sexual self-control, loving, monogamous unions would be the happy result. They believed that the institution of marriage as it existed was unjust. In *Cupid's Yokes*, Ezra Heywood called marriage "coerced consent" that "annihilates existing love and makes its revival impossible."[81] He especially disliked the compulsory aspects of marital sexuality and argued that if couples were not bound by religion and the state into indissoluble marriages in which men had excessive power economically and sexually over women, society would benefit, couples would be happier, and there would be more monogamy. Only a small minority of free lovers held what was called the "varietist" position, that men and women should be free to have sexual relations with whomever they wanted whenever they wanted.

There was no official free love position on contraception and abortion, but free love advocates had been important in promoting information on the subject ever since Mary Gove Nichols and Thomas Low Nichols published and lectured in the 1850s. Because many free lovers were anarchists, it would be difficult to argue that they held an "official" position on anything except the need to abolish traditional marriage and to reform the contemporary sexual system. In all other areas—labor, politics, education—they held diverse opinions. Very few of the sex radicals were as outspoken as Angela Heywood, married to Ezra Heywood, a frequent contributor to his newspaper, the *Word*, and a partner in the publishing business they ran out of their Princeton, Massachusetts, home. She wrote in the *Word* in 1883, after her husband had been tried and jailed for advertising douching syringes, "This womb-syringe question is to the North what the Negro question was to the South; as Mr. Heywood stood beside the slave demanding his liberation, so now he voices the emancipation of woman from sensual thraldom."[82] A free love convention held in Ravena, Ohio, in December 1873, nine months after congressional passage of the federal Comstock Law, passed resolutions that affirmed women's right to have control over their sexuality and their right to reproductive self-control.[83]

Organized feminists did not speak out against the Comstock laws, in large part, because many disliked contraception, viewing it as a threat to their demands for "voluntary motherhood." It is true that women's rights activists in the postbellum period spoke increasingly publicly about women's sexual rights in marriage; Elizabeth Cady Stanton spoke to small private groups of women on sex and marriage, and in even more intimate afternoon parlor sessions on women's need for "self-sovereignty" over their bodies and their sexual lives.[84] But she and others did not officially oppose Comstockery.

The Impact of Criminalization

The mid-nineteenth-century censorship of reproductive control drove service and information underground, with results still apparent, often tragically so, well into the mid-twentieth century. The working class women whom sociologist Lee Rainwater interviewed in Chicago in the early 1960s were no better informed and in many respects less knowledgeable about sexual physiology and controlling fertility than middle class women had been a century earlier.[85]

By criminalizing abortion and contraception, the new laws raised the specter of indictment, jail, and social opprobrium for anyone who contemplated public—and, in many cases also, private—involvement with reproductive control. Comstock quantified the results as of 1880 as follows: seized and destroyed 24,225 pounds of books and sheet stock, 14,420 stereotype plates, 165 different obscene books, 64,094 "rubber articles for immoral use," 4,185 boxes of pills and powders for abortion, 3,421 letters and packages ready for mailing at the time of dealers' arrest. He had, he said, in his possession 70,280 "open letters seized in possession of persons arrested," the names of 6,000 "dealers in obscene books and goods" listed in publishers' account books, and names and post office addresses of 901,125 people to whom "smut dealers" sent goods.[86]

The Comstock laws had a mixed impact on the circulation of contraceptive and abortive information in the last third of the nineteenth century. Magazines, journals, and newspapers scrutinized advertisements with greater care, and many refused to print anything that suggested reproductive control. One of the most successful mail-order companies, the E. C. Allen Company, kept a record of the advertisements they refused to print between 1880 and 1890. Of the 180 ads rejected as unfit for the company's literary and agricultural periodicals about one-fourth were for contraceptive devices, especially for rubber pessaries, condoms, and douches, and for abortion drugs and abortionists.[87] In other places reproductive control products continued to be advertised, sometimes openly, often in disguise. Edward Bliss Foote circumvented the Comstock laws by advertising his douching syringes in the 1880s as "Sanitary Syringes" especially "adapted to married women" to be used for "thorough cleansing and application of medicinal washes without waste."[88] Other writers disguised reproductive control advice in sections titled "On Sterility" or "Conditions Unfavorable to Pregnancy."[89]

Products continued to be available in a variety of retail stores, or sold by mail, or advertised in books, flyers, druggists' catalogues, and journals. But distribution sources and supplies were unpredictable. The Chicago druggists Morrison, Plummer & Co. warned prospective customers in 1880 that small packages "are carefully examined at the Chicago Post Office for violations of the postal regulations" and explicitly noted the prohibition on "all articles intended for the prevention of conception or procuring of abortion." They then proceeded to advertise for sale several dozen kinds of "periodical drops," emmenagogues, female pills, syringes, and pessaries.[90] The Boston drug firm George C. Goodwin & Co. listed "capotes" for sale in 1865, but not in 1874, 1876, or 1885. It did list emmenagogues, douching syringes, and pessaries.[91] In the 1870s and 1880s the supply of condoms and diaphragms in such urban areas as New York City, Philadelphia, Boston, and Chicago was reduced because vendors feared arrest, but the items were still available. At an 1886 trial in New York prosecutors introduced evidence that closed-ring pessaries were marketed with a circular describing their use as "contraceptics."[92]

The Comstock laws had a particularly dramatic impact on the dissemination of advice literature. The last two decades of the nineteenth century saw a decline both in its number and in its quality. Some established titles, such as Knowlton's *Fruits of Philosophy*, Owen's *Moral Physiology*, and Ashton's *The Book of Nature* remained in print, but only from sources increasingly viewed as disreputable; or they were available through carefully anonymous mail-order libraries. Some of the best-known works began to be sold with substantial omissions. The 1895 edition of Trall's *Sexual Physiology* still had a chapter titled "Regulating the Number of Offspring," but the contraceptive advice in it was gone.[93] The 1891 edition of Foote's *Plain Home Talk* still contained five pages on the "Prevention of Conception," but they no longer offered explicit contraceptive advice; instead, they explained Foote's trial and fine for breaking the Comstock laws, repeated earlier justifications for reproductive control, and made brief reference to "male continence," saying that "it will not be adopted to any prevailing extent in society at large." Foote was referring to the coitus reservatus method used by the communitarian society led by Noyes in Oneida, New York. He also noted that his own *Words in Pearl* was out of print, but referred interested readers to his son's *Radical Remedy in Social Science*.[94] Hollick's works remained in print without noticeable changes in his contraceptive advice, but he and his publishers became more circumspect about advertisements, no longer emphasizing, for example, that *The Marriage Guide* contained advice about the prevention of conception. In Hollick's 1873 *The Nerves and the Nervous*, an advertisement stated that *The Marriage Guide* was "a private instructor for Married People and those about to marry, both men and women in everything relating to the anatomy and physiology of the generative system, in both sexes and the process of reproduction." It omitted the following words from an earlier advertisement for the book: "Including a full description of everything that is now known respecting the prevention and production of offspring."[95]

At least three editions of Besant's *The Law of Population* were published in the United States in the 1870s and 1880s and all contained her original discussion of preventives. (An unauthorized edition published in 1889 in New York even had more contraceptive recommendations.) In his 1886 *The Radical Remedy in Social Science*, Edward Bond Foote commended Besant's work as "undoubtedly the best writing on the subject [of preventing pregnancy] now extant in England or America, being the only recent and *instructive* one which has thus far escaped prosecution; but there is more practical physiological information to impart than was put into her book. So there is room for, as well as call for, an American book."[96]

The general quality of contraceptive advice literature in the last decades of the century was inferior to that available earlier. The popular and immense work by B. G. Jefferis and J. L. Nichols, *Search Lights on Health, Light on Dark Corners*, first published in 1894 and reissued regularly until 1921, is a good example of the consequences of the Comstock laws. The advice on the "prevention of conception" actually was a confused, inaccurate jumble of warnings about the medical and legal dangers of tampering "with nature's laws," interspersed with rationales explaining why women needed preventives and discussions of withdrawal, the rhythm method, abortion, and breastfeeding. The book contained scattered advertisements for douches and suggestions about how to make douching solutions. The work was decidedly inferior in quality of advice, in organization, and in tone to even the ephemeral pamphlets of fifty years earlier. Jefferis and Nichols themselves escaped prosecution by hedging their stance on contraception with many warnings against it and by publishing simultaneously in out-of-the-way places: Parkersburg, West Virginia; Naperville, Illinois; and Ontario, Canada.[97]

The 1883 *Illustrated Science of Man and Medical Counsellor*, by Edward Zeus Franklin Wickes, who called himself "Professor Zeus Franklin," is another example of the poor quality of the late-nineteenth-century genre. The contents listed five pages dealing with contraception; more information on the subject was scattered hodgepodge throughout the book. It disparaged contraceptive methods; most of the advice was unintelligibly flowery, unreliable, and illogical. Franklin did list several spermicides and advised withdrawal, telling couples always to take a clean napkin to bed and noting: "This plan injures neither party, nor materially diminishes the pleasurable sensation of the connection. The habit once formed will be found to be more desirable and satisfactory than it at first appears." One of his engravings pictured "Animalculae killed by Astringents."[98] But even Franklin did not escape the censors. His lectures (probably on the same general topics as the book, namely marriage and sexual physiology) attracted the attention of the Boston Society for the Suppression of Vice. He was arrested when an agent, who had attended one of his lectures and tried unsuccessfully to purchase a copy of the book by pretending to be unemployed, secured a copy in some other way and used its contents to arrest Franklin. The new president of the National Liberation League, Elizur Wright, bailed him out of jail (as he had earlier victims of the Comstock laws), and 105 Bostonians signed a testimonial in his defense. One of the names on the list was "Dr. H. B. Storer," possibly a misprint for Horatio Robinson Storer, Jr., which would be ironic given Storer's antipathy to advocates of reproductive control, and especially to irregular physicians. It is also possible that Franklin or his publisher manufactured some of the names on the testimonial list, not realizing the implications of including Storer's.

Even the bestselling books of Alice B. Stockham—which expressed, in poetical and mystical language, advice on sexuality, health reform, and feminism, all with a wide appeal—were not immune from the Comstock laws. Her contraceptive advice was a retooled version of Noyes's coitus reservatus, which she called "karezza." (She disliked other methods, especially douching, withdrawal, the use of devices and drugs.) She did not condone abortion, but she was sympathetic to women who turned to it as a last resort to protect their lives and health. Though her books treated sex as a mystical experience, they nevertheless were a principal source of information about sex, marriage, and gender relations for many late-nineteenth-century Americans. Her works *Tokology* and *Karezza* were among the few recalled and listed by title by the women who responded to the Mosher questionnaire. Stockham was arrested by an agent of the Vice Society in Chicago for distributing her pamphlet *The Wedding Night*. The court judged it obscene and she was fined two hundred and fifty dollars. Furthermore, when Moses Harmon, free love advocate, anarchist and freethought editor, published parts of Stockham's *Tokology* in his radical Kansas journal, *Lucifer, the Light Bearer*, in 1905, the U.S. Post Office censored the journal.[99]

Distribution channels, too, decreased in number and variety in response to the repressions of the Comstock laws. In the last third of the nineteenth century, it became difficult to publish and distribute even the most proper books that touched on reproduction or reproductive control. Birth control publishing, therefore, increasingly became the province of small, independent, deliberately obscure entrepreneurs who relied on strategies anachronistic in the world of mass market publishing. Those involved in publishing and distributing birth control literature were seldom visible in that urban society.

Gilbert S. Baldwin, a book jobber and later a bookseller who kept *Fruits of Philosophy* available in spite of the Comstock laws, was one of those small entrepreneurs who made it possible for the public to read about reproductive control. Baldwin was a "jobber of 'railroad literature,'" which meant that he purchased cheap books and circulars in large batches and hired agents to distribute them. In the spring of 1862 he and an unnamed colleague, calling themselves "Bamford and Baldwin," distributed periodicals along the railroad lines in Chicago, probably relying heavily on boys as hawkers. They received favorable credit ratings in the next few years based on the volume of their business and the money they made. Credit raters estimated that their capital worth rose from five hundred dollars to $18,000 from 1862 to 1865, when Bamford withdrew and Baldwin opened a bookstore.[100] Sometimes listed as selling books, sometimes "notions" in the next few years, Baldwin continued to make money, and early in 1868 "G. S. Baldwin & Bro." opened branches in Toledo and Council Bluffs, Iowa. Gilbert Baldwin sold the wares in Chicago and Toledo and his brother, J. G. Baldwin, operated the Iowa branch, which, in March 1870 was "closed out by [the] sheriff. Compromised in some way." The Chicago branch ran into financial difficulties in the unstable economic climate of the early 1870s, and in June 1872 credit reporters noted that the business had "failed" and Baldwin "now is only an agent [and] has no property." Credit reporters who had earlier described Gilbert Baldwin as "a pretty decent man of good character" and "a man of family" now found him doing business "under the wing of his sister. [He] is dissipated, unreliable, [a] poor businessman—totally unworthy of credit."[101]

Many of the paperbound works Baldwin sold were police and crime stories and mild native erotica, but others were serious advice literature on marriage, sex, and reproductive control. His Chicago stock also included "imported notions" from France—ribald playing cards, erotica, and, probably contraceptives. He sold these along with the paperbound literature that was a mixture of his stock from the earlier jobbing days, French and American pornography, freethought tracts, and birth control guides including Owen's *Moral Physiology*, Knowlton's *Fruits of Philosophy*, Besant's *The Law of Population*, and a work referred to as *The Book of Nature*, probably Ashton's pamphlet.[102]

Legal and Medical Confusions

In *ex parte Jackson* in 1877 the Supreme Court ruled that the Comstock Law did not deny free speech. Not until the *Stopes* case in 1931 did the Supreme Court rule that birth control discussions were not ipso facto obscene. In the intervening fifty-four years the rulings were complicated. In an 1886 New York case the judge charged the jury that they had to decide whether the defendant had sold one gross of "womb veils" for lawful or unlawful purposes. If the sale had been to prevent disease, it was lawful, if for contraception, unlawful.[103] In 1916 birth control advocate Margaret Sanger was convicted in New York for violating the state law making it a misdemeanor to "sell, lend, or give away," to advertise, loan, or distribute any "recipe, drug, or medicine for the prevention of conception." She was charged with selling contraceptive devices at her birth control clinic. Two years later the state supreme court upheld her conviction but broadened the interpretation of the law to permit physicians to help or give advice to married people to prevent disease as well as to cure.[104] Physicians were confused, nonetheless, about what they could and could not do legally with respect to contraception. Discussions in medical journals were hampered by uncertainty because they were distributed by mail; medical schools were uncertain about teaching contraception. A doctor from Pipestone City, Minnesota, wrote to O. E. Herrick in 1882 asking for contraceptive advice and promising to destroy Herrick's letter after he read it. Herrick himself assumed, incorrectly, that it was legal to mail douching syringes.[105] Popular health journals, including the *Physiologist*, *Dr. Foote's Health Monthly*, and *New Age*, were suppressed.[106] The entrepreneurial Edward Bond Foote, a regular physician and an opponent of the Comstock laws, believed that doctors could no longer legally prescribe or advise contraceptives to save a mother's life but that they could legally perform an abortion to do so.[107] Doctors did not know for certain whether they could even, legally, discuss birth control with one another, or send information or devices through the mails, or give information privately to patients.

Many state laws regulating abortion provided a therapeutic exception that a physician could perform an abortion to save a woman's life. This narrow provision actually restricted legal abortions in the twentieth century because childbirth then became much more routinely a hospital procedure and hospital boards of physicians were required to rule on the merits of each request. In the late nineteenth century, in contrast, when most women had babies and abortions in the privacy of their homes, individual doctors did not have to consult hospital boards of their peers before performing a therapeutic abortion. The abortion laws brought doctors much more into the decision-making process; that is, they "medicalized" what had not always been a medical issue. The state laws were vague about the meaning of saving a woman's life: was a doctor to interpret that phrase as referring only to immediate, life-threatening physical conditions, or could longer-range factors be factored in? Were emotional or economic factors to be considered? Or "quality of the woman's life"? For middle class women in the late nineteenth century, then, the abortion laws may have had very limited impact. They may have had to shop around for a physician who would perform an abortion, and there may have been fewer physicians available because sectarians—and midwives as well—were being driven from the professional fold. Despite all of the obstacles neither legal nor illegal abortion disappeared, as twentieth-century statistics demonstrate. By 1966, four-fifths of all abortions were for married women, and the ratio of legal to illegal abortions was 1 to 110.[108]

The Comstock laws ushered in the era, familiar well into the late twentieth century, in which the poor and the young had access only to the most dangerous abortions—to "abortion mills" and unlicensed practitioners—while middle and upper class women could, often only with great difficulty and expense, but often successfully, find safer abortions in the loopholes "therapeutic abortion" afforded private family physicians.

Comstock, Storer, and their immediate supporters in the campaigns against contraception and abortion hoped that they could alter the direction of change in American life. To duly credit their noblest goals: they hoped to restrict fraudulent medical nostrums and to outlaw dangerous medical practices and "unqualified" irregular practitioners—all of which did need regulation. There were indeed many bogus and health-threatening remedies advertised as contraceptives and abortives and many Americans were better protected by more restrictive laws toward drugs and medical services. To the extent that the Comstock and antiabortion laws clamped down on the trade in the dangerous poisons used as abortives they had some positive effects. But their impact even on that trade is ambiguous for, although some of those drugs went off the market, other dangerous ones continued to be sold with such coded terms as "removing obstructions to menstruation" or "ergot pills."

As we have seen, however, the motives of the opponents of reproductive control were mixed, and their laudable results were outstripped by the larger legacies of their repressive campaigns. The legacy deepened class barriers by reducing the access of impoverished, single, and rural Americans to the most effective and safe methods of reproductive control. The legacy was a (temporary but unfortunate) derailment of the quiet but growing momentum for women's reproductive rights.

The most striking example of the legacy of the campaigns against reproductive control can be found in Margaret Sanger's account of her fruitless six months' search in 1913 for contraceptive information in the best libraries in America. The doctors and nurses she consulted told her that if she did not avoid the subject she would run afoul of the Comstock laws. The feminists she talked with expressed shock at the idea of a public campaign for family limitation and argued that all efforts for women's autonomy should be concentrated first on obtaining the vote. Libraries yielded no information on the "secret" women wanted. ("Why was it so difficult to obtain information on this subject? Where was it hidden? Why would no one discuss it? . . . It was like the lost trail in the journey toward freedom.")[109] Sanger searched the Library of Congress, the books in the New York Academy of Medicine, and the Boston Public Library. "At the end of six months I was convinced that there was no practical medical information on contraception available in America."

She exaggerated in order to underscore the importance of her own movement, but the symbolism of her point is crucial: the most dramatic legacy of the new social and legal policies of Comstockery was the void Margaret Sanger found where once there had been information. The combined force of the social purity legions, of the Comstocks and the Storers, and of overwhelming public acquiescence overrode a generation of commercialization and growing public discourse and drove reproductive control, if not totally back underground, at least into a netherworld of back-fence gossip and back-alley abortions.

Epilogue

It is one of those small yet fitting ironies of historical coincidence that in 1912, the same year in which Mary Poor died, Margaret Sanger embarked on a birth control crusade. The two women appear, at first glance, dramatically dissimilar: two generations apart in age: one, tightly constrained by the literal and figurative corsets of genteel Victorian society; the other, daringly casting off social fetters. One, ensconced in the domestic world of marriage and family; the other, enamored of radical political and cultural reform in Greenwich Village. And yet the disparities were not so great, for common themes profoundly touched their lives. Mary Poor, bound to home and family, recorded (and enjoyed) her sexuality, while at the same time she recorded her worries about pregnancy in her tightly controlled, elliptical private codes of ×'s and +'s. Margaret Sanger struggled in bohemian New York and in Europe to free women from the sexual conventions that bound them so tightly. They had in common acceptance and enjoyment of their sexuality and their concern about women's natural fertility and their quest to control it.

In her famous account of how she was converted to her lifelong crusade for reliable and safe birth control, Sanger described how in the summer of 1912 she was called to the Lower East Side, New York's immigrant ghetto, to care for a twenty-eight-year-old mother of three, Sadie Sachs, who was dying from a botched abortion. Sanger's constant nursing through three hot July nights and days saved Sadie Sachs's life.

This was not an unusual call for Sanger. Born and raised in the small factory town of Corning, New York, the sixth of eleven children, Margaret Higgens had learned nursing informally while still a young girl as she cared for her mother, who was dying of tuberculosis. At age fifteen, she enrolled in a program of formal nursing training at White Plains Hospital in Westchester County, New York, where she met an architect and aspiring artist, William Sanger, whom she married, in 1902, at age nineteen. For some ten years she lived the life of a suburban housewife, bearing three children but also suffering long bouts of tubercular-related invalidism, until both husband and wife, chafing at what they began to define as an overly staid middle class life, moved to Manhattan to join the artistic, cultural, and political ferment of pre–World War I Greenwich Village. Although she had disliked the social ostracism her father's outspoken freethinking had brought to her childhood in preeminently Catholic Corning, Sanger embraced the avant-garde ideas and the radicals she encountered in the salons of the Village—and slightly later in Europe—from the new forms of modern poetry and abstract paintings to the labor politics of Bill Haywood and his fellow members of the International Workers of the World, to the anarchism of Emma Goldman, and the sexual theories of Havelock Ellis and Sigmund Freud.[1] This was the beginning of her move away from the conventionalities of bourgeois American life, for in the next two decades Sanger traveled in Europe, separated from and eventually divorced her husband, openly celebrated her ideas of sexual freedom with several lovers, and, above all, found a cause: the organization of the birth control movement. In the middle of the heady early years of 1911 and 1912, however, Sanger also worked as a visiting nurse. It was her preference for obstetrical cases and her sympathy for the impoverished and desperate immigrant women in lower Manhattan which brought her to Sadie Sachs in 1912.

As Sanger's most recent and most sympathetic biographer, Ellen Chesler, explains, "Sadie Sachs may have existed in fact or may have emerged as an imaginative, dramatic composite of Margaret's experience, but the prevalence of maternal mortality and morbidity in the urban ghetto she confronted is indisputable."[2] The story, however embellished, took on enormous significance to Sanger, who describes herself as deeply moved by Sachs's desperate desire for birth control information. A physician had told Sachs that she would die from another pregnancy, but when she begged him for advice about how "to prevent getting that way again" he only laughed, told her that she could not have her cake and eat it, too, and advised that the only sure thing was for her husband to sleep on the roof. The young mother turned to Sanger, her hands clasped "as if in prayer," to implore her to tell the "secret." Sanger had to acknowledge to the young woman that she did not have the "secret." The fear of pregnancy "hung like a sword over the head of every poor woman I came in contact with," but she felt powerless to help them.

> Sometimes they talked among themselves bitterly. "It's the rich that know the tricks," they'd say, "while we have all the kids." Then, if the women were Roman Catholics, they talked about "Yankee tricks," and asked me if I knew what the Protestants did to keep their families down. When I said that I didn't believe that the rich know much more than they did I was laughed at and suspected of holding back information for money. They would nudge each other and say something about paying me before I left the case if I would reveal the "secret."

When Sanger told them that condoms and coitus interruptus "were the means used by men in the well-to-do families," the women only laughed incredulously and skeptically.[3]

One year later, when Sanger was called again to the same home to treat Sachs for another self-induced abortion, she could not save her and the young woman died. Sanger resolved to leave nursing and give women what they really needed: information about effective contraception. Finding none in America, she continued the search in Europe, seeking out the clinics of England and Holland for the information she sought. In her memoires Sanger reported returning to America in 1915 with a satchelful of contraceptive diaphragms (it may be that, indeed, she did not bring any other contraceptives—condoms or vaginal sponges, for example—or she may have preferred to emphasize the diaphragm since it became her birth control clinics' preferred contraceptive device) and a fierce determination to disperse her information and her products despite the probability of fines or imprisonment for breaking the Comstock laws.

The problems Sanger faced in the ensuing decades were not induced solely by the new legal climate. She faced, as well, the widespread cultural ambivalence, the internalized conflicts of individual women and men over reproductive control which had permitted passage of the Comstock laws in the first place. For the changes that led to new social and legal policies stimulated just as profoundly transformations in the most intimate relations between couples.

Some historians believe that reproductive control brought couples closer, indeed that smaller families were achieved only because couples cooperated so effectively. They believe that even abortion may have become less the result of a quiet, private series of actions on the part of a woman and more the result of a mutual decision by the couple, especially if a visit to a "professional" abortionist or the purchase of commercially available abortion products was involved.[4] When all is said and done, however, it is difficult to accept that the politics of marriage or the politics of gender relations were transformed only for the better by reproductive control. Some men continued to want to control sexual activity against the wishes of their wives. Horatio Storer, although notably hostile to women on fertility control issues, complained in 1867 that many husbands compelled their wives take "improper and unphysiological measures" to prevent conception.[5] Far more commonly, however, wives understandably tried to persuade or coerce their husbands to use birth control methods or to limit sexual intercourse. Discussions of family limitation were so intertwined with other issues of power in the politics of marriage—money issues only the most obvious example—that merely to raise the subject of reproductive control may have been sufficient to cause conflict in a marriage. Besant testified in her divorce trial in Britain that birth control issues had worsened her own marital relationship; her experience was not unique. William Goodell, as part of his vituperative critique of contraception, argued that unhappy marriages were caused by women's insistence on preventive techniques.[6] The diaphragm advertisements that touted a woman's ability to wear one secretly without a husband's knowledge suggest a considerable lack of openness and cooperation between husbands and wives over matters of reproductive control. Perhaps some husbands objected to contraception out of concern about a wife's fidelity. Perhaps wives wanted to wear a contraceptive pessary secretly as an added precaution while continuing to insist that a husband use withdrawal, or that he adhere to a sexual schedule based on the rhythm method and hence abstain for regular periods. Wives who wanted to control the timing and frequency of sexual intercourse may not have wanted to relinquish the power to say no. Not wanting to encourage more frequent sex, they would not have wanted their contraceptive protection—just in case—to be known.[7]

Nineteenth-century women had good reason to be ambivalent about abortion and contraception. Women wanted control over reproduction, but wanting control was not at all the same thing as achieving it. Historians have generally assumed that women welcomed this transition in power over reproduction. Yet we do not know so certainly whether it was quite so universally welcomed. Accepting responsibility for one's sexuality, calculating costs and benefits, planning ahead so the douching syringe was full and by the bed, or the vaginal sponge was adequately soaked in a spermicide, keeping careful track of menstruation, maintaining other records so the purported "safe" period would be precisely determined every month—none of these was easy or unquestionably acceptable to all women. Some women, skilled as managers of their households, talented in taking charge and in making decisions over complex domestic challenges, probably moved easily into rational calculations of fertility intervention. The young Jacksonian era woman historian Mary Ryan cites in Utica, New York, who used the period of courtship to find out how much her fiancé drank and who ascertained his views on marriage and courtship, may well have had few difficulties later making fertility control decisions.[8] Nor would this have been a problem for the women so criticized by the president of the American Association of Obstetrics and Gynecology, who wrote in 1899:

> I am sure we have all often been perplexed by the shameless confession of a handsome and what is apparently a correct young married woman that she prevents conception; even more, that she entered the marriage bed with the distinct understanding that she desires no offspring and does so because of the inconvenience it would give her. It has been my sad experience to note this antipathy to be more frequent in the young woman than in the young man.[9]

Other women, however, may well have experienced profound ambivalence about possessing or acquiring or using their own contraceptives. Many probably found the whole process acutely embarrassing, even humiliating, and, as much as women desperately longed for control over their fertility, many probably resented the implications that it was *their* duty and *their* sole responsibility. Ralph Glover had laid the issue out boldly in 1846. It was of the utmost importance, he wrote, that power of control over reproduction should be in woman's hands. But he added, "She who bears the burden and suffers the affliction should be able to protect herself and *the fault is her own if she do not.*" Harmon Knox Root argued, too, that women should not risk their health and lives with preventives that were really the responsibility of men.[10] The process by which women and men learned new methods of reproductive control, judged them, and experimented with them does not follow traditional assumptions about the "liberating" effects of birth control. Some women developed a clear understanding that they needed to depend on themselves, but many other women did not achieve notions of self-reliance so quickly, and some never achieved them at all. Serious obstacles to female autonomy were internal as well as external, and only with difficulty did women move from characteristic patterns of submissiveness into greater self-reliance and assertiveness.

Reproductive control, however widely practiced and however highly desired, was unresolved as an issue in the nineteenth century and, indeed, is still so in the twentieth century. Today we often view reproductive control as an inevitable improvement in people's lives, a liberating force bringing autonomy, enhanced sexuality, greater power over one's destiny. It certainly has been this to many; but in the nineteenth century, as today, many remained suspicious about the implications of such attempts. Reproductive control became illegal not only because of the fanaticism of a few zealots but because of its troubling implications for a broad spectrum of women and men, many of whom wanted and practiced reproductive control in the privacy of their bedrooms but failed to support it publicly when it was under attack.

To most late-twentieth-century Americans the right of a woman to control her own body requires little defense; a majority of Americans believes that adult women have a right to prevent conception and, although more controversial, to procure abortion. The right of women to reproductive self-determination—first formulated hesitatingly in the 1830s, then articulated with increasing conviction in the subsequent decades, to emerge powerfully in the 1960s as a key issue in radical feminist agendas—has gained wide public acceptance. One of the respondents in Kristin Luker's 1984 study, *Abortion and the Politics of Motherhood*, expressed this succinctly but eloquently:

> When we talk about women's rights, we can get all the rights in the world—the right to vote, the right to go to school—and none of them means a doggone thing if we don't own the flesh we stand in . . . if the whole course of our lives can be changed by somebody else that can get us pregnant by accident, or by deceit, or by force. . . . If you can't control your own body you can't control your future, to the degree that any of us can control futures.[11]

Notes

These notes contain only shortened citations for the important primary works included in the Selected Bibliography, which gives complete publication information.

Prologue

1. Norman E. Himes, *Medical History of Contraception* (New York: Schocken, 1970; 1st pub. 1936). For a good overview of the issues and the literature on the diffusion of innovations—either new ideas, values, or behaviors—and the fertility transition see Lee L. Bean, Geraldine F. Mineau, and Douglas C. Anderton, *Fertility Change on the American Frontier: Adaption and Innovation* (Berkeley: University of California Press, 1990). As an example of the belief that if people want to control fertility they will find ways to do so see the statement quoted in Hélène Bergues, *La prévention des naissances dans la famille: Ses origins dans les temps modernes* (Institut national d'études démographiques, Presses Universitaires de France, 1960), p. 22: "One can pose as a general rule that, if in a given social condition such as that of the nineteenth-century French, the number of infants is restrained, it is because the majority of parents wishes to restrain it. It is useless to search for subtle reasons; the dominant fact is simple: French families did not have many children because they did not wish to have many" (my translation). Among the historians who argue that simple folk methods achieved family limitations see Daniel Scott Smith, "Family Limitation, Sexual Control, and Domestic Feminism in Victorian America," in *Clio's Consciousness Raised: New Perspectives on the History of Women*, ed. Mary S. Hartman and Lois Banner (New York: Harper & Row, 1974), p. 123, and John Mack Faragher, *Sugar Creek: Life on the Illinois Prairie* (New Haven: Yale University Press, 1986), pp. 205–7.

2. Arguments for the ubiquity of desire for birth control can be found in Linda Gordon, *Woman's Body, Woman's Right: A Social History of Birth Control in America* (New York: Grossman, 1976), and Gordon, *Woman's Body, Woman's Right: Birth Control in America*, rev. and updated (New York: Penguin, 1990), which argues that birth control as an individual impulse has always been part of women's lives and always available. Philippe Ariès, "Interprétation pour une histoire des mentalités," in Ber-

gues, *La prévention des naissances*, pp. 314–20, on the other hand describes the process by which birth control shifted from the clandestine to the "thinkable."

3. Himes, *Medical History of Contraception*, p. 238.

4. For recent works exploring the problem of the audience see Nina Baym, *Novels, Readers, and Reviewers: Responses to Fiction in Antebellum America* (Ithaca: Cornell University Press, 1984); Mary Kupiec Cayton, "The Making of an American Prophet: Emerson, His Audiences, and the Rise of the Culture Industry in Nineteenth-Century America," *American Historical Review* 92 (1987): 597–620; Robert Darnton, "Toward a History of Reading," *Princeton Alumni Weekly*, 8 April 1987: 19–32; and William J. Gilmore, *Reading Becomes a Necessity of Life: Material and Cultural Life in Rural New England, 1780–1835* (Knoxville: University of Tennessee Press, 1989). My thinking about the issues of audiences and interpreting texts has also been greatly aided by H. Aram Veeser, ed., *The New Historicism* (New York: Routledge, 1989), and Joan Wallach Scott, *Gender and the Politics of History* (New York: Columbia University Press, 1988).

5. Mary Ware Dennett, *Birth Control Laws: Shall We Keep Them, Change Them, or Abolish Them?* (New York: Da Capo Press, 1970; 1st pub. 1926), p. 12.

6. Michel Foucault's *The History of Sexuality* vol. 1: *An Introduction*, trans. Robert Hurley (New York: Vintage, 1978), was obviously of enormous importance for this book, for he transformed the earlier paradigm and made us aware of how deeply sexuality was entrenched everywhere in Victorian culture. My book fits into this current paradigmatic shift in interpretation. Foucault showed us that sex was a powerfully pervasive subject in the nineteenth century. The discourse about birth control was part of the larger discourse on sex.

Acknowledgments and Sources

1. Linda Gordon, *Woman's Body, Woman's Right: A Social History of Birth Control in America* (New York: Grossman, 1976); Gordon, *Woman's Body, Woman's Right: Birth Control in America*, rev. and updated (New York: Penguin, 1990); Gordon, "Why Nineteenth Century Feminists Did Not Support 'Birth Control' and Twentieth Century Feminists Do: Feminism, Reproduction, and the Family," in *Rethinking the Family: Some Feminist Questions*, ed. Barrie Thorne (New York: Longman, 1982); James W. Reed, *From Private Vice to Public Virtue: The Birth Control Movement and American Society since 1830* (New York: Basic Books, 1978), and Reed, *The Birth Control Movement and American Society: From Private Vice to Public Virtue. With a New Preface on the Relationship between Historical Scholarship and Feminist Issues* (Princeton: Princeton University Press, 1984); Carl N. Degler, *At Odds: Women and the Family in America from the Revolution to the Present* (New York: Oxford University Press, 1980); James C. Mohr, *Abortion in America: The Origins and Evolution of National Policy, 1800–1900* (New York: Oxford University Press, 1978); Michael A. LaSorte, "Nineteenth Century Family Planning Practices," *Journal of Psychohistory* 4 (Fall 1976): 163–83; Angus McLaren and Arlene Tigar McLaren, *The Bedroom and the State: The Changing Practices and Politics of Contraception and Abortion in Canada, 1880–1980* (Toronto: McClelland and Stewart, 1986); Angus McLaren, *Sexuality and Social Order: The Debate over the Fertility of Women and Workers in France, 1770–1920* (New York: Holmes & Meier, 1983); McLaren, *Birth Control in Nineteenth-Century England* (New York: Holmes & Meier, 1978); Richard Soloway, *Birth Control and the Population Question in England, 1877–1930* (Chapel Hill: University of North Carolina Press, 1982).

The earlier works of J. A. Banks and Olive Banks are important for Victorian England: J. A. Banks, *Victorian Values: Secularism and the Size of Families* (Boston: Routledge & Kegan Paul, 1981); *Feminism and Family Planning in Victorian England* (New York: Schocken, 1964); *Prosperity and Parenthood: A Study of Family Planning among the Victorian Middle Classes* (London: Routledge Kegan Paul, 1954). Still useful is Peter Fryer's *The Birth Controllers* (New York: Stein and Day, 1966) and *British Birth Control Ephemera, 1870–1947, a Catalogue* . . . ([Syston, Eng.]: Baracuda Press, 1969). Important recent works on twentieth-century English birth control include: Wally Seccombe, "Starting to Stop: Working-Class Fertility Decline in Britain," *Past and Present* 126 (February 1990): 151–88; and Barbara Brookes, *Abortion in England, 1900–1967* (London: Croom Helm, 1988).

For earlier periods there is valuable information in the essays in Hélène Bergues, ed., *La prévention des naissances dans la famille: Ses origins dans les temps modernes* (Institut national d'études démographiques, Presses Universitaires de France, 1960), Orest Ranum and Patricia Ranum, eds., *Popular Attitudes toward Birth Control in Pre-Industrial France and England* (New York: Harper Torchbooks, Harper & Row, 1972). John T. Noonan, Jr., *Contraception: A History of Its Treatment by the Catholic Theologians and Canonists* (Cambridge: Harvard University Press, 1965), remains excellent.

The historical demographic literature on the nineteenth-century fertility transition grows yearly. For a sampling of recent work see: John Knodel, "Starting, Stopping, and Spacing during the Early Stages of the Fertility Transition: The Experience of German Village Populations in the 18th and 19th Centuries," *Demography* 24 (1987); James Woycke, *Birth Control in Germany, 1871–1933* (London and New York: Routledge, 1988). For an interesting earlier study see Elsie F. Jones, "Fertility Decline in Australia and New Zealand, 1861–1936," *Population Index* 37 (October–December 1971): 301–38.

Traditional stereotypes about repressed, prudish, and asexual Victorians have been challenged and dramatically revised by: Peter Gay, *The Bourgeois Experience, Victoria to Freud*, vol. 1: *Education of the Senses* (New York: Oxford University Press, 1984); John D'Emilio and Estelle B. Freedman, *Intimate Matters: A History of Sexuality in America* (New York: Harper & Row, 1988); Ellen K. Rothman, *Hands and Hearts: A History of Courtship in America* (New York: Basic Books, 1984); Karen Lystra, *Searching the Heart: Women, Men, and Romantic Love in Nineteenth-Century America* (New York: Oxford University Press, 1989).

Those who emphasize the problematic aspects of nineteenth-century marriage include Steven Seidman, "The Power of Desire and the Danger of Pleasure: Victorian Sexuality Reconsidered," *Journal of Social History* 24 (Fall 1990): 47–67; Ellen Carol DuBois and Linda Gordon, "Seeking Ecstasy on the Battlefield: Danger and Pleasure in Nineteenth-Century Feminist Sexual Thought," *Feminist Studies* 9 (Spring 1983): 7–25; and Carroll Smith-Rosenberg, "The Female World of Love and Ritual," in *Disorderly Conduct: Visions of Gender in Victorian America* (New York: Alfred A. Knopf, 1985). Those who see marriages as more companionate include Degler, *At Odds*; Reed, *From Private Vice to Public Virtue*; Gay, *Education of the Senses*; and Lystra, *Searching the Heart*. See also my Epilogue, note 4.

While these earlier histories of American reproductive control have recognized the importance of the mid-century decades, even the fullest accounts skim over them. Reed's *From Private Vice to Public Virtue* devotes only thirty-four of 381 pages to reproductive control before the Comstock laws. Gordon's *Woman's Body, Woman's Right* does devote almost a fourth of its pages to reproductive control before the 1870s, with a focus on the influence of Perfectionist religious thought and British Neo-Malthusianism on early American fertility intervention, but her book's principal focus is on a later period. She argues that there were four stages in the development of birth control as a social movement, the first being the campaign for "voluntary motherhood" in the final third of the nineteenth century (p. xv). Mohr's *Abortion in America*, which does deal with the important issue of abortion, does not discuss contraceptive products or information, so it is not a study of reproductive control as nineteenth-century Americans knew it.

Introduction

1. Lewis Grassíc Gibbon, *Sunset Song*, in *A Scots Quair* (New York: Schocken, 1981), p. 127. First published in 1946, the novel is set in Scotland in the late nineteenth and early twentieth centuries, but it is also highly suggestive of the ways Americans communicated about reproductive control even if in nineteenth-century American fiction the subject itself was not raised.

2. Mary Hunter Austin, "A Woman of Genius," in *American Voices, American Women*, ed. Lee R. Edwards and Arlyn Diamond (New York: Avon, 1973), pp. 263–64.

3. Leo Tolstoy, *Anna Karenina* (New York: New American Library, 1980), p. 635. I am grateful to Helena Wall for reminding me of this passage.

4. See Ansley Coale and Susan Cotts Watkins, eds., *The Decline of Fertility in Europe* (Princeton: Princeton University Press, 1986), which summarizes the findings of the Princeton European Fertility Project; See also J. E. Knodel, *The Decline of Fertility in Germany, 1871–1939* (Princeton: Princeton University Press, 1974); Michael S. Teitelbaum, *The British Fertility Decline: Demographic Transition in the Crucible of the Industrial Revolution* (Princeton: Princeton University Press, 1984). Gosta Carlsson, "The Decline of Fertility: Innovation or Adjustment Process?" *Population Studies* 20 (1966–67): 149–74, examines Swedish fertility restriction. Carl Mosk, "The Decline of Marital Fertility in Japan," *Population Studies* 31 (March 1979): 24–28, points out the differences in European and Japanese fertility trends.

5. The rate and pace of the U.S. fertility decline are summarized in Robert V. Wells, *Uncle Sam's Family: Issues in and Perspectives on American Demographic History* (Albany: State University of New York Press, 1985), pp. 28–56; Wilson H. Grabill, Clyde V. Kiser, Pascal K. Whelpton, *The Fertility of American Women*, Census Monograph Series (Washington, D.C.: U.S. Bureau of the Census, 1958), p. 22; and Daniel Scott Smith, "Family Limitation, Sexual Control, and Domestic Feminism in Victorian America," in *Clio's Consciousness Raised: New Perspectives on the History of Women*, ed. Mary S. Hartman and Lois Banner (New York: Harper & Row, 1974), p. 212.

6. See Kathleen Neils Conzen, "Peasant Pioneers: Generational Succession among German Farmers in Frontier Minnesota," in *The Countryside in the Age of Capitalist Transformation; Essays in the Social History of Rural America*, ed. Steven Hahn and Jonathan Prude (Chapel Hill: University of North Carolina Press, 1985), p. 279; Tamara K. Hareven and Maris A. Vinovskis, "Marital Fertility, Ethnicity, and Occupation in Urban Families: An Analysis of South Boston and the South End in 1880," *Journal of Social History* 8 (Spring 1975): 69–91; Michael R. Haines, "Fertility Decline in Industrial America: An Analysis of the Pennsylvania Anthracite Region, 1850–1900 . . . ," *Population Studies* 32 (July 1978): 327–54 (native-born and ethnic, rural and urban fertility differentials). John W. Briggs, "Fertility and Cultural Change among Families in Italy and America," *American Historical Review* 91 (December 1986): 1129–45, looks at twentieth-century ethnic fertility.

7. See Ellen Chesler, *Woman of Valor: Margaret Sanger and the Birth Control Movement in America* (New York: Simon & Schuster, 1992), pp. 150–51. Histories of immigrant women, such as Susan Glenn's imaginative *Daughters of the Shtetl* (Ithaca:

Cornell University Press, 1990), although looking closely at mother-daughter relations, have not investigated fertility control issues.

8. Late nineteenth-century and twentieth-century African-American fertility rates are discussed in: Joseph A. McFalls, Jr., and George S. Masnick, "Birth Control and the Fertility of the U.S. Black Population, 1880–1980," *Journal of Family History* 6 (1981): 89–106; and Phillips Cutright and Edward Shorter, "The Effects of Health on the Completed Fertility of Non-White and White U.S. Women Born between 1867 and 1935," *Journal of Social History* 13 (1979): 191–217. There has been less attention to reproductive control among African Americans. See Chapter 2, notes 63–65, for the few commonly cited sources.

9. Nancy Grey Osterud, *Bonds of Community: The Lives of Farm Women in Nineteenth-Century New York* (Ithaca: Cornell University Press, 1991), pp. 72–80, argues that there is statistical evidence for family limitation by mid century among New York farm families, but that there is no evidence about how or why couples attained it. She, nevertheless, argues that farm couples were not motivated by women's desires for relief from pregnancy or by "domestic feminism" but rather by desires to preserve their property for fewer children so as to ensure one child's having adequate means to maintain them in old age. John Mack Faragher, *Sugar Creek: Life on the Illinois Prairie* (New Haven: Yale University Press, 1986), pp. 253–54, notes that in rural Sugar Creek the ratio of children under 10 to women aged 16–45 declined 22.4 percent from 1830 to 1840, 14.6 percent from 1840 to 1850, and 14.3 percent from 1850 to 1860. Hal S. Barron, *Those Who Stayed Behind: Rural Society in Nineteenth-Century New England* (Cambridge: Cambridge University Press, 1984), p. 26, notes a 57 percent decline in the child-woman ratio in areas of rural New England from 1800 to 1840. John Modell, "Family and Fertility on the Indiana Frontier, 1820," *American Quarterly* 23 (1979): 615–34, notes the steady decline in one frontier area. Maris A. Vinovskis, "Socioeconomic Determinants of Interstate Fertility Differentials in the U.S. in 1850 and 1860," *Journal of Interdisciplinary History* 6 (1976): 375–96, believes that the fertility decline in urban and rural areas, 1800–1850, paralleled each other. Richard A. Easterlin, "Factors in the Decline of Farm Fertility in the U.S.: Some Preliminary Results," *Journal of American History* 63 (1976): 600–614, notes that the striking decline in rural white fertility throughout the United States is not explained by differential mortality rates. Richard A. Easterlin, George Alter, and Gretchen A. Cundran, "Farms and Farm Families in Old and New Areas: The Northern States in 1860," in *Family and Population in Nineteenth Century America*, ed. Tamara K. Hareven and Maris A. Vinovskis (Princeton: Princeton University Press, 1978), p. 65, note the significant impact of family limitation practices on northern white fertility.

10. See Catherine Clinton, *The Plantation Mistress: Woman's World in the Old South* (New York: Pantheon, 1982), pp. 152 and 205; Anne Scott, *The Southern Lady: From Pedestal to Politics, 1830–1930* (Chicago: University of Chicago Press, 1970), pp. 38–39. Richard H. Steckel, "Antebellum Southern White Fertility: A Demographic and Economic Analysis," *Journal of Economic History* 40 (1980): 331–50, concludes that there was no family limitation in the South. Jan Lewis and Kenneth A. Lockridge, "'Sally Has Been Sick': Pregnancy and Family Limitation among Virginia Gentry Women," *Journal of Social History* 22 (1988): 5–19.

11. Daniel Scott Smith, "'Early' Fertility Decline in America: A Problem in Family History," *Journal of Family History* 12 (1987): 73–84, questions the reliability of the customary indices for the nineteenth-century U.S. decline, especially the reliance historians have placed on census data. Smith suggests more studies of motivation, nuptiality, and ages at marriage to account for the decline. These challenges are particularly noteworthy given Smith's pathbreaking earlier work, "Family Limitation, Sexual Control," pp. 119–36.

Most studies of the American birth rate decline suggest that birth control played a part, but few have explored it in depth. The classic study is Yasukichi Yasuba, *Birth Rates of the White Population in the United States, 1800–1860: An Economic Study*, Johns Hopkins University Studies in Historical and Political Sciences, ser. 79:2 (Baltimore: Johns Hopkins University Press, 1962), pp. 22, 187. Warren G. Sanderson, "Quantitative Aspects of Marriage, Fertility, and Family Limitation in Nineteenth-Century America," *Demography* 16 (1979): 339–58, considers deliberate family limitation.

12. F. M. L. Thompson, *The Rise of Respectable Society: A Social History of Victorian Britain, 1830–1900* (Cambridge: Harvard University Press, 1988), pp. 53–70.

13. See Everett M. Rogers, *Communication Strategies for Family Planning* (New York: Free Press, 1973), pp. 32–37. Also, Rogers, *Diffusion of Innovations* (New York: Free Press of Glencoe, 1962). The gap between knowledge, acceptance, and practice is called the "KAP-gap."

14. Charles Knowlton, *A History of the Recent Excitement in Ashfield* (Ashfield, [Mass.]: n.p., 1834).

15. Knowlton, *A History of the Recent Excitement*, n.p.

16. In *Boston Investigator*, 9 August 1854, advertisement by Thomas Low Nichols.

17. Stanton is cited in Ellen Carol DuBois, "Outgrowing the Compact of the Fathers: Equal Rights, Woman Suffrage, and the U.S. Constitution, 1820–1878," *Journal of American History* 74 (1987): 856. Edward Bond Foote, *The Radical Remedy in Social Science* (1886): 79.

18. See Alcott, *Physiology of Marriage* (1866), p. 180, and William Goodell, "Clinical Lecture on Conjugal Onanism and Kindred Sins," *Philadelphia Medical Times* 2 (1872): 161–63.

19. The E. C. Allen Papers, Scrapbook of Unpublishable Advertisements, Historical Collections, Baker Library, Harvard Graduate School of Business Administration.

20. Theodore Reik, *Of Love and Lust* (New York: Cudahy, 1957), p. 598, describes the terminology used by late-nineteenth-century Viennese women: "When women want to discuss sexual matters they use different expressions when speaking together and when speaking before men. . . . When I was a young man the Viennese girls said: 'My aunt will visit me on Thursday' when they wished to indicate to other women in the presence of men that they expected their monthly period on this day. This phrase replaced another one which expressed the fear that 'Thursday will be bad weather.'"

21. Christine Stansell, *City of Women: Sex and Class in New York, 1789–1860* (New York: Knopf, 1986), elaborates the significance of the remnants of the libertine tradition in men's and women's lives in New York.

22. See Stuart M. Blumin, *The Emergence of the Middle Class: Social Experience in the American City, 1760–1900* (Cambridge: Cambridge University Press, 1989), pp. 179–91; Mary P. Ryan, *Cradle of the Middle Class: The Family in Oneida Co., New York, 1790–1865* (Cambridge: Cambridge University Press, 1981).

23. This issue is discussed in: Mary P. Ryan, *Women in Public: Between Banners and Ballots, 1825–1880* (Baltimore: Johns Hopkins University Press, 1990); Paula Baker, *The Moral Frameworks of Public Life: Gender, Politics, and the State in Rural New York, 1870–1930* (New York: Oxford University Press, 1991), chap. 3; and Nancy A. Hewitt, *Women's Activism and Social Change: Rochester, New York, 1822–1872* (Ithaca: Cornell University Press, 1984).

24. Reproductive control is not discussed in: Faye E. Dudden, *Serving Women: Household Service in Nineteenth-Century America* (Middletown, Conn.: Wesleyan University Press, 1983); Mary H. Blewett, *Men, Women, and Work: Class, Gender, and Protest in the New England Shoe Industry, 1780–1910* (Urbana: University of Illinois Press, 1988); Stansell, *City of Women*, and Alice Kessler-Harris, *Out to Work:*

A History of Wage-Earning Women in the United States (New York: Oxford University Press, 1982).

25. Prostitutes' birth control practices are not discussed in: Ruth Rosen and Sue Davidson, eds., *The Maimie Papers* (Cambridge: Feminist Press in cooperation with The Schlesinger Library of Radcliffe College, 1977); Rosen, *The Lost Sisterhood: Prostitution in America, 1900–1918* (Baltimore: Johns Hopkins University Press, 1982); Lucie Cheng Hirata, "Free, Indentured, Enslaved: Chinese Prostitutes in Nineteenth Century America," *Signs* 5 (Autumn 1979): 3–19. For a cursory examination of prostitutes' knowledge in early European history see Hélène Bergues, *La prévention des naissances dans la famille: Ses origins dans les temps modernes* (Institut national d'études démographiques, Presses Universitaires de France, 1960), chap. 4.

Chapter One

1. In the years from 1845 to 1864, Mary Poor's diaries record 162 menstrual cycles. Their average length was 28.7 days. The diaries and correspondence are in the Poor Family Papers (PFP hereafter), Arthur and Elizabeth Schlesinger Library on the History of Women in America, Radcliffe College.

2. I decoded Mary Poor's private records from markings in her pocket diaries. In all other respects, the Poors have been well studied by historians. Alfred D. Chandler, Jr., *Henry Varnum Poor, Business Educator, Analyst, and Reformer* (Cambridge: Harvard University Press, 1956), is an excellent source for Henry and Willie's careers. A great-grandson of Henry Varnum Poor, Chandler concentrates on his professional life. James R. McGovern, *Yankee Family* (New Orleans: Polyanthos, 1975), discusses their marriage, but not their fertility or sexuality. Ellen K. Rothman, *Hearts and Hands: A History of Courtship in America* (New York: Basic Books, 1984), looks at the Poors' courtship.

3. Charles F. Westoff, "Coital Frequency and Contraception," *Family Perspectives* 6 (1974): 136–41, reports average coital frequencies for women under forty-five years old with husbands present as 6.8 (for four weeks) in 1965 and 8.2 in 1970.

4. Chandler, *Henry Varnum Poor*, notes that Mary Poor gathered the family papers together for preservation. See also the penciled note at the top of a letter 2 February, 1858, "The last letter I wrote to my mother," which suggests that she may have done some editing of the papers.

5. The erasures were far from complete or thorough: 1865 is well erased; in 1866 there are many erasures and only a few discernible "×'s"; in 1867 in spite of sporadic erasures not all were removed. From 1869 to 1871 none was erased. The interpretive difficulties are further compounded by other changes Mary made in the record. In 1857 she began to mark the "×'s" in the front of her almanac on a one-page calendar of the year. In 1875 she began making slight slashes rather than "×'s" by certain dates. Two years later, when she was fifty-seven and Henry was sixty-five, she stopped keeping sexual records altogether.

Despite the shortcomings, the data are remarkably consistent. Six years of sexual records are not erased: three early in the Poors' marriage, 1848 through April 1852, and three later in the marriage, 1869–71. The frequencies for the unerased years compare well to the less reliable erased years. The unerased years 1849–51 show total yearly intercourse frequencies of 75, 75, and 69, only slightly higher than the subsequent three erased years: 60/(42) in 1852, 66/(59) in 1853, and 64/(58) in 1864. The bias in calculating the erased data will be toward an undercount. Similarly, the yearly totals for the unerased later years, 1869–70, of 54, 52, and 46, compare with the total of 58 in 1867 and 54/(53) in 1871, both years in which the "×'s" were erased.

The sexual record required especially meticulous decoding, for I could not assume that the "×'s" denoted sexual intercourse until I had verified that Henry was home in every instance, and that there were no marks when he was away. As it turns out, Mary was not the only one in her family to keep records of sexual activity. Her maternal uncle, Lewis Tappan, wrote passages about sex in his diary, but his granddaughter erased some and tore two pages out of the diary before giving it the Library of Congress. See Bertram Wyatt-Brown, "Three Generations of Yankee Parenthood: The Tappan Family, a Case Study of Antebellum Nurture," *Illinois Quarterly* 38 (Fall 1975):19.

6. Peter Gay, *The Bourgeois Experience, Victoria to Freud*, vol.1, *Education of the Senses* (New York: Oxford University Press, 1984), relies heavily on a similar diary record kept by Mabel Loomis Todd. Her "×'s" marked menstruation, and she, like Mary Poor, kept a record of sexual intercourse. Gay believes that it was "for prudential as much as for passionate reasons" because she and her lover used a combination of rhythm and coitus interruptus.

7. Chandler, *Henry Varnum Poor*, p. 9.

8. Chandler, *Henry Varnum Poor*, p. 23.

9. MPP to Lucy Pierce Hedge, 13 March 1859, PFP.

10.. MPP to Lucy [Hedge], 4 March 1852, PFP.

11. Stephen Nissenbaum, *Sex, Diet, and Debility in Jacksonian America: Sylvester Graham and Health Reform* (Westport, Conn.: Greenwood Press, 1980). Ronald G. Walters, "The Erotic South: Civilization and Sexuality in American Abolitionism," *American Quarterly* 25 (1973): 177–201, discusses the interest of antislavery reformers in Graham's theories.

12. MPP to parents, 16 August 1848, PFP. Mary Poor fits well into the developing "mode of mothering" of the early to mid nineteenth century discussed in Nancy Schrom Dye and Daniel Blake Smith, "Mother Love and Infant Death, 1750–1920," *Journal of American History* 73 (1986): 329–53. Her diary and letters reflect her "richer, more intense relationships" with her children and her interest in their differing personalities.

13. See J. J. Dupâquier and M. Lachiver, "Sur les débuts de la contraception en France ou les deux malthusianismes," *Annales E.S.C.* 24 (1969): 1391–1406. They define birth intervals over forty-eight months as sterile or deliberately contraceptive. In Mary Poor's case we know that the intervals were not physiologically sterile.

14. See Louise Kantrow, "Philadelphia Gentry: Fertility and Family Limitation among an American Aristocracy," *Population Studies* 34 (March 1980): 28, Table 8. In this study the birth intervals (rather than conception intervals) of elite Philadelphia women married between 1826 and 1875 showed average intervals between marriage and first *birth* (rather than conception) to be 14.2 months compared with Mary Poor's birth interval of 14 months.

15. HVP to MPP, 10 September 1843, PFP.

16. MPP to parents, 7 July 1844, PFP.

17. MPP to parents, 8 May 1845, PFP.

18. MPP to parents, 8 June 1845, addition dated 26 June, PFP.

19. MPP to parents, 10 November 1844, PFP.

20. MPP to parents, 9 February 1845, PFP.

21. MPP to parents, 11 December 1848, PFP.

22. MPP to Lucy Hedge, 27 January 1850, PFP.

23. Diary of Mary Poor, 28 December 1851, PFP.

24. Diary of Mary Poor, August 1851 entries, PFP.

25. See Joel Shew, *The Water-Cure Manual* (New York: Cady & Burgess, 1847), and Shew, *Midwifery and the Diseases of Women* (New York: Fowlers & Wells, 1853).

26. MPP to mother, 19 May 1853; MPP to Lucy Hedge, 17 August 1853, PFP.

27. MPP to mother, 9 June 1853, PFP.

28. MPP to Lucy Hedge, 10 July and 17 August 1853, PFP.

29. MPP to "Sister," 1 November 1853 (folder 182), PFP.

30. MPP to Fenoline, 5 August [1854], PFP. Mary Poor gave this an incorrect date of 1855 later.

31. See also the despairing letters she wrote her mother and sisters, especially MPP to her mother, 16 December 1855, PFP.

32. MPP to mother, 16 December 1855, PFP.

33. MPP to HVP, 19 July 1860, PFP.

34. MPP to HVP, 22 July 1860, PFP.

35. MPP to HVP, 11 June 1862, PFP.

36. MPP to Lucy Hedge, 11 December 1861, PFP.

37. MPP to Fenoline, 15 April 1861, PFP.

38. MPP to HVP, 30 June 1863, PFP.

39. MPP to HVP, 23 and 24 August 1863, PFP.

40. HVP to MPP, 27 August 1863, PFP.

41. HVP to MPP, 31 August 1863, PFP.

42. MPP to HVP, 20 September 1863, PFP.

43. MPP to HVP, 27 June 1852, PFP.

44. HVP to MPP, 12 July 1846, PFP; MPP diary, 1868.

45. Nichols, *Esoteric Anthropology* (1853). Alcott, *The Physiology of Marriage* (1866), attributed stillbirths, abortions, and feeble children to parental sex during pregnancy. Orson S. Fowler warned in his popular *Amativeness; or, Evils and Remedies of Excessive and Perverted Sensuality*, 40th ed. (New York: Fowler and Wells, [c. 1842]), that sex during pregnancy "sows the seed of sensuality in the child."

46. Gardner, *Causes and Curative Treatment of Sterility* (1856), p. 18. Mary noted in her diary that she had read Gardner's *Old Wine in New Bottles*, his account of a year spent in Paris, in which among other topics he discussed prostitution and venereal diseases. Gardner was unusual in his counting advice. (See Chapter 3, note 100.)

47. Day 1 on the graph represents the day Mary Poor marked a + in her menstrual records. Each coitus was then calculated according to its timing in her cycle. For example, if 10 April were a + day, then sexual intercourse on 15 April would be calculated as Day 6 of the menstrual cycle.

48. I have plotted the Poors' sexual frequencies according to day in the menstrual cycle for individual conception intervals, but it is unclear whether the differences in the patterns represent genuine attempts at some variant of the rhythm method—perhaps various experimentations to determine Mary's infertile days—or whether the data is skewed by the difficulties deciphering her erased ×'s.

49. See John C. Barrett and John Marshall, "The Risk of Conception on Different Days of the Menstrual Cycle," *Population Studies* 23 (1969): 455–61; P. A. Lachenbruch, "Frequency and Timing of Intercourse: Its Relation to the Probability of Conception," *Population Studies* 21 (1967): 23.

50. From Robert's birth until her miscarriage in 1851, for example, 34 percent of all sexual intercourse was in Mary's most fertile period; in the long interval between Lucy and Quita, 38 percent occurred in mid cycle.

51. MPP diary, 26 March 1851, PFP.

52. Mary Gove Nichols, *Experience in Water-Cure* (New York: Fowlers & Wells, 1850), chap. 8.

53. Quoted in Elizabeth Tyler Coleman, *Priscilla Cooper Tyler and the American Scene, 1816–1889* (N.P.: University of Alabama Press, 1955).

54. Napheys, *The Physical Life of Woman* (1872), p. 96; William T. Lusk, "Abortion," *Medical and Surgical Reporter* 33 (1875): 461–65; "Weaning," *Cincinnati Lancet and Observer*, n.s. 10 (1867): 436–42.

55. J. Van Ginneken, "Fertility Regulation during Human Lactation: The Chance of

Conception during Lactation," *Journal of Biosocial Science*, Supplement 4 (1977); J. Van Ginneken, "Prolonged Breastfeeding as a Birth Spacing Method," *Studies in Family Planning* 5 (1974): 204.

56. Russell Thacher Trall, *The Hydropathic Encyclopedia* (New York: Fowlers & Wells, 1852): "Food, Dress, Clothing for Infants."

57. MPP to mother, March to August 1854, PFP.

58. MPP to mother, 26 November, n.y. [1856]; MPP to Lucy, 30 December 1860, PFP.

59. Elizabeth Blackwell to Emily Blackwell, 12 May, n.y. [c.1854], Blackwell Family Papers, Library of Congress; and Ishbel Ross, *Child of Destiny: The Life Story of the First Woman Doctor* (New York: Harper, 1949), pp. 87–88. For Mary Gove Nichols's beliefs, see Nichols, *Esoteric Anthropology*, p. 190.

60. HVP to MPP, 27 August 1863, PFP.

61. HVP to MPP, 31 August 1863, PFP.

62. Lewis and Lockridge, "'Sally Has Been Sick': Pregnancy and Family Limitation among Virginia Gentry Women," *Journal of Social History*, Fall 1988: 5–19.

63. Schrom Dye, "Mother Love," pp. 338, 346, discusses women's anxieties surrounding their changing maternal role.

64. John Knodel, "Starting, Stopping, and Spacing during the Early Stages of the Fertility Transition: The Experience of German Village Populations in the 18th and 19th Centuries," *Demography* 24 (1987): 143–62, argues that spacing was not as significant as family limitation in the villages he studied. Wally Seccombe, "Starting to Stop: Working-Class Fertility Decline in Britain," *Past and Present* 126 (1990): 161, does not credit birth spacing as significant either. Lee L. Bean et al., *Fertility Change on the American Frontier: Adaptation and Innovation* (Berkeley: University of California Press, 1990), make a revisionist argument that fertility control could have been effected by child spacing even early in the marriage cycle.

65. Maris A. Vinovskis, *Fertility in Massachusetts from the Revolution to the Civil War* (New York: Academic Press, 1981), pp. 118–21, discusses the lack of individual-level studies of the relationship between modernization and fertility.

Chapter Two

1. Governor Bradford's ms. "[History] Of Plimmoth Plantation" (1630–1650), cited in Norman E. Himes, *Medical History of Contraception* (New York: Schocken, 1970; 1st pub. 1936), p. 225.

2. See Cornelia Hughes Dayton, "Taking the Trade: Abortion and Gender Relations in an Eighteenth-Century New England Village," *William and Mary Quarterly* 3d ser., 48 (1991): 19–49. This is a detailed analysis of a remarkably richly documented case.

3. Dayton, "Taking the Trade," pp. 24–25, 32.

4. See Laurel Thatcher Ulrich, *Good Wives* (New York: Oxford University Press, 1980), p. 196.

5. Daniel Scott Smith and Michael Hindus, "Premarital Pregnancy in America, 1640–1971: An Overview and an Interpretation," *Journal of Interdisciplinary History* 5 (1975): 537–70.

6. See Carol F. Karlsen, *The Devil in the Shape of a Woman: Witchcraft in Colonial New England* (New York: Vintage, 1989), p. 141.

7. See Roger Thompson, *Sex in Middlesex: Popular Mores in a Massachusetts County, 1649–1699* (Amherst: University of Massachusetts Press, 1986), pp. 10–11.

8. Laurel Thatcher Ulrich, *A Midwife's Tale: The Life of Martha Ballard, Based on Her Diary, 1785–1812* (New York: Knopf, 1990), p. 193, found little evidence of birth control in Hallowell, Maine, in the eighteenth century. John D'Emilio and Estelle B. Freedman, *Intimate Matters: A History of Sexuality in America* (New York: Harper & Row, 1988), p. 26, argue that demographic evidence from New England reveals that few married women limited family size. For fertility data see: Daniel Scott Smith, "The Demographic History of Colonial New England," *Journal of Economic History* 32 (1972): 172; Lorena S. Walsh, "'Til Death Us Do Part': Marriage and Family in Seventeenth-Century Maryland," in *The Chesapeake in the Seventeenth Century: Essays on Anglo-American Society*, ed. Thad W. Tate and David Ammerman (Chapel Hill: University of North Carolina Press, 1979): 126–52.

9. See Helena M. Wall, *Fierce Communion: Family and Community in Early America* (Cambridge: Harvard University Press, 1990), p. 81 and Afterword.

10. See Vance Randolph, *Ozark Superstitions* (New York: Columbia University Press, 1947), p. 95.

11. D'Emilio and Freedman, *Intimate Matters*, p. 26.

12. Alan Macfarlane, *The Family Life of Ralph Josselin, a Seventeenth-Century Clergyman* (Cambridge: Cambridge University Press, 1970), p. 201.

13. Ulrich, *A Midwife's Tale*, p. 195.

14. See Mary Beth Norton, *Liberty's Daughters: The Revolutionary Experience of American Women, 1750–1800* (Boston: Little, Brown, 1980), pp. 74–75.

15. Norton, *Liberty's Daughters*, pp. 74–75.

16. Cited in Nancy F. Cott, "Eighteenth Century Family and Social Life," in *A Heritage of Her Own: Toward a New Social History of American Women*, ed. Nancy F. Cott and Elizabeth H. Pleck (New York: Simon and Schuster, 1979), p. 119.

17. See Page Smith, *Daughters of the Promised Land: Women in American History* (Boston: Little, Brown, 1970), p. 232.

18. See Ann Leighton, *Early American Gardens "For Meate or Medicine"* (Boston: Houghton Mifflin, 1970), p. 140.

19. Leighton, *Early American Gardens*, pp. 140, 308. Culpeper's *Dispensatory* in 1720 was the first medical book with a hard binding to be published in the thirteen colonies.

20. See Ely Van De Warker, "The Detection of Criminal Abortion, II. Abortion from Medication," *Journal of the Gynecological Society of Boston* 5 (1871): 236; [Richard Foreman, "a Cherokee Doctor"], *The Cherokee Physician; or, Indian Guide to Health* (Chattanooga: James W. Mahoney, 1845), p. 207.

21. Leighton, *Early American Gardens*, p. 140.

22. Macfarlane, *The Family Life of Ralph Josselin, a Seventeenth Century Clergyman*, p. 83. Macfarlane believes that some of Jane Constable Josselin's five miscarriages were deliberate (p. 201), although he does not suggest how.

23. For centuries rue had a reputation for procuring abortion, probably because it is capable of causing uterine contractions late in pregnancy much as ergot does. Rue was sometimes used as a substitute for ergot in nineteenth-century medicine. See Ely Van de Warker, "The Criminal Use of Proprietary or Advertised Nostrums," *New York Medical Journal* 17 (1873): 23–35; Augustus K. Gardner, "An Essay on Ergot with New Views of Its Therapeutic Action," *New York Journal of Medicine*, n.s. 11 (1853): 206–32.

24. Quoted in Thompson, *Sex in Middlesex*, pp. 25–26, 78.

25. Culpeper, *The English Physician* (London, 1799).

26. Leighton, *Early American Gardens*, p. 218.

27. Folklorists have long noted that practices which some cultures believed enabled conception are considered abortifacient in others.

28. Other anthelmintics also had reputations as abortives including wormseed (*Anthelminticum*), inula, *Artemisia vulgaris*, and tansy seeds.

29. Leighton, *Early American Gardens*, p. 264.

30. Charles F. Millspaugh, *Medicinal Plants*, 2 vols. (Philadelphia: John C. Yorston, 1892), reprinted as *American Medicinal Plants* (New York: Dover, 1974), pp. 463–64. See also Ohio Folklore Collection, Center for the Study of Comparative Folklore and Mythology, UCLA, for references to mint teas and to pennyroyal tea causing abortions.

31. See Edward P. Claus, *Pharmacognosy* (Philadelphia: Lea & Febiger, 1970); also William B. Woodman and Charles M. Tidy, *Forensic Medicine and Toxicology* (Philadelphia: Lindsay & Blakiston, 1877), p. 664.

32. The *Merck Index* (Rahway, N.J.: Merck, 1968) warns against use of aloes in advanced pregnancy. The principle ingredient, aloin, can cause severe intestinal cramps and kidney damage to users. Ely Van De Warker, "The Detection of Criminal Abortion, III," *Journal of the Gynecological Society of Boston* 6 (1871): 350–55.

33. Robert G. Potter et al., "Applications of Field Studies to Research on the Physiology of Human Reproduction: Lactation and Its Effects upon Birth Intervals in Eleven Punjab Villages, India," *Journal of Chronic Diseases* 18 (1965): 1125–40, concluded that lactation may extend that period of sterility. Moni Nag, *Factors Affecting Human Fertility in Non-Industrial Societies: A Cross-Cultural Study*, Yale University Publications in Anthropology 66 (New Haven: Department of Anthropology, Yale University, 1962), p. 79.

34. See Robert M. May, "Human Reproduction Reconsidered," *Nature* 272 (1978): 491–95.

35. Quoted in Cecil K. Drinker, *Not So Long Ago: A Chronicle of Medicine and Doctors in Colonial Philadelphia* (New York: Oxford University Press, 1937), p. 54.

36. Quoted in Daniel Blake Smith, *Inside the Great House: Planter Life in Eighteenth-Century Chesapeake Society* (Ithaca: Cornell University Press, 1980), p. 37.

37. Norton, *Liberty's Daughters*, p. 233.

38. William Cadogan, *An Essay upon Nursing and Management of Children* (London, 1748). This had at least ten editions by 1772. William Buchan, *Advice to Mothers* (Philadelphia, 1804), cited Cadogan's 10th edition of 1769.

39. Macfarlane, *The Family Life of Ralph Josselin*, p. 87, argues for much class and individual variation in weaning ages in seventeenth-century England, although the practice among the yeoman class and above generally ranged from twelve to eighteen months.

40. *New York Daily Tribune*, 13 January 1851.

41. See George D. Sussman, *Selling Mothers' Milk: The Wet-Nursing Business in France, 1715–1914* (Champaign: University of Illinois Press, 1982), and Sussman, "The Wet-Nursing Business in 19th Century France," *French Historical Studies* 9 (1975): 304–28.

42. See R. Sauer, "Infanticide and Abortion in Nineteenth-Century Britain," *Population Studies* 32 (1978): 81–93; George K. Behlmer, "Deadly Motherhood: Infanticide and Medical Opinion in Mid Victorian England," *Journal of the History of Medicine* 34 (1979): 403–27. For American infanticide cases see Peter C. Hoffer and N. E. H. Hull, *Murdering Mothers: Infanticide in England and New England, 1558–1803*, Linden Studies in Anglo-American Legal History (New York: New York University Press, 1981).

43. Emily Blackwell to Marion Blackwell, 17 November 1876, box 69, Blackwell Family Papers, Library of Congress.

44. W. H. Schieffelin & Co., *Catalogue* (New York: n.p., 1871).

45. MPP to parents, 28 January 1849, PFP.

46. The best discussions of the literature on lactational sterility are in C. Tietze,

"The Effect of Breastfeeding on the Rate of Conception," *International Population Conference* (New York, 1961), vol. 2: 129–36. See also Ryder and Westhoff, *Reproduction in the U.S.*, p. 335.

47. E. Gautier and L. Henry, *La population de Crulai paroisse normande*, Travaux et documents, Cahier n. 33, pp. 146, 154. L. Henry, *Anciennes familles genévoises*, p. 135. Henry found statistical evidence that women whose infants died before reaching their first year had, on average, a five-month shorter interval before the next birth than women whose infants lived and who, presumably, continued to breastfeed their infants and derive the minimal protection of lactation.

48. John Knodel, "Natural Fertility in Pre-Industrial Germany, *Population Studies* 32 (1978): 481–510. Other scholars question how widespread the understanding of lactational sterility really was. Etienne Van de Walle and Francine Van de Walle, "Allaitement, sterilité et contraception: Les opinions jusqu'au XIXe siècle," *Population* 27 (1972): 685–701, argue that lactational sterility was not well known in Europe before the eighteenth century.

49. I am not arguing that changes in breastfeeding practices contributed to the decline in fertility in eighteenth-century America. Studies of Sturbridge and Nantucket, Massachusetts, conclude that changes in breastfeeding practices cannot account for declining family size. Nancy Osterud and John Fulton, "Family Limitation and Age at Marriage: Fertility Decline in Sturbridge, Massachusetts, 1730–1850," *Population Studies* 30 (1976): 486, note that if there were changes they were in the direction of earlier weaning and faster use of supplemental food—both of which would have reduced the contraceptive protection of lactation.

50. Jean-Louis Flandrin, *Families in Former Times: Kinship, Household, and Sexuality*, trans. Richard Southern (Cambridge: Cambridge University Press, 1979), pp. 207–38.

51. H. Temkin-Greener and A. C. Swedlund, "Fertility Transition in the Connecticut Valley, 1740–1850," *Population Studies* 32 (1978): 40. In Connecticut Valley villages the first stage occurred among some of the couples married between 1721 and 1760 (evident by an unusual variance and range in family sizes and some statistically significant increases in birth intervals). The second stage occurred among couples married between 1740 and 1780 (evident from substantially longer birth intervals and a decline in the mean age at which women bore their last child). Stage three, with a marked drop in family size but shorter birth intervals (perhaps because couples wanted children earlier in their marriage and felt more confident about their ultimate ability to limit the total number), occurred between 1760 and 1800.

52. Temkin-Greener, "Fertility Transition," pp. 27–41, found evidence of family limitation in the couples marrying from the 1760s to 1790s in Franklin County, Massachusetts; see also Osterud and Fulton, "Family Limitation": 481–94.

53. See Edward Byers, "Fertility Transition in a New England Commercial Center: Nantucket, Ma., 1680–1840," *Journal of Interdisciplinary History* 13 (1982): 17–40. Byers relied on two classic indices (age-specific marital fertility rates and the age of mothers at their last birth) to argue that the Quaker couples who predominated on the island were practicing deliberate family limitation. Barbara J. Logue, "The Whaling Industry and Fertility Decline: Nantucket, Ma., 1660–1850," *Social Science History* 8 (1983): 427–55, disagrees with Byers.

54. Robert V. Wells, "Family Size and Fertility Control in Eighteenth-Century America: A Study of Quaker Families," *Population Studies* 25 (1971): 73–82, notes that Pennsylvania Quaker women born before 1730 seem to have made no attempt to control family size, but there was consistent statistical evidence of deliberate family limitation among the wives born from 1731 to 1755, all of whom had finished childbearing by 1800. Barry Levy, *Quakers and the American Family: British Settlement in the Dela-*

ware Valley (New York: Oxford University Press, 1988), notes that by the 1760s Pennsylvania Quakers began to see their resources as finite and began to control family size, but he does not discuss how they did so.

55. Rich samplings of fertility intervention folklore are scattered in the *Journal of American Folklore* and in the files at the Center for the Study of Folklore at UCLA, which I used with the thoughtful aid of the late Wayland Hand.

56. James Axtell, ed., *The Indian Peoples of Eastern America: A Documentary History of the Sexes* (New York: Oxford University Press, 1981), p. 23, on Iroquois families. John Mack Faragher, *Sugar Creek: Life on the Illinois Prairie* (New Haven: Yale University Press, 1986), p. 114, attributes low Kickapoo fertility to long periods of sexual abstinence, prolonged nursing, herbal remedies for contraception and abortion, and occasional infanticide. James H. Merrell, *The Indians' New World: Catawbas and Their Neighbors* (New York: W. W. Norton, 1989), p. 140, notes that the Catawbas practiced abortion and infanticide.

57. See Axtell, *The Indian Peoples of Eastern America*, pp. 10, 95.

58. See Virgil Vogel, *American Indian Medicine* (Norman: University of Oklahoma Press, 1970); Harold E. Driver, *Indians of North America* (Chicago: University of Chicago Press, 1961).

59. Benjamin Gale to Eleazar Wheelock, 21 July 1769, quoted in Axtell, *The Indian Peoples of Eastern America*, p. 22.

60. Michael A. Weiner, *Earth Medicine—Earth Foods: Plant Remedies, Drugs, and Natural Foods of the North American Indians* (New York: MacMillan, 1972), lists it as an Indian emmenagogue. See also Millspaugh, *American Medicinal Plants*, pp. 37–40, for a discussion of *Cimefuga racemosa* as oxytocic and abortive.

61. See Millspaugh, *American Medicinal Plants*, pp. 58–60, and Clarence Meyer, *American Folk Medicine* (New York: Thomas Y. Crowell, 1973).

62. See David L. Cowen, "The History of Pharmacy and the History of the South," printed lecture given at the University of Georgia, Athens, 30 March 1967; copy in the Massachusetts School of Pharmacy Library.

63. Matthew Gregory Lewis, *Journal of a West India Proprietor 1815–1817* (Boston: Houghton Mifflin, 1929), pp. 314–15.

64. Cited in Herbert G. Gutman, *The Black Family in Slavery and Freedom, 1750–1925* (New York: Pantheon Books, 1976), p. 80.

65. See Gutman, *Black Family in Slavery and Freedom*, p. 81.

66. Jacqueline Jones, *Labor of Love, Labor of Sorrow*, pp. 19, 35. In the postbellum period, because of poor nutrition and health care, black fertility declined and did not begin to rise again until at least 1910 (pp. 88, 91). The question of why slave fertility was so high has triggered intense debates among historians, some arguing that this was a result of forced breeding, while others insist that it was slaves' own choice, that children were a solace and an emotional support in the hardships of slavery.

67. See Elizabeth Fox-Genovese, *Within the Plantation Household: Black and White Women of the Old South* (Chapel Hill: University of North Carolina Press, 1988), pp. 323–24. Michael P. Johnson, "Smothered Slave Infants: Were Slave Mothers at Fault?" *Journal of Southern History* 47 (1981): 493–520.

68. Linda Brent, *Incidents in the Life of a Slave Girl* (San Diego, Calif.: Harcourt Brace Jovanovich, 1973), pp. 59–60 (originally pub. 1861). I am grateful to Rena Fraden for bringing this to my attention.

69. See Mechal Sobel, *The World They Made Together: Blacks and Whites in Eighteenth-Century Virginia* (Princeton: Princeton University Press, 1987).

70. Marie Campbell, *Folks Do Get Born* (New York: Rinehart, 1946), p. 85. A colonial midwife's duties are detailed in Laurel Thatcher Ulrich, *A Midwife's Tale: The Life of Martha Ballard, Based on Her Diary, 1785–1812* (New York: Knopf, 1990). John

Demos, *Entertaining Satan: Witchcraft and the Culture of Early New England* (New York: Oxford University Press, 1982), discusses the association of midwifery with witchcraft.

71. See Thomas R. Brendle and Claude W. Unger, *Folk Medicine of the Pennsylvania Germans: The Non-Occult Cures* [Norristown, Pa.], Pennsylvania German Society Proceedings, 45 (1935).

72. For a valuable recent analysis of the historiography see James Gilreath, "American Book Distribution," *Proceedings of the American Antiquarian Society* 95 (1985): 501–83. For almanacs the best source is still Marion Barber Stowell, *Early American Almanacs: The Colonial Weekday Bible* (New York: B. Franklin, 1977) and for chapbooks, Harry Weiss, "American Chapbooks, 1722–1842," *Bulletin of the New York Public Library* 49 (1945): 587–96.

73. See Otho T. Beall, Jr., *"Aristotle's Masterpiece* in America: A Landmark in the Folklore of Medicine," *William and Mary Quarterly* 20 (1963): 207–22.

74. Quotations from Thompson, *Sex in Middlesex*, pp. 85–86, and Richard Mercer Dorson, *American Folklore* (Chicago: University of Chicago Press, 1959), p. 60.

75. Joan M. Jensen, *Loosening the Bonds: Mid-Atlantic Farm Women, 1750–1850* (New Haven: Yale University Press, 1986), pp. 115–20, discusses the access of rural folk to almanacs from country stores or at farmers' markets. Women, too, owned them.

76. See Norton, *Liberty's Daughters*, pp. 72–84, and Paul C. Nagel, *The Adams Women: Abigail and Louisa Adams, Their Sisters and Daughters* (New York: Oxford University Press, 1987).

Chapter Three

1. Clelia Duel Mosher, "Statistical Study of the Marriage of 47 Women," in "Study of the Physiology and Hygiene of Marriage with Some Consideration of the Birth Rate," Clelia Duel Mosher Papers, Archives, Stanford University. I am grateful to the Schlesinger Library for allowing me to use their microfilm of the questionnaires. See Carl Degler, *At Odds: Women and the Family from the Revolution to the Present* (New York: Oxford University Press, 1980), pp. 262–66, and John D'Emilio and Estelle B. Freedman, *Intimate Matters: A History of Sexuality in America* (New York: Harper & Row, 1988), pp. 175–78.

2. Alcott, *The Physiology of Marriage* (1866), p. 190.

3. Owen, *Moral Physiology* (1858), Appendix to 5th ed., p. 80.

4. Joan M. Jensen, *Loosening the Bonds: Mid-Atlantic Farm Women, 1750–1850* (New Haven: Yale University Press, 1986), p. 28, notes that historians are mystified by how withdrawal was learned and transmitted. She is incorrect, however, that this was the practice among the Oneida Perfectionists. Their method, "coitus reservatus," was different (requiring that a man never come to orgasm but gradually lose tumescence while inside a woman). For arguments that withdrawal was "close to being a self-evident method of contraception," see John T. Noonan, Jr., *Contraception: A History of Its Treatment by the Catholic Theologians and Canonists* (Cambridge: Harvard University Press, 1965), p. 10, while P. P. A. Biller, "Birth-Control in the West in the Thirteenth and Early Fourteenth Centuries," *Past and Present: A Journal of Historical Studies* 94 (1982): 5–7, argues that it was well understood in the medieval West from the twelfth century on. Orest Ranum and Patricia Ranum, eds., "Introduction," *Popular Attitudes toward Birth Control in Pre-Industrial France and England* (New York: Harper Torchbooks, Harper & Row, 1972), p. 6., argue that couples did not know withdrawal in the Middle Ages. M. K. Hopkins, "Contraception in the Roman Empire," *Comparative*

Studies in Society and History 8 (1965–66): 124–51, argues that withdrawal needed to be learned.

5. Owen, *Moral Physiology* (1858), p. 78. Charles Knowlton, *Fruits of Philosophy* (Philadelphia, 1839), p. 8, made a similar comment about how easily people could think up withdrawal for themselves. Rebutting his critics who said that knowledge of "checks" would lead to illegitimate sex, Knowlton argued that if a couple had already become so "familiar" as to douche to prevent conception "they would practice the 'way' or drawback . . . [even] if no such book as this had ever been written."

6. Margaret Jarman Hagood, *Mothers of the South* (New York: Norton, c.1939; rpt. ed. 1977), p. 123.

7. Owen, *Moral Physiology* (London, 1842), p. 38.

8. Quoted in Degler, *At Odds*, p. 211.

9. Owen, *Moral Physiology* (1858), p. 76.

10. Studies of the effectiveness of individual birth control methods employ estimates of the number of pregnancies which would result if one hundred women used the method for one year. The base line is the estimate that with no birth control whatsoever eighty to ninety of the one hundred women would become pregnant in the first three to four months. In some contemporary studies, couples relying solely on withdrawal had only five to ten pregnancies per 100 woman years, while in others the failure rate was thirty-eight. Anna L. Southam, "Contraceptive Methods: Use, Safety, and Effectiveness," in *Family Planning and Population Programs: A Review of World Developments*, ed. Bernard Berelson (Chicago: University of Chicago Press, 1966).

11. See Robert W. Kistner, *Gynecology, Principles and Practice*, 2d ed. (Chicago: Year Book Medical Publishers, 1971), p. 676, and Christopher Tietze, "The Use-Effectiveness of Contraceptive Methods," in *Research in Family Planning*, ed. Clyde V. Kiser (Princeton: Princeton University Press, 1962), p. 362.

12. Owen, *Moral Physiology* (1831, 1st ed.), p. 65.

13. Owen, *Moral Physiology* (1858), p. 86.

14. William Potts DeWees, *A Compendious System of Midwifery . . .* , 12th ed. (Philadelphia: Blanchard and Lea, 1853), p. 42. Nichols, *Esoteric Anthropology* (1853), pp. 171, 173, argued that pregnancy could result from semen left anywhere in the vagina; Soule, *Science of Reproduction and Reproductive Control* (1856), p. 64, noted that "withdrawal of the penis before emission" was a "sure prevention" as long as not even the smallest particle of semen got into the vagina.

15. Hollick, *The Marriage Guide* (1860), chap. 7.

16. Letter to the editor from "X.Y.Z.," [Philadelphia] *Medical and Surgical Reporter* 59 (1888): 600; W. R. D. Blackwood, letter to the editor, [Philadelphia] *Medical and Surgical Reporter* 59 (1888): 698; Thomas E. McArdle, "The Physical Evils Arising from the Prevention of Conception," *American Journal of Obstetrics and Diseases of Women and Children* 21 (1888): 934–37; S. G. Moses, "Marital Masturbation," [St. Louis] *Courier of Medicine* 8 (1882): 168–73.

17. Cooke, *Satan in Society* (1876), p. 146.

18. William Goodell, "Clinical Lecture on Conjugal Onanism and Kindred Sins," *Philadelphia Medical Times* 2 (1872): 161–63.

19. See Moses, "Marital Masturbation," pp. 168–73.

20. L. Bolton Bangs, "Some of the Effects of 'Withdrawal,'" *Transactions of the New York Academy of Medicine*, 2d ser. 9 (1893): 119–24. Another patient, thirty-three years old in 1893, who had been married for five years with no children, did not want the expense of children so he "pulled out" during sexual intercourse, which he and his wife had every day early in their marriage and at least twice a week later.

21. Letter to the editor from "X.Y.Z.": 600; Blount, *A Talk to Mothers*, no pagination. Sigmund Freud, *Pre-Psychoanalytic Publications and Unpublished Drafts*, vol. 1,

The Standard Edition of the Complete Works (London: Hogarth Press and the Institute of Psycho-Analysis, 1966), 181–83.

22. Quoted in R. P. Neuman, "Working Class Birth Control in Wilhelmine Germany," *Comparative Studies in Society and History* 20 (1978): 419. Annie Besant, *The Law of Population: Its Consequences and Its Bearing Upon Human Conduct and Morals* (1878), p. 33, noted that although French doctors believed that withdrawal might be harmful to women, its universal practice in France attested otherwise.

23. Besant, *The Law of Population* (1878), p. 33.

24. Owen, *Moral Physiology* (1831, 1st ed.), p. 65.

25. Owen, *Moral Physiology* (1858), p. 65.

26. [Glover], *Owen's Moral Physiology* (1846), p. 115.

27. Mauriceau [pseud.], *The Married Woman's Private Medical Companion* (1847), p. 143, warned as well that withdrawal had the effects of onanism on health.

28. Dunne and Derbois, *The Young Married Lady's Private Medical Guide* (1854), chap. 17.

29. Cooke, *Satan in Society* (1870), p. 146.

30. Ashton, *The Book of Nature* (1861), p. 42.

31. Bangs, "Some Effects of 'Withdrawal,'" p. 119. Daniel Scott Smith, "Family Limitation, Sexual Control, and Domestic Feminism in Victorian America," in *Clio's Consciousness Raised: New Perspectives on the History of Women*, ed. Mary S. Hartman and Lois Banner (New York: Harper & Row, 1974), pp. 130–32.

32. Napheys, *The Physical Life of Woman* (1870), pp. 97–99.

33. References to coitus reservatus among twelfth- through fifteenth-century Catholic theologians are in Noonan, *Contraception*, pp. 296, 336–38, 447. The Oneida Community has been well studied. Maren Lockwood Carden, *Oneida: Utopian Community to Modern Corporation* (Baltimore: Johns Hopkins Press, 1969); Louis J. Kern, *An Ordered Love: Sex Roles and Sexuality in Victorian Utopias: The Shakers, the Mormons, and the Oneida Community* (Chapel Hill: University of North Carolina Press, 1981).

34. John Humphrey Noyes, *Male Continence* (1872), p. 10.

35. Noyes, *Male Continence*, p. 24.

36. John Humphrey Noyes, *The Bible Argument* (Oneida, N.Y.: The author, 1848). This had several editions but was out of print by 1872. Noyes reprinted all the essential points in the book except the chapter on male continence in his *Strange Cults and Utopias of Nineteenth Century America* (Philadelphia: J. B. Lippincott, 1870; rpt. ed., *History of American Socialisms*, New York: Dover, 1966).

37. See Sidney Ditzion, *Marriage, Morals, and Sex in America: A History of Ideas*, expanded ed. with a new chapter by the author (New York: W. W. Norton, 1953), p. 172.

38. See Foote, *Plain Home Talk* (1873), pp. 876–78, quoting Noyes, *Male Continence*; Alice Bunker Stockham, *Karezza: Ethics of Marriage* (1897), pp. 22–23, 120.

39. Kellogg, *Plain Facts for Old and Young*, chapter "Prevention of Conception."

40. Society Proceedings, *Journal of the Gynaecological Society of Boston* 4 (1871): 290.

41. James Caleb Jackson, *American Womanhood: Its Peculiarities and Necessities*, 3d ed. (Dansville, N.Y.: Austin, Jackson, 1870), pp. 47–48.

42. Goodell, "Clinical Lecture on Conjugal Onanism," pp. 161–63; David E. Matteson, Letter to the editor, *Medical and Surgical Reporter* (Philadelphia) 59 (1888): 759–60.

43. "The Fashionable Crime," *Michigan Medical News* 3 (1880): 341.

44. Editorial, "Criminal Abortion," *Kansas City Medical Record* 3 (1884): 121.

45. Mosher, "Statistical Study" Cases 3, 5, 10, 13, 17, 18, 19, 20, 27, 28, 29, 30, 32, 33, 36, 37, 41, 42, 44 all used the douche method at times.

46. Knowlton, *Fruits of Philosophy*; Soule, *Science of Reproduction and Reproductive Control*, pt. 4: "The Prevention of Conception."

47. Becklard, *Physiological Mysteries and Revelations* ([1845]), pp. 35–45 and chap. 10. The divorce case is cited in Degler, *At Odds*, p. 236.

48. Trall, *Sexual Physiology* (1866), p. 207.

49. No author, "Death from the Cold Douche," *Medical and Surgical Reporter* 54 (1886): 532.

50. J. C. Gleason, "A Medico-Legal Case of Abortion Followed by Conviction of the Accused Abortionist," *Boston Medical and Surgical Journal* 101 (1879): 185–92.

51. W. H. Schieffelin & Co., *Catalogue of Prices Current* (New York, 1871); George C. Goodwin & Co., *Catalogue of Prices Current* (Boston, 1874, 1876, 1885); A. A. Mellier, *Illustrated Catalogue and Prices Current of Drugs, Medicines, and Chemicals* (St. Louis, 1877); W. A. Week & Co., *Illustrated Yearbok of Pharmaceutical Information and General Useful Recipes and Catalogue of Prices Current* (Chicago, 1872); John H. Nelson, *The Druggists' Cost Book* (Cleveland, 1879); John W. Perkins & Co., *Catalogue of Drugs and Chemicals, Druggists' Sundries . . .* (Portland, Ma., 1895).

52. Goodwin & Co., *Catalogue* (Boston, 1885), p. 174, advertisement for Albert H. Essex's "National Syringes." See especially the "combination syringe."

53. See John Mack Faragher, *Women and Men on the Overland Trail* (New Haven: Yale University Press, 1979), p. 193.

54. *The U.S. Practical Receipt Book; or, Complete Book of Reference . . . by a Practical Chemist* (Philadelphia: Lindsay & Blakiston, 1844), cited in *America's Working Women: A Documentary History, 1600 to the Present*, ed. Rosalyn Baxandall et al. (New York: Vintage, 1976), p. 17.

55. Fuller & Fuller Co., *Catalogue* (Chicago, 1885): "Patent and Proprietary Articles"; Rust Brothers and Bird, *Catalogue* (Boston, 1880); McKesson & Robbins, *Catalogue* (New York, 1879).

56. *Affleck's Southern Rural Almanac*, edition for Vicksburg, Miss. (N.p.; 1851), p. 114, advertised these from the Genuine Medicine Warehouse, New Orleans.

57. Dunne and Derbois, *The Young Married Lady's Private Medical Guide* (1854), Letters, Appendix.

58. Hollick, *The Marriage Guide* ([1852]), p. 400.

59. Mauriceau [pseud.], *The Married Woman's Private Medical Companion* (1847), advertisement footnote, pp. 15–18.

60. Thomas Hersey, *The Midwife's Practical Directory* (1836), p. 90.

61. In Besant, *The Law of Population* (1889), pp. 31–32.

62. Fuller & Fuller Co., *Catalogue* (Chicago, 1872, 1885); Goodwin & Co., *Trade Catalogue* (Boston, 1880), p. 268.

63. See Boston Women's Health Book Collective, *The New Our Bodies Ourselves* (New York: Simon and Schuster, 1973), pp. 223, 255, 518.

64. Kistner, *Gynecology: Principles and Practice*, p. 676, estimates 37.8 failures per 100 woman years; Southam, "Contraceptive Methods: Use, Safety, Effectiveness," chap. 29, cites failure rates from 21 to 41, although she does not list the sources.

65. Deborah A. Dawson, Denise J. Meny, and Jeanne Clare Ridley, "Fertility Control in the U.S. before the Contraceptive Revolution," *Family Planning Perspectives* 12 (March–April 1980): 77, notes that even women who reported douching solely for personal cleanliness rather than for contraception had longer intervals between births than did noncontraceptive users. See also Ronald Freedman, Pascal K. Whelpton, and Arthur A. Campbell, *Family Planning, Sterility and Population Growth* (New York: McGraw-Hill, 1959), pp. 174–75, 408–10.

66. "How Much Pressure Can Be Obtained by Compressing the Bulb of a Davidson Syringe?" *American Journal of Obstetrics* 19 (1886): 951–52, while not directly ad-

dressing the effectiveness of contraceptive syringes, raised questions about the efficacy of the Davidson syringe for gynecological therapeutics.

67. Grindle, *The Female Sexual System* (1864), p. 162.

68. O. E. Herrick, "Abortion and Its Lesson," *Michigan Medical News* 5 (1882): 9. Blount, *A Talk to Mothers*, advised using a fountain syringe.

69. Dubois, *Marriage Physiologically Discussed* (1839), p. 91, advised vitriol drops; Hersey, *Midwife's Practical Directory* (1836), p. 90, advised alum; Ashton, *The Book of Nature* (1861), pp. 38–40, recommended astringents, white vitriol, sulphate, or chloride of zinc.

70. Robert L. Dickinson, "Household Contraceptives," *Journal of Contraception* 1 (1936): 43–46, found that four tablespoons of household vinegar per quart of water was a powerful spermicide. German and English investigators similarly found that un-thinned table vinegar killed sperm in a test tube within ten seconds, dissolving them within one minute. Two tablespoons of thinned table vinegar per liter of water killed all sperm within fifteen seconds.

71. Leo Shedlovsky, "Some Acidic Properties of Contraceptive Jellies," *Journal of Contraception* 2 (1937): 147–55, argued that the contraceptive effectiveness depended less on the initial acidity of the substances in the gel than on the final vaginal pH after dilution by vaginal and cervical fluids. Also see the editorial "pH and Contraceptive Action," p. 159. For an opposing opinion critical of the spermicidal properties of most acids, alkaloids, and inorganic salts see John R. Baker, "Laboratory Research in Chemical Contraception," *Eugenics Review* 27 (1935): 127–31.

72. Shedlovsky, "Some Acidic Properties," p. 148.

73. No author, "Soap as a Household Contraceptive," *Journal of Contraception* 3 (1938): 205, describes a study in which 1,179 Russian women in the 1930s relied on tampons soaked in water in which a chestnut-sized piece of soap had been dissolved. Only six pregnancies ocurred in one year. Leo Shedlovsky, "The Composition of Some Commercial Contraceptive Jellies," *Journal of Contraception* 4 (1939): 179–88, argued that "surface active substances have desirable spermicidal properties."

74. David R. Climenko, "The Spermicidal and Allied Properties of a Mixture of Sodium Sulfo-dioctylsuccinate and Maleic Acid," *Journal of Contraception* 3 (1938): 149–54. The study also found saponin to be a vaginal irritant.

75. International Planned Parenthood Federation, *Family Planning for Midwives and Nurses* (1971), argues that salt douches are dangerous.

76. Knowlton, *Fruits of Philosophy* (1832), p. 60. Baker, "Laboratory Research in Chemical Contraception," pp. 127–31, argued that of the inorganic salts only mercuric chloride was an effective spermicide. The only other three substances he recommended as spermicides were hydroquinone, catechol, and resorcinol. This selection is noteworthy in that catechol was commonly used as a medicinal astringent in nineteenth-century medicine under the name "catechu" and was therefore available to women if they had wanted it as a douching solution.

77. Knowlton, *Fruits of Philosophy* (1839), pp. 84, 80.

78. Nichols, *Esoteric Anthropology* (1854), p. 173, advised using cold water immediately before and after intercourse. Soule, *Science of Reproduction*, pt. 4, advised douching with 15 to 20 grains of tannin in one pint of water five or six hours before intercourse so as to close off the cervix and then to follow coitus with a cold-water douche. He weakened the advice by saying that a woman could sometimes safely delay douching for four to five hours if necessary.

79. Hersey, *Midwife's Practical Directory*, p. 90. Knowlton, *Fruits of Philosophy* (J. Watson, [1834]), recommended douching immediately after intercourse. Nichols, *Esoteric Anthropology*, p. 173, advised "immediate, deep and thorough" douching. Others who recommended douching immediately after intercourse included Larmont, *Medical*

Adviser and Marriage Guide (1864), who advised four syringes of warm water immediately after intercourse.

80. Anonymous, *Reproductive Control* (1855), p. 53.

81. William P. Brewer, "Questions in Relation to Gynecological Subjects, with Answers," *New Orleans Medical and Surgical Journal* 2 (1874–75): 918.

82. Herrick, "Abortion and Its Lesson," p. 9.

83. Webb J. Kelly, "One of the Abuses of Carbolic Acid," *Columbus Medical Journal* 1 (1882–83): 433–36.

84. F. Wallace Abbott, "Limitation of the Family," *Massachusetts Medical Journal* 10 (1890): 337–47.

85. William Pawson Chunn, "The Prevention of Conception: Its Practicability and Justifiability," *Maryland Medical Journal* 32 (1985): 340–43. Chunn was a physician in Baltimore.

86. Knowlton, *Fruits of Philosophy* (1833), p. 133.

87. See David P. Handlin, *The American Home: Architecture and Society, 1815–1915* (Boston: Little, Brown, 1979); John R. Stilgoe, *Borderland: Origins of the American Suburb, 1820–1939* (New Haven: Yale University Press, 1988), pts. 2 and 4.

88. Chunn, "Prevention of Conception," 340–43.

89. Matteson, Letter to the editor, 759–60.

90. William Goodell, *Lessons in Gynecology* (Philadelphia: D. G. Brinton, 1879), pp. 90–102.

91. Henry M. Field, "Medication by the Use of Vaginal and Rectal Suppositories," *Journal of the Gynecological Society of Boston* 6 (1872): 307. Field, like Goodell, probably had a wide influence because he was a professor of materia medica and therapeutics at Dartmouth. See also Northern Medical Association Symposium, "Uterine Displacements," *Medical and Surgical Journal* 2 (1850): 249–53; "The Hot Water Vaginal Douche," *Michigan Medical News* 3 (1880): 13–14.

92. "A Vaginal Douche," *Columbus Medical Journal* 1 (1882): 315–16.

93. "Medical Book" and Scrapbook of the Advertisements of the Lydia E. Pinkham Company, 1875–1953, in the Lydia E. Pinkham Papers, Schlesinger Library. The Pinkham Company's income from the sales of the syringe and douching solution was $1,700 annually in the late 1870s.

94. Félix Pouchet, *Théorie positive de la fécondation des mammifères* (Paris: Libraire encyclopédique de Roret, 1842), cited in Pouchet, *Théorie positive de l'ovulation spontanée et de la fecondation des mammifères et de l'espèce humaine, basée sur l'observation de toute la série animale* (Paris: J.-B. Bailliere, 1847).

95. Pouchet, *Théorie positive de la fécondation*, pp. 275–76.

96. Pouchet, *Théorie positive de la fécondation*, p. 273.

97. Adam Raciborski, *De la puberté et de l'âge critique chez la femme, au point de vue physiologique, hygiénique et médicale et de la ponte périodique chez la femme et les mammifères* (Paris: J.-B. Bailliere, Libraire, 1844), pp. 130–31.

98. Raciborski, *De la puberté*, p. 135.

99. Sir James Simpson, the eminent British physician, read Raciborski's work and recommended his contraceptive timetable to friends and patients, not all of whom found it effective: one irate father complained to Simpson: "He's a damned rascal that Raciborski." [George R. Drysdale], *Physical, Sexual, and Natural Religion with the Solution of the Social Problem by a Student of Medicine* (London: Edward Truelove, 1855), p. 348.

100. Augustus K. Gardner, *The Causes and Curative Treatment of Sterility* (1856), p. 18. Gardner's advice ranks among the least reliable of the era since he advised counting from the first day of menstruation instead of the end and recommended waiting only ten days.

101. Storer, *Why Not? A Book for Everywoman* (1867), Preface.

102. Noonan, *Contraception*, p. 439.

103. The rhythm method theories of Avrard were reported, with some discrepancies, in: *Cincinnati Lancet and Observer* 10 (1867): 57; "Monthly Period of Infecundity," *Richmond Medical Journal* 5 (1868): 204–5; and "Agenesis in France," *Medical and Surgical Reporter* 17 (1867): 177.

104. Kellogg, *Plain Facts for Old and Young* (1880), p. 235, and section titled "Prevention of Conception: Its Evils and Dangers." Cooke, *Satan in Society* (1876); Felissa Brunswick, *Life's Best Secret* (n.p.,[1894]) has similar advice. Cowan, *Science of a New Life*, p. 111, believed that coitus should take place only to produce children; nevertheless he wrote that women were unlikely to conceive during two weeks of every menstrual period.

105. Duffey, *What Women Should Know* (1873), p. 133; Elizabeth Blackwell, *The Human Element in Sex*, 2d ed. (n.p.,1884), p. 77.

106. Henry Oldham, "Clinical Lecture on the Induction of Abortion," *London Medical Gazette* 9 (1849): 48. The American physician William Tyler Smith believed, however, that the ovular theory of menstruation could be considered definitely proven. See the *London Medical Gazette* n.s. 9 (1849): 930.

107. Dunne and Derbois, *Young Married Lady's Private Medical Guide* (1854), pp. 207–9.

108. Loombe Atthill, *Clinical Lectures of Diseases Peculiar to Women*, 2d ed., rev. and enl. (Philadelphia: Lindsay & Blakiston, 1873), Lecture 3: "Menstruation and Amenorrhea"; ibid., 5th ed., 1878. These were the American editions of a popular British text.

109. A. Reeves Jackson, "The Ovulation Theory of Menstruation: Will It Stand?" *Transactions of the 26th Meeting of the Illinois State Medical Society* (1876), pp. 143–44. Jackson was surgeon-in-chief at the Women's State Hospital of Illinois and a lecturer on the diseases of women at Rush Medical College.

110. Goodell, "Clinical Lecture on Conjugal Onanism," pp. 161–63.

111. Trall, *The Hydropathic Encyclopedia* (1852), Appendix: "Theory of Conception," in Trall, *Sexual Physiology* (1867), pp. 206–7.

112. Trall, *Sexual Physiology* (1867), pp. 206–7.

113. Trall, *Sexual Physiology* (1867), pp. 206–7.

114. For wrong notions of the sterile period see Mosher Questionnaires, Cases 5, 20, 29, 41. For more correct versions see Cases 1, 11, 14, 27. For additional information on attitudes about the sterile period see Cases 12, 15, 18, 19, and 23.

115. See G. I. M. Swyer et al., "The Scientific Basis of Contraception," *Population Studies Supplement: Towards a Population Policy for the United Kingdom* 24 (1970): 34–47, Table 1.

116. Consider two women, each with regular 28-day cycles but different durations of menstruation. The one with a three-day flow must wait seven days after menstruation to reach what researchers today consider to be the beginning of the infertile period. The woman with a five-day flow would have to wait only five days. Or, consider women following the era's worst advice—to wait only one to eight days after menstruation. If these women all had five-day menses, the woman with a twenty-day cycle would be better off than one with a thirty-two-day cycle. The former would approach the actual infertile period only about five days after menstruation, the latter would have almost seventeen days to wait.

117. Besant, *The Law of Population* (1878), p. 33, noted that the rhythm method was unreliable but that "we can scarcely say more than that women are far less likely to conceive midway between the menstrual periods than either immediately before or after them."

118. Cowan, *Science of a New Life* (1874), recommended waiting 8–14 days; Larmont, *Medical Adviser and Marriage Guide* (1864), said 10–12; Napheys, *The Physical Life of Woman* (1870), said 10–12; Trall, *Sexual Physiology* (1867), said 10–12; Pancoast, *The Ladies' Medical Guide and Marriage Friend* (1859), said 12–14; Duffey, *What Women Should Know* (1873), said 10–12; Ezra Heywood, *Cupid's Yokes* (Princeton, Mass.: Cooperative Publishing Co., n.d.), said 10–12.

Chapter Four

1. Alcott, *The Physiology of Marriage* (1866), pp. 182–83. Biographical information on Alcott is in Hebbel E. Hoff, "The Centenary of the First American Physiological Society Founded at Boston by William A. Alcott and Sylvester Graham," *Bulletin of the History of Medicine* 5 (1973): 687–734.

2. Horatio Robinson Storer, "The Criminality and Physical Evils of Forced Abortions," *American Medical Association Transactions* 16 (1866): 739.

3. Hugh S. Pomeroy, *The Ethics of Marriage* (New York: Funk and Wagnalls, 1888), p. 58.

4. The importance of sexual themes and anxieties is particularly well discussed in Ronald G. Walters, "The Erotic South: Civilization and Sexuality in American Abolitionism," *American Quarterly* 25 (1973): 177–201.

5. See Stephen Nissenbaum, "Careful Love: Sylvester Graham and the Emergence of Victorian Sexual Theory in America, 1830–1840" (Ph.D. diss., University of Wisconsin, 1968), pp. 4, 72; Ronald G. Walters, *Primers for Prudery: Sexual Advice to Victorian America* (Baltimore: Johns Hopkins University Press, 1975).

6. The best source on Owen is still Richard William Leopold, *Robert Dale Owen* (Cambridge: Harvard University Press, 1940). There is no full-length biography of Knowlton, but important material in Robert E. Riegel, "The American Father of Birth Control," *New England Quarterly* 6 (1933): 470–90; and on both men, see manuscript fragments in the Norman E. Himes Archive, Countway Library, Harvard School of Medicine. The Rare Book Room also holds unpublished manuscripts on Owen and Knowlton by Mary Lee Esty. Other information is in Peter Fryer, *The Birth Controllers* (New York: Stein and Day, 1966), and in James W. Reed, *From Private Vice to Public Virtue* (New York: Basic Books, 1978). See also their own writings, especially Knowlton, *A History of the Recent Excitement in Ashfield* (Ashfield, Mass., October 1834); Knowlton, *A History of the Recent Excitement in Ashfield*, pt. 2 (n.p., September 1835); and Robert Dale Owen, "An Earnest Sowing of Wild Oats," *Atlantic Monthly* July 1874: 67–78, and *Threading My Way* (New York: G. W. Carleton, 1874).

7. See note 143.

8. The Countway Library Rare Book Room has a copy of what is probably the first edition. Owen concluded his second article "The Population Question," *Free Enquirer* 23 October 1830, saying "the physiology of the subject [of checking population] I do not think fit to discuss in this periodical. But it is my intention to write a little treatise on the subject." In that same issue he inserted an announcement: "In a Few Weeks Will Be Published *Moral Physiology*." Other evidence from the *Free Enquirer* suggests that Owen published an edition in November or December and sent it to subscribers, friends, and prominent people. The *Free Enquirer* (3 November 1830) carried an advertisement for the tract; the 27 November 1830 issue mentions a typographical error in the tract which might cause readers some confusion; the 18 December 1830 issue contains a letter from a young woman who had clearly already read *Moral Physiology*. Not until 8 January 1831 did the *Free Enquirer* state that *Moral Physiology* was printed and ready for the general public.

9. The exact publication dates of the early editions are unclear. After the first edition in late 1830 or early 1831, the second and third editions were issued, both with the imprint "New York: Published by Wright & Owen, 1831" and identical to the first. A fourth edition was published 28 May 1831. The exact date of the fifth edition is unclear. An "Appendix to the fifth edition," signed by RDO, was dated 25 June 1831, although Leopold, *Robert Dale Owen*, p. 80, believes that it was issued 13 August 1831. Norman Himes, *Medical History of Contraception* (New York: Schocken, 1970; 1st pub. 1936), could not locate a sixth edition; he lists a seventh edition as "New York: Wright & Owen, 1834." He also lists an unnumbered edition, "New York: Beacon Office (84 Roosevelt St), n.d. [c. 1833–34], 96p." in private hands. Himes did not see this edition, but noted that it contained publisher's notes and may have mentioned a chemical contraceptive. I believe that this was put out by Gilbert Vale, editor at that time of the freethought New York newspaper *Beacon*. Leopold lists an 1839 edition put out in New York by Gilbert Vale after Owen lost his bid for the U.S. Congress, although I have not found a copy. An eighth edition (a copy of which is at the New York Public Library) was put out in New York by G. W. and A. J. Matsell in 1835. It appears to have been made from the same plates as the first edition now at Countway. Owen may have given the plates to the Matsells, although Himes believes that it was unauthorized. Finally, for the 1830s, Himes cites what he believes to be a pirated, possibly unique copy: "*The Moral physiology; a treatise on popular questions, or means devised to check pregnancy. By a physician*. (New York: Printed for the author, 1836), 76p. 15 1/2 cm." This I have not located.

There is no comprehensive bibliography of *Moral Physiology* and there is considerable disagreement between the two best sources, the listings in Leopold, *Robert Dale Owen*, and Himes, *Medical History of Contraception*, with the *The National Union Catalog of Pre-1956 Imprints* (*NUC*) differing from both, although some of the NUC editions turn out to be listed incorrectly. I am not including for discussion the numerous English editions, authorized and unauthorized.

10. Leopold notes five editions in the 1840s, all without place imprints except one, "New York, 1846." Himes and the *NUC* list only two in the 1840s—the pirated editions put out by Ralph Glover. In Owen, "An Earnest Sowing of Wild Oats," p. 77, we glimpse Owen's embarrassment about *Moral Physiology*. Although he went into great detail about his youthful theological views and the other "heresies which brought us reproach," the memoir, written when Owen was in his seventies, does not mention birth control or *Moral Physiology* until a brief few sentences at the end, where he noted that he wrote the book to rebut Malthus's solutions to population growth.

11. Owen, *Moral Physiology* (1858).

12. Owen, *Moral Physiology* (1873) and (1875). Both were identical to the 1858 Vale edition and I believe that they were reprints using Vale's plates and a new title page. Owen, *Moral Physiology* ([1872?]) and Owen, *Moral Physiology* (1881).

13. Robert Dale Owen, "The Population Question," *Free Enquirer*, 16 and 23 October 1830.

14. Owen, *Moral Physiology* (1831, 1st ed.), pp. 48–49.

15. Owen, *Moral Physiology* (1831, 1st ed.), p. 65.

16. Owen, *Moral Physiology* (1831, 1st ed.), p. 66.

17. Only Becklard, *Physiological Mysteries and Revelations* (1844), chap. 3, also mentioned the importance of birth control for single women.

18. Owen, *Moral Physiology* (1831, 1st ed.), p. 69.

19. Owen, *Moral Physiology* (1831, 1st ed.), p. 67.

20. Owen, *Moral Physiology* (3d ed. 1831), postscript to the preface.

21. In England during the winter of 1833, Owen reported receiving communications that cast doubt on withdrawal. Perhaps personal experience aided his doubts, for in

either January or February his wife, Mary Jane, conceived their first child. In an April 1833 edition of *Moral Physiology* Owen suggested once again the sponge method, although no subsequent editions contained this alteration. Cited in Leopold, *Robert Dale Owen*, p. 117.

22. The best advice Owen apparently could devise for giving women better reproductive control was that women should refuse sexual intercourse "with any man void of honour," that is, any man who would not practice withdrawal reliably, and that American women become more practical and less prudish about the topic of preventive checks: "A French lady of the utmost delicacy and respectability will in common conversation say as simply (ay and as innocently whatever the self-righteous prude may aver to the contrary) as she would proffer any common remark about the weather: 'I have three children: my husband and I think that is as many as we can do justice to and I do not intend to have any more.'" Owen, *Moral Physiology* (London, 1842), pp. 23–24.

23. Owen, *Moral Physiology* (1831, 1st ed.), preface.

24. See Himes, *Medical History of Contraception*, pp. 220–23.

25. Richard Carlile, "What Is Love?" *Republican* 11 (1825): 548–50.

26. [Glover] *Owen's Moral Physiology* (1846), p. 112. In the 1850s Glover published *The Family Physician*, which according to the *National Union Catalog of Pre-1956 Imprints* is the only section still extant of his larger work, *A Treatise on Orthopedic Surgery and Hernia* (New York: A. Baptist, jr. printers, [c. 1853]). This would have contained his reprint of *Moral Physiology*. I have been unable to find any further information about Ralph Glover. He is probably not the Glover who published Becklard's *Physiological Mysteries* (New York: Holland and Glover; 1844).

27. [Glover], *Owen's Moral Physiology* (1846), pp. 101–14. The advertisement in the New York *Herald*, 1 September 1846, is cited in John Paull Harper, "'Be Fruitful and Multiply': The Reaction to Family Limitation in Nineteenth-Century America" (Ph.D. diss., Columbia University, 1975).

28. Himes, *Medical History of Contraception*, p. 473.

29. In Owen, *Moral Physiology* (1858), pp. 85–89.

30. Quoted in Knowlton, *A History of the Recent Excitement in Ashfield* (October 1834).

31. Knowlton, *History of the Recent Excitement*.

32. Knowlton, *History of the Recent Excitement*, pt. 2.

33. Himes, *Medical History of Contraception*, p. 227 notes that the Boston medical publisher, a Mr. Campbell, may have issued this edition, or else that it came directly from the initiative of the Harvard Medical School faculty. Campbell's son informed Himes that his father sold a copy of the work to William James. The subscription edition was labeled "tenth edition" but I have found no references to the fifth through ninth editions and no copies of such editions seem to be extant. If such editions were, indeed, issued, we know nothing about who published them, when they came out, or what changes they incorporated. The "tenth edition," except for corrected spelling errors, is identical to the fourth edition of 1839.

34. Knowlton, *Fruits of Philosophy* (Wilson ed. [18—]); Knowlton, *Fruits of Philosophy* (Wilson ed. [1897]). Wilson is also associated with an edition published in San Francisco in 1891. See Selected Bibliography.

35. Information on Wilson was culled from imprints of Knowlton's works and from an advertisement on the back cover of Besant's *Law of Population* (1893). Wilson is not listed in the R. G. Dun & Co. Collection for Chicago. In addition to Knowlton's work, he distributed freethought works by Voltaire, Paine, and Ingersoll as well as sensational literature such as *The Mysteries of Chicago: The Crimes and Dissipations, the Dark Side of Chicago Told in Plain Language*. Similarly, there are no records of the

W. H. M. Smythe or "The Stein Co." that put out editions of *Fruits of Philosophy* probably in the 1880s. Another edition, credited without a date to the International Publishing Co., may have come from Frank Rivers, who was arrested by Comstock in December 1877 using the pseudonym "The International Publishing Co." to advertise "the book the English government are trying to suppress and the postal authorities refuse to carry in the mails." See the Ledger of Arrests, New York Society for the Suppression of Vice Collection, Library of Congress.

36. Knowlton, *Fruits of Philosophy* (1839), p. 8.

37. Knowlton, *Fruits of Philosophy* (1839), p. 16.

38. Knowlton, *Fruits of Philosophy* (1832), p. 38.

39. Knowlton, *Fruits of Philosophy* (1833), p. 133; Knowlton, *Fruits of Philosophy* (London, [c. 1834]), p. 35.

40. Knowlton, *Fruits of Philosophy* (1839), pp. 37–47.

41. Knowlton, *Fruits of Philosophy* (1839), p. 20.

42. Knowlton, *Fruits of Philosophy* (1839), pp. 97–98.

43. Knowlton, *Fruits of Philosophy* (1832), p. 60.

44. Knowlton, *Fruits of Philosophy* (1832), p. 63; (1833), p.129.

45. Knowlton, *Fruits of Philosophy* (1832), p. 34.

46. Knowlton, *Fruits of Philosophy* (1833), p. 135.

47. Knowlton, *Fruits of Philosophy* (1833), p. 134.

48. Knowlton, *Fruits of Philosophy* (1839), pp. 80–82, 85.

49. Knowlton, *Fruits of Philosophy* (1839), p. 85.

50. His articles in the *Boston Medical and Surgical Journal* in 1844 make it clear that he saw primarily women. See especially Charles Knowlton, "Abscess of the Lungs," *Boston Medical and Surgical Journal* 28 (1843): 319–73.

51. Knowlton, *Fruits of Philosophy* (1832), p. 58. He then quoted Owen on the benefits of withdrawal, without adding any of his own thoughts.

52. Knowlton, *Fruits of Philosophy* (1833), p. 125.

53. Knowlton, *Fruits of Philosophy* (1839), p. 8.

54. Knowlton, *Fruits of Philosophy* (1832), p. 1.

55. Knowlton, *Fruits of Philosophy* (1839), p. 86.

56. Quoted in William J. Gilmore, *Reading Becomes a Necessity of Life: Material and Cultural Life in Rural New England, 1780–1835* (Knoxville: University of Tennessee Press, 1989), p. 269.

57. See John Tebbel, *A History of Book Publishing in the United States* (New York: Bowker, 1972), 1: 542, citing the definition of Frank Luther Mott that to be a "bestseller" a book's total sales had to equal one percent of the population of the United States for the decade in which it was published. This meant a title had to sell 125,000 copies in the 1830s and 175,000 in the 1840s.

58. Owen, "An Earnest Sowing of Wild Oats," p. 77.

59. The first edition of *Fruits of Philosophy*, 63 pages, was 3 × 2 1/2 inches; the second edition, similarly small, was a stubby 158 pages. The third has a type surface less than two and a half inches and is 190 pages long. This third edition did not include a table of contents or imprint on the title page, although the copyright named Knowlton. A number of other reproductive control and sexual advice works of the 1830s and 1840s were pocket-sized for easy concealment: Becklard, *Physiological Mysteries and Revelations* (1842, 1844), and Hollick, *The Origin of Life* . . . (1846, 1847), all about 3 × 5 inches.

60. Mauriceau, [pseud.] *The Married Woman's Private Medical Companion* (1847).

61. Becklard, *Physiological Mysteries and Revelations* (1842, 1844), Dubois, *Marriage Physiologically Discussed* (1839). The impact of Owen's and Knowlton's works was great. Some of the birth control and sexual physiology literature of the 1830s and

1840s affected by them include: Hall, *The Mother's Own Book* (1843) and *Womanhood* (1845); Hersey, *The Midwife's Practical Directory* (1834, 1836); Hollick, *The Origin of Life* (1846, 1847), and *Outlines of Anatomy and Physiology* (1846); Mauriceau [pseud.], *The Married Woman's Private Medical Companion* (1847).

62. See Donald M. Scott,"The Popular Lecture and the Creation of a Public in Mid-Nineteenth-Century America," *Journal of American History* 66 (1980): 791–809; Carl Bode, *The American Lyceum, Town Meeting of the Mind* (Carbondale: Southern Illinois University Press, 1959).

63. We need a detailed historical study of itinerant lecturing. It is touched on in histories of medicine and in biographies, but we have no general treatment of the subject.

64. No author, "Itinerant Lecturers on Anatomy and Physiology," *Boston Medical and Surgical Journal* 71 (1864): 443–44.

65. See Sally Gregory Kohlstedt, "Physiological Lectures for Women: Sarah Coates in Ohio, 1850," *Journal of the History of Medicine* 33 (1978): 75–81. This lecturer may have been the same Sarah Coates who served as secretary pro tem at the Salem, Ohio, Convention for Women's Rights, 19 April 1850. See *History of Woman Suffrage*, ed. Elizabeth Cady Stanton (Rochester, N.Y.: n.p., 1881), 1: 103.

66. *New York Daily Tribune*, 10 February 1851, advertising notice.

67. See Frederick C. Waite, "Dr. Lydia Folger Fowler," *Annals of Medical History*, n.s. 4 (1932): 290–97.

68. Knowlton, *Fruits of Philosophy* (1839), intro. and p. 88. Knowlton lambasted three "unprincipled persons who have attempted to write popular physiological treatises on generation . . . and have consequently presented the reader with a jumble of truth and error, of science and obscenety [sic] which . . . must have been productive of quite as much mischief as benefit." He meant the author of *Aristotle's Masterpiece*, Canfield, and Jean Dubois, author of *Marriage Physiologically Discussed*, whose second edition was published in 1839.

69. Canfield, *Practical Physiology* (1850). There is some evidence that the book saw several printings in the 1840s. Becklard's *Physiological Mysteries and Revelations* (1845) was printed "with a supplement from Canfield's Sexual Physiology, on Coquetry, Venereal Madness, Marriage, etc." The twenty-page supplement did not contain any of Canfield's birth control information. When Canfield copyrighted his book in 1849, he said in a "prefix" that he had revised the work slightly to renew the copyright, but because it was stereotyped he could not change every word. This, too, suggests earlier editions, although I have found no further references to them. Knowlton expressed his anger in *Fruits of Philosophy* (1839), intro.

70. Scattered information on Canfield is available in Albert Post, *Popular Free-thought in America, 1825–1850* (New York: Columbia University Press, 1943). The *National Union Catalog* contains useful information about his publications. Bruce Laurie, *Working People of Philadelphia, 1800–1850* (Philadelphia: Temple University Press, 1980), p. 81, quotes Canfield's sympathy with the Catholics "as men, as republicans, and as members of a persecuted sect."

71. Canfield, *Practical Physiology*, pp. 74, 81.

72. Canfield, *Practical Physiology*, pp. 31, 33.

73. Mary Elizabeth Wieting, *Prominent Incidents in the Life of Doctor John M. Wieting, Including His Travels with His Wife around the World* (New York: G. P. Putnam's Sons, 1889), p. 5. There is no information on Wieting in *Index Medicus* (1889) or the R. G. Dun & Co. Collection.

74. Hollick, *The Marriage Guide* [1852]), intro. to 1st ed.. F. Harrison Doane, the editor and translator of Dunne and Derbois, *The Young Lady's Private Medical Guide*, (1854), pp. 206–7, also complained about Wieting, citing him by name as one of the

speakers currently publicizing erroneous notions about the rhythm method. Doane had medical offices at 1 Tremont Street in Boston, where Wieting often lectured. Doane's twelve-page appendix inserted into the Dunne book advertised his private practice specializing in women's diseases and his ten-dollar "Anti-Conception Compound"— either a douching solution or an abortifacient.

75. Wieting, *Prominent Incidents*, p. 5.

76. Hollick, *Outlines of Anatomy*, advertising section quoting the *St. Louis Intelligencer* on Hollick's style.

77. See Lewis Perry, *Childhood, Marriage, and Reform: Henry Clarke Wright, 1797–1870* (Chicago: University of Chicago Press, 1980), pp. 70, 232, 231.

78. Wright, *The Unwelcome Child* (1858), letter 5. See also Wright, *Anthropology; or, The Science of Man* (Cincinnati: E. Shepard; Boston: Bela Marsh, 1850), for his justifications of studying sex, love, and human nature and his influential *Marriage and Parentage* (1854) most influential. Like other sex radicals of his day, Wright was anxious and fearful of sexuality. It is in this context that any birth control recommendations he might have made must be viewed. He believed sexuality should be kept under careful control and that women were best suited for doing this. Husbands, he said, should let their wives decide when and how frequently to have sexual intercourse. If Wright was reticent about contraception, he forcefully opposed abortion. Even so, he was deeply empathic to women who had no recourse but abortion.

79. Information on Hollick is scattered and sparse. John C. Harrison, *Quest for the New Moral World: Robert Owen and the Owenites in Britain and America* (New York: Scribner's, 1969), pp. 218–22, discusses the Owenite phase of his career. Joseph McCabe, *A Biographical Dictionary of Modern Rationalists* (n.p.: n.d.), p. 355, refers to Hollick. Credit reporters rated him favorably in 1864: "Is called a smart man in his line of business, of excellent character, very attentive and careful . . . his reputation and standing with the Faculty is very good." New York City, vol. 376, p. 259, R. G. Dun & Co. Collection. There is some information in an unpublished manuscript by Mary Lee Esty held in the Rare Book Room, Countway Library. Esty did remarkable detective work, uncovering Hollick's descendants and some information about his life in New York. See also James W. Reed, *From Private Vice to Public Virtue: The Birth Control Movement and American Society since 1830* (New York: Basic Books, 1978), pp. 11–13.

80. See Reed, *From Private Vice to Public Virtue*, p. 11. Hollick may have worked at the Manchester Lying-In Hospital, for several of his later books refer to practices there.

81. Hollick's *The Matron's Manual of Midwifery*, copyrighted in 1840, was in its 100th edition in the early 1850s. *The Origin of Life*, published in New York and St. Louis in 1845, went through ten editions that year and continued to be reprinted until 1902. *The Marriage Guide*, first published in 1850, was in its 300th edition around 1877, its 500th in 1883. Other titles did well too: *The Male Generative Organs*, copyrighted in 1840, saw a 300th edition in 1884; *A Popular Treatise on Venereal Diseases*, copyrighted in 1852, had fifty editions that year. Three of Hollick's works were translated into Spanish in 1863.

82. Hollick, *Outlines of Anatomy and Physiology* (1846). Advertising notices from newspapers make it possible to trace some of Hollick's travels.

83. Hollick, *The Origin of Life* (1846), "Note on the Subject of Menstruation and the Ovaries." These four pages at the end of the book before the Addendum cited Raciborski's discoveries, which Hollick interpreted to mean that, unlike animals who could conceive only irregularly, human conception was nearly always possible.

84. Hollick, *The Marriage Guide* (1852), preface.

85. Hollick, *The Marriage Guide* (1852), p. 224. See also Chapter 3 for Hollick's rhythm method ideas.

86. Hollick, *The Marriage Guide* (1860), p. 204.

87. Hollick, *The Marriage Guide* (1860), pp. 206–8.

88. Hollick, *The Marriage Guide* (1852), has birth control references scattered throughout. The reference to ergot is on pp. 323–32, a full-page "Notice: Prevention of Conception" offering private advice by mail if the rhythm method fails (p. 400); the chapter on sperm reports that the French knew drugs which kill sperm instantly and also notes that electrical charges are spermicidal (p. 173). Hollick, *A Popular Treatise on Venereal Diseases* (1852), p. 353, contains advertisements for condoms, pessaries, and aphrodisiacs. Hollick, *The Matron's Manual of Midwifery and the Diseases of Women during Pregnancy* (New York and Boston: T. W. Strong, 1849), p. 10, advertised condoms available by mail.

89. In Hollick, *Outlines of Anatomy and Physiology* (1846), p. 3, from a letter in the *Boston Courier*, 3 June 1844.

90. Hollick, *Outlines of Anatomy and Physiology* (1846), "Notice of Dr. Hollick's Lectures and Books," advertising supplement.

91. Hollick, *Outlines of Anatomy and Physiology* (1846): "Notices of Dr. Hollick's Lectures and Books."

92. Hollick, *The Origin of Life* (1846), Preface.

93. Lewis Masquier, *Sociology; or, The Reconstruction of Society, Government and Property* (New York: Pub. by the author, 1877), contains seven pages at the end of the book about Hollick, unnumbered and titled "The Nerves and the Nervous."

94. New York City, vol. 376, p. 259, R. G. Dun & Co. Collection.

95. Theodore Zeldin, *France, 1848–1945*, 2 vols. (Oxford: Clarendon Press, 1973), vol. 2: *Intellect, Taste, and Anxiety*, p. 1157.

96. Hall, *The Mother's Own Book* (1843); Hall, *Womanhood* (1845). Sparse biographical on Hall comes from internal evidence in his books and from *The National Union Catalog of Pre-1956 Imprints*. See Chapter 6 for the relationship between Hall and the inventor of a contraceptive diaphragm in the 1840s.

97. Hall, *The Mother's Own Book*, p. 54.

98. Hall, *The Mother's Own Book*, p. 60; *Womanhood*, p. 80.

99. Hall, *The Mother's Own Book*, pp. 53–55, and *Womanhood*, chaps. 22, 23.

100. Hall, *Womanhood* (1845), chaps. 8, 21, deal with suppressed menstruation. See also chaps. 22 and 23.

101. An important exception is the work of Regina Morantz-Sanchez, especially "Making Women Modern: Middle-Class Women and Health Reform in Nineteenth-Century America," pp. 346–58, in *Women and Health in America*, ed. Judith Walzer Leavitt (Madison: University of Wisconsin Press, 1984).

102. Celia M. Eckhardt, *Fanny Wright: Rebel in America* (Cambridge: Harvard University Press, 1984), is the best source. See also Nancy Woloch, "Frances Wright at Nashoba," in *Women and the American Experience* (New York: Knopf, 1984), pp. 151–66; and Barbara Taylor, *Eve and the New Jerusalem: Socialism and Feminism in the Nineteenth Century* (New York: Pantheon, 1983), pp. 65–70. Wright's views can also be traced in her extensive writings in the *Free Enquirer*.

103. Frances Wright, *A Plan for the Gradual Abolition of Slavery in the United States without Danger of Loss to the Citizens of the South* (Baltimore, 1825), suggested gradual emancipation through a system of cooperative labor in which slaves would pay for their costs and the profits would go toward emancipation. This process would end slavery, Wright believed, without pecuniary loss to the slaveowners.

104. Wright was powerfully moved by the senior Robert Owen's "Declaration of Mental Liberty," on 4 July 1826 at New Harmony, in which he attacked "a Trinity of the most monstrous evils that could be combined to inflict mental and physical evil": private property, "absurd and irrational systems of religion," and marriage "founded on

individual property." Cited in Arthur Bestor, *Backwoods Utopias: The Sectarian Origins and the Owenite Phase of Communitarian Socialism in America, 1663–1829*, 2d ed., enl. (Philadelphia: University of Pennsylvania Press, 1970), p. 222. Like Owen, Wright believed that marriage should be dissolvable through divorce and that if love did not remain the basis of marriage it was little more than legal prostitution.

105. Quoted in *Free Enquirer*, 4 March 1829, in an untitled article on Wright's lecture tour.

106. *Free Enquirer*, December 1828 and February 1829; the *Free Enquirer*, 4 March 1829.

107. Paul Boyer, "Frances Wright," in *Notable American Women 1607–1950*, vol. 3, ed. Edward T. James (Cambridge: Belknap Press of Harvard University Press, 1971), makes this argument, as do Nella Fermi Weiner, "Of Feminism and Birth Control Propaganda, 1790–1840," *International Journal of Women's Studies* 3 (1980): 411–30, and Catherine Clinton, *The Other Civil War: American Women in the Nineteenth Century* (New York: Hill & Wang, 1984), p. 66. Eckhardt does not go this far. She says that Wright liked Carlile's *Every Woman's Book*, but she does not discuss Wright's ideas about birth control.

108. Reprint of a letter from "W" about Wright's lectures in New York City, *Free Enquirer*, 25 February 1829.

109. Wright, "An Answer to Vindicia," *Free Enquirer*, 4 March 1829.

110. *Free Enquirer*, 22 July 1829.

111. See Eckhardt, *Fanny Wright*, p. 226.

112. Owen explained as his motivation that he had been goaded into writing *Moral Physiology* by a dispute with the New York Typographical Society over his purported support for Carlile's *Every Woman's Book*. See the exchange of letters between Owen and S. Woodworth, W. E. Dean, and W. H. Clayton reprinted in *Free Enquirer*, 9 October 1830, pp. 399–400, and Owen, *Moral Physiology* (1831), Preface.

113. Owen and Wright continued to correspond after her marriage. He published her occasional articles in the *Free Enquirer*, including her mixed reaction to his prospectus for *Moral Physiology*. She believed that it would "contain many useful observations," but she was pessimistic about its reception given the "hypocrisy" and "ignorance" in society. See her letter quoted in "Editorial," *Free Enquirer*, 5 March 1831. Eckhardt, *Fanny Wright*, pp. 233, 290, is unusually imprecise about Wright's estrangement from Owen, and it remains something of a mystery, but a powerful testimony to Fanny's continuing emotional difficulties. In March 1837 to Owen's surprise she published an editorial against him in the *Boston Investigator*. Then for several months she sent him embittered letters concerning financial matters. She apparently believed that he had cheated her by not repaying promptly enough money she loaned him in 1831. Owen, *Threading My Way*, p. 323, wrote that he had needed an older and wiser mentor than Wright in his youth: "I required to be restrained, not urged; needed not the spur but the guiding-rein."

114. Mary Sargeant Nichols [Mary Gove Nichols], *Mary Lyndon; or, Revelations of a Life: An Autobiography* (New York: Stringer and Townsend, 1855).

115. See Hebbel E. Hoff, "The Centenary of the First American Physiological Society Founded at Boston by William A. Alcott and Sylvester Graham," *Bulletin of the History of Medicine* 5 (1937): 687–734.

116. Mary S. Gove [Mary Gove Nichols], *Lectures to Women on Anatomy and Physiology with an Appendix on Water Cure* (New York: Harper, 1846). This is a reissue of an 1842 book with the appendix added.

117. See John B. Blake, "Mary G. Nichols, Prophetess of Health," *Proceedings* [of the American Philosophical Society] 106 (1962): 219–34.

118. Irving T. Richards, "Mary Gove Nichols and John Neal," *New England Quar-*

terly 7 (1934): 335–55. Blake, "Mary Gove Nichols," notes that she was denounced by some Quakers and by some newspapers that said that her lectures were obscene although Blake does not identify them.

119. No author, "Lectures to Ladies on Anatomy and Physiology," *Boston Medical and Surgical Journal* 26 (1842): 97–98. Grace Adams, *The Mad Forties* (New York: Harper, 1942), p. 20, cites Bennett's disapproval.

120. See Bertha-Monica Stearns, "Two Forgotten New England Reformers," *New England Quarterly* 6 (1933): 59–84. *The National Union Catalog of Pre-1956 Imprints* lists several of Nichols's novels from the 1840s: *The Lady in Black, Ellen Ramsay, Raffle for a Wife.*

121. Mary S. Gove Nichols, *Experience in Water-Cure* (New York: Fowlers & Wells, 1850), a twenty-five-cent pamphlet. There is information on their views in the short-lived *Nichols' Journal of Health, Water-Cure, and Human Progress* (1853–ca. 1858).

122. Nichols, *Esoteric Anthropology* (1853), pp. 163–64, discusses female ovaries using the pronoun "we": "while zoosperms are formed by millions . . . we have but one or two, or in rare cases, three to five, ova perfected once a month."

123. Nichols, *Esoteric Anthropology* (1853), p. 151; page 192 noted that the "surgical" method of abortion was simplest and least dangerous.

124. Stephen Pearl Andrews, ed., *Love, Marriage, and Divorce and the Sovereignty of the Individual: A Discussion by Henry James, Horace Greeley, Stephen Pearl Andrews, Including the Final Replies of Mr. Andrews Rejected by the Tribune* (New York: Stringer & Townsend, 1853), p. 70.

125. Nichols, *Esoteric Anthropology* (1853), pp. 173, 161.

126. Nichols, *Esoteric Anthropology* (1853), p. 190.

127. Elizabeth Blackwell to Emily Blackwell, [August] 1853, in the Blackwell Family Papers, Library of Congress; Elizabeth Blackwell, *Pioneer Work* (1985), p. 162.

128. *Una:* "Parentage," September 1854; "Woman and Marriage," November 1853; and "Reasons Why Woman Should Define Her Own Sphere," February 1853. Davis did not write any of these articles, but as editor and proprietor she surely chose or even sought out writers whose opinions approximated her own. See Alice Felt Tyler, "Paulina Kellogg Davis," in *Notable American Women.*

129. Harriot K. Hunt, *Glances and Glimpses; or, Fifty Years Social, Including Twenty Years Professional Life* (Boston: John P. Jewett, 1856), p. 122.

130. Hunt, *Glances and Glimpses*, pp. 139–40.

131. Quoted in Ann Douglas Wood, "'The Fashionable Diseases': Women's Complaints and Their Treatment in Nineteenth-Century America," in *Women and Health in America*, ed. Leavitt, p. 231.

132. Stanton, *History of Woman Suffrage*, 1:106–10, has "Address to the Women of Ohio," said to be written by Jones.

133. See Keith E. Melder, "Jane Elizabeth Hitchcock Jones," *Notable American Women.*

134. See Ellen Carol DuBois, ed., *Elizabeth Cady Stanton, Susan B. Anthony: Correspondence, Writings, Speeches* (New York: Schocken, 1981), pp. 94–97.

135. See Lois W. Banner, *Elizabeth Cady Stanton: A Radical for Woman's Rights* (Boston: Little, Brown, 1980), pp. 110, 124. Banner says in several places in her book that Stanton focused her feminist theories and actions on the centrality of birth control, but she does not specifically document it.

136. William Leach, *True Love and Perfect Union: The Feminist Reform of Sex and Society*, 2d ed. with a new introd. (Middletown, Conn.: Wesleyan University Press, 1989), p. 54, notes that women's physiological societies helped women learn about sex and reproduction before the Civil War.

137. Sara B. Chase, "Responsibility of Sex," from the Truth Seeker Tracts, Scientific Series 5, read before the New York Liberal Club, 9 July 1875.

138. See D. M. Bennett, *Anthony Comstock, His Career of Cruelty and Crime* (New York: Liberal and Scientific Publishing House, 1878).

139. See Harper, *'Be Fruitful and Multiply,'* pp. 202, 243; George F. MacDonald, *Fifty Years of Freethought* (New York: Truth Seeker Company, 1929; rpt. New York: Arno Press, 1972), p. 287.

140. New York City, vol. 389, p. 193, R. G. Dun & Co. Collection, reports from 1879 to 1890.

141. The spacing of the couple's six children suggests that they were able to delay and prevent pregnancy at times. Information is scanty about their exact births, so only approximate birth intervals can be presented below:

Marriage, 12 April 1832

Florence Dale Owen (born November 1833;
  died summer 1834) = 19 months

Florence Dale Owen [II] (born 1836) = 26–37 months

Julian Dale Owen (born 1837) = 9–23 months

Ernest Dale Owen (born 1839; died 1845) = 25–34 months

Rosamond Dale Owen (born 1846) = 73–83 months

Ernest Dale Owen [II] (born 1850) = 49–59 months

142. The conception intervals of the Knowltons' children are:

Marriage, 17 April 1821

Charles Lorenzo (born 3 May 1824) = 28 months

Melvinia Lucy (born 5 August 1826) = 18 months

Stephen Owen (born October 1828) = 17 months

August Comfort (born 15 November 1831) = 28 months

Willis (born 2 May 1837) = 57 months

143. See Leopold, *Robert Dale Owen*, p. 108.

144. [Charles Knowlton], *Address of Dr. Charles Knowlton before the Friends of Mental Liberty at Greenfield, Ma. and Constitution of the United Liberals of Franklin Co., Ma.* (Boston: J. P. Mendum, 1845). Thirteen members signed the founders' membership roll. The only other woman was Elizabeth Temple, the daughter of the Knowltons' friend, Philo Temple, of Deerfield.

145. Will of Charles Knowlton and other legal documents relating to the estate. Greenfield Co. Courthouse, Greenfield, Mass. Knowlton made the will out in 1847 before he left home "for an indefinite time." He left Tabitha, "in whose judgment and thrift I have confidence" in charge of the three children still at home (aged 19, 16, and 10), all real estate and household possessions including "diverse notes and accounts" worth one thousand dollars. If he died and she survived him, she was to receive $350 worth of the personal property and the use of one-half of the real estate whether she remarried or not. It was this last that Tabitha challenged, because Knowlton had acquired more property by 1850.

146. Probate Records of Greenfield County, Mass.

Chapter Five

1. Abner Kneeland, *A Friend to Free Inquiry: A Review of "Fruits of Philosophy; or, Private Companion of Young Married People" by Charles Knowlton, Author of "Modern Materialism"* (Boston: Abner Kneeland, [1833–34]), cited by Norman E. Himes, *Medical History of Contraception* (Baltimore: New York: Schocken, 1970; 1st pub. 1936), p. 450.

2. See Roderick S. French, "Liberation from Man and God in Boston: Abner Knee-land's Free-Thought Campaign, 1830–1839," *American Quarterly* 32 (1980): 202–21; Leonard W. Levy, *Blasphemy in Massachusetts: Freedom of Conscience and the Abner Kneeland Case* (New York: Da Capo, 1973).

3. Ellis Gray Loring to William H. Channing, Boston, 10 October 1847, "Notes, Etc. on the Abner Kneeland Controversy" (henceforth Kneeland File), b MS. Am 1428 (145) at Houghton Library, Harvard University. The quotations are Loring's interpreta-tion of the indictment. Accounts of the trial are also in Abner Kneeland, *A Review of the Trial, Conviction, and Final Imprisonment in the Common Jail of the County of Suffolk of Abner Kneeland, for the Alleged Crime of Blasphemy, Written by Himself* (Boston: George A. Chapman, 1838), at the American Antiquarian Society.

4. Loring to Channing, 10 October 1847, Kneeland File, Houghton Library, Har-vard University.

5. The petition and signatures are in Kneeland File.

6. Loring to unnamed correspondent, 9 October 1843, Kneeland File.

7. [Samuel Dunn Parker], *Report of the Arguments of the Attorney of the Com-monwealth at the Trials of Abner Kneeland for Blasphemy in the Municipal and Su-preme Courts in Boston, January and May 1834* ([Boston]: Beals, Homer, 1834), pp. 86–87. A copy is in the Boston Athenaeum, which has a few other Kneeland materials. It is possible that Parker did not give this lengthy reading from Knowlton's book but inserted it later into his pamphlet, much as congressmen still insert speeches into the *Congressional Record*, but there is no suggestion in the pamphlet that such was the case.

8. Parker, *Report of the Arguments*, p. 81.

9. Information on the Matsells is scarce and scattered: Walter Hugins, *Jacksonian Democracy and the Working Class: A Study of the New York Workingmen's Move-ment, 1829–37* (Stanford: Stanford University Press, 1960), p. 103; Robert Dale Owen, "An Earnest Sowing of Wild Oats," *Atlantic Monthly* 34 (July 1874): 74, recalls Matsell as an "excellent young man of fifteen . . . to whom we paid two dollars a week."

10. *Boston Investigator*, 12 June 1835, advertisement.

11. Hugins, *Jacksonian Democracy*, p. 103 says that Matsell was forced out as police chief in 1857 by in-fighting between the mayor and the state legislature. *The National Union Catalog of Pre-1956 Imprints* entry on G. W. Matsell lists a pamphlet, *Answer of and Protest of George W. Matsell, Police Commissioner and President of Police of the City of New York to Charges Made against Him, the Commissioner of Police, by the Mayor of the City of New York, 7 October 1875* (New York: J. X. Browne, 1875), which suggests that he continued on. In the post of police chief he became alarmed about street crime and juvenile delinquency and like certain other urban reformers in mid century, about "the dangerous classes"—a term popularized by Children's Aid Society reformer Charles Loring Brace, whom Matsell knew. Christine Stansell, *City of Women: Sex and Class in New York, 1789–1860* (New York: Knopf, 1986), pp. 194–95, 203–6, 209, is hostile to Matsell for his "alarmist exposé" of crime and children in the streets and for his "unabashed drive toward self-aggrandizement."

12. See Seymour J. Mandelbaum, "Ann Trow Lohman," *Notable American Women, 1607–1950*, vol. 2, ed. Edward T. James (Cambridge: Harvard University Press, 1971).

13. See Albert Post, *Popular Freethought in America, 1825–50* (New York: Co-lumbia University Press, 1943), p. 48. Biographical details about Vale can be pieced together from scattered references in Richard W. Leopold, *Robert Dale Owen* (Cam-bridge: Harvard University Press, 1940); Lewis Masquier, *Sociology; or, The Recon-struction of Society, Government, and Property* (New York: Pub. by the author, 1877), pp. 105–6; and Sidney Ditzion, *Marriage, Morals, and Sex in America: A History of Ideas* (New York: Norton, 1953), pp. 120–22, and in the 1830s from the *Boston Investi-gator*.

14. Samuel Palmer Putnam, *Four Hundred Years of Freethought* (New York: The Truth Seeker Company, 1894), p. 526; Hugins, *Jacksonian Democracy and the Working Class*, pp. 95–96.

15. See Chapter 4, note 9 and the Selected Bibliography.

16. Owen, *Moral Physiology* (1858), pp. 86–87, 81, 85–89.

17. Owen, *Moral Physiology* (1858), p. 33.

18. *Boston Investigator*, 10 September 1856, advertisement.

19. Post, *Popular Freethought*, p. 50.

20. See Ditzion, *Marriage, Morals, and Sex in America*, pp. 116, 120–22. The *Beacon* was not an insignificant newspaper, for it had one thousand subscribers in 1842—the height of its popularity.

21. Post, *Popular Freethought in America*, is the best basic source. Sidney Warren, *American Freethought, 1860–1914* (New York: Gordian Press, Inc., 1966), is also useful.

22. See George E. Macdonald, *Fifty Years of Freethought* vols. 1 and 2 (New York: Truth Seeker Company, 1929; reprt. Arno Press, 1972). Macdonald was an active freethinker for over fifty years.

23. Bruce Laurie, *Working People of Philadelphia, 1800–1850* (Philadelphia: Temple University Press, 1980), discusses Philadelphia freethinkers; see also Anthony F. C. Wallace, *Rockdale: The Growth of an American Village in the Early Industrial Revolution* (New York: Norton, 1972), pp. 246–55; Sean Wilentz, *Chants Democratic: New York City and the Rise of the American Working Class, 1788–1850* (New York: Oxford University Press, 1984), pp. 153–57.

24. Quoted in Post, *Popular Freethought*, p. 54.

25. Post, *Popular Freethought*, p. 130.

26. *Boston Investigator*, 22 July 1840, 17 March 1841, 9 October 1850.

27. *Free Enquirer*, 29 October 1828.

28. At certain times, irregularly and erratically, the *Boston Investigator* listed the actual titles of the books they delivered to agents; at other times they gave the initials and the states of the customers ordering specific titles. The editors did this as a primitive accounting system, but the practice illustrates the extensiveness of the demand for "liberal" reading materials. I have searched certain issues of the *Boston Investigator* between 1831 and 1860 at random. Sometimes the editors noted sending "pamphlets on physiology," or, after listing a number of books by title, they noted sending "pamphlet of information." I suspect that these were Owen's or Knowlton's birth control pamphlets. Examples are a shipment of tracts 27 January 1858 to D. Cooke of Michigan and the "tracts" sent to K. Graves, Ohio, 26 December 1855. S. Bosworth, Connecticut, 10 February 1858, received a *Manual of Nutritive Care* and a "pamphlet of information." The names may have been pseudonyms. A "John Burns" in St. Clair, Michigan, received Hollick's *The Marriage Guide* and *Male Generative Organs*, according to the 28 February 1855 issue of the *Boston Investigator*. The *Michigan State Gazeteer and Directory* (1856) lists no Burns in St. Clair. Similarly, J. Warner of Millville, Wisconsin, bought *Fruits* according to the 18 July 1855 issue. The *Wisconsin State Directory* (1857–58) lists no such name, either under booksellers or any business connected to books. Also see *Cleveland Liberalist*, 1 July 1837 and 10 May 1854 under "Business Items."

29. Quoted in [no author], "Case of Abortion Procured by Violence," *American Medical Recorder* (Philadelphia), 8 (1825): 461–62. For another example see John Brooks, "A Case of Abortion . . . ," *New England Journal of Medicine and Surgery* 10, n.s. 5 (1821): 105–10.

30. The histories of nineteenth-century American medicine I have found most helpful are: Guenter B. Risse et al., eds., *Medicine without Doctors: Home Health Care in American History* (New York: Science History Publications, U.S.A., 1977); William G.

Rothstein, *American Physicians in the Nineteenth Century: From Sects to Science* (Baltimore: Johns Hopkins University Press, 1972); Paul Starr, *The Social Transormation of American Medicine* (New York: Basic Books, 1982); Joseph K. Kett, *The Formation of the American Medical Profession: The Role of Institutions, 1780–1860* (New Haven: Yale University Press, 1968). There is much valuable analysis in Regina Markell Morantz-Sanchez, *Sympathy and Science: Women Physicians in American Medicine* (New York: Oxford University Press, 1987) and "Professionalism, Feminism, Gender Roles: A Comparative Study of Nineteenth Century Medical Therapeutics," *Journal of American History* 67 (1980): 568–88.

31. The roots of medical sectarianism and the rise of the health reform movement are complex. They are explored in: William Bentley Walker, "The Health Reform Movement in the United States, 1830–1870" (Ph.D. diss., Johns Hopkins University, 1955), and more recently in James H. Cassedy, "Why Self-Help? Americans Alone with Their Diseases, 1800–1850," in Risse et al., *Medicine without Doctors*.

32. See Rothstein, *American Physicians*, pp. 125–51 and passim.

33. New York City, vol. 334, p. 1917, R. G. Dun & Co. Collection, "Mattson Manufacturing Co. Syringes."

34. *Bangor Gazette*, 30 November 1844, advertisement.

35. Kneeland, *A Review of the Trial*, p. 43. *Independent Botanic Register*, 1 (1835–36): 63, lists Kneeland among the Thomsonian agents. He published *A Portrait of the Conduct of Elias Smith towards Dr. Samuel Thomson . . . by a Thomsonian* (Boston: Printed at the office of the Boston Investigator, 1832), and it is possible that he published the third edition of Thomson's *New Guide to Health* in Boston in 1832, although the imprint lists only the publication place and date.

36. Hersey, *The Midwife's Practical Directory* (1836), preface. Information about Hersey comes from *Index Medicus* (1880–89) and internal evidence in his publications and newspaper.

37. Hersey issued a circular describing the work in October 1834 and distributed the work to wholesale dealers at one dollar a copy. By June 1835 he explained in the *Independent Botanical Register* that not all the orders for his book could be filled but that copies were in the hands of agents "to favor an extensive diffusion of the knowledge of the work." The next year he issued the second edition.

38. Hersey, *The Midwife's Practical Directory* (1836), p. 60.

39. Hersey, *The Midwife's Practical Directory* (1836), p. 87.

40. Cited in James C. Mohr, *Abortion in America: The Origins and Evolution of National Policy, 1800–1900* (New York: Oxford University Press, 1978), pp. 61–62.

41. The water cure has been well studied by historians. See especially Susan E. Cayleff, *Wash and Be Healed: The Water-Cure Movement and Women's Health* (Philadelphia: Temple University Press, 1987), and Kathryn Kish Sklar, "All Hail to Pure, Cold Water!" in *Women and Health in America*, ed. Judith Walzer Leavitt (Madison: University of Wisconsin Press, 1984), pp. 246–54.

42. See Howard A. Kelly and Walter L. Burrage, "Russell Thacher Trall," *Dictionary of American Medical Biography* (New York: D. Appleton, 1928), and *New York Times*, 26 September 1877, Obituary.

43. Trall, *Sexual Physiology* (1867), pp. 213, xi.

44. Trall, *Sexual Physiology* (1867), pp. 207, 210–11, 213.

45. Trall, *The Hydropathic Encyclopedia*, p. 58, and app.: "Theory of Conception." Trall, *Pathology of the Reproductive Organs* (Boston: B. Leverett Emerson, 1861), contained advertisements for Davidson's Patent Syringe.

46. For arguments about the similarities among medical sectarianism and the fostering of self-reliance see especially Ronald L. Numbers, "Do-It-Yourself the Sectarian Way," in Risse et al., *Medicine without Doctors*, pp. 49–64.

47. Kett, *Formation of the American Medical Profession*, discusses the importance of women in the Thomsonian movement, but the phenomenon deserves closer scrutiny. Regina Morantz-Sanchez argues that women, by participating in antebellum health reform, helped carve out and legitimize new roles within the family and society. See her "Nineteenth Century Health Reform and Women: A Program of Self Help," in Risse et al., *Medicine without Doctors*, especially pp. 73–90, and "Making Women Modern: Middle-Class Women and Health Reform in Nineteenth-Century America," in Leavitt, *Women and Health in America*, pp. 346–58.

48. *Free Enquirer*, 23 October 1830, "Announcement"; 15 January 1831, editorial.

49. See Leopold, *Robert Dale Owen*, p. 73.

50. "Communications," *Free Enquirer*, 18 December 1830.

51. Owen, "Sowing," p. 73.

52. Knowlton was charged under the state common law because there were few state laws against obscenity until the late 1830s. Even prosecutions under the common law were rare. A section of the Tariff Act of 1842 was amended to give the Customs Office the power to confiscate and to bring suit to destroy "obscene or immoral prints" and pictures. See Michael Grossberg, *Governing the Hearth: Law and Family in Nineteenth-Century America* (Chapel Hill: University of North Carolina Press, 1985), pp. 157–59.

53. Charles Knowlton, *A History of the Recent Excitement in Ashfield*, pt. 2 (September 1835). This one-page handbill was all Knowlton published of the promised second installment to his 1834 pamphlet with the same title. It is in the Antiquarian Society in Worcester, Mass.

54. Charles Knowlton, *A History of the Recent Excitement in Ashfield* (Ashfield, [Mass.], 1834), p. 9 and passim.

55. Knowlton, *A History of the Recent Excitement*. Also, Frederick G. Howes, *A History of the Town of Ashfield, 1742–1910* (Ashfield, Mass.: n.p., 1914), "Churches in Ashfield."

56. Howes, *A History of the Town of Ashfield*, "Churches in Ashfield."

57. G. J. Barker-Benfield, *The Horrors of the Half-Known Life: Male Attitudes toward Women and Sexuality in Nineteenth-Century America* (New York: Harper & Row, 1976), pt. 3, is the best biography of Todd.

58. John Todd, *Serpents in the Dove's Nest* (Boston: Lee and Shepard, 1867); *Cincinnati Lancet and Observer* 10 (1867); advertisement.

59. Editorial, *Boston Medical and Surgical Journal* 76 (1867): 145.

60. Andrew Nebinger, *Criminal Abortion: Its Extent and Prevention* (n.p.: "extracted from the Transactions of the Medical Society for Pennsylvania," 1876).

61. For other references to religion and abortion see the editors' comments (no author, no title), *Boston Medical and Surgical Journal* 76 (1867): 145.

62. Daniel Garrison Brinton to Horatio Robinson Storer, Media, Pa., March 1898, B Ms C55.2 Rare Book Room, Countway Library of Medicine, Harvard University. This may be the same Brinton who published William Goodell's *Lessons in Gynecology* in Philadelphia, in 1879, and a second edition in 1880. Brinton had been editor of the *Medical and Surgical Reporter* in Philadelphia for decades, sponsoring and tolerating numerous artilces sympathetic to "the prevention of conception." [Anonymous], "Abortion," *Medico-Legal Journal* 7 (1889): 170–87, commends the Jews for not practicing abortion.

63. Cited in French, "Liberation from Man and God," p. 206.

64. Owen, *Moral Physiology* (1830), preface to the 1st ed. Nor were such fears solely on this side of the Atlantic. The *London Examiner* in 1832 sought stronger laws against abortion on the grounds that if women could obtain abortions at will, all sexual restraint would collapse and "the bonds which hold society together would be broken

asunder." Quoted in R. Sauer, "Infanticide and Abortion in Nineteenth-Century Britain," *Population Studies* 32 (1978): 84.

65. See John Paull Harper, "'Be Fruitful and Multiply': The Reaction to Family Limitation in Nineteenth-Century America" (Ph.D. diss., Columbia University, 1975), argues that the opposition from public figures was based mainly on their fears about demographic change, particularly the declining native birth rate. Carroll Smith-Rosenberg, "The Abortion Movement and the AMA, 1850–1880," *Disorderly Conduct: Visions of Gender in Victorian America* (New York: Knopf, 1985), pp. 217–44, also discusses the opposition to abortion in these terms.

66. *Advertiser and Patriot* (Boston), 9 April 1838, report of the Kneeland trial, cited in French, "Liberation from Man and God," p. 213.

67. Kneeland, *A Review of the Trial*, pp. 13, 114; Parker, *Report of the Argument*, p. 36.

68. William T. Davis, *History of the Bench and Bar of the Commonwealth of Massachusetts* (Boston: Boston Historical Co., 1895; rpt. ed. New York: Da Capo Press, 1974), vol. 2, "Franklin County."

69. French, "Liberation from Man and God," p. 216.

70. Benjamin F. Thomas, *Sketch of the Life and Judicial Labors of Chief-Justice Shaw* (Boston: John Wilson and Son, 1868). Davis, *History of Bench and Bar in Massachusetts*, p. 245, notes Shaw's membership on the Harvard Board of Overseers, the Boston Public Library Society, the Massachusetts Historical Society, the Society for the Propagation of the Gospel among the Indians, and the Academy of Arts and Sciences.

71. Wilentz, *Chants Democratic*, p. 188.

72. Quoted in Celia M. Eckhardt, *Fanny Wright: Rebel in America* (Cambridge, Harvard University Press, 1984), p. 216. Wilentz, *Chants Democratic*, pp. 183–211, analyzes the Working Men's Movement, Skidmore's role and faction. See also Edward Pessen, *Most Uncommon Jacksonians: The Radical Leaders of the Early Labor Movement* (Albany: State University of New York Press, 1967) and "Thomas Skidmore, Agrarian Reformer in the Early American Labor Movement," *New York History* 25 (1954): 280–94.

73. Skidmore was one of eleven candidates nominated by the new Working Men's party for the New York State assembly in 1829 and he was almost elected. He lost power during postelection in-fighting orchestrated in part by Robert Dale Owen and George Henry Evans. Owen and Skidmore fundamentally distrusted each other's solutions to American social and economic problems. Owen viewed Skidmore as a dangerous radical whose hostility to private property would give the entire workingmen's movement an anarchic association. Skidmore was suspicious of Owen as a conservative member of the propertied class who did not have the best interests of working people at heart, and he distrusted Owen as a "political dreamer."

74. Thomas Skidmore, *Moral Physiology Exposed and Refuted* (New York: Skidmore & Jacobus, 1831).

75. Thomas Skidmore, Letter, *Free Enquirer*, 2 October 1830.

76. Leopold, *Robert Dale Owen*, p. 82.

77. See Robert F. Berkhofer, Jr., "A New Context for a New American Studies," *American Quarterly* 41 (1989): 588–613.

78. See Joel Perlmann and Dennis Shirley, "When Did New England Women Acquire Literacy?" *William and Mary Quarterly* 48 (1991): 51, with a good review of the historical literature on American literacy.

79. William J. Gilmore, *Reading Becomes a Necessity of Life: Material and Cultural Life in Rural New England, 1780–1835* (Knoxville: University of Tennessee Press, 1989), Table 7-4, pp. 250, 205–19, 150–51, 160–61, challenges the "trickle-down" hypothesis that knowledge circulated from elites to nonelites. His book illustrates a complex circulation system for print-culture distribution.

80. Jacob Abbott, *New England and Her Institutions* (Boston, 1835), p. 25, cited in Nancy F. Cott, *The Bonds of Womanhood: 'Woman's Sphere' in New England, 1780–1835* (New Haven: Yale University Press, 1977), p. 10 n6.

81. No author, *American Journal of Education* 5 (May 1830): 222.

82. Joseph F. Kett and Patricia A. McClung, "Book Culture in Post-Revolutionary Virginia," *Proceedings of the American Antiquarian Society* 94, pt. 1 (1984): 97–147, concluded that book ownership did not increase in Jacksonian era Virginia but that women became a more significant part of the reading public.

83. Wallace, *Rockdale*, pp. 114–17.

84. Post, *Popular Freethought*, records large crowds at freethought events in the 1830s, some as large as six and seven hundred, although Wilentz, *Chants Democratic*, p. 171, argues that as of 1829 the freethinkers attracted no more than a few hundred devoted followers. The *Boston Investigator* reported two to four hundred people attending freethought events in the mid 1830s.

85. Laurie, *Working People of Philadelphia*, p. 70.

86. Richard D. Brown, *Knowledge Is Power: The Diffusion of Information in Early America, 1700–1865* (New York: Oxford University Press, 1989), pp. 161–67, looks at roles of women in the diffusion of knowledge and the constraints on them.

87. See Gilmore, *Reading Becomes a Necessity*, pp. 124–25.

88. See Allan R. Pred, *Urban Growth and the Circulation of Information: The United States System of Cities, 1790–1840* (Cambridge: Harvard University Press, 1973), pp. 279, 186.

89. Knowlton, *A History of the Recent Excitement*.

90. Kneeland, *A Review of the Trial*.

91. Howes, *A History of the Town of Ashfield*.

92. Will of Charles Knowlton, Probate Records; land transactions in the Registry of Deeds, Franklin County Courthouse, Greenfield, Mass.

93. Knowlton, *A History of the Recent Excitement*.

94. There is important scattered information in his miscellaneous medical writings, such as: Knowlton, "Abscess of the Lungs," *Boston Medical and Surgical Journal* 28 (1843): 369–73; Knowlton, "Erysipelas and Puerperal Fever," *Boston Medical and Surgical Journal* 30 (1844): 89–95.

95. See John Mack Faragher, *Sugar Creek: Life on the Illinois Prairie* (New Haven: Yale University Press, 1986), pp. 100–101, 205–7.

96. Faragher, *Sugar Creek*, p. 177.

97. See John Mack Faragher, "Open-Country Community: Sugar Creek, Illinois, 1820–1850," p. 239, in *The Countryside in the Age of Capitalist Transformation: Essays in the Social History of Rural America*, ed. Steven Hahn and Jonathan Prude, (Chapel Hill: University of North Carolina Press, 1985). David Jafee, "One of the Primitive Sort: Portrait Makers of the Rural North, 1760–1860," in Hahn and Prude, discusses village cultures receiving information from different types of itinerants.

98. Brown, *Knowledge Is Power*, pp. 158–59: agricultural reformers tried to persuade farmers to trust information derived from printed sources in the early nineteenth century.

99. Jafee, "One of the Primitive Sort," p. 113. Faragher, *Sugar Creek*, however, argues that money was rarely exchanged in Sugar Creek transactions before mid century.

100. For discussions of the numerical size, geographical spread, and class appeal of Thomsonian see Rothstein, *American Physicians*, pp. 125–51; Starr, *The Social Transformation of American Medicine*, pp. 47–54; and Kett, *The Formation of the American Medical Profession*, pp. 106–7.

101. Mauriceau [pseud.], *The Married Woman's Private Medical Companion* (1847), chap. 2, "Conception."

102. Michael B. Katz and Mark J. Stern, "Fertility, Class, and Industrial Capitalism: Erie Co., New York, 1855–1915," *American Quarterly* 33 (1981): 63–92, argue that fertility first declined among the "new business class" but that other groups quickly followed as industrial capitalism altered the costs of raising children and expectations about children's futures. F. Barry Smith, "Sexuality in Britain, 1800–1900: Some Suggested Revisions," in *A Widening Sphere: Changing Roles of Victorian Women,* ed. Martha Vicinus (Bloomington: Indiana University Press, 1977), pp. 182–98, suggests that birth control in Victorian Britiain may have "percolated up from the self-instructed," self-employed, upwardly mobile but blocked working class artisans and freethinkers with "privatized ethics."

103. Stuart M. Blumin, *The Emergence of the Middle Class: Social Experience in the American City, 1760–1900* (Cambridge: Cambridge University Press, 1989), and Mary Ryan, *Cradle of the Middle Class: The Family in Oneida County, New York, 1790–1865* (Cambridge: Cambridge University Press, 1981), analyze the middle classes. For the working classes: Wilentz, *Chants Democratic.* Peter Knights, *The Plain People of Boston, 1830–60: A Study in City Growth* (New York: Oxford University Press, 1971), has a far more detailed breakdown of professional categories for antebellum Boston.

104. See Pessen, *Most Uncommon Jacksonians,* chap.: "The Attack on Malthusianism."

105. See Ryan, *Cradle of the Middle Class,* p. 157.

106. Cited in Paul G. Faler, "Cultural Aspects of the Industrial Revolution: Lynn, Mass., Shoemakers and Industrial Morality 1826–1860," in *American Workingclass Culture: Explorations in American Labor and Social History,* ed. Milton Cantor (1979), p. 142. Angus McLaren, *Birth Control in Nineteenth-Century England* (New York: Holmes & Meier, 1978), discusses opposition to birth control in the working class press.

107. Historians disagree about this issue of whether birth control was imposed from without or within. Paul G. Faler, *Mechanics and Manufacturers in the Early Industrial Revolution: Lynn, Ma., 1800–1860* (Albany: State University of New York Press, 1981), argues for the social control view; Ronald G. Walters, *American Reformers, 1815–1860* (New York: Hill & Wang, 1978), is critical. Wilentz, *Chants Democratic,* pp. 40–46, emphasizes the attempts of the General Society of Mechanics and Tradesmen in shaping mechanics' morality and work habits. Charles E. Rosenberg, "Sexuality, Class, and Role in Nineteenth Century America," *American Quarterly* 25 (1973): 131–53, argues that lower middle and working classes found reform ideology useful. For a broader analysis of the reform-as-social-control model see Laurence Kohl, "The Concept of Social Control," *Journal of the Early Republic* 5 (1985): 21–34.

108. Stephen Nissenbaum, *Sex, Diet, and Debility in Jacksonian America: Sylvester Graham and Health Reform* (Westport, Conn.: Greenwood Press, 1980).

109. New York Census 1850 lists twenty-five lodgers at Trall's establishment. The lodgers also included two lawyers, a physician, and a publisher. Trall lived at the establishment as well, with his thirty-four-year-old wife and five-month-old son.

110. Faler, *Mechanics and Manufacturers,* notes that "loyalists" constituted a bare majority of Lynn's workers. Laurie, *Working People of Philadelphia,* uses the same three categories in identifying responses among the Philadelphia workers he studied.

111. See T. S. Ashton, *Economic and Social Investigations in Manchester, 1833–1933* (London: P. S. King, 1934), pp. 18–19, 141. The society was concerned about the large circulation of "immoral and irreligious publications." In particular they noted that four hundred copies of Paine's *Age of Reason* and eight hundred copies of his *Rights of Man* sold in 1834, most to workers.

112. Wilentz, *Chants Democratic,* pp. 153–57, notes that Wright and Owen "nourished a radical culture in the heart of the mechanics' wards" in New York City.

Their Broome Street Hall of Science was the "nerve center of freethought" in New York City. See Laurie, *Working People of Philadelphia*, Table 8, p. 72. Laurie notes that the Free Enquirers emphasized self-education and temperance but descried total abstinence.

113. See Wilentz, *Chants Democratic*, p. 409. Forty percent of the leaders supporting Robert Dale were journeymen, 25 percent were shopkeepers, retailers, and petty professionals. Among the Skidmore faction there were more master craftsmen, manufacturers, and small masters than among the Owenites.

114. See Stansell, *City of Women*, p. 146; Mary H. Blewett, *Men, Women, and Work: Class, Gender, and Protest in the New England Shoe Industry, 1780–1910* (Urbana: Univesity of Illinois Press, 1988).

115. See Stansell, *City of Women*, pp. 130–37, 121–27.

116. Stansell, *City of Women*, p. 54.

117. See Introduction, n. 25.

118. See Anne M. Butler, *Daughters of Joy, Sisters of Misery: Prostitutes in the American West, 1865–90* (Urbana: University of Illinois Press, 1985), pp. 15, 24n63.

119. The only contemporary discussion I have found is Webb J. Kelly, "One of the Abuses of Carbolic Acid," *Columbus Medical Journal* 1 (1883): 433–36, which cites case histories of prostitutes douching with carbolic acid.

120. Margaret Byington, *Homestead: The Households of a Mill Town* (Pittsburgh: University of Pittsburgh Press, 1974; rpt. of the 1910 ed.), pp. 38–39, assesses the spending patterns and budgets of ninety workers' families. John Modell, "Patterns of Consumption, Acculturation, and Family Income Strategies in Late Nineteenth-Century America," in *Family and Population in Nineteenth-Century America*, ed. Tamara K. Hareven and Maris Vinovskis (Princeton: Princeton University Press, 1978), pp. 296–340, discusses the methodological problems when one analyzes workers' consumption and income.

121. See Edward D. Andrews, *The Community Industries of the Shakers*, New York State Museum Handbook 15 (Albany: The University of the State of New York [Press], 1932), p. 91.

122. See Edgar W. Martin, *The Standard of Living in 1860* (Chicago: University of Chicago Press, 1942), pp. 394–95.

123. Knowlton, *Fruits of Philosophy* (1832), p. 62. He noted condom prices on pp. 59–61, but omitted prices in later editions. Advertising circular for "Dr. Cameron's Patent Family Regulator," reprinted in *Women of America*, ed. Carol Berkin and Mary Beth Norton (Boston: Houghton Mifflin, 1979), pp. 266–67.

124. See Martin, *The Standard of Living in 1860*, pp. 394–95.

125. Wallace, *Rockdale*, pp. 173–75, notes the mill operatives who bought books or subscribed to a newspaper in the 1830s.

126. Owen, "An Earnest Sowing of Wild Oats."

127. [Charles Knowlton], *Address of Dr. Charles Knowlton before the Friends of Mental Liberty at Greenfield, Massachusetts, and the Constitution of the United Liberals of Franklin Co., Massachusetts* (Boston: J. P. Mendum, 1845).

128. Inventory of Estate of William Russell of Deerfield, Mass., in Franklin Co. Courthouse, Greenfield, Mass. Russell's estate was worth $2442.86 when he died—making him in Knight's definition part of the category of "proprietors, managers, officials" with over $1000 in personal property but less than $5000 total worth.

Chapter Six

1. The reference to Nichols's letter is from an advertisement in *Boston Investigator*, 9 August 1854. The Selected Bibliography contains full citations for these shorter

works. Some of the works were once in the Library of Congress, catalogued under "the prevention of conception," but the booklets can no longer be found. These include: Mary Daisy Hindmarsh, *Married Ladies' Guide; or, Longer Life for Women* (n.p., 1894); W. R. King, *The Hidden Law of Nature Discovered* (Cullman, Ala.: Beckert & Johnson, 1879); J. W. Luse, *The Married Ladies' Private Guide to Health and Happiness. Giving the Information that Every Married Lady Should Have* (Clyde, Ohio: n.p., 1883); Madame Moore, *The Wife's Secret of Power* (New York: Madame Moore, c. 1871); Dan Newcomb, *How Not To and Why; or, Arguments Based upon Physiological, Moral, and Social Relations, in Favor of Preventing Conception and Giving the 'Ways and Means' in Plain Language* (Chicago: A. W. Penny, 1872); [B. C.] Ross, *Conception: The Process; Method of Prevention without Any Expense or Any Hindrance to Perfect Intercourse* (Independence, [Kans.]: Printed for the author, 1877); G. W. Warren, *A Confidential Letter to the Married* (Cleveland, Ohio: n.p., 1854); Daniel Winder, *A Rational or Private Marriage Chart. For the Use of All Who Wish to Prevent an Increase of Family* (Mansfield, Ohio: n.p., 1858); J. T. Willie, *The Ladies Present; Containing Information for the Married and Those about to Marry* (n.p., 1854).

2. The Selected Bibliography lists these works in full, but of special note are those by Cowan, Dunne, Foote, Grindle, Hollick, Larmont, Napheys, Nichols, Pancoast, Root, and Trall.

3. Anonymous, *Reproductive Control* (1855).

4. New York Society for the Suppression of Vice Collection, vol. 2, Ledger of Arrests, 1872–1884, Manuscript Division, Library of Congress, Washington, D.C.

5. New York [State], New vol. 165, p. 74, and New vol. 166, p. 183, R. G. Dun & Co. Collection. Credit-rating reporters consistently filed favorable assessments of the company's financial success from 1874 to 1883, noting in 1878, "No question that they are making money—over sixty thousand last year," estimating receipts averaging $500 a day in October 1879, and estimating Soule's worth at nearly $500,000 in 1883.
The evidence linking Soule's Hop Bitters Company with birth control is indirect. The New York Society for the Suppression of Vice arrest records refer to a product, "Neutraline," which Soule purportedly advertised for the prevention of conception.

6. [Glover], *Owen's Moral Physiology* (1846), Editor's Preface.

7. Nichols, *Esoteric Anthropology* (Cincinnati, 1853), is 3 inches by 5 inches.

8. Ashton, *The Book of Nature* (1861), preface.

9. Dunne and Derbois, *The Young Married Lady's Private Medical Guide*, chap. 17.

10. Napheys, *The Physical Life of Woman* (1872), "Limitation of Offspring," pp. 91–99.

11. Soule, *Science of Reproduction*, p. 4.

12. Anonymous, *Reproductive Control*, pp. 21–39, "Prevention Defended."

13. [Beach], *The Habits of a Well-Organized Married Life*, p. 6.

14. [Beach], *The Habits of a Well-Organized Married Life*, pp. 2–3.

15. Ashton, *The Book of Nature* (1861), p. 42, was one of the few to heartily recommend withdrawal: "a plan which every person of good breeding should adopt for its cleanliness alone. . . . It is indeed a refinement of social intercourse—a triumph of mind which thus controls even the laws and instincts of our nature!" There is no information on Ashton in the R. G. Dun & Co. Collection or in *Index Medicus* (1889 ed.).

16. Soule, *Science of Reproduction*, p. 64.

17. Ashton, *The Book of Nature* (1861), pp. 61–63.

18. Pancoast, *The Ladies' Medical Guide and Marriage Friend* (1859), chaps. 6 and 7; Nichols, *Esoteric Anthropology*, chaps. on generation, impregnation, and the evolution of the fetus; Besant, *The Law of Population* (1889), p. 30. Soule, *Science of Repro-*

duction, pt. 2, discussed "seminal secretions," "semen and animalculae," and, more briefly, "the Fallopian tubes." In Part 3 he explained "The Philosophy of Conception," much of it taken without credit from Hollick's arguments about the purported timing of ovulation. Ashton, *The Book of Nature* (1861), discussed the "male generative organs," "the ovaries," "the time and manner of impregnation." Edward Bliss Foote added 102 pages in *Medical Common Sense* between 1858 and 1864, doubling the illustrations and adding advice on birth control, embryology, a theory of sexual intercourse, barrenness, impotence, and women's generative organs.

19. Neither edition of William Goodell, *Lessons in Gynecology*—(Philadephia: D. G. Brinton, 1879), reprinted in 1887, 3d ed., enl. and rev. in 1891—had information on reproduction. Nor did Theodore Gaillard Thomas, *A Practical Treatise on the Diseases of Women* (Philadelphia: n.p., 1868). Thomas Addis Emmet, *The Principles and Practice of Gynecology*, 3d ed., thoroughly rev. (Philadelphia: Henry C. Lea, 1884), had no information on reproduction, sperm, or fertilization, although there is a chapter on ovulation and menstruation. William Tyler Smith, *The Modern Practice of Midwifery: A Course of Lectures on Obstetrics* (New York: Robert M. DeWitt, 1858), devoted little space to conception.

20. Knowlton, *Fruits of Philosophy* (London, [c. 1834]), chap. 2, "On Generation"; Knowlton, *Fruits of Philosophy* (1839), chap. 2.

21. Among the historians who have suggested sexual abstinence as one of the ways nineteenth-century couples limited fertility are John Mack Faragher, *Sugar Creek: Life on the Illinois Prairie* (New Haven: Yale University Press, 1986), p. 205; Nancy Grey Osterud, *Bonds of Community: The Lives of Farm Women in Nineteenth-Century New York* (Ithaca: Cornell University Press, 1991), p. 73.

22. Anonymous, *Reproductive Control*, p. 55.

23. Becklard, *Physiological Mysteries and Revelations* (1844), had sixteen engravings; Hollick, *The Origin of Life* (1846), had "fine colored engravings on stone." Hollick, *The Diseases of Woman* (1849), had colored plates and engravings. Nichols, *Esoteric Anthropology* (1853), had drawings of the sperm, male organs, ovaries with ova, but no drawings of the female organs of reproduction. Larmont, *Medical Advisor and Marriage Guide* (1864), had nearly one hundred "electrotyped engravings." Ashton, *The Book of Nature* (1861), contained colored engravings, including one opposite the title page of a nude woman. Foote, *Plain Home Talk* (1873), had two hundred illustrations. John Tebbel, *A History of Book Publishing in the U.S.* (New York: R. R. Bowker, 1972), 1: 549, notes that physiological texts began to use pictures in the 1850s and colored plates in the 1890s, so apparently the birth control literature pioneered in this use.

24. The *Exhibition Catalogue of the Massachusetts Charitable Mechanics Association* (Boston, 1856) said of the pamphlet sold with the Mattson & Co. Family Syringes, "The little book sold with it is a good compilation and worth many times the purchase price." George C. Goodwin & Co. *Catalogue* (Boston, 1885), p. 378, advertisement for Mattson's syringes, pictures two boxes, each with "Mattson's Family Syringe, with Family Guide," and "Mattson's Irrigator Syringe, with Anatomical Chart, for the Use of Ladies" on the cover of each box.

25. William A. Rothacker, "The Prevention of Conception," *Cincinnati Lancet and Clinic*, n.s. 10 (1883): 287–90.

26. Byrn, *The Physiology of Marriage* (1872), p. 105, and Byrn, *Al-ma-kan-tur Circle* (1857). It cost twenty-eight cents. Byrn disapproved of abortion, but sold abortifacient pills, sent anywhere "free from detection . . . so no one would suspect that they were medicines" by mail for one dollar. His "Married Woman's Private Medical Cabinet" consisted mainly of recipes to promote suppressed menstruation or check hemorrhaging. He advised douching for health, without mentioning contraception. Byrn is a

good example of an officially trained M.D. deeply involved in mail order sales of medi-cines, devices, and books. See James R. Masterson, "The Arkansaw Doctor," *Annals of Medical History* 2 (1940): 30–51.

27. Root, *The People's Medical Lighthouse* (1853, 1854).

28. John Paull Harper, "'Be Fruitful and Multiply': The Reaction to Family Limita-tion in Nineteenth-Century America" (Ph.D. diss., Columbia University, 1975), p. 23, gives examples of birth control ads in Boston and New York newspapers in the 1830s. Frank Luther Mott, *History of American Magazines, 1741–1850* (New York: Appleton, 1930), 2:185, cites as an example of cheap periodicals the *Arena*, edited by Thomas Low Nichols. I have been unable to locate it.

29. *Sporting Times and Theatrical News*, 25 March 1871; random issues 1870–73.

30. I found no ads in random issues of the *Ladies Repository* (1850), the *Home Magazine* (Philadelphia, 1854 and 1870), *Christian Parlor Magazine* (New York, 1846 and 1852), or *Gleason's Pictorial* (Boston, 1853). One of the few periodicals with ads was Harper's *New Monthly Magazine*, but the number varied greatly year to year. Random searches, November 1870 to October 1881, of *Scribners Monthly* turned up no advertisements. Mott, *History of American Magazines*, 3:9, states that in the post–Civil War period *Scribners*, which became *Century*, was the first high-class magazine to carry numerous ads and that *Lippincotts* carried the second greatest number in the 1870s.

31. New York Society for the Suppression of Vice Collection, vol. 2, Ledger of Ar-rests, 1872–84.

32. Root, *The People's Medical Lighthouse* (1854), contained advertisements and tes-timonials in the back of the book for his newspaper which I have not been able to locate. Frederick Hollick, ed., *People's Medical Journal, Devoted to the Dissemination of Popular Information on Anatomy, Physiology, the Laws of Health, and the Cure of Disease*, illustrated by engravings (New York: T. W. Strong) 1 (1853) and 2 (1854). A subscription cost twenty-five cents a year or three cents an issue. Hollick extensively advertised his sexual and birth control advice book *The Marriage Guide* in the news-paper.

33. Root, *The People's Medical Lighthouse* (1854), pp. 394–98, testimonial letters. Even though it is quite probable that Root wrote many of the testimonials himself, he would have had little reason to fabricate all the small details, so they are useful evi-dence.

34. See Jean Burton, *Lydia Pinkham Is Her Name* (New York: Farrar, Straus, 1949), p. 189.

35. Dr. S. Morse, *Indian Root Pills Almanac* (n.p., 1888), advertised "Dr. S. Morse's Indian Root Pills" as a female medicine "to purify the blood and remove ob-structions. . . . A box of these pills is a medical companion at certain periods. From one to three should be taken every day until relief is obtained."

36. J. Miller, "Criminal Abortion," *Kansas City Medical Record* 1 (1884): 295–98.

37. John Todd, *Serpents in the Dove's Nest* (Boston: Lee and Shepard, stereotyped, 1867). For an extended discussion of Todd see G. J. Barker-Benfield, *The Horrors of the Half-Known Life* (San Francisco: Harper & Row, 1976), chaps. 12, 14.

38. Hugh S. Pomeroy, *The Ethics of Marriage* (New York: Funk & Wagnalls, 1888), p. 156. He was unclear about what the circular advertised.

39. Cooke, *Satan in Society* (1876), pp. 23, 213.

40. Advertisements, vol. 328 (1898), Lydia E. Pinkham Papers (hereafter LEPP), Schlesinger Library, Radcliffe College. Harmon Knox Root's testimonial letters at the end of *The People's Medical Lighthouse* indicate that he, too, used this method. A letter from "Harvey J. Bliss" of Boston reported learning about Root's products when "fortunately one of Dr. Root's circulars was thrown into our house."

41. Lydia E. Pinkham MS (n.d.), box 123, folder 2493, LEPP.

42. Copy of undated advertisement advising taking the "Vegetable Compound" in case of delayed menstruation until "the flow was well established," Advertisements, vol. 379 LEPP; for douching advertisements see Advertisements, vols. 328 and 537; for suggestions about what Pinkham may have told women who wrote to her for personal advice on reproduction, see the manuscript of her text for women, box 123, folder 2493, LEPP. See Rust Brothers & Bird, *Catalogue* (Boston, 1891), advertisement for Lydia E. Pinkham's "Blood Purifier."

43. See Ronald J. Zboray, "The Transportation Revolution and Antebellum Book Distribution Reconsidered," *American Quarterly*, 38 (1986): 53–71; and W. S. Tryon, "Book Distribution in Mid-Nineteenth Century America, Illustrated by the Publishing Records of Ticknor & Fields, Boston," *The Papers of the Bibliographical Society of America* 41 (1947): 210–30. Raymond Howard Shove, "Cheap Book Production in the United States" (Ph.D. diss., University of Illinois, 1937), is still useful.

44. *New York Tribune* 29 September 1857 and 18 November 1857, discussion of publishers of "obscenity." *Day's Doings*, 24 August 1872, advertisements for Martin Dutton & Co., selling *Things You Ought to Know: Complete Marriage Guide and Treatise on Sexual Physiology*, "one dollar by mail."

45. My analysis of birth control publishers and distributors is based on nearly one hundred names of publishers, printers, translators, distribution agents, and book-sellers, names I gleaned from imprints of variant editions, advertisements, and *The National Union Catalog of Pre-1956 Imprints*. I was able to locate information on some 25 percent of the names. My principal sources were the R. G. Dun & Co. Collection and histories of publishing, especially John Tebbel, *A History of Book Publishing in the U.S.* (New York: R. R. Bowker, 1972).

46. It is suggestive that Clyde, Ohio—a small town not far from Lake Erie—was the source of the birth control advice pamphlet by J. W. Luse, *The Married Ladies' Private Guide to Health and Happiness. Giving the Information That Every Married Lady Should Have* (1883), was also the locale of the first play-publishing house in the West from 1870 to 1914, established by Albert D. Ames, who owned the printing press. Tebbel, *A History of Book Publishing*, 2: 613.

47. Examples of subscription publishers who touched on birth control in the second half of the nineteenth century include Hiram Rulison's Queen City Publishing in Cincinnati, John Cowan's self-publishing subscription company, and the Fireside Publishing Company in Philadelphia, which published four editions of Eliza B. Duffey's *What Women Should Know* between 1873 and 1893. The company, which did only subscription publishing, was a profit-making venture consisting of a state senator, a lawyer, and the manager, Henry C. Altemis, a young Philadelphian from a prominent family. Philadelphia, vol. 158, p. 307, R. G. Dun & Co. Collection.

48. Cowan's *The Science of a New Life* was first issued in 1869 in New York simultaneously by Fowlers and Wells and by J. S. Ogilvie. In 1871, Cowan issued a subscription edition from New York and one in German in 1872. A Chicago firm, G. W. Ogilvie and Co. (possibly related to the New York Ogilvies), issued an edition in 1903. Credit-raters reported on Cowan's publishing ventures from 1871 to 1881, finding him doing a "small but safe business" publishing two to three works and selling them by canvasing agents. They noted that he graduated as a physician but had no regular practice. They rated Cowan an "honest, well-meaning young man," who in January 1875 was thought to have ample means, but who left town in June 1881 after a judgment was brought against him for an unpaid bill of $329. New York City, vol. 435, p. 200M, R. G. Dun & Co. Collection.

49. Martin L. Holbrook (1831–1902) was himself an author, of *Parturition without Pain: A Code of Directions for Escaping from the Primal Curse* (New York: Wood &

Holbrook, 1871), an editor of the *Herald of Health and Journal of Physical Culture* from 1866 to 1884, and publisher of numerous medical works under various imprints, including "Wood & Holbrook," "M. L. Holbrook," and probably "Miller, Wood & Co." The printing press at 15 Laight Street in New York City was used by various combinations of publishers. Trall himself put out his *Health and Diseases of Woman* with the imprint "Published by R. T. Trall & Co., 15 Laight St." in 1862. Miller, Wood & Co., Publishers, put out a fifth edition of Trall's *Sexual Physiology* in 1867. In 1881, 1885, and 1895 (the 1895 edition was "revised and greatly enlarged" although expurgated of all birth control information) editions were published by M. L. Holbrook Co. Holbrook held the copyright to the 1895 edition. The address 15 Laight Street was where Trall had his hydropathic boardinghouse and his Hygienic Institute.

50. See Martin Henry Blatt, *Free Love and Anarchism: The Biography of Ezra Heywood* (Urbana: University of Illinois Press, 1989), p. 119; Hal D. Sears, *The Sex Radicals: Free Love in High Victorian America* (Lawrence, Kans.: Regents Press of Kansas, 1977), pp. 168–69. Judge Blatchford also ruled that a work could be judged by a few isolated passages, not its overall content. If a jury found any part of a work obscene, the whole work had to be judged obscene. Bennett obtained considerable public support, including seventy thousand signatures on a petition presented to Congress in 1878 at hearings before the Committee on the Revision of Laws that was considering the repeal of the Comstock laws. In two of the cases Edward Bliss Foote helped pay Bennett's legal costs and bail.

51. George E. Macdonald, *Fifty Years of Freethought* (New York: Truth Seeker Company, 1929; rpt. Arno Press, 1972), has biographical details about Bennett.

52. Besant, *Marriage* (1879), advertisement on reverse of cover page.

53. New York City, vol. 411, pp. 1-B, 100GG, R. G. Dun & Co. Collection.

54. The geographical proximity of men who became business partners is worth noting. Butts lived for over a decade at 36 Dey Street, next door to the Wakefield Earth Closet Company. Sharing the building at No. 36 with Butts was J. P. Dinsmore, who manufactured patent medicines and became an associate in the earth closet business. He was probably the person who hired Butts as an itinerant agent to sell patent medicines.

55. New York City, vol. 380, p. 196; vol. 185, p. 1008; vol. 373, p. 1530; vol. 381, pp. 200–A137; vol. 439, p. 543, R. G. Dun & Co. Collection. Also see Tebbel, *A History of Book Publishing*, 1:426–29. Jewett was so poor in 1876 that he was forced to write to "old abolition companions" begging for money: Jewett to Elizur Wright, 4 January 1876 (on letterhead of the Murray Hill Publishing Company), vol. 14, Elizur Wright Papers, Library of Congress.

56. Hollick's books were also published and distributed by Nafis & Cornish in New York and by a branch, Nafis, Cornish & Co., in St. Louis in 1846, and by a Philadelphia firm, the National Publishing Company, in 1846 and 1847. Later in the century the American News Company, a large venture specializing in buying proven bestsellers and reissuing them in cheap paperbound editions for a large market, published a 300th edition of *The Marriage Guide, The Origin of Life,* and *The Nerves and the Nervous.* Information about Strong can be found in New York City, vol. 31, p. 100-I, R. G. Dun & Co. Collection, which has credit reports from 1847 to 1884. Strong retired in 1866 but retained his bookstore, and his imprint continued to appear on publications. In 1876, leaving publishing completely, he was worth over $250,000, largely from real estate speculations on Manhattan and Long Island. His earnings from publishing, however, kept him solvent when real estate prices fell in the depression of 1877. His household is listed in the New York City Federal Census in 1850 (Ward 14, microfilm roll #551, p. 241). In 1850, Strong was married to a twenty-nine-year-old Englishwoman, Hester Strong, and they had three children, all born in New York,

aged six months and four and five years. The other members of the Strong household in 1850 were a twenty-seven-year-old Pennsylvania man, probably a clerk in Strong's store, a twenty-four-year-old English woman, maybe a relative of Hester's, and two German-born female domestic servants, aged eighteen and twenty.

57. Trall, *Pathology of the Reproductive Organs* (1862), p. 8. F. Barry Smith, "Sexuality in Britain, 1800–1900: Some Suggested Revisions," in *A Widening Sphere: Changing Roles of Victorian Women*, ed. Martha Vicinus (Bloomington: Indiana University Press, 1977), p. 190, notes that radical English publishers such as the Watsons, the Holyoakes, and Edward Truelove openly advertised and sold contraceptive devices with their books.

58. Information gathered from Hollick's newspaper, *People's Medical Journal*, 1854; and New York City, vol. 376, p. 259, R. G. Dun & Co. Collection.

59. See Cincinnati, vol. 79, p. 85, R. G. Dun & Co. Collection. Credit reporters cited Rulison from 1856 to 1861. See also Tebble, *A History of Book Publishing*, 1:489, on the Queen City Publishing House. Root probably published the first few editions himself, including a fourteenth edition issued from Saratoga Springs: R. K. Root & Co., in 1857. His lengthy medical guide contained sexual, anatomical, and marital advice intermixed with discussions of lung, heart, and liver ailments. Root openly listed in the table of contents that one chapter of the book dealt with "the prevention of conception," abortion, and methods involving "suppression of the semen." He advertised condoms, "French male powders for the prevention of conception (whose use is unclear), "Dr. Root's Female Wash," probably a douching solution, and a secret discovery that he would disclose for ten dollars.

60. Philadelphia, vol. 137, p. 527, R. G. Dun & Co. Collection.

61. See Zboray, "The Transportation Revolution," pp. 53–71.

62. Massachusetts [Suffolk Co., Boston] vol. 68, pp. 311; vol. 73, p. 185, R. G. Dun & Co. Collection. Credit reporters noted that Strong was connected with Cottrell "so far as the legitimate business of the store is concerned and supplies him with the goods he sells." By 1856, Cottrell had bought out Strong's interest and in the 1860s he manufactured blank books and diaries.

63. The R. G. Dun & Co. Credit Ledgers contain no information on Ranney. Information on his addresses comes from book imprints. Ranney also published sensational pamphlets such as *The Mysteries of Mormonism* for twenty-five cents and *Danger in the Dark: A Tale of Intrigue and Priest Craft*. Ranney is not an uncommon name, but others with than surname—perhaps relatives—turn up with minor connections to reproductive control. Henry S. Ranney was one of Charles Knowlton's friends in Ashfield and was made guardian of one Knowlton daughter when Charles died. An R. H. Ranney was treasurer of the Index Association in Boston in 1876, the organization opposing book censorship. The works of George Napheys were also published according to the correspondence system. The 1872 edition of his *The Physical Life of Woman: Advice to the Maiden, Wife, and Mother* was published in Philadelphia, New York, and Boston by George Maclean, in San Francisco by F. Dewing & Co., in Cincinnati and in Chicago by E. Hannaford & Co.

64. See Zboray, "The Transportation Revolution," p. 63.

65. Kellogg, *Plain Facts for Old and Young* (1880), p. iii. In general book publishing the use of agents declined in the late nineteenth century but continued to be important for books "of a very special character," according to book historian Tryon, "Book Distribution in Mid-Nineteenth Century America," p. 219.

66. Asa K. Butts, *Man: Scientific Supplement* (1880), advertisement for Besant, *The Law of Population*.

67. Gleason, *Talks to My Patients* (1870), advertisement in the back of the book. Anonymous, *Reproductive Control* (1855), p. 55. Byrn's *The Physiology of Marriage*

(1863) was sold for twenty-five cents by male agents peddling it door to door or at railway stations.

68. Cited in Tebbel, *A History of Book Publishing*, 1:542. To be a bestseller a book had to have a total sale equivalent of one percent of the population of the United States in the decade.

69. See Mott, *American Magazines*, 1:361. I believe that Ashton's pamphlet did see a large circulation. The stereotype plates for the pamphlet probably circulated, too, because references to works titled *The Book of Nature* turn up occasionally in the advertisements for cheap literature available from agents and through the mails in the 1880s and 1890s. Stereotype plates could be a lucrative asset in nineteenth-century publishing. Hurst & Co., publishers of cheap paperbound literature and "railroad fiction" in New York City, increased their value nearly sevenfold in thirteen years, with most of their assets being stereotype plates. New York City, vol. 443, pp. 927, 992, 985, 1000, R. G. Dun & Co. Collection.

70. American editions of Besant's *The Law of Population*, for example, were published in batches of ten thousand each in 1877. It was advertised as in its "third ten thousand" in 1886.

71. Edward Bliss Foote to Elizur Wright, 1887, Elizur Wright Papers, Library of Congress.

72. Clelia Duel Mosher, "Statistical Study of the Marriage of Forty-Seven Women," in "Study of the Physiology and Hygiene of Marriage . . . ," Clelia Duel Mosher Papers, Archives, Stanford University, Case 24. John Cowan, *The Science of a New Life* (New York: Cowan, 1874), p. 110.

Chapter Seven

1. David E. Matteson, Letter to the editor, *Medical and Surgical Reporter* (Philadelphia) 59 (1888): 759–60; Foote, *The Radical Remedy in Social Science* (1886), p. 100; F. Wallace Abbott, "Limitation of the Family," *Massachusetts Medical Journal* 10 (1890): 337–47.

2. No author, "The Fashionable Crime," *Michigan Medical News* 3 (1880): 341.

3. Augustus K. Gardner, "Physical Decline of American Women," *Knickerbocker* 55 (1860): 49.

4. See John T. Noonan, Jr., *Contraception: A History of Its Treatment by the Catholic Theologians and Canonists* (Cambridge: Harvard University Press, 1965), pp. 347–48, notes that condoms, used chiefly outside marriage, became an issue for Catholic theologians in the mid-seventeenth century, for whom they at first presented no difference in principle than withdrawal.

5. B. F. Finch and Hugh Green, *Contraception through the Ages* (Springfield, Ill.: Charles C. Thomas, 1963), pp. 50–57; Norman E. Himes, *Medical History of Contraception* (New York: Schocken, 1970; 1st pub. 1936), pp. 186–202.

6. Quoted in Linda Gordon, *Woman's Body, Woman's Right: A Social History of Birth Control in America* (New York: Grossman, 1976), p. 44.

7. Mary Lee Esty, manuscript draft of articles on Robert Dale Owen and Charles Knowlton, cites these advertisements. I am grateful to James Reed for initially providing me with copies, which I have subsequently seen in the Rare Book Room at Countway Library of Medicine.

8. Kellogg, *Plain Facts for Old and Young* (1880), p. 235, chap. on "marital excess."

9. Matteson, Letter to the editor, pp. 759–60. Matteson was a physician in Warsaw, New York. Clelia Duel Mosher, "Statistical Study of the Marriage of 47 Women,"

in "Study of the Physiology and Hygiene of Marriage with Some Considerations of the Birth Rate," Clelia Duel Mosher Papers, Archives, Stanford University.

10. Mary Hallock Foote to Helena Gilder, 21 December 1878, cited in Carl Degler, *At Odds: Women and the Family in America, from the Revolution to the Present* (New York: Oxford University Press, 1980), p. 224.

11. [Beach], *The Habits of a Well-Organized Married Life* (1867), p. 6.

12. See E. J. Dingwall, *Early Contraceptive Sheaths* (n.p., 1953), quoted in Finch and Green, *Contraception through the Ages*, pp. 51–52.

13. Dubois, *Marriage Physiologically Discussed* (1839), p. 92.

14. Becklard, *Physiological Mysteries* (1842), pp. 35–45.

15. Quoted in Himes, *Medical History of Contraception*, p. 190.

16. U.S., Congress, House, *Imports-Duties, 1867–1883 Inclusive*, Misc. Doc. 49, 1884. Category 701 was "Gold-Beaters' Skins and Molds." By the late 1860s importation of animal bladders, crude guts, and other integuments, in processed and unprocessed forms, had so increased that customs listed them in five separate categories. The *New England Business Directory* (Boston: Sampson, Davenport, 1871) listed seven different Boston dealers in "Gold Beaters."

17. Gardner, *Conjugal Sins* (1874), p. 109.

18. John H. Nelson, *The Druggists' Cost Book* (Cleveland, Ohio: n.p., 1879).

19. Anonymous, *Reproductive Control* (1855), p. 41.

20. Himes, *Medical History of Contraception*, p. 196.

21. Foote, *Medical Common Sense* (1864), p. 378.

22. Blount, *A Talk to Mothers*, p. 6.

23. Goodrich Rubber Company, *Rubber, Health, and Convenience* (Akron, Ohio: n.p., 1919), p. 2.

24. See James Reed, *From Private Vice to Public Virtue: The Birth Control Movement and American Society since 1830* (New York: Basic Books, 1978), p. 15.

25. In Owen, *Moral Physiology* (1858), p. 87.

26. Ashton, *The Book of Nature* (1861), pp. 40–41.

27. Owen, *Moral Physiology* (1831, 1st ed.), p. 67; Mauriceau [pseud.], *The Married Woman's Private Medical Companion* (1847), p. 144n.

28. Ashton, *The Book of Nature* (1861), p. 41.

29. Thomas F. Chapman, *Chapman's Old Established Cash Drug House* (New York: n.p., 186[?]), p. 37.

30. W. A. Week & Co., *Illustrated Year Book* (Chicago: n.p., 1872).

31. Root, *The People's Medical Lighthouse*, testimonial letters at the end.

32. George Drysdale, *Elements of Social Science* (London, 1854), cited in Himes, *Medical History of Contraception*, pp. 233–35, wrote that condoms led to impotence, but I have not seen similar criticisms in the U.S. literature.

33. Root, *The People's Medical Lighthouse* (1854), p. 390.

34. Dr. J. Ford Thompson, speaking before the Gynecological Society of Washington, D.C., in 1888, argued that there was no proof condoms were dangerous. His opinion was cited favorably in Thomas A. Pope, "Prevention of Conception," *Medical and Surgical Reporter* 58 (1888): 522–25. A Boulder, Colorado, physician recommended "skin coverings worn by men" as the best preventives: Charles Ambrook, Letter to the editor, *Michigan Medical News* 5 (1882): 36–37; F. R. Brunner, "Is Onanism Justifiable?" *Medical Register* 3 (1888): 78–79, argued that it was better to use a condom or "onanism" than abortion to limit reproduction.

35. Hollick, *The Marriage Guide* ([1852]), p. 32; Hollick, *A Popular Treatise on Venereal Diseases* (1852), p. 353, advertises condoms.

36. Besant, *The Law of Population* (1878), pp. 32–36; (1889), p. 30.

37. Rose Williams to Allettie Mosher, Dakota Territory, 27 September 1885, quoted

in Elizabeth Hampsten, *Read This Only to Yourself: The Private Writings of Midwestern Women, 1880–1910* (Bloomington: Indiana University Press, 1982), p. 104.

38. Anonymous, *Reproductive Control*, pp. 40–51.

39. Knowlton, *Fruits of Philosophy* (1832), pp. 59–60.

40. Becklard, *Physiological Mysteries*, p. 42; Dubois, *Marriage Physiologically Discussed*, p. 91.

41. Knowlton, *Fruits of Philosophy* (London, [c.1834]), "Promoting and Checking Conception." Hollick, *The Marriage Guide* (1860), chapter 7, lists the sponge along with other popular contraceptive methods that he did not particularly like.

42. Besant, *The Law of Population* (1878), p. 33.

43. Ashton, *The Book of Nature* (1861), p. 41.

44. McKesson & Robbins, *Prices Current*, p. 107; W. A. Weed & Co., *Illustrated Yearbook of Pharmaceutical Information* (Chicago: n.p., 1872), under "Druggists' Sundries, Fancy Goods."

45. Quoted in Besant, *The Law of Population* (1878), p. 34.

46. Lydia E. Pinkham to unnamed woman, 8 November 1880, vol. 537: 48, in Lydia E. Pinnkham Papers, Schlesinger Library. This notebook is the only evidence about customers in the Pinkham Papers.

47. H. K. Mulford Co., *Price List of Pharmaceutical and Biological Products* (Philadelphia, 1899), p. 165. Weeks & Potter, *Drug Catalogue* (Boston, 1880), offered vaginal tampons with five different drugs.

48. Besant, *The Law of Population* (1889), p. 31.

49. Clarence J. Gamble, "Sponges & Tampons with Household Spermicides," in *Manual of Contraceptive Practice*, ed. Mary S. Calderone (Baltimore: Williams & Wilkins, 1964), pp. 197–99.

50. Anna L. Southam, "Contraceptive Methods: Use, Safety, Effectiveness," in *Family Planning and Population Programs: A Review of World Developments*, ed. Bernard Berelson (Chicago: University of Chicago Press, 1966), chap. 29. Southam does not list her sources for the failure-rate estimates.

51. Marie E. Kopp, *Birth Control in Practice: Analysis of Ten Thousand Case Histories of the Birth Control Clinical Research Bureau* (New York: Robert E. McBride, 1933), p. 133.

52. Matteson, Letter to the editor, pp. 759–60; Besant, *The Law of Population* (1878), pp. 33–34.

53. Abbott, "Limitation of the Family," pp. 337–47.

54. See Himes, *Medical History of Contraception*, p. 288.

55. William A. Rothacker, "The Prevention of Conception," *Cincinnati Lancet and Clinic*, n.s. 10 (1883): 288.

56. See Himes, *Medical History of Contraception*, p. 319. See also Aletta Jacobs, "A Generation of Birth Control in Holland," pp. 85–94, in *International Aspects of Birth Control*, ed. Margaret Sanger (New York: n.p., 1925), pp. 85–94.

57. Himes, *Medical History of Contraception*, p. 321; also Himes's manuscript notes on Allbutt's *Population Essays* (1892), box 21, Norman E. Himes Archive, Countway Library, in which he notes Allbutt's detailed comments on contraceptive pessaries.

58. U.S. Department of Commerce, Patent and Trademark Office, Specification of Letters Patent No. 4729, 28 August 1846, John B. Beers, "The Wife's Protector."

59. U.S. Department of Commerce, Patent and Trademark Office, Pessaries Class 128, #9286X. The name and address of the inventor are missing on the Patent Office's copy, so there is no way to verify that Hull and Hall were the same man.

60. "Dr. Cameron's Patent Family Regulator or Wife's Protector," advertising circular, Walter Scott Tarbox Mss, Suffolk Co. Courthouse, Boston, Mass.; cited in Harper,

"Reaction to Family Limitation," pp. 40–41. The records of the Tarbox case were missing when I sought them.

61. Foote, *Medical Common Sense* (1864), p. 380.

62. Cited in Himes, *Medical History of Contraception*, bibliog. Foote advertised widely that he conducted his medical practice in both English and German.

63. M. Larmont and E. Bannister, *Medical Adviser and Marriage Guide* (1864), p. 89. That they offered abortions is suggested by their advertising notices promising private rooms so that their patients could retain anonymity. [Beach], *The Habits of a Well-Organized Married Life* (1867), p. 6, described a "Womb Guard" for five dollars.

64. Trall, *Sexual Physiology* (1867), p. 213.

65. J. Marion Sims, *Clinical Notes on Uterine Surgery* (New York: William Wood, 1873), pp. 277–79. For other emphases on women's wearing contraceptive devices secretly, see William A. Rothacker, "The Prevention of Conception," *Cincinnati Lancet and Clinic*, n.s. 10 (1883): 288.

66. Ashton, *The Book of Nature* (1861), p. 38.

67. Linda Gordon, *Woman's Body, Woman's Right: A Social History of Birth Control in America* (New York: Grossman, 1976), p. 179.

68. Lee Rainwater, *And the Poor Get Children: Sex, Contraception, and Family Planning in the Working Class* (Chicago: Quadrangle, 1960), p. 157.

69. Address of the President, *Transactions of the Illinois State Medical Society* 37 (1887): 38.

70. Emily Blackwell to Elizabeth Blackwell, 14 July 1856, and Elizabeth to Emily, 11 August 1856. Elizabeth Blackwell was not even certain how to insert the pessary her sister sent. The "frizzled" comment is Elizabeth to Emily, 27 November 1854, Blackwell Family Papers, Library of Congress.

71. William Goodell, *Lessons in Gynecology* (Philadelphia: D. G. Brinton, 1879), illustrates the importance given to uterine displacements for he devotes four of the twenty-nine lessons to the use of pessaries in treating uterine malpositions.

72. McKesson & Robbins, *Prices Current* (1872); W. H. Shieffelin & Co., *Catalogue* (New York, 1871). S. M. Meek, "An Essay on Female Diseases and the Use of the Pessary in Uterine Displacements," *Southern Medical and Surgical Journal* 2 (1838): 25–36.

73. Miles F. Porter, "The Prevention of Conception," *Cincinnati Lancet and Clinic*, n.s. 10 (1883): 355. Porter was inspired to describe his two cases by Rothacker, "The Prevention of Conception."

74. About 20 percent of all women seen by gynecologists today have a slightly malpositioned uterus. This condition is rarely considered to be of anything more than statistical interest, but a century ago gynecologists considered such asymmetrical uterine positions a serious problem to be treated with pessaries, tampons, or sponges, and drugs. See also Kistner, *Gynecology, Principles and Practice*, 2d ed. (Chicago: Year Book Medical Publishers, 1971), p. 213. Goodell, *Lessons*, p. 126; F. S. Edwards, "New Intra-Uterine Pessary," *American Medical Times* (New York) 8 (1862): 8. George Granville Bantok, *On the Use and Abuse of Pessaries* (Edinburgh: n.p., 1878), defends the use of intrauterine pessaries to treat flexions.

75. Meigs, *Woman: Her Diseases and Remedies* (1854), pp. 204–5.

76. See Rothacker, "The Prevention of Conception," p. 289. John Peel and Malcolm Potts, *Textbook of Contraceptive Practice* (Cambridge: Cambridge University Press, 1969), p. 128, quotes Dr. C. F. Routh speaking to the British Medical Association.

77. Goodell, *Lessons in Gynecology*, p. 124; Walter Channing, "Effects of Criminal Abortion," *Boston Medical and Surgical Journal* 60 (1859): 134–42.

78. Ely Van De Warker, *Philadelphia Medical News* (21 February 1885), cited in

George Tiemann & Co., *Catalogue of Surgical Instruments* (New York: n.p., 1889), p. 496.

79. Tiemann, *Catalogue* (1889), pp. 494–96.

80. Nelson, *The Druggists' Cost Book.*

81. Prices are listed in: McKesson & Robbins, *Catalogue* (1879, 1883); Morrison, Plummer & Co., *The Druggist's Ready Reference* (Chicago: n.p., 1880); Van Schaack, Stevenson & Reid, *Catalogue* (Chicago, 1874); George C. Goodwin & Co., *Trade Catalogue* (Boston: n.p., 1880); Lazell, Marsh & Gardiner, *Catalogue of Prices Current* (New York: 1882); Weeks & Potter, *Drug Catalogue* (Boston, 1879).

82. U.S. Department of Commerce, Patent and Trademark Office, Patent #544,091, 6 August 1895, George J. Gladman. Also the patents granted 22 May 1894, Samuel Whitney Hinckley's "Uterus Battery." This might have worked as an IUD with a rigid stem "to rest in the neck of the womb" and a button body "to rest against the mouth of the womb and hold the device in position."

83. "Criminal Abortion," *Druggists' Circular* 2 (1858): 139.

84. Goodwin, *Trade Catalogue* (1874); Fuller and Fuller Drug Co., *Trade Catalogue* (1885).

85. Goodwin, *Trade Catalogue* (1880), p. 195.

86. Van de Warker, "Abortion from Medication. Part II of The Detection of Criminal Abortion," *Journal of the Gynecological Society of Boston* 5 (1871): 229–45; pt. 1, vol. 4 (1871): 292–305; Van de Warker, "The Criminal Use of Proprietary or Advertised Nostrums," *New York Medical Journal* 17 (1873): 23–35.

87. "The Action of the Federal Commission against Abortifacient Preparations," *Journal of Contraception*, 4 (1939): 198–99.

88. Edward Shorter, *A Short History of Women's Bodies* (New York: Basic Books, 1982), pp. 184–88, discusses abortifacients.

89. Van de Warker, "The Criminal Use of Proprietary . . . Nostrums," p. 23.

90. "Instruments of a Notorious Abortionist," *American Medical Times* 6 (1863): 34.

91. Frank Harris, *My Life and Loves*, p. 117, cited in John S. Haller and Robin M. Haller, *The Physician and Sexuality in Victorian America* (Urbana: University of Illinois Press, 1974).

92. See George W. Gay, "A Case of Criminal Abortion," *Boston Medical and Surgical Journal*, n.s. 9 (1872): 151–52; "The Causation of Sudden Death during the Induction of Criminal Abortion," *Journal of the Gynaecological Society of Boston* 2 (1870): 283–89; "Dr. Baxter," "Case of Abortion Procured by Violence," *American Medical Recorder* 8 (1825): 461–62. See the editors' discussion of the use of an elastic catheter for abortion in the *Medical and Surgical Reporter* 36 (1877): 164, and the query and answer, p. 190. Also, J. C. Gleason, "A Medico-Legal Case of Abortion," *Boston Medical and Surgical Journal* 101 (1879): 185–92.

93. Quoted in "The Liability of Physicians to a False Charge of Abortion," *Journal of the Gynaecological Society of Boston* 4 (1871): 348–49. See also L. Bolton Bangs, "Some of the Effects of 'Withdrawal'," *Transactions of the New York Academy of Medicine*, 2d ser. 9 (1893): 122.

94. James S. Whitmire, "Criminal Abortion," *Chicago Medical Journal* 31 (1874): 385–93.

95. *New York Herald Tribune*, 15 June 1841, and *Day's Doings*, June 1870.

96. W. M. Smith, Letter to the editor, "The Prevalence of Abortion," *Medical and Surgical Reporter* 33 (1875): 259.

97. Elizabeth Blackwell to Emily Blackwell, 1851–56, Blackwell Family Papers; Ishbel Ross, *Child of Destiny* (New York: n.p., 1944), p. 87, attributes Blackwell's decision to become a doctor to her abhorrence of abortion.

98. Gleason, *Talks to My Patients* (1870), p. 161.

99. James Dabney McCabe, *Lights and Shadows of New York Life* (Philadelphia: National Publishing Co., 1872; facsimile rpt., London: Deutsch, 1971), pp. 618–30, "Child Murder," discusses European-trained midwives operating lying-in institutes.

100. *Royal Commission on the Decline of the Birth-Rate and on the Mortality of Infants in New South Wales, Report*, vol. 1 (Sydney, Australia: William Applegate Gullick, Government Printer, 1904).

101. Grindle, *The Female Sexual System* (1864), pp. 165–66.

102. Quoted in John Paull Harper, "'Be Fruitful and Multiply': The Reaction to Family Limitation in Nineteenth-Century America" (Ph.D. diss., Columbia University, 1975), p. 55.

103. Grindle, *The Female Sexual System*, notice pasted in the back of the copy in the Rare Book Room at Countway Library.

104. Harper, "Reaction to Family Limitation," pp. 124–25, 168.

105. The sources differ on the details of Restell's life. Seymour Mandelbaum's entry on her in *Notable American Women* is the most authoritative to date. There is some information in [no author], *Wonderful Trial of Caroline Lohman, Alias Restell*, 3d ed. (New York: National Police Gazette [1847]), editorial, "Madame Restell and Some of Her Dupes," [New York] *Medical and Surgical Reporter* (1846), pp. 158–65, and James Dabney McCabe, *Lights and Shadows of New York Life* (London: Deutsch, 1971; facsimile of 1st ed., Philadelphia: National Publishing Co., 1872), pp. 618–30.

106. James C. Mohr, *Abortion in America: The Origins and Evolution of National Policy* (New York: Oxford University Press, 1978), p. 48. See also the article "Restell the Female Abortionist," *Police Gazette*, 21 February 1846.

107. Thomas Low Nichols, *The Lady in Black: A Story of New York Life, Morals, and Manners* (New York: The Author, 1844), p. 15.

108. McCabe, *Lights and Shadows*, p. 620. Also "Card from Madame Restell," *New York Times*, 21 August and 17 December 1856.

109. Mauriceau [pseud.], *The Married Woman's Private Medical Companion*, pp. 104–54.

110. Ledger of Arrests 1872–84, vol. 2, New York Society for the Suppression of Vice Collection, Library of Congress.

111. Foote, *Medical Common Sense* (1864), advertisement in back.

112. Editorial, *Herald of Health*, 1878, p. 35, advertising that Russell Thacher Trall's *Sexual Physiology* was sold by respectable booksellers, by itinerant agents, and by mail order.

113. [Beach] *The Habits of a Well-Organized Life*, p. 9.

114. Birth control authors illustrate how commonly peddler/agents were associated with the contraceptive and abortive trade. In mid century both Harmon Knox Root and Edward Bliss Foote warned their readers that they were contravening custom and that the condoms advertised in their books were not available from agents or peddlers.

115. See Paul J. Uselding, "Peddling in the Antebellum Economy: Precursors of Mass Marketing or a Start in Life," *American Journal of Economics and Sociology* 34 (1975): 55–66. And see Linn Jones, "General Operation of the Prophylactic and Contraceptive Law in Oregon," *Journal of Contraception* 2 (1937): 195–97; Harry Levin, "Commercial Distribution of Contraceptives in Developing Countries: Past, Present, and Future," *Demography* 5 (1968): 941–46; and Levin, "Making and Marketing Birth Control Products," in *Family Planning Programs: An International Study*, ed. Bernard Berelson (New York: Basic Books, 1969).

116. Ledger of Arrests, 1871–72, New York Society for the Suppression of Vice Collection.

117. New York [state], vol. 257, p. 3342, R. G. Dun & Co. Collection.

118. Ledger of Arrests, 1872–84, New York Society for the Supression of Vice Collection.

119. Ledger of Arrests, New York Society for the Suppression of Vice Collection.

120. *Imports & Exports, U.S., 1867–1883*, list of "Fancy Articles," pp. 156–68. In druggists' catalogues condoms were likely to be advertised in the section under "druggists sundries and fancy goods" if they were not buried in the "miscellaneous goods" section.

121. *American Druggists' Circular and Chemical Gazette* 1 (1857), advertising section.

122. Scrapbook of Unpublishable Advertisements, E. C. Allen Co. Papers, Historical Collections, Baker Library, Harvard Graduate School of Business Administration.

123. Information on Albert H. Essex and his Essex Manufacturing Company comes from advertisements and drawings in *American Druggists' Circular* 4 (1860): 352 and 8 (1864): 3; also from Goodwin & Co., *Trade Catalogues* (1885), p. 174. They are not in the R. G. Dun & Co. Credit Ledgers. Information on Henry G. Norton comes from New York City, vol. 194, March 1860–December 1874, R. G. Dun & Co. Credit Ledgers. Norton took one partner in the rubber-goods business in 1860, a twenty-nine-year-old, unmarried man who had been his principal salesman.

124. New York City, vol. 435, October 1869–November 1881, R. G. Dun & Co. Collection.

125. Massachusetts, vol. 80, reports March 1870–March 1882, R. G. Dun & Co. Collection. See also Goodwin & Co. *Trade Catalogue* (1865, 1874, 1880, 1885).

126. Trall, *Sexual Physiology* (1895), p. 261.

127. McKesson & Robbins, *Catalogue* (New York: 1872, 1879, 1883).

128. Records of Downing's Drug Store, Hanover, N.H., 1883–84; Historical Collections, Baker Library: bills for goods sent to L. B. Downing from wholesalers.

129. Chapman, *Chapman's Old Established Drug House*, claimed to be the oldest drughouse on Broadway, established in 1840 by Thomas F. Chapman, M.D. He advertised his goods in the 1860s in a forty-page circular.

130. See Vincent J. Cirillo, "Edward Bliss Foote: Pioneer American Advocate of Birth Control," *Bulletin of the History of Medicine* 47 (1973): 471–79. The Footes' third son, Alfred Herschel, born in 1871, died young.

131. See Samuel P. Putnam, *Four Hundred Years of Freethought* (New York: Truth Seeker Company, 1894).

132. Foote, *Medical Common Sense* (1859 and 1864), frontis. portraits.

133. Foote, *Medical Common Sense* (1858 and 1859). The refusal to provide advice and the criticism of methods came in a subsection enticingly titled "The Prevention of Conception," in the larger section "Essays for Married People Only." The "Card to Married People," p. 258, offered to provide advice by letter.

134. Putnam, *Four Hundred Years of Freethought*.

135. Foote, *Medical Common Sense* (1864), pp. 378–80.

136. Foote, *Plain Home Talk* (1873), pp. 876–78. Foote sometimes advertised the pamphlet by the title *Information for Married People*, but later as *Words in Pearl for the Married* because it was set in small "pearl" type for easy mailing.

137. Other titles in the pamphlet series included *Physiological Marriage* and *Continence: Foote's Reply to the Alphites*. No copies of *Words in Pearl* are known to be extant, so the advice contained in the pamphlet can be inferred only from Foote's other writings.

138. Edward Bliss Foote to Elizur Wright, 1 August 1876, Elizur Wright Papers, vol. 14, Library of Congress.

139. Anthony Comstock, *Frauds Exposed: or, How the People Are Deceived and*

Robbed and Youth Corrupted (n.p., 1880; Montclair, N.J.: Patterson Smith Reprint Series in Criminology, 1969), p. 427.

140. New York City, vol. 444, p. 1062, "Murray Hill Publishing Co., 22 Dec. 1875," R. G. Dun & Co. Collection. In the early 1870s Foote opened the company with an authorized capital of about $20,000—a company in name only, for little of the stock was owned by anyone but Foote. Murray Hill's printing was done by Trow & Sons, the largest printing establishment in New York. The Murray Hill Publishing Company also published Edward Bond Foote's *Radical Remedy in Social Science* and Annie Besant's *Marriage as It Is, Was and Should Be* (New York: Murray Hill Publishing Co., 1885).

141. New York [State], vol. 559, p. 147; New York City, vol. 381, p. 28, and vol. 381 (28 November 1877), R. G. Dun & Co. Collection. Credit reporters estimated that Foote's house at 110 Lexington Avenue was worth about $30,000. Foote reportedly "keeps a fair bank account" and was generally "believed [to be] well off."

142. Foote, *Book of Medical Sense and Nonsense* (New York: Murray Hill Publishing Co., August 1887), advertisement in the back.

143. Ledger of Arrests, vol. 2, pp. 63–64, records on E. B. Foote, New York Society for the Suppression of Vice Collection.

144. Foote, *Book of Medical Sense and Nonsense*, advertisements for "the irrigator" described as "a cyclinder of firm, soft rubber, providing for married women a more efficient means for vaginal cleansing than ordinary vaginal pipes."

145. Neil Harris, "The Drama of Consumer Desire," in *Cultural Excursions: Marketing Appetites and Cultural Tastes in Modern America* (Chicago: University of Chicago Press, 1990), pp. 174–97.

146. Richard Brown, *Knowledge Is Power: The Diffusion of Information in Early America, 1700–1865* (New York: Oxford University Press, 1989), p. 271.

Chapter Eight

1. Several studies see connections between the nineteenth-century opposition to abortion and contraception: Michael Grossberg, *Governing the Hearth: Law and the Family in Nineteenth-Century America* (Chapel Hill: University of North Carolina Press, 1985), pp. 155–95; Linda Gordon, *Woman's Body, Woman's Right: A Social History of Birth Control in America* (New York: Grossman, 1976), chaps. 1, 3, 6; James Reed, *From Private Vice to Public Virtue: The Birth Control Movement and American Society since 1830* (New York: Basic Books, 1978), pp. 34–45. For extended analyses of one or the other oppositional impulse see: James C. Mohr, *Abortion in America: The Origins and Evolution of National Policy, 1800–1900* (New York: Oxford University Press, 1978); John Paull Harper, "'Be Fruitful and Multiply': The Reaction to Family Limitation in Nineteenth-Century America" (Ph.D. diss., Columbia University, 1975); David J. Pivar, *Purity Crusade, Sexual Morality, and Social Control; 1868–1900* (Westport, Conn.: Greenwood Press, 1973); Carroll Smith-Rosenberg, "The Abortion Movement and the AMA, 1850–1880," in her *Disorderly Conduct: Visions of Gender in Victorian America* (New York: A. Knopf, 1985).

2. The legal history of abortion is in Lawrence Lader, *Abortion* (New York: Bobbs-Merrill, 1966). Also: Kristin Luker, *Abortion and the Politics of Motherhood* (Berkeley: University of California Press, 1984), p. 15.

3. See Harper, "'Be Fruitful and Multiply,'" chap. 2.

4. See Smith-Rosenberg, "The Abortion Movement," p. 219.

5. See Grossberg, *Governing the Hearth*, pp. 178–79.

6. Storer, *On Criminal Abortion in America* (1860), p. 54. Smith-Rosenberg, "The

Abortion Movement," pp. 217–44, and Grossberg, *Governing the Hearth*, pp. 159–75, discuss court cases.

7. "Brief of 281 American Historians as Amici Curiae Supporting Appellees," in *Webster V. Reproductive Health Services*, U.S. Supreme Ct., October term, 1988, p. 343n.

8. Roger Lane, *Violent Death in the City: Suicide, Accident, and Murder in Nineteenth-Century Philadelphia* (Cambridge: Harvard University Press, 1979), cited in Catherine Clinton, *The Plantation Mistress: Woman's World in the Old South* (New York: Pantheon, 1982), p. 291n6.

9. Mohr, *Abortion in America*, identifies three phases to the antiabortion laws, the third, from the 1860s to the 1880s, the most stringent. Harper, "'Be Fruitful and Multiply,'" isolates the 1840s as the decade of hardening against abortion. Smith-Rosenberg, *Disorderly Conduct*, discusses the 1840s to 1880s as a single period.

10. See Hugh S. Pomeroy, *The Ethics of Marriage* (New York: Funk & Wagnalls, 1888), app.

11. *U.S. Statutes at Large*, vol.17, 42d Cong., sess. 3, chap.259, 260, 1873.

12. *U.S. Statutes at Large*, vol.17. See also: Carol Flora Brooks, "The Early History of the Anti-Contraception Laws in Massachusetts and Connecticut," *American Quarterly* 18 (1966): 6.

13. See Mary Ware Dennett, *Birth Control Laws: Shall We Keep Them, Change Them, or Abolish Them?* (New York: Da Capo Press, 1970; Copyright 1926), pp. 10–15; C. Thomas Dienes, *Law, Politics, and Birth Control* (Urbana: University of Illinois Press, 1972), p. 40.

14. See Harriette M. Dilla, "Appendix No. 1," pp. 268–70, in Dennett, *Birth Control Laws*. Dennett, pp. 10–28, notes that in no other country was contraceptive information classified with "penalized indecency."

15. Dennett, *Birth Control Laws*, pp. 41–42, notes that Comstock expressed this opinion in a 1915 letter to the Birth Control League. State laws were reviewed in the hearings on the Cummins-Vaile bill in the 1930s: U.S. Congress, Senate, Committee on the Judiciary, *Birth Control*, including "A Digest of State Legislation Relating to the Prevention of Conception," Hearings before a Subcommittee of the Senate Committee on the Judiciary on S.4582, 71st Cong., 3d sess., 13, 14 February 1931.

16. U.S. Code *Annotations*, 18, sec. 1461. Other cases summarized in this section include rulings that the public record does not have to record the exact language or titles of obscene works, that postmarks are presumptive proof of deposit in the U.S. mail, and that it is immaterial to show that obscene passages are common to other literature.

17. *Griswold v. Connecticut*, 381 U.S. 485–86.

18. Quoted in Carl E. Schnieder and Maris A. Vinovskis, *The Law and Politics of Abortion* (Lexington, Mass.: Lexington Books, D. C. Heath, 1980), p. xv.

19. Charles Gallaudet Trumbell, *Anthony Comstock, Fighter* (New York: Fleming H. Revell, 1913). For another sympathetic account see Richard Christian Johnson, "Anthony Comstock: Reform, Vice, and the American Way" (Ph.D. diss., University of Wisconsin, 1973).

20. See Heywood Broun and Margaret Leech, *Anthony Comstock: Roundsman of the Lord* (New York: Albert & Charles Boni, 1927); Trumbell, *Anthony Comstock*, pp. 23, 48.

21. Trumbull, *Anthony Comstock*, chap. 3.

22. See Paul Boyer, *Purity in Print: The Vice-Society Movement and Book Censorship in America* (New York: Scribner, 1968), p. 6.

23. See Dennett, *Birth Control Laws*, p. 31.

24. See Broun and Leech, *Anthony Comstock*, p. 73.

25. Neither Boyer, *Purity in Print*, nor Comstock's biographies mention women as members of the early vice societies. They were, of course, involved in the broader "social purity" reform movement. See Pivar, *Purity Crusade*.

26. See Boyer, *Purity in Print*, p. 7; Johnson, "Anthony Comstock," p. 58.

27. Pivar, *Purity Crusade*, app. A.

28. See Pivar, *Purity Crusade*; Gordon, *Woman's Body*, on the feminists involved in social-purity concerns; also George M. Fredrickson, *The Inner Civil War: Northern Intellectuals and the Crisis of the Union* (New York; Harpur & Row, 1965).

29. Grossberg, *Governing the Hearth*, details numerous examples of this impulse.

30. Leach, *True Love and Perfect Union*, chap. 4, "Sexual Ownership and the Rationalization of Sexual Desire," and p. 84; see also Gordon, *Woman's Body*, chap. 5.

31. *Congressional Globe*, 18 February 1873.

32. Broun and Leech, *Anthony Comstock*, p. 135.

33. *Congressional Globe*, 20 February 1873, p. 1525. Senator Allen G. Thurman, a Democrat from Ohio, also objected to voting on the bill without having a chance to read it. *Congressional Globe*, 18 February, p. 1437. Senator Hannibal Hamlin objected to the fact that Senator William A. Buckingham, Republican from Connecticut, tinkered with the wording of the bill on the Senate floor after it had been reported by committee and without everyone's being able to look at the exact wording.

34. *Appendix to the Congressional Globe*, 1 March 1873, 42d Cong., 3d sess., p. 168.

35. *Congressional Globe*, 20 February 1873, p. 1525.

36. Dienes, *Law, Politics, and Birth Control*, pp. 42–47. Dienes's discussion of Knowlton's legal problems is riddled with errors, so this, too, may be inaccurate.

37. We have especially little evidence about how the state Comstock laws were passed. There was next to no publicity, no public hearings, and little legislative debate. Historians have had little success tracking down actual links between the social purity forces and state legislators. Brooks, "The Early History of the Anti-Contraception Laws," p. 6, could not find specific links that she believes existed; Smith-Rosenberg, "The Abortion Movement," also believes in but does not detail the ways the AMA committees worked with state legislatures to pass the Comstock laws. Broun and Leech, *Anthony Comstock*, p. 148, describe Comstock's threatening to expose as a dealer in imported rubber goods a New York State assemblyman who opposed the state obscenity law. Comstock got the support he wanted.

38. Hugh Lenox Hodge, *An Introductory Lecture to a Course on Obstetrics* (1839); Hodge, *Foeticide, or Criminal Abortion: A Lecture* (Philadelphia: Lindsay & Blakiston, 1869). Hodge republished it with amendments after the 1854–55 session at the University of Pennsylvania. He published a fourth edition in 1872. The quotation is from Harper, "'Be Fruitful and Multiply,'" p. 30.

39. D. Humphreys Storer, "Two Frequent Causes of Uterine Disease," *Journal of the Gynecological Society of Boston* 6 (1872): 194–203.

40. Storer, "Two Frequent Causes," p. 198.

41. Editorial Notes, *Journal of the Gynecological Society of Boston* 6 (1872): 393–400.

42. Clarke's views are quoted, disapprovingly, in the untitled report of a meeting of the Gynecological Society of Boston, *Journal of the Gynecological Society of Boston* 4 (June 1871): 350–51.

43. The role and motivations of the AMA physicians in this crusade against abortion have received much scrutiny from historians. Smith-Rosenberg, "The Abortion Movement," is critical; Mohr, *Abortion in America*, is more sympathetic.

44. Le Boutillier to Horatio R. Storer, St. Anthony, Minnesota Territory, 28 March 1857, Rare Book Room, Countway Library.

45. The correspondence is in the Rare Book Room at Countway Library. The others on the committee were: Hugh L. Hodge; the sixty-three-year-old Troy, New York physician Thomas Windeatt Blatchford; Edward H. Barton from South Carolina; A. Lopez from Arizona; the thirty-nine-year-old Charles A. Pope, professor of anatomy and physiology at St. Louis University; William Henry Brisbane of Wisconsin; and young Alexander Jenkins Semmes, professor of physiology at Savannah Medical College. Storer persuaded Charles A. Pope (1818–70) of St. Louis to present the report with him to the AMA: Pope to Storer, St. Louis, 24 March 1857 and 18 March 1859.

46. Hodge to Storer, 30 March 185[9?], Philadelphia; Samuel David Gross to Storer, 19 March 1859, Philadelphia.

47. [Storer], "Report on Criminal Abortion," *Transactions of the AMA* 12 (1859): 75–78, and "Criminal Abortion," *North American Medico-Chirurgical Review* 3 (1859): 64–72. Storer, "Cases Illustrative of Criminal Abortion," *American Journal of Medical Science*, n.s. 37 (1859): 314–18.

48. Storer to Massachusetts Medical Society, Boston, 27 January 1859, and Report of Committee to Investigate the Controversy with the AMA, Boston, 5 October 1870, Countway Library.

49. James Clarke White to Storer, 15 February 1865; Storer to [?] Ropes, Newport, R.I., 2 January 1877, discusses Storer's financial responsibility for the *Journal.*

50. [Storer], "The Criminality and Physical Evils of Forced Abortions," *American Medical Association Transactions* 16 (1866): "Origin of the Essay" [Intro.].

51. Ely Van de Warker, "The Detection of Criminal Abortion, Part I," *Journal of the Gynecological Society of Boston* 4 (May 1871): 292–305; "Part II" 5 (October 1871): 229–45; "Part III" 5 (1871): 350–70; and "The Criminal Use of Proprietary or Advertised Nostrums," *New York Medical Journal* 17 (1873): 23–35.

52. See Ronald T. Takaki, *Iron Cages: Race and Culture in Nineteenth-Century America* (New York: Knopf, 1979), chap. 2.

53. See Kristin Luker, *Abortion and the Politics of Motherhood* (Berkeley and Los Angeles: University of California Press, 1984), p. 32.

54. Broun and Leech, *Anthony Comstock*, p. 26.

55. Storer, "The Criminality and Physical Evils," pp. 726, 732, 734.

56. Horatio R. Storer, "Contributions to Obstetric Jurisprudence: The Abetment of Criminal Abortion by Medical Men," *New York Medical Journal* 3 (1866): 424; Storer, *Why Not?* pref. to 2d ed..

57. Storer to Burt Green Wilder, 18 December 1872, quoted in William Leach, *True Love and Perfect Union: The Feminist Reform of Sex and Society*, 2d ed. (Middletown, Conn.: Wesleyan University Press, 1989), p. 95. Leach uses this, incorrectly I believe, as an example of Storer's arguing for the importance of sexual intercourse in marriage. I believe that Storer aimed rather to denigrate coitus interruptus, coitus reservatus, and the use of condoms.

58. William Goodell, "Clinical Lecture on Conjugal Onanism and Kindred Sins," *Philadelphia Medical Times* 2 (1892): 161–63; Goodell, "The Dangers and the Duty of the Hour," *Maryland State Medical and Chirurgical Faculty Transactions* (1881): 71–87. Augustus K. Gardner, "Physical Decline of American Women," *Knickerbocker* 55 (1860): 37–52, and Gardner, *Conjugal Sins*; S. G. Moses, "Marital Masturbation," [St.Louis] *Courier of Medicine* 8 (1882): 168–73. Joseph M. Toner, "Abortion in a Medical and Moral Aspect," [1861?], box 97 Medical Writings, Toner Collection, Library of Congress, argued that there was no difference in morality between contraception and abortion. E. M. Buckingham, "Criminal Abortion," *Cincinnati Lancet and Observer*, n.s.10 (1867): 139–43, severely criticized married women who used preventives.

59. Smith-Rosenberg, "The Abortion Movement," p. 235. Mohr, *Abortion in America*, pp. 179–89, analyzes the antiabortion campaign in terms of feminism and antifeminism.

60. Quoted in Broun and Leech, *Anthony Comstock*, p. 134.

61. See Martin Henry Blatt, *Free Love and Anarchism: The Biography of Ezra Heywood* (Urbana: University of Illinois Press, 1989), pp. 71–74.

62. Broun and Leech, *Anthony Comstock*, pp. 67, 133, note without further comment his love of Maggie and the child's adoption. Comstock's particular vendetta against abortionists, especially such women as Madame Restell, is also noteworthy. The first thing he did after arriving in Washington to introduce his bill before Congress was to write entrapping letters to ten abortionists.

63. See George K. Behlmer, "Deadly Motherhood: Infanticide and Medical Opinion in Mid-Victorian England," *Journal of History of Medicine* 34 (1979): 404.

64. Editorial, [D. G. Brinton] "The Limitation of Births," [Philadelphia] *Medical and Surgical Reporter* 44 (1881): 382–84.

65. Review of *Is It I? A Book for Every Man, Leavenworth Medical Herald* 1 (1868): 269–70.

66. E. P. C. [Edmund Potts Christian], "The Abortion Case," *Ohio Medical and Surgical Journal* 10 (1858): 212–18.

67. William Pawson Chunn, M.D., "The Prevention of Conception: Its Practicability and Justifiability," *Maryland Medical Journal* 32 (1894–95): 340–43. Henry I. Bowditch, a member of the Committee on Criminal Abortion for the Suffolk, Massachusetts, District Medical Society, also objected in 1857 to Storer's denunciation of contraception. Bowditch later signed a testimonial in favor of Zeus Franklin, who was prosecuted under the Comstock laws for his *Illustrated Medical Counseller, or Marriage Guide* (New York: Mutual Benefit Publishing Co., 1883).

68. The quotation is from O. E. Herrick, "Specialties," *Michigan Medical News* 4 (1881): 40–41. Herrick argued that douching would eliminate abortion, and gave detailed instructions in his article and probably to his patients. He invented a "galvanic uterine supporter" and various types of trusses. Herrick, "Abortion and Its Lesson," *Michigan Medical News* 5 (1882): 7–10; Herrick, "Prevention of Conception," *Michigan Medical News* 5 (1882): 59–60, and U.S. Patent Office, Pat. #222399, 9 December 1879, "Galvanic Uterine Supporter" to Orris E. Herrick.

69. Editorial, *Michigan Medical News* 4 (1881): 34–35.

70. Charles Ambrook, Letter to the editor, *Michigan Medical News* 5 (1882): 36–37. See also Phoebe French, M.D., "Prevention of Conception," *Michigan Medical News*, 5 (1882): 71–72. C. Willston, Letter to the editor, *Michigan Medical News*, 5 (1882):23–24, quoted Goodell's rebuttal of Herrick's arguments that birth control was safe.

71. James T. Whittaker, "Experiments in Reproduction," *Transactions of the Ohio Medical Society* (Cincinnati, Ohio) 26 (1871): 229–40.

72. F. R. Brunner, M.D., "Is Onanism Justifiable?" *Medical Register* (Philadelphia) 3 (1888): 78–79.

73. Thomas A. Pope, "Prevention of Conception," *Medical and Surgical Reporter* (Philadelphia) 59 (1888): 522–25. W. R. D. Blackwood, "The Prevention of Conception," *Medical and Surgical Reporter* 59 (1888): 394–96, opposed abortion but supported birth control especially if a woman's life was in danger or if the parents were "diseased." L. Huber of Rocky Ford, Colorado, "The Prevention of Conception," *Medical and Surgical Reporter* 59 (1888): 580–81, wrote that doctors faced "a continuous demand" for information on reproductive control "no matter what ranks or classes of society he serves." He approved giving help.

74. "The Prevention of Conception," *Cincinnati Medical News*, n.s. 19 (1890): 303–

8. This was a report of the Proceedings of the Detroit Medical and Literary Association.

75. For examples of doctors giving information to their patients see Letter to editor from X.Y.Z., [Philadelphia] *Medical and Surgical Reporter* 59 (1888): 600, and Letter to editor from David Matteson, [Philadelphia] *Medical and Surgical Reporter* 59 (1888): 759–60.

76. Edwin M. Hale, *On the Homeopathic Treatment of Abortion,* cited in Mohr, *Abortion in America,* p. 173. See Harper, "'Be Fruitful and Multiply,'" p. 173, for a discussion of Hale's ambivalence.

77. Hale, *A Systematic Treatise on Abortion* (Chicago: C. S. Halsey, 1866), pp. 30–34. By 1878, Hale's *The Medical, Surgical, and Hygienic Treatment of Diseases of Women* (New York, 1878) contained a detailed discussion of the use of sulphate of zinc, tannin, and warm water as spermicides, the French pessary and cap, and cold water injections for birth control, cited in Wilson Yates, "Birth Control Literature and the Medical Profession in Nineteenth Century America," *Journal of the History of Medicine and Allied Sciences* 32 (January 1976): 52.

78. See Sears, *The Sex Radicals,* pp. 34–41.

79. The founding of the Liberal League and its role in fighting Comstockery is discussed in Martin Henry Blatt, *Free Love and Anarchism: The Biography of Ezra Heywood* (Urbana: University of Illinois Press, 1989); Sears, *The Sex Radicals,* pp. 36–41; and George E. MacDonald, *Fifty Years of Freethought,* vols. 1 and 2 (New York: Truth Seeker Company, 1929; rpt. Arno Press, 1972).

80. Leach, *True Love and Perfect Union,* pp. 137–38.

81. Quoted in Blatt, *Free Love and Anarchism,* p. 100.

82. Angela Heywood, *The Word,* January 1888, p. 2. Quoted in Blatt, *Free Love and Anarchism,* p. 146.

83. See Blatt, *Free Love and Anarchism,* p. 109. John Spurlock, "The Free Love Network in America, 1850–60," *Journal of Social History,* Summer 1988: 767, does not address free-love attitudes toward reproductive control except to note that free lovers believed in less frequent sexual intercourse.

84. See Ellen Carol DuBois, ed., *Elizabeth Cady Stanton: Susan B. Anthony: Correspondence, Writings, Speeches* (New York: Schocken, 1981), pp. 95, 56, 66. Stanton spoke much earlier than this about a woman's need for sexual control of her body, but generally in private correspondence with women friends.

85. Lee Rainwater, *And the Poor Get Children* (Chicago: Quadrangle, 1960).

86. Anthony Comstock, *Frauds Exposed; or, How the People Are Deceived and Robbed, and Youth Corrupted* (1880), rpt. ser. in Criminology (Montclair, N.J.: Patterson Smith, 1969), p. 435. Dennett, *Birth Control Laws,* p. 47, found no official record of U.S. indictments for people who broke the Comstock laws by giving contraceptive information. Dennett's appendix lists twenty-three well-known cases before 1926, three of which involved Sanger and three involved Emma Goldman. There were many violations but few prosecutions. In Comstock's own record of his "victories," in *Frauds Exposed,* only 5 percent were contraceptive cases. DeRobigne Bennett, *Anthony Comstock: His Career of Cruelty and Crime* (New York: Liberal and Scientific Publishing House, 1878), cited twenty-seven prosecutions, five of which were for contraceptive information.

87. Scrapbook of Unpublishable Advertisements, E. C. Allen Company Papers, Historical Collections, Baker Library, Harvard Graduate School of Business Administration. The Allen Company also rejected advertisements promising cures for impotence and venereal diseases, for erotic photographs and books, marriage manuals, women's beauty aids—mainly arsenic preparations—and "fancy French playing cards."

88. Edward Bliss Foote, *Book of Medical Sense and Nonsense* (New York: Murray Hill Publishing Company, 1887), one of Foote's dime pamphlets.

89. Foote, *The Radical Remedy* (1886), used this latter wording.

90. Morrison, Plummer & Co., *The Druggist's Ready Reference* (Chicago, 1880).

91. George C. Goodwin & Co., *Trade Catalogue* (Boston: New England Patent Medicine Warehouse, 1865, 1874, 1876, 1885); A. A. Mellier, *Mellier's Illustrated Catalogue and Prices Current* (St. Louis: n.p., 1877), listed four types of "capotes/cundrums" under Druggists' Sundries; Van Schaack, Stevenson, & Reid, *Catalogue* (Chicago: n.p., 1874), listed ten kinds of condoms in their index. The H. K. Mulford Company, *Price List of Pharmaceutical and Biological Products* (Philadelphia: n.p., 1899), continued to advertise emmenagogues and vaginal tampons. E. L. Patch Co., *Price List* (Stoneham, Mass.: n.p., 1891, 1897, 1900), continued to offer emmenagogues and ergot preparations. Vaginal and "intrauterine" suppositories made of spermicides continued to be sold for twenty-five cents per dozen: Luyties Homeopathic Pharmacy Co., *Catalogue and Price List* (St. Louis: n.p., 1896).

92. Foote, *The Radical Remedy*, p. 99n.

93. Trall, *Sexual Physiology* (1895). Trall, *Sexual Physiology* (London, 1922), was also expurgated.

94. Foote, *Plain Home Talk* (1891), pp. 876–80.

95. Hollick, *The Nerves and the Nervous* (New York: American News Company, n.d. [copyright 1873]), advertisements in the back. Hollick, *The Matron's Manual of Midwifery* (1849), p. 468, has the unexpurgated ad. For other ads mentioning the prevention of conception see Hollick, *Male Generative Organs* ([1862]), p. 450; Hollick, *The Diseases of Woman*, 49th ed. (New York: T. W. Strong, n.d.), p. 269; Hollick, *A Popular Treatise on Venereal Diseases* ([1852]), p. 353.

96. Foote, *The Radical Remedy* (1886), p. 59. After the suicide of George Napheys in 1876, his publisher kept his *The Physical Life of Woman* in print, including most of his contraceptive advice, although that advice changed. In 1870, Napheys warned against douching as harmful to women and withdrawal as harmful to men. An 1891 edition omitted that discussion altogether: *The Physical Life of Woman* (1870), pp. 97–99; compare with the new stereotype edition put out in Philadelphia in 1891.

97. B. G. Jefferis and J. L. Nichols, *Search Lights on Health* . . . (1904), pp. 240–45, 246–47. Another example of the genre in the late nineteenth century is Anonymous, *The Cottage Physician for Individual and Family Use* . . . , with an introduction by George W. Post (Springfield, Mass.: King-Richardson, 1898), which contained nothing on contraception other than a vaguely worded hint against practicing the rhythm method (p. 568) and a paragraph descrying abortion. Elsewhere in the book, however, the author provided recipes for making "regulating pills" (p. 531), quoted John Cowan's *The Science of a New Life* about the timing and effectiveness of the safe period, and advised breastfeeding a child for nine to twelve months. On the page immediately following their warning about quacks' "preventive remedies," the authors advertised a vaginal syringe, and injections of salt water, borax, or vinegar "for cleanliness."

98. Zeus Franklin, *Illustrated Science of Man and Medical Counsellor* . . . (New York: Mutual Benefit Publishing and Manufacturing Company, c. 1883). The table of contents ended with p. 127 but the book contained 322 pages. The latter portion of the book is numbered erratically with pages bound in incorrect sequence. Six pages (203–8) discuss the limitation of offspring, but are not listed anywhere so that a reader could locate them efficiently. The advice was a jumble of quotes from Knowlton, Owen, Hollick, Malthus, and John Stuart Mill with little of practical value. The engravings are almost identical to plates in Ashton's *The Book of Nature* (1861).

99. See Sears, *The Sex Radicals*, p. 262.

100. Chicago, vol. 27, p. 339, vol. 31, p. 76, R. G. Dun & Co. Collection. The credit reports on Baldwin lasted from 1862 to 1873.

101. Ohio [Lucas County], vol. 119, pp. 503–11; Iowa [Pottawattamie Co.], vol. 44, pp. 120F, 120Z4, R. G. Dun & Co. Collection.

102. Besant, *Marriage: As It Was* (N.P.: People's Popular Liberal Library, n.d.), has an advertisement on the back cover for G. S. Baldwin, 1998 Clark Street, Chicago, listing a dozen titles of books available, including the birth control literature and "French playing cards." The R. G. Dun & Co. entries make mention of his notions.

103. Foote, *The Radical Remedy*. In a 1912 case, *Ackley v. U.S.*, the defendant was found guilty even though the article might have had a legitimate use and might not have worked to prevent conception.

104. David M. Kennedy, *Birth Control in America: The Career of Margaret Sanger* (New Haven: Yale University Press, 1970), chap. 8, argues that from the beginning of Margaret Sanger's career until 1930 no court construed the federal statutes with regard to contraception. Kennedy believes that the state laws had more effect than the federal statute. Kennedy points out that the federal and state laws confused the legal atmosphere. Kennedy also argues that by 1935 there was a "free flow of contraceptive literature and materials through the U.S. mails" for physicians.

105. Herrick, "Abortion and Its Lesson," pp. 7–10.

106. Broun and Leech, *Anthony Comstock*, p. 62.

107. Foote, *The Radical Remedy*, pp. 85–90, citing the Comstock laws.

108. See Luker, *Abortion and the Politics of Motherhood*, p. 97.

109. Margaret Sanger, *My Fight for Birth Control* (Fairview Park, Elmsford, N.Y.: Maxwell Reprint Co., Division of Maxwell Scientific International, 1931), p. 58.

Epilogue

1. See David M. Kennedy, *Birth Control in America: The Career of Margaret Sanger* (New Haven: Yale University Press, 1970), chap. 1.

2. See Ellen Chesler, *Woman of Valor: Margaret Sanger and the Birth Control Movement in America* (New York: Simon & Schuster, 1992), p. 63.

3. Margaret Sanger, *My Fight for Birth Control* (Fairview Park, Elmsford, N.Y.: Maxwell Reprint Co., Division of Maxwell Scientific International, 1931), pp. 49, 53.

4. Carl Degler, *At Odds: Women and the Family in America from the Revolution to the Present* (New York: Oxford University Press, 1980), p. 209, argues that there would not have been such a substantial decline unless both husband and wife cooperated closely with each other. The century's fertility decline, to Degler, is "a concrete measure of the closeness of intrafamilial relations." He sees the declining white birth rate as a measure of married couples' mutuality and cooperation as much as it was a reflection of female assertiveness. Other historians who hold with the cooperation model include: Nancy Grey Osterud, *Bonds of Community: The Lives of Farm Women in Nineteenth-Century New York* (Ithaca: Cornell University Press, 1991), pp. 74–75; James Reed, *From Private Vice to Public Virtue: The Birth Control Movement and American Society since 1830* (New York: Basic Books, 1978), p. 30; Karen Lystra, *Searching the Heart: Women, Men, and Romantic Love in Nineteenth-Century America* (New York: Oxford University Press, 1989), pp. 77–84. Joan M. Jensen, *Loosening the Bonds: Mid-Atlantic Farm Women, 1750–1850* (New Haven: Yale University Press, 1986), p. 28, believes that nineteenth-century men and women most likely cooperated to restrict fertility, probably using "abstention" in the later years of marriage. John Mack Faragher, *Sugar Creek: Life on the Illinois Prairie* (New Haven: Yale University

Press, 1986), p. 206, believes that family limitation was achieved beginning in the 1840s by active cooperation between husband and wife, "by abstinence from sexual intercourse, or by abortion." J. A. Banks and Olive Banks, *Feminism and Family Planning in Victorian England* (New York: Schocken, 1964), pp. 125–26, note that middle class British husbands in the 1860s and 1870s must have cooperated with wives to limit family size but not necessarily out of concern for their wives. Doctors on both sides of the birth control issue saw little evidence that husbands were concerned about a wife's health; instead the costs of children concerned men.

The marriages of the feminist-abolitionists studied by Blanche Hersh came close, she believed, to being "partnerships of equality," with husbands and wives cooperating to limit the size of their families (they were well below the average for their era). Hersh believes that they accomplished this limitation by sexual abstinence and withdrawal. Like the well-known Angelina Grimke and Theodore Weld, a number of other antebellum antislavery reformers, "sexual perfectionists," were eager to restrain all their appetites and plagued with guilt about stirrings of sexual passion. Blanche Glassman Hersh, *The Slavery of Sex: Feminist-Abolitionists in America* (Urbana: University of Illinois Press, 1978), pp. 209–11, 244–48.

James C. Mohr, "Abortion in America," in *Women's America: Refocusing the Past,* ed. Linda K. Kerber and Jane De Hart Mathews (New York: Oxford University Press, 1982), pp. 179–89, argues that mid-nineteenth century couples arrived at mutually acceptable fertility priorities that "mooted in advance the question of which one was more responsible for the abortion decision."

5. Storer, *Why Not?* (1867), preface; Storer, "The Still Prevalent Ignorance of Differential Diagnosis," *Journal of the Gynaecological Society of Boston* 5 (1871): 136–39, an exchange between Storer and several other physicians about husbands who forced wives to have abortions. See also Phoebe French, "Prevention of Conception," *Michigan Medical News* 5 (1882): 71–72. French, a physician in Big Rapids, Michigan, said that many of her patients came wanting birth control because their husbands wanted no more children. The Catholic church in France in the nineteenth century heard numerous confessions from women fearful that they were sinning because their husbands insisted on practicing coitus interruptus to prevent pregnancy. See John T. Noonan, Jr., *Contraception: A History of Its Treatment by the Catholic Theologians and Canonists* (Cambridge: Harvard University Press, 1965), pp. 400–402.

6. William Goodell, "The Dangers and the Duty of the Hour," *Maryland State Medical and Chirurgical Faculty Transactions,* 83d Session (1881): 71–87. Besant's remark is cited in Arthur H. Nethercot, *The First Five Lives of Annie Besant* (Chicago: University of Chicago Press, 1960). Elaine Tyler May, in *Great Expectations: Marriage and Divorce in Post-Victorian America* (Chicago: University of Chicago Press, 1980), p. 90, found no divorce cases in 1880s Los Angeles in which the conflict was the wife's refusal to have children, but four in the 1920s. Such actions, because they were against the husband's will, were regarded as sufficient grounds for divorce. Wally Seccombe, "Starting to Stop: Working-Class Fertility Decline in Britain," *Past and Present* 126 (1990): 155, 161, 173–75, provides documentation of the conflicts created in working-class British marriages in the early twentieth century over who would practice what birth control methods. Although he cites a few instances of cooperation, the bulk of his evidence concerns the ways that "avoiding intercourse . . . wracked marital relations with tension, bitterness and alienation."

7. James Ashton, *The Book of Nature* (1861), p. 38.

8. Mary P. Ryan, *Cradle of the Middle Class: The Family in Oneida Co., New York, 1790–1865* (Cambridge: Cambridge University Press, 1981), p. 180.

9. James E. Free, Letter to the editor, [Philadelphia] *Medical and Surgical Re-*

porter (1888): 726. A patient with four children asked Free, "Now doctor, what shall we do to keep from having babies?" His only advice was to stop permitting her husband "sexual indulgence."

10. [Ralph Glover], *Owen's Moral Physiology* (1846), p. 104. Emphases added. Root, *The People's Medical Lighthouse* (1854), pp. 342–44, 390–93.

11. Kristin Luker, *Abortion and the Politics of Motherhood* (Berkeley: University of California Press, 1984), p. 97.

Selected Bibliography
of Literature of Reproductive Control Advice, 1830–1880

Alcott, William Andrus. *The Physiology of Marriage.* 27th thousand. Boston: Dinsmoor and Company, 1866; reprint ed., New York: Arno Press and The New York Times, 1972. [First published anonymously in 1855.]

Anonymous. *Aristotle's Compleat Masterpiece, in Three Parts: Displaying the Secrets of Nature in the Generation of Man.* . . . n.p., n.d.

Anonymous. "By an American Physician." *Reproductive Control; or, A Rational Guide to Matrimonial Happiness. The Right and Duty of Parents to Limit the Number of Their Offspring According to Their Circumstances Demonstrated. A Brief Account of All Known Modes of Preventing Conception.* . . . Cincinnati: n.p., 1855, in *Birth Control in Nineteenth-Century America.* New York: Arno Press Reprint, 1974.

Ashton, James. *The Book of Nature, Containing Information for Young People Who Think of Getting Married, on the Philosophy of Procreation and Sexual Intercourse; Showing How to Prevent Conception and to Avoid Child-Bearing. Also, Rules for Management during Labor and Child-Birth.* New York: Published by Wallis and Ashton, 1861. [Copyright 1859, Benjamin H. Day, So. District of New York. NUC lists 4 other editions: New York: Ashton, 1860; New York: Brother Jonathan Office, 1865; New York: Brother Jonathan Office, 1870; and New York: n.p., [19??].]

[Beach, Madames, Putney and Company.] *The Habits of a Well-Organized Married Life. By a Married Woman.* [New York: n.p.], 1867.

Becklard, Eugene. *Know Thyself: The Physiologist; or, Sexual Physiology Revealed.* Boston: Bela Marsh, 1859; reprint ed. in *Sex for the Common Man: Nineteenth Century Marriage Manuals.* New York: Arno Press Reprint, 1974.

——. *Physiological Mysteries and Revelations in Love, Courtship, and Marriage: An Infallible Guide-Book for Married and Single Persons in Matters of the Utmost Importance to the Human Race.* . . . Translated by Philip M. Howard from the 3d Paris ed. New York: n.p., 1842.

With revisions and additions of the 6th Paris ed. New York: Holland & Glover, 1844.

With a supplement from Canfield's Sexual Physiology, on Coquetry, Venereal Madness, Marriage, etc. Philadelphia: John B. Perry, 1845. [The supplement, pp. 179–92, has nothing on birth control, reproduction, or douching.]

Bergeret, L. F. E. *The Preventive Obstacle; or, Conjugal Onanism; The Dangers and Inconveniences to the Individual, to the Family, and to Society of Frauds in the Accomplishment of the Generative Functions.* Translated by P. De Marmon from the 3d French ed. New York: Turner & Mignard, Printers & Publishers, 1870.

Besant, Annie. *The Law of Population: Its Consequences and Its Bearing upon Human Conduct and Morals.* 2d ten thousand ed. Author's American ed. from the 25th thousand English ed. New York: Asa K. Butts, Radical Freethought Publishing House, 1878.

3d ten thousand. Author's American ed. from the 35th thousand English ed. Bound Brook, N.J.: A. K. Butts, 1886.

New York: Henry Sumner, Publisher, 1889. [Copyright to Henry Sumner.]

34th thousand New American ed. from 35th thousand English ed. Valley Falls, Kans.: Fair Play Publishing Co., [1889].

San Francisco: n.p., 1893. ["The Readers' Library. Issued Monthly. No. 8. Subscription, $3.00 per year. Entered at San Francisco P.O. as 2d class mail matter." 73 pp., no copyright.]

——. *Marriage: As It Was, As It Is, & As It Should Be.* New York: A. K. Butts, 1879.

The People's Popular Liberal Library, No. 13 (N.p.: Published for the trade, n.d. [c. 1880s?]).

Blount, Anna Ellsworth. *A Talk to Mothers by a Doctor Who Is Herself a Mother.* N.p., n.d.

Byrn, Marcus Lafayette. *The Al-ma-kan-tur Circle and Calendar of Love. Containing Revelations and Mysteries, Facts and New Discoveries Never Before Offered to the Public, Being of the Greatest Importance to Both Married and Single Persons of Both Sexes.* New York: Published by the author, 1857. Contains "The Married Woman's Private Medical Cabinet."

——. *The Physiology of Marriage and the Philosophy of Generation, Being a Confidential and Reliable Friend for Medical and Scientific Consultation on Subjects of Vital Importance.* Contained in *Useful Knowledge; or, The Repository of Valuable Information.* N.p.: M. Lafayette Byrn, 1872.

Canfield, Russel. *Practical Physiology, Being a Synopsis of Lectures on Sexual Physiology, Including Intermarriage, Organization, Intercourse, and Their General and Particular Phenomena.* Philadelphia: J. Wixon & Co., 1850. [Copyright 1849, E. District Pa.]

[Cooke, Nicholas Francis]. *Satan in Society. A Plea for Social Purity. A Discussion of the True Rights of Woman, Marital and Social.* Chicago: Lakeside Series, issued monthly by subscription, 1893.

——. *Satan in Society. By a Physician.* Cincinnati: C. F. Vent; Baltimore, Md.: Edward F. Hovey, 1876; reprint ed., New York: Arno Press, 1974.

Cowan, John. *The Science of a New Life*. New York: Cowan & Co., Publishers, 1874; reprint ed., New York: Source Book Press, 1970.

Dixon, Edward H. *Woman and Her Diseases, from the Cradle to the Grave. Adapted Exclusively to Her Instructions in the Physiology of Her System and All the Diseases of Her Critical Periods. With An Appendix on the Propriety of Limiting the Increase of Family*. 10th ed. New York: A. Ranney, 1857.

Dubois, Jean. *Marriage Physiologically Discussed*. 2d ed. Translated by William Greenfield from the French. New York: Printed for the Booksellers, 1839; reprint ed. in *Sex for the Common Man: Nineteenth Century Marriage Manuals*. New York: Arno Press Reprint, 1974.

Duffey, Eliza B. *The Relations of the Sexes*. New York: Wood & Holbrook, 1876.

——. *What Women Should Know. A Woman's Book About Women, Containing Practical Information for Wives and Mothers*. Philadelphia: J. M. Stoddart & Co., 1873; reprint ed., New York: Arno Press Reprint, 1973.

Dunne, P. C., and A. F. Derbois. *The Young Married Lady's Private Medical Guide*. 4th ed. Translated with notes from the French by F. Harrison Doane. [Boston]: Published for the Proprietor, 1854.

Evans, Elizabeth Edson Gibson. *The Abuse of Maternity*. Philadelphia: J. B. Lippincott, 1875.

Foote, Edward Bliss. *Medical Common Sense Applied to the Causes, Prevention, and Cure of Chronic Diseases and Unhappiness in Marriage*. Philadelphia: Duane Rulison, 1859.
   Rev. and enl. ed. New York: Published by the author, 1864.

——. *Plain Home Talk about the Human System, and Habits of Men and Women, the Causes and Prevention of Disease, Our Sexual Relations and Social Natures, Embracing Medical Common Sense Applied to Causes, Prevention, and Cure of Chronic Diseases, the Natural Relations of Men and Women to Each Other, Society, Love, Marriage, Parentage, etc*. New York: Murray Hill Publishing Co., 1873, 1876, 1891.

Foote, Edward Bond. *The Radical Remedy in Social Science; or, Borning Better Babies through Regulating Reproduction by Controlling Conception. An Earnest Essay on Pressing Problems*. New York: Murray Hill Publishing Co., 1886.

Gardner, Augustus K. *The Causes and Curative Treatment of Sterility with a Preliminary Statement of the Physiology of Generation*. New York: DeWitt & Davenport, Publishers, 1856.

——. *Conjugal Sins against the Laws of Life and Health and Their Effects upon the Father, Mother, and Child*. Rev. ed. New York: Hurst & Co., Publishers, 1874.

Gleason, R[achel] B. *Talks to My Patients, Hints on Getting Well and Keeping Well*. New York: Wood & Holbrook, 1870.

[Glover, Ralph]. *Owen's Moral Physiology; or, A Brief and Plain Treatise on the Population Question, with Alterations and Additions by Ralph Glover, M.D.* New York: R. Glover, 2 Ann St., 1846.

——. *Owen's Moral Physiology . . . by Glover*. 3d ed., with alterations and additions. New York: R. Glover, 1847.

Grindle, H. D. *The Female Sexual System; or, The Ladies' Medical Guide*. New York: n.p., 1864.

Hall, Alfred G. *The Mother's Own Book and Practical Guide to Health; Being a Collection of Necessary and Useful Information. Designed for Females Only.* Rochester, N.Y.: n.p., 1843.

——. *Womanhood: Causes of Its Premature Decline, Respectfully Illustrated. Being a Review of the Changes and Derangements of the Female Constitution, a Safe and Faithful Guide to Mothers during Gestation, before and after Confinement, with Medical Advice of the Most Salutary and Important Nature to All Females. Also Sixty Vegetable and Domestic Recipes with Directions.* 2d ed., rev. and enl. Rochester, N.Y.: E. Shepard, 1845.

Hersey, Thomas. *The Midwife's Practical Directory; or, Woman's Confidential Friend; Comprising Extensive Remarks on the Various Casualties and Forms of Disease.* . . . Columbus, O.: Clapp, Gillett & Co., 1834.

——. *The Midwife's Practical Directory; or, Woman's Confidential Friend: Comprising Remarks on the Various Casualties and Forms of Disease Preceding, Attending and Following the Period of Gestation, with An Appendix.* 2d ed., enl. and improved. Baltimore: Published by the author, 1836. [Copyright 1835.]

Hollick, Frederick. *The Male Generative Organs in Health & Disease.* . . . 300th ed., rev. and with additions. New York: Excelsior Publishing House, [1884]. [Copyright 1849, 1872, 1884.]

——. *The Marriage Guide: or, Natural History of Generation; a Private Instructor for Married Persons and Those About to Marry, Both Male and Female: in Every Thing Concerning the Physiology and Relations of the Sexual System and the Production or Prevention of Offspring—Including All the New Discoveries Never Before Given in the English Language.* New York: T. W. Strong [1852].
    200th ed., enl. and improved. New York: T. W. Strong, 1860.

——. *The Matron's Manual of Midwifery and the Diseases of Women during Pregnancy and in Child Bed.* 47th ed., much impr. New York: T. W. Strong. [Copyright 1848.]
    New York: T. W. Strong, 1849.

——. *The Origin of Life: A Popular Treatise on the Philosophy and Physiology of Reproduction in Plants and Animals, including the details of human generation with a full description of the male and female organs.* 10th ed. New York: Nafis & Cornish; St. Louis: Nafis, Cornish & Co., 1846. [Copyright 1845.] I have not been able to locate editions before this tenth edition. The book appeared in 1845 and went through ten editions that year.
    17th ed. New York: Nafis & Cornish; St. Louis: Nafis, Cornish & Co., 1847.

——. *The Origin of Life and Process of Reproduction in Plants and Animals.* New York: American News Company Subscription Book Dept. [copyright 1878.]

——. *A Popular Treatise on Venereal Diseases, in All Their Forms.* . . . New York: T. W. Strong, 1852.

Jefferis, B[enjamin] G[rant], and J[ames] L[awrence] Nichols. *Light & Life or the Royal Road to Health and Happiness.* Charlotte, N.C.: C. H. Robinson & Co., 1903.

——. *Search Lights on Health, Light on Dark Corners. A Complete Sexual Science and Guide to Purity and Physical Manhood, Advice to Maiden, Wife and Mother. Love, Courtship, and Marriage.* Parkersburg, W.Va.: White Publishing Co., 1904. [Copyright 1894, J. L. Nichols, Washington, D.C.]

Kellogg, John Harvey. *Plain Facts for Old and Young*. Burlington, Ia.: Segner & Condit, 1880.

[Knowlton, Charles.] *Fruits of Philosophy; or, The Private Companion of Young Married People. By a Physician*. New York: n.p., 1832. [Copyright 1831 in District of Rhode Island. 63pp. This is the first edition.]

Fruits of Philosophy; or, The Private Companion of Young Married People. By Charles Knowlton, M.D. 2d ed., with additions. Boston: n.p. 1833. [Copyright 1833 by Charles Knowlton, Massachusetts. 158pp. Internal evidence suggests that the publisher was Abner Kneeland at the office of the *Boston Investigator*.]

Fruits of Philosophy; or, The Private Companion of Adult People. 4th ed., with additions. Philadelphia: F. P. Rogers, Printer, 1839. [Copyright: Eastern District of Pennsylvania. Introduction is dated 4 September 1839.]

Fruits of Philosophy; or, The Private Companion of Adult People. 10th ed., with additions. Boston: Published by subscription. 1877. [128pp.]

Fruits of Philosophy: An Essay on the Population Question. By Charles Bradlaugh and Mrs. Annie Besant. 3d new ed. with notes. London: Publishing Company, [1877]. [Copyright: "Entered according to an act of Congress 1877 by Excelsior Importing Co., Covington, Ky." Library of Congress. Himes believes that this was printed in the United States. I found no such company in Covington, Ky., in the R. G. Dun Credit & Company Collection.]

Fruits of Philosophy: An Essay on the Population Question by Charles Knowlton, M.D., New York. New ed. Chicago: Printed for the proprietors by W. H. M. Smythe, [ca. 1878]. [No prefaces; Drysdale footnotes are omitted; no appendix. Same birth control advice as 2d ed. Otherwise apparently based on the Bradlaugh-Besant edition. 32pp.]

Fruits of Philosophy: A Treatise on the Population Question by Charles Bradlaugh and Mrs. Annie Besant. Chicago, Ill.: G. E. Wilson, Publisher. n.d. [The publisher's address is given as 312 State Street. The Library of Congress incorrectly dates it 1870. The *National Union Catalogue* dates it "18—."]

Fruits of Philosophy: A Treatise on the Population Question by Charles Bradlaugh and Mrs. Annie Besant. Chicago: The Wilson pub. co., [1897]. [Wilson's address is given as 413 Wabash Ave. "Wilson's library of fiction, v. 4, no. 3. Annual subscription $3.00. Issued monthly. 10 March 1987." 87pp. The publisher's preface refers to him as "Dr. Knowles."]

Fruits of Philosophy: A Treatise on the Population Question. Edited by Charles Bradlaugh and Annie Besant. New York: Published by The Truth Seeker Company, 33 Clinton Place, n.d. [After 1877.]

Fruits of Philosophy: A Treatise on the Population Question by Charles Bradlaugh and Annie Besant. 2d new ed. New York. International Pub. Co., n.d. ["Bequest of Mrs. Henry Draper, 1915." 58pp.]

Fruits of Philosophy: A Treatise on the Population Question. By Charles Bradlaugh and Mrs. Annie Besant. [Chicago]: International Publishing Company, [189?]. [Bookplate: "Albert Thorndike, Esq., 17 October 1917. 58pp.]

Fruits of Philosophy. N.p., n.d. [47pp. and 1 page of appendix. Has Drysdale footnotes.]

Fruits of Philosophy; or, The Private Companion of Adult People, by Charles Knowlton, M.D. Edited with Introduction by Norman E. Himes, with medical emendations by Robert Latou Dickinson. Mt. Vernon, N.Y.: Peter Pauper Press, 1937.

British Editions

Fruits of Philosophy; or, The Private Companion of Young Married People. 2d ed. reprinted from the American. London: J. Watson. [c.1834.] [Watson's address is listed as 18 Commercial Place, City Road, Finsbury. Adjoining the Mechanics Hall of Science. 40pp. Contains Appendix, n.d. from the *Boston Investigator*. Identical to 2d U.S. ed.]

Fruits of Philosophy; or, The Private Companion of Young Married Couples. London: James Watson, [1841?]. [Watson's address is 3, Queen's Head Passage, Paternoster Row. 40pp. No *Boston Investigator* appendix.]

Fruits of Philosophy: An Essay on the Population Question. 2d new ed., with notes, 90th thousand. London: Freethought Publishing Company, n.d. [Publisher's address is 28, Stonecutter. Copyright is to Annie Besant and Charles Bradlaugh. It was published after the 1877 Bradlaugh-Besant prosecution. Contains medical notes by "G.R."—George Drysdale.]

Fruits of Philosophy. Knowlton. N.p., n.d. [Penciled on verso of front cover is "Published by William Robinson, Newcastle-upon-Tyne, c. 1878–79." Bound with English pamphlets and broadsides from the Malthusian League, Bancroft Library, University of California, Berkeley.]

Fruits of Philosophy: An Essay on the Population Question by Charles Knowlton, M.D. Newcastle-on-Tyne: W. Robinson, Bookseller, 1886. [Robinson's address is 18 Book Market.]

Fruits of Philosophy: An Essay on the Population Question. Newcastle-on-Tyne: J. B. Barnes, Printer and Stationer, 1889. [Address is Black Boy Yard, Groat Market.]

Editions of Fruits I Refer to in the Book but Have Not Actually Seen:

Fruits of Philosophy; or, The Private Companion of Young Married People. 3d ed., with additions. Boston: n.p., 1834. [190pp. "almost a miniature book." "Preface by the publisher" signed "Ashfield 1834." Copyright names Knowlton.]

Fruits of Philosophy. . . . San Francisco: The Reader's Library, 1891. 87pp.

Fruits of Philosophy. . . . Chicago: Stein Co., n.d. 94pp.

Fruits of Philosophy. . . . 2d new ed. Chicago: Garden City Pub. Co., [187?]. 22pp.

Larmont, Martin, and Co. *Medical Adviser and Marriage Guide Representing All the Diseases of the Genital Organs of the Male and Female, with the Most Complete and Practical Works on the Physiological Mysteries and Revelations of the Male and Female Systems, with the Latest Experiments and Discoveries in Reproduction Illustrated Anatomically and Fully with Plates, Everything Pertaining to the Male and Female Genital Systems. . . .* New York: Published by E. Warner, 1864. [The NUC lists five editions, the first in 1854, a 20th in 1856, a 30th in 1859, one in 1864, and one copyrighted in 1870.]

Mauriceau, A. M. [pseud. for Ann Trow Lohman, Charles Lohman, and/or Joseph Trow]. *The Married Woman's Private Medical Companion, Embracing the Treatment of Menstruation or Monthly Turns during Their Stoppage, Irregularity, or Entire Suppression, PREGNANCY and How IT MAY BE DETERMINED: With the Treatment of Its Various Diseases. Discovery to PREVENT PREGNANCY: Its Great and Important Necessity Where Malformation or Inability Exists to Give Birth. To Prevent Miscarriage or Abortion When Proper and Necessary. TO EFFECT MISCARRIAGE When Attended with Entire Safety. CAUSES AND MODE OF CURE OF BARRENNESS OR STERILITY.* New York: n.p., 1847; reprint ed., New York: Arno Press, 1974. [Himes lists six editions from 1847–1885; *NUC* lists nine editions, 1847–1860. The 1847 copyright is to Joseph Trow, brother of Ann Trow Lohman, whose alias was "Madame Restell." Joseph Trow published an 1885 ed. in New York.]

Meigs, Carles DeLucena. *Woman: Her Diseases and Remedies: A Series of Letters to His Class.* 3d ed., rev. and enl. Philadelphia: Blanchard and Lea, 1854.

Mysteries of Man; or, Esoteric Anthropology. . . . New York: Davies, 1862. [This widely circulating work was probably a pirated version of Nichols's work.]

Napheys, George H. *The Physical Life of Woman: Advice to the Maiden, Wife, and Mother.* Philadelphia: George Maclean, 1869.
> Philadelphia, New York, Boston: George Maclean; Cincinnati: E. W. Hannaford & Co., 1870.
> Philadelphia, New York, Boston: George Maclean; San Francisco: F. Dewing & Co.; Cincinnati and Chicago: E. Hannaford & Co., 1872.
> New stereotype ed. rewritten, enl. rev. Philadelphia: J. G. Fergus & Co., 1873.
> New stereotype ed. with final corrections of the author. Philadelphia: David McKay, 1891.

——. *The Transmission of Life, Counsels on the Nature and Hygiene of the Masculine Function.* 3d ed. Philadelphia: J. G. Fergus & Co., 1871.

Nichols, Thomas Low. *Esoteric Anthropology: A Comprehensive and Confidential Treatise on the Structure, Functions, Passional Attractions and Perversions, True and False Physical and Social Conditions, and the Most Intimate Relations of Men and Women.* Port Chester, N.Y.: By the author, 1853.
> Cincinnati: Watkin, Nicholson (c.1853). [Copyrighted 1853, So. District New York but cites the N.Y. Stereotype Association, 201 William St.]
> [New York]: Published by the author at his Reform Book Store, 1854. [Nichols identified himself as "Principal (sic) of American Hydropathic Institute.]
> 15th ed. London: W. Foulsham & Co., n.d. [c.1916–17?].

Editions I Have Not Seen
> New York: Published by T. L. Nichols, 1855.
> *Mysteries of Man: or, Esoteric Anthropology.* New York: Davies & Kent, 1861.

Noyes, John Humphrey. *Male Continence.* Oneida, N.Y.: Published by the Oneida Community, Office of the Oneida Circular, 1872. [Noyes published a pamphlet, *The Bible Argument*, in 1848, of which one chapter was titled "Male Continence." This chapter he later published as a separate pamphlet.]

Owen, Robert Dale. *Moral Physiology; or, A Brief and Plain Treatise on the Population Question.* New York: Published by Wright and Owen, 359 Broome St., 1831. [This is probably a first edition, although it is not catalogued as such at Countway Library. It has 72 pages, 19-1/2 cm. in size with autograph notes signed "E. B. Scott; R. C. Larrabee, and S. Herves."]

    3d ed. New York: Wright & Owen, 359 Broome St., 1831. [This photoduplicated copy of the 3d ed. is at Widener Library. It has penciled marginal notes by Norman E. Himes, who donated the copy to the library.]

    8th ed. New York: G. W. & A. J. Matsell, 1835.

    10th ed., with Notes by the Publisher, embodying all Modern discoveries, illustrated by anatomical & physiological engravings. New York: G. Vale, 1858. [This important edition of Owen's tract was published in October 1858 in New York by Gilbert Vale. It may have been a reprint of an edition Vale published in 1839. At some point, Vale added text, engravings, and publisher's notes that included his recommendations about reproductive control. It also has the Appendix to the 5th ed.]

    10th ed., with Notes by the Publisher [of the 5th ed.] Embodying All Modern Discoveries, Illustrated by Anatomical and Physiological Engravings, with the Appendix to the 5th ed. Boston: Published by J. P. Mendum at the office of the Boston Investigator, 1875. [Vale's edition was republished verbatim in 1875 by Josiah P. Mendum, editor of the freethought journal in Boston.]

English Editions

    London: James Watson [1831?].

    5th ed. with appendix. London: J. Watson, 5 St. Paul's Alley, 1842.

    London: Published for James Watson by Holyoake & Co., 147 Fleet St., 1859; reprint ed. in *Birth Control and Morality in Nineteenth Century America, Two Discussions.* New York: Arno Press, 1972.

    New ed. London: E. Truelove, 256 High Highborn, n.d. [Countway Library has catalogued this 1831, but it is probably later because the cover cites Owen as the author of "Footfalls on the Boundary of Another World," which was not published until the 1860s. It contains the Preface to the 8th edition, London, September 1832, and the Appendix to the 5th edition. It contains text not in the first New York edition.]

Pancoast, Seth. *The Ladies' Medical Guide and Marriage Friend, Elementary Epigenemal Expositions: Procreation, Health, Beauty, Longevity.* Philadelphia: Published by the author, stereotyped by George Charles, 1859.

——. *The Ladies New Medical Guide, an Instructor, Counseller, and Friend in All the Delicate and Wonderful Matters Peculiar to Women.* Philadelphia: John E. Potter & Co., 1890. [This is identical to the 1859 edition.]

Pomeroy, Hugh S. *The Ethics of Marriage.* New York: Funk & Wagnells, 1888.

Pouchet, Felix Archimede. *Théorie positive de l'ovulation spontanée et de la fécondation des mammifères et de l'espèce Humaine, basée sur l'observation de toute la serie animal, avec atlas.* Paris: J. B. Bailliere, 1847.

Raciborski, Adam. *De la puberté de l'âge critique chez la femme, au point de vue physiologique, hygienique, et medicale et de la ponte periodique chez la femme et less mammifères.* Paris: n.p., 1844.

Root, Harmon Knox. *The People's Medical Lighthouse: A Series of Popular and Scientific Essays on the Nature, Uses, and Diseases of the Lungs, Heart, Liver . . . also a Key to Consumption . . . and Marriage Guide. . . .* 2d ed. New York: Published by the Proprietor, 1853.

    8th ed. New York: Published by the Proprietor, 512 Broadway, and A. Ranney, 195 Broadway; Cincinnati: H. M. Rulison, 1854.

    10th ed. rev., with 65 rare and interesting engravings. New York: Published by Adolphus Ranney, 195 Broadway: Cincinnati: H. M. Rulison, 1854.

Royal Commission on the Decline of the Birth-Rate and on the Mortality of Infants in New South Wales. *Report,* vol. 1. Sydney, Australia: William Applegate Gullick, Government Printer, 1904. [Himes said that he saw two volumes of this study, but I can find no proof that a second volume was ever printed. The second volume was supposed to contain all the materials expurgated from volume 1, particularly all the evidence about birth control availability, advertisements, and evidence about use.]

Soule, J. *Science of Reproduction and Reproductive Control; the Necessity of Some Abstaining from Having Children, the Duty of All to Limit Their Families according to Their Circumstances Demonstrated. Effects of Continence—Effects of Self-Pollution and Abusive Laws and Philosophy of Impregnation with an Explanation of the Seminal Animalcules and Female System. With all the Different Modes of Preventing Conception and the Philosophy of Each.* Stereotype ed. Cincinnati: n.p., 1856.

Stockham, Alice Bunker. *Karezza, Ethics of Marriage.* Chicago: Alice B. Stockham & Co., 1897.

———. *Tokology: A Book for Every Woman.* 29th ed. Chicago: Sanitary Publishing Co., 1885.

    Rev. ed. Chicago: Alice B. Stockham & Co., 1897.

Storer. Horatio Robinson. *On Criminal Abortion in America.* Philadelphia: J. B. Lippincott, 1860.

———. *Why Not? A Book for Everywoman.* Boston: Lee and Shepard, 1866; 2d ed., 1867.

Trall, Russell Thacher. *The Hydropathic Encyclopedia . . . with an Appendix on the Theory of Conception.* New York: Fowlers & Wells, Publishers, 1852.

———. *Sexual Physiology: A Scientific Exposition of the Fundamental Problems in Sociology.* New York: Wood & Holbrook, Hygienic Institute, 1866. [Notes on this edition, probably the 1st, are in the Norman E. Himes Papers, Box 121, Countway Library.]

    5th ed. New York: Miller, Wood & Co.; London: J. Burns, 1867.

    Sexual Physiology and Hygiene. Rev. and greatly enl. New York: M. L. Holbrook: London: L. N. Fowler & Co., 1895.

———. London: Simpkin, Marshall, Hamilton, Kent & Co., Ltd., 1922.

Wright, Henry Clarke. *Marriage and Parentage; or, The Reproductive Element in Man, as a Means to His Elevation and Happiness.* Boston: Bela Marsh, 1854.

    2d ed., enl. Boston: Bela Marsh, 1855.

    5th thousand, Boston: Bela Marsh, 1866.

———. *The Unwelcome Child; or, The Crime of an Undesigned and Undesired Maternity.* Boston: Bela Marsh, 1858.

Index